This Ugly Civilization

THIS UGLY CIVILIZATION

Ralph Borsodi

foreword by

Harry Elmer Barnes

new introduction by

Bill Sharp

UNDERWORLD AMUSEMENTS

Find out more about this book and its author at:
www.ThisUglyCivilization.com

Typeset, designed and edited by Kevin I. Slaughter.

Rev.: X.XXI.MMXXI

isbn 978-1-943687-22-0

Underworld Amusements
www.UnderworldAmusements.com

The publisher would like to thank
Bill Sharp, Karen Stupski, Mark A. Sullivan,
Trevor Blake and Michael Moynihan.

A further special dedication from the publisher to artist
and botanist Rita B. Eames, wife of Cornell botanist Arthur J. Eames.
It was her former copy we transcribed for this new edition.

Dedicated to

MYRTLE MAE BORSODI

Whose Courage, Initiative and Resourcefulness
Made the adventure possible
Which inspired this book
And for whose patient cooperation in its production
A tribute of mere words is wholly
Inadequate

2019 INTRODUCTION
Bill Sharp

Ralph Borsodi's *This Ugly Civilization* (1929) launched a new career for him that spanned nearly a half-century. The timing of the book was important. It came out on the eve of the Great Depression.

There were three basic themes in *This Ugly Civilization*:

- A critique of modern industrial civilization.
- Achieving personal economic independence.
- Maximizing individual potential.

In this new introduction I will outline, in brief, how each of these themes developed over the course of Borsodi's long and productive life.

Early Life

Borsodi was born, probably in Vienna, in 1888. His father immigrated to New York City and established a successful printing business. Borsodi learned the printing and advertising business as a youth. He was largely self-educated. It appears he attended but a few years at a private school and never attended college. He was a voracious reader with a keen and retentive mind. He had his own apartment at fifteen.

Borsodi became a successful, independent, businessman—a consulting economist in New York City with major corporate clients.

Henry George

Borsodi was brought up in the Georgist tradition. His father was active in the movement. As a youth Ralph edited the organization's newsletter, conducted classes and made speeches. In 1919 he was elected its chairman.

Henry George has been recognized as the first original American economist. George lived during the expansive years of the settlement west of the Mississippi River. This was the epic of the American frontier—that great historical experiment in self-reliance as the continent was settled and put under the plow. Alexis de Tocqueville, in 1832, provided a great insight into the pre-industrial American culture. The agrarian tradition wasn't to last. Towards the end of he nineteenth century the frontier era came to a close.

This self-reliant spirit also drove business and industrialization. As businesses got big, they dramatically changed the way we lived. The role of the individual in the life of the nation's economy and civil life was transformed. Industrialization eroded many of the virtues that had defined American culture. Farmers moved to the city and became workers. Workers became parts of the great economic machine.

There was a popular reaction to industrial dominance and the loss of American tradition. It was called the Populist movement. George was a leader of this movement. His basic theme was land. The small farm had been the foundation of American economic and social life since the first settlement of the continent by Europeans. With the new economy, speculators bought up land and this made it harder for the family farm to thrive. George and followers wanted to reestablish the agrarian ideal much as expressed by Thomas Jefferson at the founding of the American Republic. Their solution was to put land into public trust and tax only what was produced on it.

Homesteader

In 1920 Borsodi bought a small farm near Suffern, New York and established his homestead. He continued to commute to the city for his business. He then bought additional property and built a large, fine, stone house (which still stands on a beautiful setting). He called this homestead Dogwoods for the trees that adorned the property.

Economic Independence

During the 1920's Borsodi steadily developed his homesteading model. It is clear that his intent was to help others achieve the type of economic independence he sought. He invited friends from the city to visit weekends and learn homesteading skills. In a very real sense, Borsodi's homestead was an experiment. As an accountant he kept careful records. This he first documented in *This Ugly Civilization.*

Borsodi took a lot of inspiration for his homestead from a leading Georgist, Bolton Hall. Borsodi's father, William, and Hall were friends. William printed two of Hall's books, *Free America* (1904) and *Three Acres and Liberty* (1906), both pioneering works on back-to-the-land. William Borsodi collaborated with and wrote an introduction to Hall's *A Little Land and Living* (1908). Ralph drew on these books to design his exemplary homestead. He put the theory into action and told a compelling story. In 1933, at his publisher request, he published *Flight From the City: An Experiment in Creative Living on the Land.* It is a classic handbook for family homesteading.

Economic Criticism

While by no means anti-capital, Borsodi was highly critical of the industrial economy of his day. He was not alone in his distaste for industrial civilization.

I should point out that for Borsodi, these critiques took the form of a statement of the problem. The problem was the impact of industrialization and centralization on society and the resulting assault on human dignity and self-determination. Borsodi worked to find a solution to these problems.

Above all Borsodi was an individualist, a libertarian if you will. He believed everyone had the right to live his or her own life. He believed that liberty was achieved not by political largess but through self-education and development of one's innate capacities to live a self-determined life. For Borsodi, like Thoreau, the best government was the least government. Borsodi believed that small communities could produce much of what they needed (as they had in the past) and manage their own affairs. There is simply no need for a centralized economy or government.

Prior to *This Ugly Civilization*, Borsodi published two other critical books (and a manual on accounting). *National Advertising Versus Prosperity* was published in 1923 and *The Distribution Age* in 1927. These two books were about advertising and retail distribution, his fields of expertise. He was critical of the centralization of the economy these caused. He believed they added unnecessary cost and he believed they produced inferior goods.

In 1933, at the depth of the Great Depression, Borsodi published *Prosperity and Security: A Study in Realistic Economics. Prosperity and Security* is a detailed analysis of what he considered the causes of the Great Depression.

Jumping ahead, to complete his list of critical books, following World War II Borsodi published *Inflation is Coming and What to Do About It.* It was a critique of Keynesian (central government controlled) economic policy. It was published again during the inflationary 1970s.

In 1956, following a long tour of Asia, Borsodi published *The Challenge of Asia: A Study of Conflicting Ideas and ideals. The Challenge of Asia* explored the social and economic impact of development in what was then called third world countries. Borsodi believed that such development would demolish the culture and economic self-determination of these countries.

Towards the end of his life he wrote a masterwork on economics, *Wealth and Illth*, but it didn't get published.

All of these books followed the same basic theme Borsodi articulated in *This Ugly Civilization*—a critical analysis of economic centralization. Borsodi disliked centralization in any form. He detested communism and found no merit in socialism. Borsodi believed that centralization, in the economy, government, education and social institutions, was dehumanizing.

Borsodi Declaration of Independence

In a real sense, *This Ugly Civilization* was Borsodi's Declaration of Independence. It was, as I suggested, the founding document for the work that would occupy him for the rest of his life.

Serialized in three parts in *The New Republic*, *This Ugly Civilization* brought Borsodi considerably public recognition. There are a number of stories about people who went back to the land after reading the book including such as the iconic homesteaders Scott and Helen Nearing. Eleanor Roosevelt (Franklin was then Governor of New York) paid a visit to Dogwoods.

In 1933, at the Depth of the Great Depression, Borsodi was called on to advise the Dayton Homesteading Project. Dayton, as had other American communities, set up a homesteading project to provide relief for displaced workers. Borsodi worked with participants to create their homesteads. They started with local funds but money for building houses and other structures ran out. Against Borsodi's advice, the homesteaders opted for government control of the project. Borsodi returned to his home at Suffern. Fact is, Federal funding did not appear and the Dayton project failed. Most of the Federal homesteading projects failed. In Borsodi's view, this was an unsurprising and inevitable miscarriage of centralized government.

School of Living

Back at Suffern, Borsodi opened the School of Living. From the beginning he believed that the foundation of personal independence was education. He believed the failure of the Dayton project was largely due to members having little understanding of how to achieve an independent lifestyle. They lacked a philosophy for living a self-determined life. He included a report on the Dayton experiment in the 1935 edition of *Flight From the City*. In that edition, he also published the charter of the School of Living.

It is clear that Borsodi had a strong educational bias from youth. It was a core principle. It was clear that he wanted to share things he had learned. But he was a lot more than an educator. He was a visionary, an innovator and an organizer. Part of his vision was a community surrounding the School. That School is intended to address the practical needs of life and this includes the life-long development of individual potential. He set out to realize this vision.

Land is fundamental to Borsodi's vision. He was disappointed but not surprised by the failure of the Federal takeover at Dayton. He was also disappointed by the lack of success of Henry George's land reform plan. That plan required political action. Little had been achieved after nearly a half-century. Borsodi developed an alterative approach, a private land trust.

The first of Borsodi's communities, and the icon of his model, was established a short distance from his homestead near Suffern at Bayard Lane (historic marker on Route 202 north of Suffern). He established a private land trust account, acquired 40 acres, and sixteen people settled on (mostly two acre) homesteads. He established a building fund and a building guild to construct homes and other structures. The homesteaders leased their land but owned their house and other structures. At the center of the community, on four acres, Borsodi constructed a building to house the School of Living. It had a library, office, a large meeting room, a large kitchen and rooms up stairs for visitors. The School staff maintained their own garden.

Decentralism

An essential idea in all of Borsodi's work is decentralism. For him it seems something of an inalienable right to be free of coercion. Centralism in any form is about coercion.

The problem of industrial centralism is found in the two books prior to *This Ugly Civilization*. *TUC* represents a shift of gears, so to speak, into overcoming the effects of centralization. The New Deal—massive centralization of the US economy starting in 1933, and even more egregious examples in Germany, Italy, Russia and Japan—I believe made the problem crucial to Borsodi's emerging mission. The failure of the Dayton experiment was a wakeup call. Characteristically, he responded within a matter of weeks with the School of Living. This gave Borsodi an organizational foundation.

In 1937, Borsodi and a wealthy Georgist friend, Chauncey Stillman, who had provided financial support to Borsodi's work, and Herbert Agar, a Southern Agrarian, started a journal. They called it *Free America*, I believe following Bolton Hall's use of this title for one of his books. *Free America* attracted a considerable number of subscribers. It had a mailing list of over 3,000. They used the journal to mobilize the decentralist movement. Borsodi became a leader in this movement. Mildred Loomis called Borsodi the "Decentralist Prophet." Others have recognized his leadership in the movement.

During the 1940's, following the accelerated massive centralization of government and industry during World War II, the School of Living journal was titled *The Decentralist*. We know that Mildred prepared a decentralists bibliography during this time.

From at least 1945 Mildred's primary job was to publish the School of Living periodicals. She did so throughout her life. That year she started *The Interpreter*. It was addressed to decentralist and homesteaders across the country. The subtitle of early issues read: "A Semi-monthly Comment of the Current Events for People Concerned with the Achievement of Normal Living Through Education and Decentralization." For eight years it went out twice monthly, then monthly. In 1947 *Free America* shut down and *The Interpreter* took over the mailing list. In 1957 the School of Living publication name was changed to *Balanced Living*, reflecting an increased focus on holistic learning and living, and in 1963 to *A Way Out.* A few years later a newsletter was started titled *Green Revolution*, which promoted Borsodi's evolving integral education model and a renewed homesteading campaign. The banner of the *Green Revolution* continued to carry the word "Decentralized."

Education and Living

World War II brought an end to Borsodi's homestead community experiment. Good paying jobs became plentiful and young men went off to war. Following the war he transferred the School of Living headquarters to Ohio, under the direction of Mildred Loomis.

Mildred Loomis was drawn to Borsodi after reading *This Ugly Civilization*. She was a graduate student at Columbia at the time. She visited Borsodi at his homestead, she participated in the Dayton, Ohio homesteading experiment, and she worked with him at Suffern for a year before starting her own homestead, with husband John, near Dayton. Mildred and Borsodi worked in close collaboration to the end of his life and she carried on his legacy to the end of hers. She has been, justifiably, called the cofounder of the School of Living.

Mildred and John established a model homestead. They exemplified the life Borsodi advocated. They were economically independent. They taught homesteading. Mildred became the center of a large homesteading network that stretched across the country.

Mildred's job was Director the Education for the School of Living (she was also a Trustee). One of her major attractions to Borsodi was his work in education. She had always been an "A" student. She was one of the first women to receive a degree in business and economics. She had worked as a teacher. She used her savings, during the Great Depression, to do graduate work for the purpose of improving her capacity as a human being. I believe Borsodi's model of alternative education was her foremost interest.

Borsodi had a very different idea about education. He was, as noted, self-educated. He had little faith in public education. As a student of American history he was acutely aware of the role of education in a democracy, as envisioned by Jefferson. Borsodi's objective was personal freedom, liberty, independence, self-determination, self-reliance—you choose the word. He was committed to helping others learn to lead lives of their own choosing. This vision deeply appealed to Mildred.

Problem-Centered Education

During World War II Borsodi continued to develop his educational model. In 1948 he published his two-volume *Education and Living*. It came out of nearly two decades of work following *This Ugly Civilization*. I consider it his best work.

In *This Ugly Civilization* Borsodi wrote about quality mindedness and the barriers to achieving it: educational barriers. In *Education and Living* he offered a problem-centered approach to learning and an idea he called "normal" living. "Normal Living" is a development of the idea of the quality mind and the life thus achieved. "Normal" is not the average; it is the balanced, holistic, way he believed human beings should live. It is about optimal living or "the good life."

Borsodi first proposed his problem-centered framework as early as 1940 when he stated in a presentation:

> Believing that the full development of each human being is the supreme value, the School of Living has as its primary purpose to assist adults in their study and use of the accumulated wisdom of mankind.
>
> Believing that such study and use of wisdom is best facilitated by being related to the universal and perpetual living experience of human beings, the School of Living aims to assist adults in becoming aware of and defining the major problems of living common to all

people.

Borsodi's problem-centered system had evolved over a period of years. In *Education and Living* there were then thirteen problems. The problems of living are not separate, isolated issues. They belong to a whole, a universal system. They are like, and were later represented as, the spokes of a wheel joined at the center. We may address each problem in turn but we must also ask how they relate to each other.

The problem-centered method is not merely a method for solving problems. It is a teaching tool that develops personal capacity. It fosters critical thinking. It is a program for seeking the essence of what it means to live as a human being. It seeks to define root causes. It works for effective solutions.

The problem framework is also an efficient way to more readily access information about solving the problem. Borsodi found the subject-centered approach to education inadequate. He rejected the narrow specialization it encourages. Human problems have a variety of causes. We need access to information that is pertinent. Borsodi organized the School of Living library around this structure.

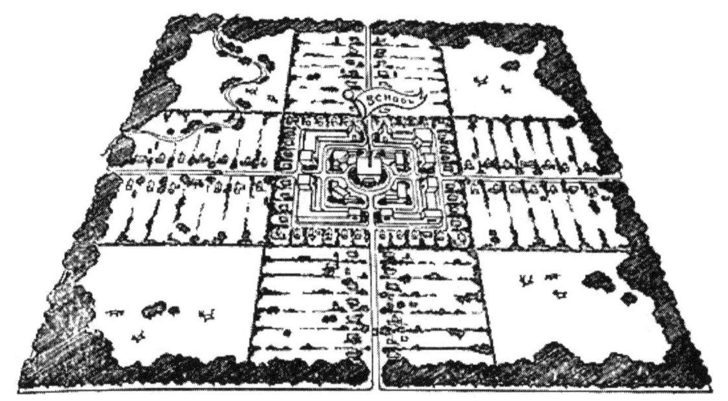

In *Education and Living*, Borsodi further developed his idea of the school as the center of a small community. Since we no longer have the institutions around which a successful community can be formed, the School of Living assumes that role: Not a courthouse, not a church, but a school. This is not a school in any way like those then or today. The School of Living is a locally managed learning program that seeks to bring out the best of our humanity and to promote strong lives and communities.

Education and Living is about learning and living. It is about life-long, adult education. It is about learning and un-learning. It is, above all, about applying what one learns to daily life.

Florida and India

Education and Living brings to a close a highly productive, nearly 30 year, phase of Borsodi's work. Borsodi's wife, Myrtle Mae, died shortly after *Education and Living* was published. He remarried, sold his Dogwoods homestead in 1950, and moved to a community in Florida set up along the lines he had proposed.

Borsodi had barely settled in Florida when he and his new wife, Clare, took a long cruise to Asia. As noted above, he made a close study of the impact of western industrialization that he later published as *The Challenge of Asia*. Back in Florida, with the encouragement of friends, he started a university-level experimental program founded on the problem-centered system. This was a productive period in the development of a formal educational model for personal independence and self-reliance. While the university experiment did not gain traction, it engaged a number of notable people of the time in a conversation about an education appropriate for the time. The problem-centered system and the structure of the universal problems were thoroughly reworked.

In 1958 there was yet another major shift but I consider this more of a continuation of the work Borsodi started in Florida. That year, Gandhian educators, whom he had met on his tour of Asia, invited Borsodi to India. He spent several years there hosted by a small rural university organized much along the lines he had proposed. Responding to their request, he summarized his major principals in his *Pan-Humanist Manifesto.* This pamphlet, even more than *This Ugly Civilization*, is Borsodi's Declaration of Independence. It was well received in India. Gandhi was an ardent decentralists. It was published in the US as the *Decentralist Manifesto.*

While in India, with the support of young Indian scholars, Borsodi worked on his extensive files on the problems of living. He completed *The Education of the Whole Man* (published 1963). In that book he elaborated his problem-centered and integral educational system. It provides much of the theory behind Borsodi's system.

Borsodi, after a serious illness, returned to the US in 1961 and settled in Exeter, New Hampshire where he spent the remainder of his life. The period between 1950, and his move to Florida, and 1961, when he returned to the US, represented an important period in Borsodi's work. The university experiment at Melbourne and the close support of friends in India allowed him to elaborate and formalize his model. *The Education of the Whole Man* brought this phase to a close.

Final Phase

In 1961 Borsodi turned 73. After settling in and some time for rest, he went back to work. In addition to speaking and extensive correspondence, he completed four major projects.

The first of these was a final book on his problem-centered system. Borsodi brought four steamer trunks full of his research materials back to the US. Mildred and a young Indian Scholar, who came to the US for the purpose, took the trunks to her homestead in Ohio and sorted these materials. There were perhaps 8,000 pages. They produced a 700 page typed summary. Borsodi published his classic *Seventeen Problems of Man and Society* in 1968. He devoted a chapter to each of the seventeen problems. He continued to work on the extended manuscript for several years. His archive records at the University of New Hampshire contain some 12,000 pages of this manuscript. The University of New Hampshire awarded him a doctorate degree for his work in education.

Borsodi proposed a separate volume for each of the problems. He completed one of them, *Wealth and Illth,* I believe in 1972. Mildred Loomis spent time with him finalizing the manuscript, now lost. An earlier rough draft is in the University of New Hampshire archives.

In addition to writing, Borsodi established two organizations during this last phase of his life. He and close associate Bob Swann, founder of the Schumacher Society, incorporated the International Independence Institute (III) in 1967. The mission of the III was to establish and promote land trust. It was modeled after the private trust Borsodi established thirty years earlier. It had a presence in the US, Europe and India. It became the foundation of community land trust. Swann became one of the leading advocates of this model.

Borsodi developed the idea for an inflation-proof local currency. He called it the Constant. It was well accepted in Exeter, supported by several banks, and became a model for local currencies in the US and elsewhere. He created another organization to support it. One objective of a local currency is to create an independent local economy that remains stable and secure despite national and global economic instabilities. Bob Swann also became a champion of local currency.

Ralph Borsodi died in 1977 just short of his 90th birthday. A brief list of his accomplishments include:

- He wrote twelve books, co-authored another and finished a major, unpublished, manuscript.
- He wrote over 100 articles, lectured, and conducted seminars and workshops.
- Developed a groundbreaking integral, adult education program.
- Honorary doctorate from the University of New Hamp-

shire.

- Founded multiple organizations including:
- School of Living (1934 to present).
- Melbourne University (1952 – 1957).
- International Independence Institute (1967).
- Independent Arbitrage International (1973).
- During World War II he wrote a peace plan that anticipated a (decentralized) United Nations.
- Pioneer homesteader: he not only built a model homestead, he made the business case for it.
- Developed small-scale appropriate technology
- Developed private land trust model for foundin.g homesteading communities.
- Formed two land trust communities and advised others.
- Developed prototype local currency.
- Recognized leader of the decentralist movement.
- Championed organic food and diet and food reform.

Coda

At root, Borsodi sought to remake modern culture—not to replace it but to create an alternative that would allow the greatest personal independence for those who chose to participate.

Borsodi and Loomis pursued this objective with single-minded determination. They had a considerable influence. They knew the work was not done. They had hoped others would come forward to carry on the system.

Century Twenty-one

This Ugly Civilization was published in 1929. What, it is fair to ask, is the relevance of a book published 90 years ago? Let me ask: Is our civilization any less ugly? Are our lives any more secure?

Borsodi's ugly civilization touched on unpleasant esthetics but it was mostly about the psychological pathology of living in such an environment. Factories and commercial buildings produced a style of architecture Frank Lloyd Wright called "American Ugly." But of greater importance, it was about the dehumanization of mass culture driven by a mindless commercialism.

Following World War II, the US was the greatest manufacturing economy on the planet. We had a massive war industry and a world market of devastated countries. Commercial development in the US brought shopping malls, big-box stores, shopping strips along highways, outlet malls, and cookie-cutter retail outlets. It brought suburban housing developments and crowded freeways. Main streets became derelict. *More* ugly.

Globalization in the 1980s further changed the economic environment with devastating impact on many American towns and cities. The ugly, smoke-belching factories became rusting brownfields. As industry moved off shore, where labor was cheap, small, locally owned manufacturers closed. They couldn't compete.

There are today hundreds of once vibrant but now shrinking and distressed communities. As I write this, my hometown has the distinction of being the number one fastest shrinking city in the US. I saw this happen. A vibrant local economy imploded. Long drives along America's back roads give you a view of shuttered storefronts, dead mills and dilapidated houses. You don't see much of this from the interstate highways. Over 80% of American's now live in cities.

As global population continues to grow geometrically, demand for non-renewable resources, including land and water, increases. Energy crises occur. Obesity and addiction are on the rise. Life expectancy has flattened if not declined for younger generations. We have been in a state of virtual war since the beginning of the century. We have a vast new, well-armed, homeland defense bureaucracy. As they say, it's not a pretty picture.

This is also the problem with climate change. In the draft of

Wealth and Illth, Borsodi wrote about the impact of environmental degradation on the economy. A lot of environmental legislation came out then but climate change has rewritten the sustainability equation.

As an economist, Borsodi was concerned with the business cycle: recurring recessions. He saw it as a product of the industrial economy. *This Ugly Civilization* anticipated the Great Depression. Since World War II there has been a recession on the average of seven years. The twenty-first century has given us two major recessions, including the Great Recession. That was 2008. Recovery was painfully slow.

Many people still expect governments, non-profits and institutions to solve their problems and make life feel good. So, on a scale of one to ten, how is that working for you?

Much of the psychological stress people feel comes from change. The rate of change continues to accelerate. But change is addictive—we've come to crave it. Massive change is destabilizing. I think it safe to say, about our future prospects, that if we had a dashboard, there would be a lot of blinking and buzzing.

Psychologist and others have published reams about the effect of modern society on our psychic state. There are a lot of self-help books. There are lots of blogs. There are lots of articles and web pages about looking good and feeling good—interspaced with lots of advertisements about how to buy what you need to do that. Advertising, as Borsodi wrote long ago, is driving this craving.

Alienation is no longer a common word. It describes a state of unhealthy detachment from society. This is the real ugliness Borsodi wrote about. He went to the root of the problem: how do you feel? And, characteristically, he moved directly into a solution. First of all you can develop a self-sufficient, homesteading lifestyles. But of greater importance is a program of study and work that doesn't seek to make you just feel better but to make you a better person. That is about climbing out of the morass. It is about achieving a mental state of freedom, independence, and self-reliance.

Individuality can be a positive or negative feeling. Our society is fragmenting and mandates individuals take care of themselves. Many find this unsettling if not frightening. That need not be the case. For Borsodi and friends, individuality was a desirably ideal. But he knew that it takes learning, education, to achieve the knowledge, skills and mental preparation to lead a self-determined and self-fulfilling life.

Where Next?

We are steadily bombarded by news and advertisements, that tell us how bad things are. "Ain't it awful?" is not, however, a statement of a problem. It's like talking about the weather. It is a problem only if you personally feel the "pain." And this society is about making you not feel the pain. It's about easy outs. It's about our "comfort zone."

Borsodi was about challenging pet assumptions. He was about getting down to what troubles us, defining the problem and finding an effective solution. I believe we could benefit by reviving the Borsodi/Loomis legacy. Republishing *This Ugly Civilization* is a great start. I plan to have the joint biography of Borsodi and Loomis completed in 2020, on the one-hundredth anniversary of Borsodi starting his homestead (1920).

Two Thoughts

Two things I would like to close with. First, I should point out that Borsodi's direction was not retro. His issue with the economy wasn't science, technology and industry; it was the way it was carried out. Indeed, Borsodi introduced appropriate technology nearly 30 years before Schumacher was credited with it. He had a radio very soon after it got started. For him, technology was for our use, not to dominate us. He is by no means alone in that view.

I would also like to again stress that the individual is the focus of this work. Borsodi clearly understood that the foundation of the good society is the individual operating at capacity. He made that crystal clear in *This Ugly Civilization* and in book after book to the end of his long and productive life. As I've written about in my own work, we are in desperate need of men and women with the capacity to address and solve the problems of our day. We are desperately in need of learning programs that help individuals achieve such capacity. Borsodi's problem-centered framework I find a highly useful tool for clarifying thought and mobilizing action.

BILL SHARP
State College, PA
September, 2018

1933 FOREWORD
Harry Elmer Barnes

Mr. Ralph Borsodi has written one of the most challenging and important books of recent years. During the height of the madness of 1929, when the book was first published, it was easy to ignore it. Indeed, to many people Mr. Borsodi's arguments seemed fantastic in the face of Coolidge "prosperity," high wages and rising prices. Now that four years of depression have vindicated so many of them, his program—which seemed so impossible a few years ago—is rapidly becoming the only way out for many of those staggered by the insecurities of modern industrialism.

The most striking and dramatic aspect of the book is its slashing attack upon the ugliness, oppressiveness and irrationality of our factory system, as run under the present profit motive in an era of speculative business enterprise.

There is nothing completely new about this. The traditions of John Ruskin, William Morris and others, and their assault upon the repulsive and repressive nature of our machine age and factory system, are old and familiar. That Mr. Borsodi has done the job again in effective fashion in terms of our present economy is not in itself an epoch-making contribution to the literature of social and economic criticism. Nor is his proposal to escape by building up self-supporting domestic units on the land wholly novel.

Far more fundamental and much more truly challenging is Mr. Borsodi's relentless exposure of the shallow and superficial nature of the most sacred shibboleths of contemporary civilization.

Mr. Borsodi is sufficiently well informed and realistic to recognize that the factories are but a product and a symbol of underlying principles and processes. Behind them, their operation and the disposition of their products, is a dominant philosophy.

There is the current doctrine that the well-being of the human race is to be assured chiefly, if not exclusively, through mass factory production and business prosperity. Efficiency and economy in the operation of the factory are designed to insure high productivity. Expert advertising will market the products. Large sales insure high profits. Such profits enable the employers to offer high wages and steady employment. Permanent work and good wages are to make it possible for the employees to buy more and, hence, to speed up consumption. Greater consumption is to lead to the placing of larger orders at the factories, and so on around the circle.

But at no point have we been willing to raise the basic question as to whether the greater consumption means greater happiness and larger satisfaction with life.

Greater consumption, indeed, but greater consumption for what? This is a question with which Henry Ford has never grappled. To do so would involve him in obvious embarrassment, if not in destructive confusion.

Our current business philosophy has passed through three stages. The first was that of the crude days of industrial expansion following the early period of machine-factory production. It was the public-be-damned era. Immediate profit was all that concerned the business man. Large profits could only be insured, it was believed, by depressing wages. This was proved a fallacy which, if persisted in, would lead to the disintegration of capitalistic enterprise.

So some employers then came to understand that if they were to find a market for an ever larger supply of goods they would have to pay decent wages in order that the worker might be an effective consumer. High wages meant general prosperity, and well diffused prosperity meant extensive consumption.

We are now entering upon a third stage of analysis and evaluation. This will introduce qualitative, moral and sociological considerations. The judgments demanded can no longer be exclusively those of the bookkeeper. Tentatively accepting the doctrine of greater consumption as a means of assuring human happiness, we are coming to ask such questions as, consumption for what? Consumption of what? How much consumption? What price consumption? And the like.

It is the fact that Mr. Borsodi rocks to its very foundations the whole philosophy of the present era of mass-production that gives his book real significance. It may not convince us and it may not convert us, but it will be a thick-headed or irresponsible person who can read the book without being moved to reconsider his economic and social philosophy and, perhaps, his whole way of living.

Sooner or later, we shall have to deal with the question of whether we are to live to consume or to consume to live. When we face this issue it will be necessary to do more than call conferences of industrial leaders or radical agitators.

Mr. Borsodi is sensible and realistic enough not to launch an undiscriminating blanket attack upon machines and factories. The machines have enormously contributed to lessening human effort and to increasing our productive power. Only when introduced in factories have they become a menace to mankind. Even a factory is not in itself inherently destructive of human well being. Factories which manufacture essential products render a great social service. It is the factories which manufacture non-essential or harmful products and are linked up with irresponsible types of modern advertising that menace the welfare of humanity.

The core of the whole matter is to be found in the changed philosophy of production and consumption which accompanied the establishment of the factory:—"Before the coming of factory production commerce devoted itself to producing what the buying public wanted, rather than to marketing what producers fabricated."

In 1929 Mr. Borsodi's devastating critical analysis of the fundamental deficiencies and thoughtlessness of industrial civilization seemed far more important and convincing than his proposal for escape. The factories and factory machines were busy everywhere, and escape from them in large numbers seemed impossible. In 1933 the situation is different. Millions are leaving the city to return to the country.

Whether we follow Mr. Borsodi to the country or stay in our congested cities, we must face the question of what really constitutes a satisfactory life and how both factories and farms can be employed to produce it.

Mr. Borsodi answers this question by placing before us an economic philosophy based upon a twelve year experiment with domestic machinery and production for use. If the depression lasts long enough, millions may turn to production for use, domestic machinery, the decentralization of electric power, and what Mr. Borsodi calls self-sufficient homesteads as the instruments for achieving the good life.

Even if one believes that we shall solve our current industrial problems primarily by curbing speculative piracy and insuring high wages, while preserving the system of mass production, he will find Mr. Borsodi's book of real value. For, under the most favorable outcome, many will be unable to find work within the industrial system. Automatic machinery is likely to throw more and more out of work. Therefore, though Mr. Borsodi's program should prove an incidental and secondary line of defense against poverty and confusion, it is, nevertheless, bound to be highly significant. Several millions of Americans, at least, are destined to find this their only practicable mode of relief.

To those to whom Mr. Borsodi has directly addressed his book —the men and women he calls quality-minded, artists, teachers, scientists, poets and all those belonging to the cultured minority—his program will prove particularly interesting at this time. For it points to a way in which they might do what Mr. Borsodi has done: make themselves economically independent enough to end any subservience on their part to contemporary business, social and political pressures.

HARRY ELMER BARNES

1933 PREFACE

IN the four years between 1928, when Herbert Hoover was triumphantly elected President of these United States, and 1932, when he was repudiated, American public opinion has undergone a complete revolution. It has changed not only from Republicanism to Democracy in politics, from dryness to wetness on the liquor question—it has changed from sublime faith in American economic institutions to a bitter dissatisfaction with them.

Belief in the "new era" of permanent expansion, and faith that mass production and high wages, in accordance with the ideas of Henry Ford, would abolish poverty, have in these four years given way to doubt and despair, to desire for change and search for security. The selfsame people who four years ago laughed at forecasts of disaster and who called those who criticized the tendencies of American civilization "Jeremiahs," have now lost their self-assurance. Most of them are groping around for some new magic to replace the old, and many of them are turning to the new gospel of economic planning to give some meaning to the struggle for life.

In 1928, during the peak of the great boom, I wrote *This Ugly Civilization.* The book was published just before the collapse of the boom in the fall of 1929. In spite of the fact that reviewers were kind to the book and were good enough to pay it the tribute of lengthy consideration—even when they disagreed with its argument—public interest in the book was small. When it appeared the public still believed in the permanence of the new era, and for months after the debacle in Wall Street in October of that year, few people were ready to give up their convictions that the decline would merely prove a temporary break in the movement toward bigger and better business. In the spring of 1930 it will be remembered, there was a decided improvement in business. Prices in the securities market began to rise again. Business responded to the stimulus of the glittering promises which the President, Andrew Mellon (then Secretary of the Treasury), Charles E. Mitchell (then president of the National City Bank of New York), John D. Rockefeller, Sr., and other political, industrial, and financial leaders made. It was only after this movement collapsed in the summer of 1930 and all the optimistic statements began to prove illusory that faith and hope began to decline. As the depression dragged its weary way, month after month and year after year, with prices declining continuously and unemployment increasing steadily, the doubts of intelligent men and women as to the magic of the gospel of mass production and high-pressure selling made a hearing possible for the message in *This Ugly Civilization.*

By that time the book was out of print.

As the depression has continued, spreading misery far and wide, requests for the book and for information about it have kept pouring in on me. The correspondence from those who had heard about the Borsodi experiment, or who read the book or the earlier *New Republic* articles, has been extraordinary. Men and women from all over the country, and even from Europe, keep asking for more and more details about "how to go Borsodi." Proposals to establish colonies began to be made to me. In Dayton, Ohio, plans for multiplying such an experiment as mine in a large way are be ing sponsored by social agencies. Individual families which have in one way or another tried out the idea, have been writing me about their experiences.

Two things make me feel that a reissue of the book is now justified. One, the number of requests I receive for information about the way of life of which I am an advocate; the other the fact that in the four years since the book was written our new experiments in domestic production have immensely strengthened the case for what I have called the organic homestead. Our experiments with home weaving in particular warrant revising upward what I originally said about the economy and desirability of shifting cloth production from *production for sale* in our textile mills to *production for use.* Hence what I wrote five years ago as theory on the subject of domestic weaving has in this edition been revised on the basis of our experience with weaving during the past three years.

At the present time the world needs to be shown that there is some practical plan which men and women anywhere can adopt for securing food, clothing, and shelter—the essentials of life which requires them neither to wait for a revival of business nor to wait for some revolutionary reform of the existing social system. Those who are looking for some way to security and independence—for a satisfactory way of life in a crazy world in which everything seems suddenly to have become insecure—and who wish to achieve comfort and beauty in life here and now, may find in this book a new approach to the solution of the economic riddle.

RALPH BORSODI
March, 1933

1929 PREFACE

THIS book in its present form is an attempt, still largely unsatisfactory to myself, to project certain ideas evolved from a quest of comfort—material and philosophical—in some respect quite different from that which engages most of us today.

If I have ventured to step from the humdrum practicality of economics to the sacred and dangerous precincts of philosophy, it is because philosophers generally seem to forget that the acquisition of food, clothing and shelter is prerequisite to the pursuit of the good, the true and the beautiful. Epistemology, ethics and esthetics acquire reality only if related to economics.

While not too sanguine about my success in venturing into this field, the book cannot wholly fail if here and there it spurs men and women to free themselves from the ugliness of this civilization. If it directs the attention of even a few thinkers to the questions with which it deals, I will feel fully justified in having published it.

It is impossible to acknowledge my indebtedness to all from whom I have taken counsel in the preparation of this book, but special mention must be made of my friend Guy M. Carleton, with whom I have discussed almost every point in it, and who has been good enough not only to study the manuscript, but to make many suggestions for its improvement.

RALPH BORSODI
Suffern, NY
August, 1929

CONTENTS

BOOK II
The Conquest Of Comfort

Part IV | The Material Aspect

Part V | The Philosophic Aspect

L'Envoi

BOOK I

THE QUEST OF COMFORT

Since humanity came into being man hath enjoyed himself too little: that alone, my brethren, is our original sin.

—*Thus Spake Zarathustra.*

PART I
THIS UGLY CIVILIZATION

Shame, shame, shame—
that is the history of man.

—*Thus Spake Zarathustra*.

CHAPTER I
THIS UGLY CIVILIZATION

THIS is an ugly civilization.

It is a civilization of noise, smoke, smells, and crowds—of people content to live amidst the throbbing of its machines; the smoke and smells of its factories; the crowds and the discomforts of the cities of which it proudly boasts.

•

The places in which the people work are noisy. The factories are filled with the recurring, though not the rhythmic, noises of machines and the crash and clatter incidental to their operation. The offices, too, are noisy with the rat-tat-tat of typewriters, the ringing of telephones, the grinding of adding machines. The streets on which the people move about, and around which they work and play, resound with the unending clatter of traffic—the roar of motors, the squeaks of brakes, the shrieks of sirens, and the banging of street cars. And even the homes in which they are supposed to rest are noisy because they are not only packed close together but built tier on tier so that the pianos, phonographs, and radios in them blare incongruously above, below, and on all sides of them.

The people of this factory-dominated civilization accept its noisiness. For noise is the audible evidence of their prowess; the inescapable accompaniment of their civilization's progress. The greater the noise, the greater the civilization.

•

The people of Pittsburgh, a city of more than half a million souls, live in a cloud of soot. Soot shuts out the sun by day; the moon and stars by night. Soot blackens Pittsburgh's churches and courthouses; its humble dwellings and towering office buildings. It creeps and sifts into Pittsburgh's homes. It smuts the walls, the draperies, the rugs, the furnishings in Pittsburgh's homes. In Pittsburgh people accept a sooty civilization because soot makes Pittsburgh great.

The people of Chicago, a city of over three million souls, live under an encircling and overpowering smell. At breakfast, at luncheon, at dinner: while working and playing; awake and asleep; Chicago's millions inhale penetrating smells from the mountains of dung and offal in its great stockyards. The greater the smells the stockyards make, the greater their contributions to Chicago. In Chicago people accept a smelly civilization because smells make Chicago great.

The people of New York, a city of over six million souls, shuttle back and forth morning and night between their flats at one end and their jobs at the other end of a series of long underground tubes. Twice each work day throughout their lives New Yorkers push and are pushed into their noisy, sweaty, obscenely crowded subways, elevated railroads, street cars and busses. In New York people accept a civilization of crowded homes, crowded streets, crowded stores, crowded offices, crowded theatres because crowds make New York great.

Pittsburgh is not our only sooty factory city; Chicago is not our only smelly stockyards town; New York is not our only crowded metropolis. The cities of the country differ from one another only in degrees of sootiness, smelliness, noisiness and crowdedness. What is most discouraging, those not so sooty as Pittsburgh, nor so smelly as Chicago, nor so crowded as New York, aspire to equal these three shining jewels of our civilization in the very things that make for ugliness.

•

Travel on the Erie Railroad from New York to Buffalo and you will see how this civilization scars what should be one of the most beautiful regions of the world. The train moves through a countryside that is one unending delight—a succession of hills and valleys, fields and streams of entrancing loveliness. From the time it leaves the factory dotted area of northern New Jersey, which the sprawling cities of Jersey City, Passaic and Paterson make hideous, it travels through a region that should inspire all of those who dwell in it to the building of beautiful places in which to work and play.

Instead, the cities and towns are eyesores, especially those that contain factories, and most of them do; made more hideous because of the contrast between the dingy places built by men and the natural beauty about them. What the factory has left undone to mar the country seems to have been done by the signs and billboards advertising factory products; by the huddle of stores and warehouses in which factory products are distributed; by the drab, box-like houses in which dwell the makers of factory products. Between the factory itself and these by-products of a factory dominated countryside all has been done that could be done to make the country ugly.

•

Above all, this civilization is ugly because of the subtle hypocrisy with which it persuades the people to engage in the factory production of creature comforts while imposing conditions which destroy their capacity for enjoying them. With one hand it gives comforts—with the other hand it takes comfort itself away.

The servitude to the factory which it enforces uniformly upon all men harnesses skilled workers and creative individuals in a repetitive treadmill which makes each muscle in their bodies, every drop of blood in their veins, the very fibres of their being, cry out in voiceless agony that they are being made to murder time—the irreplaceable stuff of which life itself is composed.

For America is a respecter of things only, and time—why time is only something to be killed, or butchered into things which can be bought and sold.

•

Wherever the factory dominates, there you will find the factory-generated waste of human life and natural resources, and the noise, soot, smell and crowds of industrialized America.

For the misdirection of human energy which destroys beauty is neither exclusively American nor exclusively modern. Ugliness has existed in all ages and is to be found among all the peoples of the earth. The tragic universality of the "misfortune" to which Friedrich Nietzsche calls attention in *Thus Spake Zarathustra* has made ugliness the common curse of mankind. Says Nietzsche:

> There is no sorer misfortune in all human destiny, than when the mighty of the earth are not also the first men.

For "the mighty of the earth," when bereft of wisdom, have to devote themselves ruthlessly to perpetuating their own might. This is the genesis of the interminable warfare waged by predatory quantity-minded men upon the quality-minded men who seek to make the world a more beautiful place in which to live.

Substitute "church" for "factory" and the argument of this book applies equally well to the situation of mankind when Voltaire waged his war with *l'Infame*. Hypatia the church tore to pieces. Bruno it burned at the stake. Copernicus and Galileo it terrorized into temporary silence. What the church did when it had full sway to the quality-minded individuals who sought to make the world a more intelligent place was similar in essence, although far worse in kind, to that which the factory does today.

Substitute "slavery" for "factory" and the argument applies equally to that period of history when mankind accepted the idea that heredity and power gave to limited numbers of men the right to enslave others. Nothing in all history is more vile than the institution which permitted a "noble" Roman to cripple Epictetus, because he owned him! What slavery did when it flourished to the quality-minded individuals, both slave and free, who sought to make life more beautiful, was no different in essence from that which the factory does today.

Substitute "absolutism" for "factory" and the argument applies equally to every period and every place in which kings, princes and nobles wielded absolute powers. What absolutism did wherever it had sway to quality-minded individuals was similar in essence to what the factory does today.

The civilizations dominated by the church, by slavery and by absolutism were each in their way ugly. But the superstitions, cruelties, and injustices which marred them were the symptoms and not the true causes of the perhaps incurable disease from which all of them suffered.

The institutions which dominated those civilizations, just as the factory dominates ours, expressed the activities of acquisitive, predatory, ruthless, quantity-minded types of men. Because these powerful but inferior types impose their wills upon superior types of men, the individuals who mitigate the tragedy of life—those who have contributed all the beauty to be found amidst the wealth of folly and waste in the world—are penalized and handicapped in their work.

Under penalty of all that is dear to men—work, comfort, fellowship, even life itself—they are forced to subscribe to the false facts, false hopes, false fears, false tastes of the conventions of their times. The penalties for failure to conform have varied from burnings-at-the-stake, the favorite method when the church dominated civilization, to starvation-into-accepting-a-place-in-the-factory system, the favorite method now that the factory dominates civilization.

•

America has not yet permitted the factory, officially, to take over the government. America still gives, officially, lip-service to the rights of the individual. But factory-dominated America is slowly but surely destroying its idealists by making laws, schools and all other popular institutions "practical." Already the factory has created a factory folkway. In America "business as usual" is not a mere slogan—it is a holy and patriotic virtue.

But look at Russia. In Russia proscription of the nonconformist is practiced—after socialization—on an even greater scale than in capitalistic America.

There the factory is supreme.

There the factory has taken over the government.

And there all men are being forced to conform to the needs of the factory, precisely as in ancient Sparta they were forced to conform to the needs of the state, and in the Middle Ages to the needs of the church.

•

And now let me try to tell you why it is that I have come to the conclusion that it is the factory—the gross abuse of the factory—that has produced this ugly civilization.

•

For it *is* an ugly civilization.

It is ugly because of its persistent failure to concern itself about whether the work men do, and the things they produce, and above all the way they live, create the comfort and understanding essential if mankind is to achieve an adequate destiny.

And it will remain ugly and probably become uglier year by year until the men who are able to mitigate its ugliness free themselves to do so.

CHAPTER II
MACHINES

All civilizations have been ugly. They could not well avoid it.

But this civilization is unique. Machines make it possible for this one to be beautiful, and yet it is in many respects indescribably uglier than the civilizations that have preceded it.

For this civilization, instead of using machines to free its finest spirits for the pursuit of beauty, uses machines mainly to produce factories—factories which only the more surely hinder quality-minded individuals in their warfare upon ugliness, discomfort, and misunderstanding.

•

Consider, for instance, the persuasive and eloquent apology for the factory which Mr. Glenn Frank has recently written and which he entitled *The Machine Age*.[1] Among contemporary students of our civilization Mr. Frank has no superior in equipment and experience for the task of defending our "machine civilization" from those who venture to criticise it. He is a practical man, with years of business experience under Mr. E. A. Filene of Boston, the head of the largest men's and women's clothing store in the world. He is a forceful writer, with the skill in expressing himself to be expected from a man for so many years the editor of the *Century*. He is an erudite man, for he is the president of the University of Wisconsin, one of the best exemplars of the higher education in these machine-dominated states.

And yet Mr. Frank makes the serious mistake of taking a facile phrase, the machine age, too seriously. To speak rhetorically of a machine age is permissible if the inferences drawn are merely rhetorical. But it is not permissible to assume that "machine age" is a self-defining term and that no obligation exists for defining it as carefully as every general concept should be defined when it is used as a basis for broad generalizations. In the absence of definition I can truthfully say that I am heartily in favor of my kind of machine age and very much opposed to Mr. Glenn Frank's kind of machine age. Plainly, if we are to understand each other, we must define our terms.

Mr. Frank fails not only to define adequately the term which gives his thesis its title but he uses it interchangeably with such expressions as "the machine," "machine industry" and "machine civilization"—expressions which he likewise fails to define.

Certainly Mr. Frank, who says he has spent every hour which he could steal from his profession for the past ten years in research for a correct understanding of American civilization, ought not to fall into this error. And yet if so well equipped a student fails in this way to penetrate beneath surface appearances it is not surprising that defenders and critics of the machine age both make the same mistake.

It is a rather common mistake. Most of those who criticise the machine and nearly all of those who defend it show clearly that they do not really understand the machine.

The time has come to understand it. The time has come to begin the discussion anew with a better definition of the thing that occasions the dispute. Perhaps we shall then find ourselves a little nearer to the discovery of what is probably the wisest course of conduct upon which mankind may enter with respect to the machine.

•

In India, where criticism and defense of the machine is in the realm of practical politics, the failure to define the term "machine" has led to a considerable confusion among the followers and the opponents of Mohandas Karamchand Gandhi.

Writing with deep appreciation of the revival of domestic spinning, Gandhi says:

> Slowly but surely the music of perhaps the most ancient machine of India is once more permeating society.[2]

But in the same book in reply to the charge that he is opposed to machinery and progress he says:

> Do I want to put back the hand of the dock of progress? Do I want to replace the mills by hand-spinning and hand-weaving? Do I want to replace the railway by the country cart? Do I want to destroy machinery altogether? These questions have been asked by some journalists and public men. My answer is: *I would not weep over the disappearance of machinery or consider it a calamity.*[3]

I have taken the liberty of italicising the line which makes it very plain that two different kinds of machines are referred to in the two quotations. In the first, Gandhi speaks approvingly of the growing use of the machines of *one kind.* In the other, he says that he would not weep over the actual disappearance of machines of *another kind.*

Evidently there is real need not only for a definition of the term "machinery" but also for the drawing of a distinction between the two kinds of machinery to which Gandhi referred.

•

According to the dictionary, very nearly every kind of mechanical contrivance which does not fall plainly into the category of tools, falls into that of machines. The dictionary makes it clear that the term "machine" is applicable to innumerable mechanical appliances, many of them antedating the application of power to machinery and many of them very different from those which are conjured up in the mind when we think of modern machines.

If we forget the dictionary definition of machines, it is very easy to forget that machines are very old; that machines were used to perform the work of the world long before the industrial revolution. What the industrial revolution brought upon us was not the machine but the application of power to the operation of machines. Power did not introduce mankind to the machine. Power merely revolutionized the manner in which man used the machine.

What is called the industrial revolution was really the economic, social and political changes caused by the transfer of machinery from the home and workshop to the mill and factory.

It is quite possible that the application of power to machinery resulted in a reduction in the amount of machinery used per capita. The spinning wheel was certainly a piece of machinery. It is extremely doubtful whether the number of spinning machines per capita is as great as the number when practically every home boasted several spinning wheels and many kinds of spindles. It is doubtful whether the number of looms per capita is as great as before the introduction of the power loom. It is doubtful whether the number of iron mills, flour mills, and lumber mills per capita is as great as when every neighborhood included a number of them.

What did result from the application of power to machinery was the gradual abandonment of machine production in the home and workshop and its transfer to the mill and factory. An even more unfortunate result was the fact that this transfer blighted the development of the technique of domestic production for nearly two hundred years. Only since the development of the internal combustion engine and of the electric motor has a technique of domestic production been developed which makes it possible for the family to compete with the factory.

•

It is easy to forget that the distinctive feature of our present industrial civilization is not so much our machine technique as it is our factory technique. It is the impressive use of machinery by the factory that makes us forget that there is a significant distinction between the domestic machine and the factory machine.

Factory machines, important as they are in our present civilization, are by no means the only type of machines which are characteristic of this age of ours. In the discussion of this question this other type of machinery is almost invariably overlooked. Critics and defenders of the machine age forget that our domestic machines include sewing machines, vacuum cleaners, washing machines, mangles, refrigerating machines, cake mixers, meat grinders, polishing and scrubbing machines, and of course automobiles. In addition, suburbanites and farmers use bread mixers, cream separators, fruit presses, steam pressure cookers, mechanical churns, automatic pumping systems, lighting plants, saw mills, grist mills, all of which are distinctly domestic and not factory machines. Obviously it is not these machines which Mr. Glenn Frank has in mind when he speaks of machines; of a machine age; of machine industry; of machine civilization. Yet these domestic machines are indubitably machines, often power driven, and they are indubitably characteristic of the times; perhaps even increasingly characteristic. The industries which are producing these domestic machines are growing rapidly, a growth of ominous significance for many non-essential and undesirable factories.

•

The distinction between the factory machine and the domestic machine is very important. For domestic machines are generally waging economic warfare with factory machines.

The domestic sewing machine is at war with the factory sewing machine.

The domestic washing machine and domestic mangle are at war with a whole group of laundry machines.

The domestic refrigerating machine is at war with the machines in the artificial ice-factories.

The domestic steam pressure cooker is at war with the machines in the canneries and packing houses.

The domestic cream separator and churn are at war with the butter-making machines in the creameries.

The domestic flour and grist mill is at war with the four mills, feed mills and cereal mills with their legions of brands and gayly colored cartons.

Even the family automobile and auto truck, by a logical extension of the term factory, may be said to be at war with factory machinery—with the railroads and the trolley cars which produce mass-transportation as compared to the individual transportation produced by the individually owned automobile. Young as they are as means of transportation, the automobile and the auto truck have already served largely to relegate the mass-producers of transportation to that heavy-hauling for which they are best adapted. As domestic machines are perfected, as they approach more nearly to the state of perfection to which the automobile has already attained, it is possible that they may tend to restrict factory production to that heavy-manufacturing to which the factory is best adapted.

Some manufacturers are well aware of this conflict between the two types of machines. The laundries of the country and the manufacturers of machines for use in laundries became alarmed several years ago at the great increase in the sale of domestic washing machines and mangles. Improvements in these domestic machines, especially the attachment of electric motors to them, threatened to check the abandonment of home washing upon which the future prosperity of the laundries and the manufacturers of laundry machinery was dependent. The of the largest manufacturers of laundry machinery in America, The American Laundry Machinery Company of Cincinnati, Ohio, began a general advertising campaign to urge the women of the nation to use laundries rather than to do their washing at home. A "Visitors' Week Laundry Party" was made a part of this campaign and promoted by this company as an annual event. During this week the laundries of the country invite housewives to visit their plants. This one company spends about a quarter of a million dollars annually to keep America safe for the factory idea of washing our dirty linen.

Could anything more clearly demonstrate the fact that there is a fundamental difference between the two types of machines? Machinery is used by the laundries to destroy domestic laundering, but machinery is also being used in the home to maintain it. If home laundering survives, it will be because the domestic machinery has been sufficiently perfected to free housewives from the drudgery of old fashioned scrub-boards and sad-irons. They will have been freed from this drudgery just as surely as if they had turned to the laundries to free them though they would still have useful but not such heavy work to do in the home. If the laundry prevails, the housewives will be freed from wash tubs and ironing boards, *but only on condition that many other women work in laundries.* Who that knows something of the conditions of labor in our laundries will say that this would mean a net gain in the beauty of civilization?

•

This illustration can be duplicated in one field after another and in all cases the conclusion to which one is driven as to the net social result is the same.

If mankind is not to be made into appendages to machines, then domestic machines must be invented capable of enabling the home to meet the competition of the factory—the right kind of machinery must be used to free man from the tyranny of the wrong kind of machinery.

It is not the machine, therefore, but the factory which needs consideration at the hands of thoughtful people.

It is the factory, not the machine, which proliferates at a rate which man has found impossible to control, and which is so relentlessly mechanizing the whole of life and reducing all (except the relatively few blessed with administrative genius) to mere cogs in a gigantic industrial machine.

It is the factory, not the machine, which makes railroads and steamship lines absolute necessities and which makes city and country dependent upon our lines of mass-transportation.

It is the factory, not the machine, which is reducing all men and all commodities to a dead level of uniformity because the factory makes it impossible for individual men and individual communities to be self-sufficient enough to develop their own capacities.

It is the factory, not the machine, which destroys both the natural beauty and the natural wealth of man's environment; which fiiis country and city with hideous factories and squalid slums, and which consumes forests, coal, iron and oil with a prodigality which will make posterity look back upon us as barbarians.

It is the factory, not the machine, which is responsible for the fact that we now make things primarily for sale rather than primarily for use; that we make things as cheaply as possible instead of as substantially as possible.

It is the factory, not the machine, which encourages wastefulness and which makes us measure products in terms of money instead of in terms of the labor involved in making them and the worth of the materials of which they are composed.

It is the factory, not the machine, which tends to decrease the number of men engaged in production and which condemns more and more people to the idiotic task of flunkeying for one another.

It is the factory, not the machine, which is responsible for the class antagonisms and for the foolish and often bloody strikes which disgrace the supposedly enlightened and progressive industrialized countries.

It is the factory, not the machine, which is destroying the skilled craftsman to whom work is a means of self-expression as well as a means of support.

It is the factory, not the machine, which creates the citizen who lacks a sustained interest in government; which destroys the initiative and self-reliance of men by making them into mere machine-tenders and clerks in factory offices.

It is the factory, not the machine, which has transformed man from a self-helpful into a self-helpless individual and which has changed mankind from a race of participators in life to a race of spectators of it. By destroying the economic foundations of the home it has robbed men, women and children of their contact with the soil; their intimacy with the growing of animals, birds, vegetables, trees and flowers; their familiarity with the actual making of things, and their capacity for entertaining and educating themselves. If we live in flats and hotels, eat from tin cans and packages, dress ourselves in fabrics and garments the design of which we only remotely influence, and entertain ourselves by looking at movies, baseball and tennis and listening to singing and music, it is due to the fact that we have applied the factory technique, not the machine technique, to sheltering, feeding, clothing, and entertaining ourselves.

Finally, it is the factory, not the machine, which is responsible for the extension of the soul-deadening repetitive labor that is the greatest curse of this civilization. Not only are the natural-born robots of the nation condemned to perform the same identical operation hour after hour and day after day, but those who are capable of creative work in the crafts, the arts and the professions are forced to conform to repetitive cycles because the factory leaves open no field in which they may exercise their talents and live. In some cases it entirely destroys the market for their services; in others, it limits the market to a small part of what it should be in a great civilization. We have a great market only for the mass-producers of culture—for mass-art: rotogravure; for mass-literature: newspapers and magazines; for mass-drama: movies. This is the ugliest crime of which the factory, not the machine, is guilty. Accepting the democratic dogma that the individual, no matter how gifted, must be subordinate to the welfare of the mass, mankind is forgetting that the destruction of conditions which make it possible for superior individuals to impose their tastes upon society means the destruction of any really desirable way of life for all of the race.

•

The trouble with Mr. Glenn Frank and the apologists for the factory is just this: they accept without question what is the most dangerous social myth of this factory-dominated civilization. They do not realize that *the idea that mankind's comfort is dependent upon an unending increase in production is a fallacy.*

It is more nearly true to say that happiness is dependent not on producing as much as possible but on producing as little as possible. Comfort and understanding are dependent upon producing only so much as is compatible with the enjoyment of the superior life. Producing more than this involves a waste of mankind's most precious possessions. It involves a waste of the only two things which man should really conserve—the two things which he should use with real intelligence and only for what really conduces to his comfort. When he destroys these two things, he has destroyed what is for all practical purposes irreplaceable. These two things are *the natural resources of the earth and the time which he has to spend in the enjoyment of them.*

When he produces more things than are necessary to good living, he wastes both of them; he wastes time and he wastes material, both of which should be used to make the world a more beautiful place in which to live, and life in it more beautiful than it is today.

CHAPTER III
EFFICIENCY

GO where you will in America; ask whomever you meet, "What of man's quest of comfort?" and they will say: "Make a large factory to flourish where only a small factory flourished before; that is the way to comfort."

For in industrialized America everybody has finally come to believe that a high standard of living is impossible without mass production, without mass distribution and without mass consumption.

And now when everybody has finally come to believe, the very foundations of our factory civilization are becoming less and less secure.

Something inherent and ineradicable; something which tends to offset the low costs of factory production; something which interferes with the contribution of the factory to material well being; something which reveals that a factory civilization cannot be the end of mankind's quest of comfort, is making itself visible.

This thing we must now seek.

•

Why did the factory come into being? How did the factory come to its present-day dominance of all the activities of mankind? What is likely to be the effect of the innumerable efforts now under way to regulate and socialize it?

Some of these questions have been much discussed from certain aspects. They have, however, been too much discussed in connection with burning controversies between capital and labor and between capitalism and socialism. There has been too little discussion based upon objective studies of the factory itself, and the factory system of production, distribution, and consumption.

We have been very much like two groups of men heatedly discussing the question of how rapidly automobiles should be driven. One group, fixing its attention upon such matters as the condition of the highways and the safety of pedestrians, insists that no automobile ought to be permitted to travel at a speed in excess of ten miles per hour. The other group, fixing its attention upon other matters altogether, such as the great boon which presumably flows from any increase in the speed of transportation, insists that the automobile should be compelled to travel at the highest rate of speed at which it can be driven. But both approaches to the question look too much to factors outside of the automobile itself. An objective approach to the question would first of all involve a study of the optimum speed at which the automobile should travel—the speed which would enable it to deliver the maximum of service at the minimum of cost—and then it would consider what changes would have to be made in the highways and in the rules regulating traffic so as to make it possible for the automobile to travel at that speed with maximum safety.

So we must approach this matter of understanding the factory system. It is useless to describe the factory, factory products, factory workers, and all the consequences which flow from the factory system until we study the economic force which brought the factory and the factory system into being and which has ever since been at work sustaining and promoting it. The factory is not a phenomenon of nature like a mountain or a river. It is an artifice of man. It is as distinctly an artificial creation as the mountain or river is distinctly a natural creation. To understand the inner significance of the factory, we must therefore take account of the motives which actuated man in producing it and which are responsible for its spread all over the world.

Having considered these preliminary questions we must then ask ourselves: What types of products lend themselves to factory production? What is the size to which the factory of necessity tends to develop? What are the methods by which factories have to be managed and controlled? These questions must be answered objectively: by a study of the factory itself and the system which is necessary if it is to function most perfectly as a factory. Only in this way will it be possible to distinguish between what is accidental and what is inherent in the factory.

Child labor, for instance, is certainly a social calamity which seemingly the factory inflicts upon mankind. But it is in reality a calamity which has its origin in the unregulated private ownership of the factory and the factory system. It can be ended at any time, either by adequate legal regulation with continued private ownership, or by the abolition of private ownership and the substitution of state ownership. It is no more an inherent attribute than smoke or smell, underpayment or unemployment and similar present day evils, all of which can be eradicated by mere changes in factory organization, operation or ownership.

Finally we must try to answer certain questions which have to do with the future of the factory and of factory civilization.

The whole world is being industrialized. The process of industrialization which took over fifty years in Japan could now be executed in about one-fifth of that time. Within a decade Italy and Russia, India and China, Mexico and Latin America may be so industrialized that exportation of many of the commodities which other nations are now supplying them will practically cease. Industries in all countries will then be forced to look only to their domestic markets for outlets for their production.

Will the intense rivalry which will then develop between factories striving to sell enough to keep their machines operating to capacity reduce prices to levels involving long periods of operation at a loss? Will the competition between the factories produce an excess of losses over profits in industry as a whole? Will the competitive demoralization which today exists in the coal industry and the textile industry and the food industry spread to all industries? Will some form of cooperative control be necessary in order to insure continuance of production? Will socialism be the ultimate solution of the problem of producing the things mankind needs and desires when private industry will cease producing them because it cannot do so at a profit?

•

I am firmly convinced that this objective study of the factory and the factory system for which I am pleading will make it clear that the industrialized nations will ultimately be driven to the socialization of production and distribution. The magnitude of the social problems which are being created by industrialization; the need for outlets for factory products; the public demand for social control of the factory, will force socialization upon the nations.

When the present period of corporate ownership reaches its point of optimum development; when ownership of stocks and bonds shall be nationwide; when management shall have increasingly been turned over to industrial engineers; when the captains of industry will find it less and less possible to keep the huge enterprises which they direct from wiping out profits in competitive struggles for orders for their plants, there will develop a general acquiescence in some form of social liquidation of private ownership of the factory.

There are already plenty of straws to show which way the wind is blowing. Today, at the very time when the United States Chamber of Commerce solemnly issues pronunciamentos in favor of less and less interference by government in business, American industry itself is actually engaged in building legal and statutory foundations for consolidation, for monopoly, and for government regulation. Evidently there is something inherent in the factory—in a system of production which gets larger and larger all the time, which tends to consolidation, regulation, socialization; some force of which business men generally are not cognizant and to which they continue to voice hostility even after they have accepted it in practice.

Upon this point, let me quote Mr. Paul M. Mazur, one of the partners in the banking firm of Lehman Brothers, New York:

> Consolidation . . . offers the solution of other problems of American industry. In many cases the existence of uncontrolled competitive effort has made profit for some American industries impossible. For nearly five years the textile situation has presented a most un alluring picture. Here and there textile corporations have been successful, but, by and large, the entire industry lias presented most depressing profit figures to its owners. Decrease of sales and inefficient management have contributed in important measure to the unhappy situation. But the existence of a large number of highly individualized corporate units and the resulting competition have been the fundamental causes of the lean years during which the textile business has starved

upon half rations. The need for keeping the wheels and looms of mills running has encouraged the sale of goods at unprofitable prices. And any bulge in demand that might have been momentarily created has been inundated with a tremendous supply that resulted from the desire of each mill to get its full share of the apparently available sales market. The selling custom of the industry also added to the problem of the mill. The plan whereby the whole sales responsibility is turned over to an independent sales agency—called commission merchant or f actor—grew originally out of the necessity of financing the production of the mills, but it has transferred the ownership of the sales market for the products of the mill from the producer to the commission agent.

The necessity of controlling production and eliminating the guerilla warfare that results from unlimited competition actually screams for consolidation within the textile industry in America. Moreover, the wisdom of the producer's possessing unquestioned title to his own sales agency and his own sales market can only prompt the inclusion of the function of sales among the processes of the new consolidated units which are inevitable in the industry. The problem is already serious—almost tragic in New England—and it will become more serious as Europe begins to pay its annual interest charges in the textile values which she is so well fitted to create.

With mergers the textile business of America may be able to prosper; without mergers, its hope of rehabilitation is desperate indeed.

The textile situation is merely the most aggravated case of competitive disease in American industry. As time goes on and the demand for volume continues, the road of consolidation will be more and more frequently trod. Such a road will carry industry to competitive safety, even to the security of monopoly, unless the Sherman Law and the Clayton Act present effective barriers to the development of mergers.[4]

Recognition of these facts is not confined to industrialized America. In industrialized Germany students of this question are saying that the epoch of the freedom of German industry and commerce is rapidly and inevitably drawing to a close. A new era is dawning which fulfills Marxist prophecies of Government control. This was the gist of a recent article by Dr. E. Schmalenbach, a professor at the University of Cologne, whose knowledge of economics was considered by the Government so extensive that he was made chairman of the commission entrusted in 1927 with the investigation of the Ruhr mining situation.

"The predictions of the founder of Marxism are being fulfilled before our eyes, but the present industrial leaders will protest if they are told that they are the executors of Marx's testament," Dr. Schmalenbach wrote.

While the industrialists are not trying to bring about economic restraint, he adds, they are tools in the hands of evolution. Continued improvement in labor-saving machines is largely responsible for the unavoidable change, aided and abetted by the growing intensity of capitalism in making human hands more and more superfluous. The costs of production have been increasing constantly, and the time must come when they are so high as no longer to balance consumption.

German industry and commerce are now at the crossroads, and nineteenth-century freedom is about to be lost and replaced by restraint at the hands of the Government, he said. The transition will come within a period of a few years only. Objections by trusts and cartels to supervision will not prevent or even retard the change of the entire economic system, but their resistance will actually accelerate the process of change.

Dr. Schmalenbach finds no cause for public worry about the operation of the new system even though it involves the abandonment of the present largely free competitive system. Monopolies will soon be assisted to maintain themselves in supreme power. He illustrates this contention by using the coal industry of Europe as an example. Possession of coal mines under the old system is a curse instead of a blessing for England, Germany, France, and Belgium since competition forces them to bear heavy losses through selling at prices below the cost of production to countries having no coal. This practice under the new system would be discontinued and selling would be done at prices fixed to protect against loss.

Directors of large cartels and monopolies, the Professor contends, show the same lack of comprehensive outlook as did the German Princes at the time of the founding of the German Empire.

He concludes:

> The Bismarck who could drill patriotism into them has not yet been found. The "new system of restraint" will quickly show its superiority to the present system. I am convinced that in the near future we shall reach a condition under which large corporations will receive their monopolies from the State, which, at the same time, will compel them, by strict supervision, to live up to their duties. This development cannot be prevented by the present warfare against State control.[5]

The consolidations of which American business men like Mr. Mazur speak so hopefully, and the monopolistic evolution which economists like Professor Schmalenbach consider inevitable, may ultimately end in socialization, as Karl Marx predicted. For it is improbable that the consuming public would long submit to exploitation by uncontrolled private monopoly. The industrialized nations might not turn to communism, but the very least form of socialization which they would adopt would involve public regulation. "Private" business would be subject to regulation much as are railroads, street cars, electric and gas companies and other privately owned public utilities today.

Strangely enough both the business men and the economists pleading the cause of the huge armies of investors, and the reformers and socialists pleading the cause of the consuming public are in agreement about the desirability of developing the factory system, the desirability of integrating industry, the desirability of utilizing the powers of the government in order to promote the production and distribution of factory products. Both believe in mass production, in mass distribution, in mass consumption. Socialization, if it ever arrives, as Russia tends to show, will mean a change of directors, but not of direction. We may substitute commissars for capitalists, but we will be continuing along the same line of serialized, standardized, socialized production, distribution and consumption.

I do not believe that socialization is unavoidable. It may come, but if it does come, it will not be because the state has no alternative except to take over the management of the Frankensteins which our captains of industry have been creating. When it does come, it will be because the herd-minded masses will again do what they have so often done in the past, follow the leadership of quantity-minded men who deliberately reject the alternatives which quality-minded men evolve.

I am opposed to the whole tendency toward making the individual a cog in huge factory systems of production and distribution, quite without regard to whether the systems are to be individually, corporately or governmentally owned.

Complete socialization would be the final step in the process of making man the servant of his own machines, the first step of which was taken when factories were first erected.

The improvements in the status of the workers for which socialists hope, if society through officials of some kind takes the place of the present owners of industry, will not solve the problem of the quest of comfort. For socialists consider man too much merely as one of the elements in the processes of production and distribution and do not sufficiently consider how men individually should live if mankind generally is to enjoy the good life.

•

The modern factory with its application of power to the operation of heavy and expensive machinery came into existence during the latter part of the eighteenth century. Individual desire for profits, for huge profits, for profits which make present day factory profits relatively insignificant, was responsible for its birth.

The first factories were established at a time when nearly all "boughten" products were slowly fabricated by individual craftsmen. The factory products were naturally sold either at the prevailing high prices or at prices only a little lower than those of craft-made products. The combination of power-driven machinery and factory methods cut the cost of making goods to fractions of the cost upon which the prevailing level of prices was based. Manufacturers could undersell the craftsmen and still make themselves rich in a comparatively short lime. Profits that now seem fabulons were made because the public was accustomed to the high "handicraft" level of prices. High profits continued until production of craft-made products virtually ceased; until factory-made goods took possession of the market, and until competition between rival manufacturers brought prices down to a level which gave consumers part of the lower costs of factory production. During this period, manufacturing fortunes had time to become firmly established factors in world economics and the process of investing and reinvesting manufacturing profits in still additional factories had time to enlist the cupidity of an army of quantity-minded men.

The foundations for modern mass-production, mass-distribution, and mass-consumption were laid.

The factory-made fortunes introduced into the economy of the world a type of capital different in many respects from any which had up to that time been evolved. First of all, this capital was infinitely more mobile. Even the fixed capital of the manufacturer was more mobile than the fixed capital, if one may call it that, which formed most of the wealth of the upper classes before the industrial revolution. Pre-factory wealth consisted mainly of land and houses, of all forms of capital the most immobile. Land, which was the principal source of income of the wealthy, was practically fixed in quantity. It increased in value only with the increase in population. This was a very slow process because, until comparatively recent times, wars and plagues regularly decimated the population. Livestock and agricultural products, jewelry, precious metals, furnishings and other forms of pre industrial wealth, were all things which could at that time be accumulated only slowly.

With the coming of the factory all this was changed. The factory revealed the golden secret of rapid capital turn-over. The profits from the factory accumulated in the form of cash, bills and accounts receivable, and stocks of goods, all of them forms of wealth which were exceedingly mobile. Even profits in the form of additions to plant and equipment, while less mobile than the other forms of factory wealth, were still not so immobile as land.

The unending stream of factory-created profits was invested in more and more factories.

Facilities for banking and trading were stimulated into feverish growth.

Joint stock companies and limited liability companies began to take the place of individual and partnership forms of factory ownership.

The instrumentalities for speculation were developed and made ready for the period of expansion which began with the coming of the canal and the railroad and which has continued without respite since that time.

•

Sir Richard Arkwright, the father of the cotton-spinning industry, and perhaps even father of the modern system of factory production and distribution, furnishes an example of the rapidity with which fortunes were accumulated through the organization, operation, and marketing of the products of the factory. He was the youngest of thirteen children of very poor parents. The parents had Little enough to give to any of their children either of education or of other more substantial advantages, and by the time this was distributed among so large a brood, each was the recipient, so far as fortune was concerned, of about as near to nothing as is conceivable. He began life as a barber. Dealing in human hair and dyeing it by a process of his own enabled him to accumulate a little wealth. In 1767 he gave up this business and began his real career, first as an exploiter of inventions dealing with spinning, and after the manufacture of yarn was firmly established, as a speculator and trader in the yarn markets. Less than twenty years later he was the head of businesses representing a capital in excess of 200,000 pounds. He had become many times a millionaire by modern standards. Nothing in the previous history of mankind had been discovered which made it possible to create peacefully such a fortune in so short a period of time. The only way in which wealth had previously been accumulated rapidly was by seizure and conquest, or by currying the favor of those who were already wealthy and powerful. Before the factory these were the only alternatives available to power-seeking men who objected to the slow process of acquiring riches by inheritance or by minute accretions in land values as population increased.

Arkwright lived to be showered with honors and attention. A grateful British king knighted him. He died enormously wealthy, the progenitor of the modern captain of industry, the man who showed Britain what could be accomplished by a nation led by men like himself. Historians tend to neglect the men who followed in his footsteps; but economists cannot afford to do so. Their lives furnish demonstration after demonstration of the proposition that factories came into being in the beginning, and continue to this day to be established because individuals like Arkwright see in each new field of production enormous opportunities for profit—the opportunity to sell a factory product at a high profit to a public still used to a non-factory level of prices, or willing to pay a high price for a new product because of the higher prices or greater disadvantages of the product which it displaces.

•

These high profits explain the present day dominance of our economic life by the factory system of production, distribution and consumption. Enormous sums accumulate in the hands of relatively wealthy factory owners. That they should invest these sums in the erection of more factories, in the production of the raw materials they need for them, and the development of systems of transportation for both the raw materials and the finished products, is only natural. For they cannot consume these sums in good living, no matter how ostentatiously they may spend money. They do not know enough about art, science and history to use them to really beautify the earth.

They can only invest them and re-invest them.

So capital is always accumulating in their hands, just as it is accumulating in their banks, in their business corporations, their insurance companies and even in their endowments and foundations.

Ingenious, cunning, ruthless, with appetites whetted by gargantuan visions, they are encouraged by the existence of all this capital to develop new industries. The capital accumulated in textiles makes it easier to make fortunes in railroads, and in turn to make fortunes in brewing and distilling; in iron and steel; in meat-packing and flour-milling, and today in automobiles, in movies and in radio.

Every advance in science is seized upon to extend the factory system. Those first to operate successfully factories which take advantage of new scientific developments win the greatest profits. Nearly every new factory product and new factory process creates at least one great fortune when it is new. Kerosene produced the Rockefeller fortune; refined sugar the Havemeyer fortune; reapers produced the McCormick fortune; cash registers the Patterson fortune; cameras the Eastman fortune and automobiles the Ford fortune.

Bonanza profits on new products, fortunately for the public, stimulate the building of factories in the new fields. As soon as production in a new field is sufficiently developed to insure profits, the factories in it tend to multiply often at geometric progressions. The time in which the mass production of a new product can be pushed past the experimental stage has persistently been shortened. What took decades to accomplish in the case of the steam railroad has taken a single generation in the case of the automobile. Mass production, which had to develop by trial and error methods in the early days of the factory, can today be applied to making any product as soon as the market for a product proves large enough to justify the necessary investment in automatic machinery.

The radio vacuum tube and the radio receiver industry, as soon as the products themselves were developed, sprang into mass production. So great was the capital inflow into the industry and so efficient the machinery and techniques used in the factories, that within a few years the volume of production frequently exceeded the absorption capacity of the market.

•

The world is rapidly becoming one vast factory. The frontier of the agricultural civilizations of the past was marked by the clearings of the pioneer settlers. Where the pioneer was there was the agricultural frontier. The frontier of our modern industrial civilizations is marked by belching smokestacks. Where the factory is and the region where no factories have yet been erected begins, there is the industrial frontier. Farther and farther into the "backward" regions of the earth goes that frontier.

If we assume that the first distinctly industrial community was Manchester, in which Arkwright established the factory production of yarn, then the first industrial frontier was in that tight little island that contains England. By 1850, the industrialists had dotted England with factories. Then the factories began to appear across the channel in Europe and simultaneously across the Atlantic in North America. Now only Asia and Africa and part of South America and Australia remain to be industrialized—the last frontiers which the factory will have to conquer before the whole world will have been industrialized.

Sometimes I see the factory as a reincarnation of the fabled Wandering Jew. Where the Wandering Jew directed his footsteps, there came the Black Plague. Restlessly the Wandering Jew pushed on into every region of the globe. Behind him he left regions writhing in miseries as to the source of which the sufferers were ignorant.

So it has been with the factory.

Wherever the factory establishes itself, there it introduces its special form of ugliness.

Restlessly the factory pushes on into every region of the globe. One after another the non-industrial cultures and civilizations go down before it. Highly developed civilizations like those of the Japanese and the East Indians succumb to it precisely as do the primitive cultures of the South Sea Islanders or the African negroes. Into each region it introduces distresses and discomforts as to the source of which the populace is largely ignorant.

•

In every country where the factory has been established long enough; in every nation in which the factory has precipitated those grave social problems which we shall later consider in some detail, efforts to socialize the factory—to make it subservient to society—inevitably develop. These efforts, although rarely inspired directly by socialism, are yet vindications of Marx, Engels, and Lassalle. For socialization and functionalization of the factory are predicated upon the basic idea that the uncontrolled private ownership of the means of production and distribution is responsible for practically all of the social maladies of the world.

If every individual were willing to sacrifice freedom and initiative in the economic field, society might succeed—as the socialists believe—in eliminating every trace of exploitation from the factory system. But the elimination of exploitation by the abolition of private ownership of production and distribution does not reach the root of the trouble. The factory's ineradicable attributes would still remain to plague mankind. Socialization or functionalization of the factory will never produce the utopia for which so many idealists are working. Socialization must fail as a remedy because it does not treat with the real disease which the factory system has inflicted upon mankind.

Socialization must fail because it contains no balm for efficiency-scourged mankind.

For the efficiency that is the quintessence of factory civilization is the real disease which the factory has inflicted upon mankind.

And efficiency would remain to rob mankind of comfort no matter what form management and ownership of the factory might take.

The factory must be efficient. It can survive only by becoming more and more efficient.

It has to be efficient under private management and ownership. It would have to be efficient even if private management and ownership were changed to public.

Mankind's comfort would have to be sacrificed on the altar of the great god efficiency under socialism precisely as it has to be under capitalism because the *factory system ceases to be economic unless it is efficient enough to absorb the institutional burden which is its inescapable concomitant.*

•

What is the nature of this institutional burden? And what is its significance?

With domestic production--indeed with almost any non-factory system of production—the price which is paid, or if you prefer, the sacrifice which is made in order to satisfy the individual's desire for any commodity, may be resolved into three costs: the cost of the labor necessary in fabricating the commodity; the cost of the materials used; and the incidental expenses not directly classifiable under either of these two heads. These three costs are analogous to what are usually called the direct material cost, the direct labor cost, and the shop expense of the factory, the three comprising the manufacturing cost of a factory product.

With factory production these three costs are, of course, much lower than with domestic production.

Factory production makes it possible to effect savings on the cost of material by purchasing in large quantities, by eliminating waste and by utilizing by-products. It makes revolutionary savings on the cost of labor possible through the division of labor and the use of labor-saving machinery. Finally, it makes almost equally large savings possible in the shop or factory expenses. These factory expenses—the non-productive labor of firemen, engineers, oilers, etc., the materials such as coal, oil, materials for repairs which are not directly chargeable against any unit of product, and of course the rent, taxes, insurance, depreciation, etc.—are distributed over the large number of units of the products made by the factory, and are therefore materially smaller than the incidental expense per unit under domestic production.

•

But these savings are somewhat offset by three *new* factory costs which have no real counterparts under domestic production: the transportation costs on materials and supplies; the general office expenses of the manufacturer, and the profits which have to be added if the manufacturer is to be compensated for his effort and enterprise.

The factory's transportation costs on materials and supplies are hardly compatible with any expenses incurred in domestic production. With domestic production consumption takes place at the point of production. But with large scale production it is almost impossible to find both a sufficient supply of raw materials and a sufficient market for all that is produced at the place where the factory is located. Transportation of both the raw materials and the finished products is often necessary. Transportation of one or the other is almost inevitable.

The factory's general expenses are new and hardly comparable to any of the costs involved in domestic production because advertising and selling expenses, credit costs, and accounting and other office expenses have their reason for being only because the factory has to sell what it produces.

And for the same reason the manufacturer's profit is hardly comparable to anything existing under domestic production. The elaborate structure of interest on bonds and bank loans; dividends on stock, and the various forms which remuneration for risks and management take, are non-existent under a system of non-factory production where the capital investment—no factory machinery being used—is negligible.

But if these three costs were the only costs constituting the institutional burden of the factory system, efficiency would not present so menacing an aspect. These three new factory costs are only a part of the full institutional burden. Some of the more important of the other costs are wholesaling transportation and warehousing costs, wholesaling expenses, wholesaling profits, retailing transportation and warehousing costs, retailing expenses, retailing profits.

Factory production must be efficient enough to carry the burden of all these distribution costs because, with a volume of production in excess of the demands of the market in its immediate neighborhood, some such costly system of distribution is necessary. It must be efficient enough to carry the burden of all transportation costs and distributors' expenses and profits in addition to the costs of its own which are usually lumped together under the term "overhead."

Let the factory fail to absorb these costs and it becomes impossible for it to supply consumers as economically as they can produce for themselves or buy from a custom maker. Mankind would then find a revival of domestic and custom production worth while.

The following diagram which compares the costs in a system of non-factory production with the costs in a system of factory production presents the situation graphically:

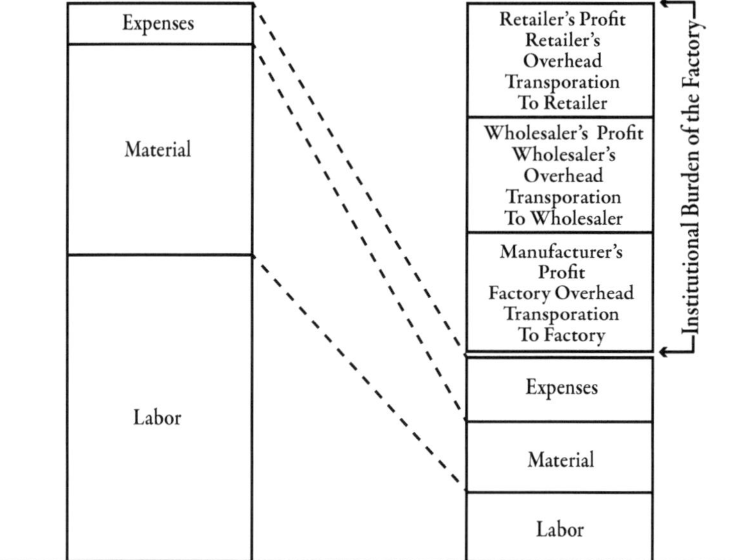

The diagram makes graphic the fact that what the consumers of factory products are supposed to gain through the lowering of the direct cost of manufacturing—through lower costs of material, labor and direct factory expense—they tend to lose in what I have called the institutional burden of the factory system.

•

With factory production large capital is necessary for plant, machinery and materials. It is secured by borrowing; by forming partnerships; by incorporation. Interest, profits, and dividends are used to pay those who furnish capital. Depreciation and obsolescence of plant and equipment form a major problem; the larger the machinery, the greater is not only the necessity of providing for wear and tear, but of setting up reserves to make it possible to acquire new machines and to use new processes wherever their invention makes the use of older machinery unprofitable.

Overhead is relatively large not only because of these expenses but because of the high cost of superintendence. The larger the factory, the greater the superintendence. Large numbers of workers cannot be directed by the methods which were efficient enough when a master workman was producing, under the handicraft system, surrounded by a group of apprentices. The military system of management, in which all power and authority emanate from one man who keeps control of all details is inexpensive but it is efficient only in the small shop. In the factory, the departmental system develops inevitably. Work is divided into departments each under absolute control of one man who is in turn under the control of a superintendent who gives general instructions and holds the department foremen responsible for results. In the largest factories, combinations of what are known as the functional system and the departmental system of management are used. The work of management is divided so that each supervisor shall have as few functions as possible. There are gang bosses, speed bosses, inspectors, repair bosses, planning department representatives and of course corresponding "office" supervisors: designers, planners, record keepers and cost clerks. Similar additions to the overhead develop in the office of the factory. There are office managers, personnel managers, sales managers, advertising managers and traffic managers. When more than one plant has to be supervised or a number of branch offices must be managed a whole hierarchy of higher supervisors are necessary: above the superintendents of the plants there are engineers, auditors, general managers, treasurers, presidents and finally directors. All tend to absorb the reductions in manufacturing costs which are made possible by the factory machinery and factory methods.

•

If the mass of goods produced by the factory is to be absorbed, mass distribution has to be provided. Time and place utilities have to be created. Distant markets must be secured. The goods must be warehoused at convenient points in anticipation of seasonal demand. Mass consumption must be created through salesmanship and advertising. As a result, approximately two-thirds of what the consumer of today pays for the products of the factory is payment for distributing the product; less than a third is payment for manufacturing it.

I have discussed the distribution question in detail in *The Distribution Age*, and the part advertising plays in the creation of mass consumption in *National Advertising vs. Prosperity*. In these two books, I have assembled what seems to me irrefutable evidence that as factories grow larger and larger, as the industrialization becomes more and more complete, distribution costs rise higher and higher. In 1870 only 10% of the working population of the United States was engaged in transporting and distributing the commodities then produced. Ten years later, this increased to 11%. In the next ten years it increased to 14%. By 1900, it was 16%. The average rise during these 30 years was about 1½% per decade. Beginning with 1900, the rate of increase became progressively more rapid. By 1910, it had jumped to 20%. By 1920, fifty years after it was only 10%, it had become 25%. Even if the rate of progression ceases to increase, within the next fifty years there will be one worker engaged in transportation and distribution for every worker engaged in farming or manufacturing.

•

As the factory increases in size—as the contribution of labor to production becomes smaller and that of machinery and power larger—the institutional burden becomes greater and greater. We find almost a natural law governing the growth of factories: the larger the factory, the greater the inverse relationship of the general overhead and distribution costs to labor and material costs. The problems of efficiency of operations and of volume of sales increase in importance, while those of wages and of raw material costs decrease in importance. Indeed, in spite of the intensity of modern competition, a Henry Ford can afford to pay higher wages than prevail in the general labor market and to use the most expensive of raw materials, and still accumulate a gigantic fortune. He can do this because his product is still relatively a new one and his industry still immature. He can secure volume distribution at low cost, and he has the necessary skill to operate a gigantic factory efficiently. As the automobile industry reaches maturity, however, this will become more and more difficult.

In young industries, like the automobile industry, efficiency produces enormous profits.

In old industries, like the textile industry, only the most rigorous efficiency enables the manufacturer to avert bankruptcy. Management in a textile mill is a race between covering the over head and going into bankruptcy.

In new industries, profits are the spur to efficiency.

In old industries, survival is the spur to efficiency.

•

The factory has to be operated with an efficiency proportioned to the institutional burden because only to a limited extent can it raise prices to cover increasing overhead and distribution costs.

The individual factory cannot raise prices beyond a certain limit because of the competition of rival factories.

A whole industry cannot raise prices beyond a certain limit because its products would drive consumers either to the products of other industries or to the production of the goods for themselves.

An individual bakery cannot raise the price of bread, for instance, beyond the neighborhood price without losing its business to rival bakeries. If all the bakeries in the country were consolidated, or bread baking were taken over by society, the price of bread could still not be raised beyond a certain point because consumers would then be driven to baking bread for themselves. When prices are raised to the point fixed by these limits, further margins for overhead and distribution costs can only be secured by increased efficiency in production.

As long as the factory management is efficient and the sales volume adequate, the overhead is covered; interest and dividends are paid; the securities of the corporation rise in value. If the factory management is inefficient, and the overhead is not covered, capital charges are not met. The securities then depreciate in value until the equities they represent are completely dissipated. The corporation operating the factory then fails. Liquidation of its assets turns the factory over to a new corporation.

The new corporation may represent "stronger hands." The factory is then absorbed and operated as a part of a merger or consolidation of some kind. Occasionally, however, the factory which has been taken over is not operated at all. Production is concentrated in other factories owned by the new corporation. Often, however, the new corporation is not strong enough to in dulge in this drastic method of insuring profits. It may merely represent new capital which acquires the plant and the machinery at a bargain and hopes to operate the factory successfully because its investment is smaller than that of the corporation which failed.

It is an ingenious system. Considering it objectively, it produces for mankind with amazing reliability. It will continue to function at least as well as it does today, as long as scientific management devises new wrinkles in efficiency to offset rising overhead and distribution costs.

•

The institutional burden is largely an inherent attribute of the factory system. Mere changes in methods of control and ownership will not eliminate it.

Socialism, for instance, would abolish all the present charges for rent, interest, and profit. Theoretically this would reduce the cost of capital. Theoretically this would eliminate the surplus profits of capitalists. Actually, the saving would be negligible because in taking over all factories not only would the gains of the successful factories be taken over, but all the losses of the unsuccessful ones.

Cooperation, on the other hand, would operate the distribution system in the interest of consumers and the factory system in the interests of the producers and workers. Theoretically the consumers would be insured against exploitation by the "middle-men." Theoretically the producers and workers would be protected against exploitation by the factory owners, Actually, the protection hoped for could be realized only through the agency of exceptionally able and honest management and not through any elimination of the institutional burden of the factory system itself.

For most of the costs of producing and distributing factory products consist of items which would remain no matter what the form of control or what the kind of ownership. Some economic efforts must be made in order to accumulate capital, and whatever the form these efforts take, consumers must be charged enough to pay the actual cost of accumulating and using the capital. Some economic efforts must be made for meeting depreciation and obsolescence in buildings, machinery, and materials. And again consumers must be made to pay for the actual cost of maintaining and replacing the equipment essential to the factory. And distribution also has tangible and very real economic costs, and consumers must be made to pay these costs if the factory's products are to be made available when consumers want them and in the places where consumers want to procure them. There are other items in the institutional burden which cannot be escaped by any mere change in control—changes of fashion affecting demand, new methods which make old machinery worthless, and new industries which tend to render the old ones un-economic.

Thus there is no escape from the conclusion that the institutional burden of the factory system as a whole cannot be eliminated by a shift of factory control from individual owners to corporations; from corporations to trusts and from trusts to government departments.

•

The economic obligation to be efficient cannot be evaded by abolishing private ownership of the factory and outlawing private profit. Socialization may actually increase the overhead and so make an even more rigorous efficiency in production necessary.

Overhead expenses, transportation and distribution costs and practically all the costs which comprise the institutional burden of the factory system are not arbitrary inventions of capitalism.

The state owned and operated factory would labor under substantially the same inherent and unavoidable compulsion to be efficient as does the privately owned factory. If it failed in efficiency, it would be unable to furnish the public goods at a cost as low as that provided by the privately owned factory. The truth about the cost of its products could be concealed from the public by making production a state monopoly and thus preventing privately owned factories from making odious price comparisons. Making it impossible for the public to buy from an alternative source of supply would enable the state owned factory to survive, but the factory would nevertheless be an economic failure. It would absorb more labor and more material than similar factories under capitalism and yet furnish the public a smaller quantity of finished goods.

Thus we are driven to conclude that no matter what the form of control and ownership, the compulsion to operate the factory efficiently is inherent and inescapable. It must be operated efficiently or fail as a factory, with individual losses under private ownership; with government losses under public ownership.

Efficiency is, therefore, the quintessence of the factory system. Efficiency determines where factories are located; what equipment is used in them; how large they are to be; what methods and practices are to prevail in their operation. For only if they are efficient can they absorb the functional handicap of the institutional bur den and deliver an economic product to the public.

•

We are indebted to the late Frederick Winslow Taylor, the founder of scientific management, for the first exposition of the principle that factory efficiency is dependent upon the application to factory operations of the laws which govern maximum production from the machinery, the materials and the labor available to the management. Factory efficiency is high or low in accordance with the extent to which the management can make the workers accommodate themselves to the formulæ which the efficiency engineers evolve. It is not, therefore, the native capacity of the workers, much less their personal desires about work, which determines how they work in the efficient factory. It is the factory's impersonal necessities that determine how the workers must work. And the management must discover its factory's necessities or fall behind in the competition with those which do.

An illustration from *The Principles of Scientific Management* gives some idea of what the factory can afford to pay for the development of formulæ that lead to greater efficiency. In the fall of 1880, William Sellers, President of the Midvale Steel Company, asked Taylor to conduct a series of experiments designed to answer two questions which would add greatly to the efficiency of all the company's machine work. At the time the experiments were begun it was believed that it would not take more than six months to develop the necessary formulæ. As a matter of fact, the experiments were carried on, with occasional interruptions, for 26 years and from $150,000 to $200,000 was spent in making them.

Taylor was asked by Sellers to provide the company with a set of rules that would enable the managers of the factories to answer two questions:

First, at what cutting speeds should the machinists operate the various metal cutting machines at which they work;

Second, what feeds should they use in their machines?

"They sound so simple," said Taylor, "that they would appear to call for merely the trained judgment of any good mechanic. In fact, after working 26 years, it has been found that the answer in every case involves the solution of an intricate mathematical problem, in which the effect of twelve independent variables must be determined."

•

Once such formulæ have been found, they impose themselves upon all factories.

The Midvale Steel Company discovers a new and more efficient method of production. It cuts its costs and lowers its prices; enlarges its sales and increases its profits.

In order to meet the Midvale Steel Company's competition, competing steel companies must adopt the new methods. They must become equally efficient or they must reconcile themselves to more or less speedy failure.

Both the owners of the factories and the factory workers find themselves forced to conform to the necessities of a Frankenstein, the inevitability of which both accept, precisely as both owners and slaves once accepted the inevitability of slavery.

And there is no escape from this inevitability of efficiency by an abandonment of private ownership. There is only one escape: that is by an abandonment of an further development of the factory. This would stabilize efficiency at the standard which prevails today. But it is an escape in some respects worse than the evil to be remedied.

Efficiency, more efficiency, still more efficiency—this is what the factory itself imposes upon mankind, not only with regard to production, as in the instance just cited, but also in every detail of factory operations, beginning with the purchase of raw materials, the management of labor, accounting, credit, and finance, and ending with marketing, selling, and advertising. Taylor summarizes it as:

> Science, not rule of thumb. Harmony, not discord.
> Cooperation, not individualism.
> Maximum output, in place of restricted output.
> The development of each man to his greatest efficiency and prosperity.[7]

•

Cooperation and not individualism is implicit in the factory system. As efficiency increases, cooperation will therefore increase. With maximum efficiency the goal, cooperation will not be dispensed with once it is attained within individual factories. Cooperation inside factories will be followed by cooperation between factories, and finally, by cooperation between all the factors in production and distribution. Efficiency thus imposes upon the factory-dominated world a process of integration, centralization and finally, if uncontrolled private monopoly is not to be permitted to exploit the public, some form of socialization.

Added impetus is being given to this tendency, especially in the older industries, by the threatening aspect of over industrialization. Under our present economic regime factories, as we have seen, tend to proliferate at a constantly accelerating rate. They would probably increase similarly under any other regime in which policy was in the hands of a quantity-minded class of managers and rulers. But under present day conditions, the immediate consequence of over-industrialization to the individual factory owner, and therefore to the workers and those dependent upon the operation of the factory for a market for raw materials and supplies, is a reduction of net income.

With more factories than are really needed seeking to market their products, and to operate at least at such a proportion of their total capacity as will enable them to meet overhead expenses, prices frequently fall below the cost of production.

Industries in which this state of affairs has become chronic many branches of the textile industry and certain branches of the food industry—are social and economic menaces. What they produce is sold at low "distress" prices to the public, but the communities in which the factories are located suffer from the unemployment and underpayment of labor, and from the loss of profits and the bankruptcies of the owners of the factories. These factory towns become economic plague spots, in which consuming-power for the products of other industries is at a very low point because the residents have not income enough to buy and to consume a normal volume of commodities.

Confronted by the problem of stabilizing profits and stabilizing production, American manufacturers in spite of their boasted individualism are beginning to turn to cooperation and governmental assistance for salvation.

They are trying to solve the problem by raising prices. Prices are raised by controlling production; monopolizing raw materials; licensing patents; stimulating consumption, (usually by lessening consumption of the products of rival industries), and by cooperative price-fixing.

They are trying to solve the problem by reducing costs—by using more and more automatic machinery, by working longer hours, and by lowering wages.

And now they are beginning to try to solve the problem by enlisting the assistance of the government. The tendency in this direction is becoming plainer all the time. The oil industry furnishes an excellent illustration of it. A report of the Committee of Eleven of the American Petroleum Institute in 1925 showed that the industry at that time was unaware of the existence of any serious problem. Their report stated that the industry was confident of its ability to secure "prices that will provide a return to producers, refiners, and distributors commensurate with the risk involved and the capital invested." The total domestic output of oil, however, was only 763,743,000 barrels that year—slightly more than the average production of the four years 1923-26 inclusive. The year 1927, however, produced an output of 905, 800,000 barrels.

The industry began to discover a problem. Lower prices for petroleum and its products; increased expense for storage facilities; diminished profits and outright losses could not be ignored. Prices of leading oil stocks moved to new low levels in the face of a rise in the price of stocks generally. Even the stocks of the Standard Oil of New Jersey and Standard Oil of New York were being affected.

A Committee of Nine was formed, consisting of three representatives of the oil industry, three of the mineral section of the American Bar Association, and three of the Federal Government. This committee brought in a report radically different from that of the Committee of Eleven. It was plain to this committee that the industry had to save itself by cooperative development of oil pools by "voluntary" agreement. In order to secure the necessary "voluntary" agreements, the government was to remove any unnecessary obstacles—that, is, suspend the enforcement of the Sherman Anti-Trust Law—and in addition to bring to bear whatever pressure it "reasonably" could exert. As a step in this direction, the State and Federal antitrust laws were to be amended so as to remove unequivocally from their purview voluntary agreements looking to the restriction of output and the cooperative development and production of oil.

If this sort of cooperation in the oil industry succeeds in re storing profits, is it not plain that expansion will again set in, profits will again disappear, and still more cooperation will be needed to save the industry, and so on ad infinitum? [8]

If in spite of help from such "voluntary" cooperation the industry ultimately ceases to furnish possibilities of profits, then the owners of the industry will naturally strive to "unload" it on the government, and if the government proves reluctant about taking over the losing venture, the public's need of the products of the industry will force it to take it over.

These various efforts of American manufacturers to escape from the effects of over-industrialization, carefully concealed from the public, run counter to existing law, to existing folkways and to existing economic philosophy. They involve conventional business men and conventional economists in a maze of logical contradictions—natural consequences of the conflict between business necessity and existing statutes, customs and philosophies.

Ultimately economic necessity will prevail.

New laws, new customs, new economic theories—which permit of greater cooperation, greater integration, greater efficiency will take the place of those which prevail today.

But efficiency will remain—to whip and drive and scourge the victims of this civilization.

PART II
THE FACTORY

Lo, this is the tarantula's den!

—*Thus Spake Zarathustra.*

CHAPTER IV
THE FACTORY ITSELF

THAT ugly group of ramshackle buildings in the midst of a fertile farming country in Indiana, in which men, women and children are frenziedly packing tomatoes, corn and peas into tin cans, is a factory.

That monstrous ugly set of retorts, furnaces, coal and ore piles, in grimy, sooty Pittsburgh, in which straining and sweating men are producing iron and steel, is a factory.

That light but ugly loft with its rows and rows of sewing machines, one of dozens of similar lofts in a great rabbit-warren of a building in New York, in which hurried men and women are making clothes, is a factory.

And so is that model cotton mill somewhere in the Sunny South surrounded by its model village of brightly painted frame bungalows all as like as peas in a pod. The men, women and children may be spinning and weaving cotton goods in a model mill; they may be living in model houses, buying from a model commissary, attending a model church, and their children studying in a model school, yet the mill and its life is ugly because work, homes, movies, schools, and churches are planned and provided for the millworkers by the omnipotent corporation which plans the details of their lives precisely as it selects the looms and spindles which they operate.

•

The buildings which house the average factory—its machinery, workers, supplies and goods—are most often a collection of ugly wooden, brick, or concrete structures. Sometimes they are standard factory buildings made in a factory devoted to the factory production of factory buildings and then shipped "knocked clown" to the place where they are erected. Sometimes the buildings are what are known as "lofts"; block-like structures, each floor of which is rented by a separate factory. Occasionally the buildings are architectural "gems," but gems which conceal the fact that they exist primarily to be efficient by the thin expedient of superimposing a veneer of period architecture upon what would be much more fitting if its frankly utilitarian purposes were intelligently exploited.

•

Factories are to be found everywhere; sometimes in the country, sometimes in a suburb of a city, but oftenest in the city itself. They are found most often in the city because they prosper best in a large consuming market or near enough to one so that they secure a cheap and adequate outlet for their output. Some times, however, they are found close to the source of their raw materials, or where the materials can be secured at a minimum of expenditure for transportation. Nearly always they are located where there is a large adaptable labor population.

But no matter where they are located, city or country, they tend to concentrate population.

They are congestion makers.

Factories make the country into towns, towns into small cities, the small cities into large ones. They are the most efficient urban izers which man has yet evolved. They are therefore the best of all inflaters of land values. The hustling communities and the "realtors" who keep them hustling are forever seeking more factories.

The sequence which they worship is:

Factories;

Larger populations;

Higher realty values.

•

The factory is a slum breeder. Today it is admittedly a slum breeder but it will always be a slum breeder—Matthew Arnold to the contrary notwithstanding.

It breeds slums for two reasons.

First, it can afford to pay its workers only what the competition of other factories permits it to pay. Wages are still relatively low—too low to permit the wage earner to live outside of slums. For the factory today is in the hands of acquisitive, ruthless, quantity-minded men who find in the intense pressure of competition ample justification for exploiting labor to the uttermost limit. The factory worker is therefore paid too little to afford the time and the expense of living far from his job. The capitalistic factory therefore is a congestion breeder—a breeder of districts which are congested because men, women and children must live close to the factories to enable all the members of the family of working age to secure work.

Secondly—and this reason applies to the factory whether in the city or in the country—factory work checks any tendency toward part-time farming. The factory worker produces factory goods for others to consume; he subsists on what other factories produce for him. The factories located in the country and suburban districts make it possible for the workers to have space around their homes in which to garden. But even with space, and even if strength enough remains after the day's work, only the thriftiest workers have gardens: the vast majority get their foodstuffs out of packages and tin cans. The foreign-born workers, in whom the farming tradition is not quite dead, and the ex-farmers who take a job in the factory, both garden somewhat—for a time. But when their wives and children also begin to take places in the factory, the garden usually is abandoned. With gardening ended, the country factory surrounds itself with what might be called country slums—slums which are, if anything, more depressing than their city prototypes.

Socialization of the factory would enable the worker to get the full wages to which he is entitled, although the wages might not prove to be as high as socialists expect; they might not be even as high as the wages which capitalism finds it possible to pay. But even if real wages were higher—much higher—that would not lessen the extent to which the factory would be a slum breeder. Factory workers would live in better slums—more hygienic slums, containing apartment houses instead of tenements, and they would fill their homes with showy furnishings instead of shabby ones. There might be less squalor, but there would be no less ugliness.

•

What makes the place in which mankind today produces practically all the commodities it consumes a factory?

In the sense in which I use the term factory it applies only to places equipped with tools and machinery to produce "goods, wares or utensils" by a system involving serial production, division of labor, and uniformity of products.

In this definition certain qualifying phrases describing the factory system are used, because a mere place in which tools, machinery and power are used and in which many persons are working is not necessarily a factory. A garage doing large quantities of repair work on automobiles is much like a factory in appearance. So is a railroad repair shop. Yet neither of these lineal descendants of the roadside smithy is truly a factory.

The distinctive attribute of the factory itself is the system of serial production. It is not, as might be thought, machine production nor even the application of power to machinery. Machinery and power, it is true, make modern serial production possible but only as iron and steel make the modern automobile possible. No one would make the mistake of saying iron and steel are the automobile. No one should make the mistake of saying that power and machinery are the factory. Only the establishment in which a product of uniform design is systematically fabricated with more or less subdivision of labor during the process is a factory. Large power and heavy machinery may not even be used. A dress factory, for instance, uses little power and no heavy machinery. It is nevertheless a factory, with a factory technique of production, a factory product, a factory labor problem, a factory distribution problem, and a *pro rata* contribution to the factory blight upon civilization.

•

Production in Europe up to the beginning of the industrial revolution was of three kinds: domestic production, custom production, and guild production.

Domestic production was then, and what survives of it still is, a family function. In the peasant hut the methods of production and the products themselves were simple and rustic. In the manor houses, however, there was a considerable organization of the family and its retainers, and the products made reflected the higher standards of the upper classes. Domestic production is distinguishable from all other types because it is directed toward the making of things which the family itself consumes. Home sewing, home preserving, home washing, are surviving examples of domestic production.

Custom production, which played so great a part in the economy of the pre-industrial era, survives today in very few fields and of these custom tailoring is probably the most important. Custom production was the principal means of support of the village smithy, the village miller, the village cabinet-maker. It did not however prevent these custom workers from devoting a part of their time to husbandry. When planting and harvesting required their attention, or whenever the volume of trade slackened, it was possible for the custom producers to devote themselves to productive labor on the land.

Guild production began with the specialization of the functions of the master craftsmen. The master craftsman's life before guild production developed was a highly integrated existence. He was himself a master workman, a superintendent of his journeymen and apprentices, an employer taking risks for material, food, and wages, often a producer of his own raw materials; a merchant buying raw materials, and a shopkeeper selling finished goods. With the coming of the merchant guilds the craftsman evolved into no less than six different persons: the large merchant, the shop keeper large and small, the merchant employer, large master, small master, and journeyman.

By the beginning of the eighteenth century European industry meant far more than baking bread, making cloth, cobbling shoes, and fashioning furniture for use in the immediate neighborhood. It meant the production on a large scale of goods to be sold in distant places—cloth, docks, shoes, beads, dishes, hats, buttons. The guild members engaged in the production of these goods conformed minutely to the directions of their guilds. The guilds were thus enabled to engage in commercial operations of great magnitude and to conduct not only a national but also an international trade for their members.

•

Towards the close of the eighteenth century, Arkwright laid

the foundations for the modern factory. He began by patenting a power-spinning machine which incorporated ideas of his own with those which he filched by "business" methods from Kay and Highs and Wyatt and Paul, with all of whom he worked at one time or another. He finished laying the foundations of industrialism when he established the custom of enlisting capital not only in the manufacture of yarn by the factory system but also in the establishment of the yarn market which was indispensable to the distribution of the factory product. It was speculation in this yarn market, rather than inventing and manufacturing, which enabled him to amass the fortune which won him knighthood.

Stephenson's work in perfecting the steam railroad was almost a contemporaneous development. It was not only fortuitous in point of time: it fitted in so perfectly as to seem almost pre-ordained. As a matter of fact, the rise of the factory created such enormous demands for coal, for freight, and for travel that existing transportation facilities were utterly incapable of satisfying them. It became plain to everybody that fortunes were to be made by those who supplied the demands for transportation. When the steam railroad made it possible to haul coal and raw materials to the factory in large volume and to transport in equal volume factory products to the place where they could be sold, the last link in the chain of events which destroyed the medieval agricultural and commercial economy had been forged.

•

Enormous profits were the rule among these early manufacturers. For a long time factory spun yarn and factory woven cloth were sold in both domestic and foreign markets at prices which were based upon costs established by workshop and cottage industry. The profits were so large that the incidental horrors involved in the destruction of the livelihoods of the craftsmen were disregarded by the general public, just as the infamy of child labor, which the factories introduced, was disregarded by the entire commercial world. Tough-fibered business men, encouraged by tough-fibered economists, exploited the theory that the social gain from increased production and from the extension of foreign trade fully justified the horrors of the factory system.

It is impossible to form a sound conclusion as to the value to mankind of this institution which the Arkwrights, the Watts, and the Stephensons had brought into being if we confine ourselves to a comparison of the efficiency of the factory system of production with the efficiency of the processes of production which prevailed before the factory appeared.

A very different comparison must be made.

We must suppose that the inventive and scientific discoveries of the past two centuries had not been used to destroy the methods of production which prevailed before the factory.

We must suppose that an amount of thought and ingenuity precisely equal to that used in developing the factory had been devoted to the development of domestic, custom, and guild protection.

We must suppose that the primitive domestic spinning wheel had been gradually developed into more and more efficient domestic machines; that primitive looms, churns, cheese presses, candy molds, and primitive productive apparatus of all kinds had been perfected step by step without sacrifice of the characteristic "domesticity" which they possessed.

In short, we must suppose that science and invention had devoted itself to making domestic and handicraft production efficient and economical, instead of devoting itself almost exclusively to the development of factory machines and factory production.

The factory-dominated civilization of today would never have developed. Factories would not have invaded those fields of manufacture where other methods of production could be utilized. Only the essential factory would have been developed. Instead of great cities, lined with factories and tenements, we should have innumerable small towns filled with the homes and workshops of neighborhood craftsmen. Cities would be political, commercial, educational, and entertainment centers. The homestead would have developed in countless directions and would have continued the economic center of the family. Efficient domestic implements and machines developed by centuries of scientific improvement would have eliminated drudgery from the home and the farm.

Before we can say that the coming of the factory was a good

thing for mankind, we must ask ourselves whether this supposititious world would have been a more comfortable and beautiful world than the one in which we actually have come to live.

We must, in short, make a comparison between the factory economy which we have today and a hypothetical economy which I believe should have been developed.

I appreciate that the apologists for the factory, both the defenders of the existing capitalistic factory system, and the proponents of a reformed socialistic factory system, will join hands in saying that the introduction of any such hypothetical economy into the discussion introduces a chimerical and utopian element which renders the whole argument academic. In this respect both would claim that they are more "practical" than I. For both are subscribers to the proposition that the development of the factory is essential to the comfort of mankind. Both will therefore pride themselves on dismissing as impractical the ideas of anyone who ventures to suggest that mankind might with profit abandon much of present day factory production, precisely as mankind thought it profitable to abandon domestic, craft and guild production in the course of the industrial revolution. I insist, however, that there is ample historical precedent for envisaging such a possibility. The Arkwrights were considered by the practical men of their day hopeless theorists. The factory system of production seemed to be as different from the prevailing method of production as the hypothetical system to which I am calling attention differs from our modern factory system. Time, however, vindicated the practicability of the Arkwrights. Time may vindicate my belief in the practicability of the abandonment of our present factory system.

•

When Samuel Slater in 1790 brought to America the factory idea as it had up to that time developed in England and erected the first cotton mill at Pawtucket, R. I. nearly everything consumed in the American home was either produced in the home it self or made to order in community mills and custom workshops.

Nearly every home at that time had its "loom" room. Not every loom room contained a loom, but a very large number of them did. Most of them, however, contained yarn spinning equipment.

They contained wool-wheels and flax-wheels. They contained flax-brakes of various kinds; wool-cards and wool-combs; several kinds of reels, and of course, the ubiquitous dye-pots. The heavy wool was spun on the big wool-wheels; the lighter fibers—flax, cotton, silks and hemp—were spun on flax-wheels. With this equipment, and the assistance of custom weavers, fullers, and tailors, the American home was supplied with its textiles and clothing. The products were often of a quality that can hardly be duplicated today. The quality had to be of the best. The labor which had to be put into the production of goods made it necessary that what was fabricated should wear long enough to justify the time put into their manufacture.

Country dwellers of all classes produced practically all their own foodstuffs. The wealthy, when they dwelt in cities, usually secured their foodstuffs from their country estates. Artisans and shop workers usually combined farming with the pursuit of their crafts and so supplied the foodstuffs for their own tables. Only a very small number of homes in the cities and towns had to buy their "victuals."

The pioneer home not only produced its own foodstuffs but many of the implements with which the foodstuffs were grown and harvested, and cooked and preserved. Grist mills, bread troughs and yeast jars; churns and cheese presses; syrup-making equipment, cracker-stamps, sausage-guns, turn-spits; cider and vinegar barrels, brick ovens and smoke-houses were part of the equipment of nearly every home. The foods which could not be stored dry or packed in vegetable cellars were preserved by drying, smoking and pickling. The equipment for this purpose consisted of an amazing variety of ingenious baskets, buckets and jars. It consisted of equipment unknown today and used in arts lost to the homemakers of this age who use foods which come from factories—from dairies, sugar mills, biscuit factories, packing houses, tanneries, and bakeries. With this primitive equipment even the poorest home of those times, though it is true the fare was often coarse and sometimes monotonous, enjoyed an abundance that made it possible to indulge in the luxury of hospitality. The open latch string was a social rite which extended not only to relations, friends and neighbors, but to the strangers who travelled by the door. This system of production made possible a lavish hospitality which seems legendary in this day. The table in the better American colonial home groaned beneath the foodstuffs and po tables served, while the quantity and variety were so great that to the modern taste the old cuisine seems positively vulgar.

The production of most other things consumed in those days was much like that of foodstuffs and textiles. The homes either contained equipment which made it possible for the family to produce them—to produce its own "simples" and medicines, its own candles, its own soaps and cleansers, its own furniture and implements—or the family relied upon neighborhood artisans who operated workshops in which these things were made in conjunction nearly always with farming.

Manufacturing was confined to neighborhood industries which devoted themselves to the relatively few products that did not lend themselves to domestic manufacture. The neighborhood mills and shops used wind and water to operate their heavy machinery. The countryside was dotted with grist mills, lumber mills, forges, tanneries and potteries. Though inferior in efficiency, the neighborhood industries were superior esthetically to the factories which replaced them. They were, so to speak, country evoked. They fitted into the country, as the factory fits into the crowded city.

Slowly but surely with the advent of Samuel Slater and his imi tators, the loom room and equipment for domestic production dis appeared from the homes, and the community mills and neighborhood shops disappeared from the countryside. The question is, was this decay due to an economic insufficiency inherent in individual production or was it due to an insufficiency largely adventitious? Is it not possible that workshop and domestic producers lost in competition with the factory merely because they did not, and perhaps could not at that time, utilize the early stream of scientific progress of which the factory took advantage?

•

Production in the old-fashioned home and workshop was a laborious and time consuming process. But the things produced were durable. And they had charm and infinite variety, which the growing army of antiquarians engaged in collecting them now recognize. Both because of intrinsic quality and expressive charm, they endured. High quality, with slow depreciation, was an inevitable corollary of individual production, just as poor quality, with rapid depreciation, is an inevitable corollary of serial production. With individual production, the quality had to be good. The busy men and women of those days could not afford the luxury of shoddy materials and inferior workmanship because they could not spare the time to replace things frequently. With serial production, however, man has ventured into a topsy-turvy world in which goods that wear out rapidly or that go out of style before they have a chance to be worn out seem more desirable than goods which are durable and endurable. Goods now have to be consumed quickly or discarded quickly so that the buying of goods to take their place will keep the factory busy.

By the old system production was merely the means to an end. By the new system production itself has become the end.

Promoted by quantity-minded men combining a fanatic faith in the value of manufactures with a thirst for wealth, and assisted by government tariffs and subsidies and municipal and state gifts and grants of land and capital, factory production slowly but surely displaced individual production. It produced a higher level of wages for unskilled laborers. It made it possible for great masses of consumers to buy "goods, wares and utensils" which they had not been able to use and possess before. It created a material well-being which did not exist in the days of individual production. By using power and machinery on a new scale; by abandoning personal and custom production for serial production of uniform, standardized products, and by departmentalizing and subdividing labor, it put the ponderous and inefficient equipment in the homes and workshops out of business.

No doubt the change was inevitable. The water-wheel and the windmill put the hand-crank and the foot-treadle out of business. The steam engine put the water-wheel out of business. But now the gasoline engine and the electric motor have been developed to a point where they are putting the steam engine out of business. The modern factory came in with steam. Steam is a source of power that almost necessitates factory production. But electricity does not. It would be poetic justice if electricity drawn from the myriads of long neglected small streams of the country should provide the power for an industrial counter-revolution.

•

On the credit side of the factory and of factory production must be entered one outstanding item: the provision of a revolutionary increase in the quantities of products and commodities.

By lowering prices, the factory makes it possible for the masses of people to consume more. By lowering quality and lessening durability, it makes it necessary for them to consume more. Finally, by eliminating self-expression in the making of the products, it lessens their attachment to the things which they buy and possess. All these effects of factory production tend to make the average individual consume more, waste more, and destroy more than in the past. Superficially this has been all to the good: we now eat more, wear more clothes, live in better houses, use more furnishings and utensils, transport ourselves more speedily and freely than ever before.

Mankind has not, however, attained to this state of material well-being without paying a ghastly price in real comfort for the part which the factory played in achieving it. The material well being may be worth the price. The question which interests me is, was it necessary to have paid that price, and if unnecessary, should we not cease making similar sacrifices of comfort merely that we may still further increase our consumption of creature comforts ?

•

The first effect of the production of seemingly unlimited quantities of commodities and their being placed on sale at prices much lower than previously prevailed was to drive workshop products off the markets and to curtail if not entirely destroy domestic production. A disorganization of the economy of the world unprecedented in all history followed. An essentially agricultural economy with a small admixture of the commercialism fostered by the merchant guilds was changed violently into an essentially industrial economy with a small admixture of agriculture. The industrial revolution created a host of novel political, legal, economic and social problems:

child labor, trade unionism, universal manhood suffrage, socialism, woman suffrage, economic and sex independence of both men and women. These problems were out growths of efforts to create an equilibrium in the relations of capital and labor—a relationship at least as stable as that which had at one time prevailed between master and servant. The problem is probably unsolvable; even the socialists, who think they have a solution for it, are blithely unaware of the part played by functional and ineradicable attributes of the factory in making man subservient to his machines.

•

The second effect of the production of seemingly unlimited quantities of products was the development of a new economic basis for imperialism.

Before the coming of factory production commerce devoted itself to procuring what the buying public wanted, rather than to marketing whatever producers fabricated. Foreign commerce barely went beyond the exchange of luxury goods. Merchants were essentially importers. They exported only in order to make importation possible. The fur traders, for example, went into the wilderness to secure furs. They carried wares to exchange for them not because there was a pressure to export the wares but because wares were the instrumentalities which enabled them to get the furs the buying public sought.

Before the industrial revolution European nations developed foreign trade only because they wanted what foreign countries produced. They wanted spices, then of relatively greater importance than today—pepper and cinnamon from Egypt, Ceylon, Sumatra, Western India; ginger from Arabia, India, China; nutmeg, cloves, allspice from the Spice Islands and the Malay Archipelago. They wanted precious stones: diamonds, rubies, and pearls from Persia, India, and Ceylon. They wanted glass, porcelain, silks, rugs, tapestries, metalwork from the entire Orient. They wanted tea from China. They wanted gold and silver, furs and tobacco from America. For all these things they offered in exchange whatever Europe then produced: rough woolen cloth, arsenic, antimony, quicksilver, tin, copper, lead. European traders usually found the balance against themselves and they paid the difference in gold and silver.

The chartered commercial companies helped them to redress that balance by throwing what amounted to a taxing power against the countries from which they were importing goods. English, Dutch, French, Swedish, Danish, Scotch, and Prussian East India companies, West India companies, and companies for trading in all the various sections of the world helped to solve the "mercantilist" problem for hungry Europe for nearly two hundred years. The era of colonial expansion followed and made it still easier to meet the adverse balances by securing gold and silver and raw materials from distant colonies.

Then came the factory. Import imperialism changed into export imperialism.

With the factory came seemingly unlimited production at prices far below those of the craft produced goods of Asia, of America, of Africa. The English factory for the first time made it possible to produce more than could be absorbed by the immediate buying power of the English market. By 1860 England's production of pig iron alone was larger than that of all the rest of the world. It became necessary to export goods in order to keep the factories busy. Imperialism was given a new orientation.

Import imperialism was aggression which made it possible for the imperialist nation to get what it wanted from the conquered: silks and tea, for instance. Export imperialism, which replaced it, made it possible for the imperialist nation to sell to the conquered what it had to market: cotton yarn and cotton goods, for instance. The continuous operation of spinning frames and power looms drove the trader, and behind him his country's soldiers, in search of markets. The motive of empire ceased to be freedom to import: it became freedom to export. The early imperialistic adventures of England in India were undertaken in order to secure access to the spices, precious stones, silks and other products of India. England's present policy in India is a desperate endeavor to keep India a dumping ground for the products of British mills and factories. Empire enables British traders, as it enables the traders of all the modern imperialist nations, to keep the home-fires—in the factories—burning.

There is, of course, still a tremendous import imperialism. The industrialized nations still need raw materials—cotton, rubber, raw silk. But as scientists perfect the factory system, the need for imported raw materials becomes less and less pressing. Indigo, for instance, was at one time a raw material of which the industrialized nations imported great quantities. Then came the synthetic chemists. They made it possible for the industrialized nations to erect factories which produced dyestuffs from ordinary coal-tar. Dependence upon the imported product thus ended. The synthetic production of raw materials has unlimited possibilities, as is being shown by the rayon industry today. This synthetic imitation of silk has already rendered the highly industrialized nations less and less dependent upon the importation of raw silk. The time may come when synthetic chemistry will finally free the industrialized nations of all dependence upon imported raw materials. Chemical factories will extract the raw materials which the factories in the industrialized nations need from air, soil and water. The industrialized nations may find that they have attained the paradise of protectionist economics, the absolutely ideal "balance of trade": nothing to import and unlimited quantities of goods to export.

•

The third effect of the production of seemingly unlimited quantities of commodities was the infection of the world with that political-economic plaque which still blights mankind—the protective tariff.

To make a market for the products of its factories in other nations, export imperialism developed. To protect the domestic market against the invasion of foreign factories, tarif walls were invented. In the United States the tariff became a wall behind which its factory system was erected. Today every nation employs tariffs in some form or other, ostensibly to protect its factories against the competition of foreign factories. But tariffs, however much they may foster domestic manufacturing and free the nation from dependence upon foreign factories, are in reality differentials in favor of those industries which are able to secure high rates against those which are unlucky enough to receive low rates. And as all tarifs are enacted for the benefit of manufacturers, they tend in actual practice to create a general differential in favor of the factory and against the farm. Manufacturing is thus made supernormally profitable while agriculture is made abnormally unprofitable.

A world which accepts the dogma that man exists to produce, and which rejects the proposition that production exists for man, deserves to be plagued by protective tariffs.

Mankind might rid itself of their annoyance and dangers if economists ceased to discuss them seriously and began to ridicule them as they deserve.

•

The fourth effect of the production of seemingly unlimited quantities of products was the creation of the modern domestic distribution problem, the ushering in of the distribution age, and the facing of manufacturers with the problem of making consumers consume all that the factories were capable of producing. High pressure marketing, national advertising, installment selling, house to house canvassing are some of the fruits of the distribution age. As the distribution problem increases in magnitude, ways and means have to be found to enable consumers to consume more food, more clothing, more furniture and more transportation. The population must be made to devote more and more of its time to consumption; less and less of its time to production.

The industrial utopia will come when this principle will be carried to its logical conclusion.

In that industrial utopia men and women will, presumably, work only one day per week—and that a very short day. They will devote the rest of their time to consuming all that the factories produce for them. Greater efficiency, higher wages and lower prices will make this possible.

We shall have developed to the *n*th degree the relatively primitive consumption resorts which we possess today. Specialization and standardization of these resorts will make it possible for mankind to consume much more than it does today.

Sumptuous food resorts established in the most salubrious surroundings will entertain thousands of men and women devoting themselves wholeheartedly to food consumption. Food in car-load lots will be shipped into these resorts direct from the factories and unloaded on private sidings, while the waste from the resorts, instead of being really wasted as today in sewage systems will be pumped to synthetic converting factories through pipelines much as crude oil is now piped to the refineries.

The resorts devoted primarily to clothes consumption will be second only to the food resorts in importance. A continuous round of opportunities for the display of clothes will be furnished to those who prefer to devote themselves to the exercise of highly developed exhibitionist complexes. The opportunity to change their costumes a dozen times a day will make them happy. The latest styles will be shipped to them from the factories hourly by aeroplane and the discarded garments baled and shipped by freight to the garnetting mills.

The country will be dotted with consumption resorts of other kinds: resorts for automobile, tire and gasoline consumption; resorts for the consumption of furniture and house decorations; resorts, in fact, for the consumption of all the various commodities of which a superabundance will be provided by the factories. Man will make a virtue of his inability to "evade industry's pervasive influence or wholly escape the tyranny of manufactured things."

The present six-day work week will have been gradually reduced to the one-day week. Men and women will earn in one day enough to devote the other six days of their week to consumption. After having worked his day in the factory or office, the New Yorker of that day will be whisked in an aerial taxi to the great Hotel Avoirdupois at the top of one of the peaks in the Catskills—the resort which he has selected for his week-end. He will register at the office and be assigned a number, a room, a table and a food-class. This last will be given him only after medical examination. The resort physicians having determined his capacity to eat, the resort dietitians will then prepare the menus upon which he can best exert that capacity. Both the intake per meal and the number of meals per day will have thus been scientifically adjusted to his tastes and to his capacities. He will discard his business clothes and change to the loose, flowing robes which interfere least with his girth-line and which make it easy for him to take the exercises and the therapeutic treatments prescribed in order to keep him in fit condition to eat.

Then he will begin a six-day eating marathon of, perhaps,

twelve meals per day. Between the meals he will of course, visit the great eliminatories which will be the real pride of the Hotel Avoirdupois. All the appliance of science, manipulated by skilled physicians, nurses and masseurs, will make it possible for him to return to the table with every bit of his previous meal completely eliminated from his system. Artificial elimination of the waste, by the most delicate and pleasing modernizations of the old Roman vomitoriums, will be available day and night. This very careful technique will insure maintenance of his capacity to eat and to eat with enjoyment unimpaired. He will thus be able to consume from ten to twenty times as much food as is customary today. At the end of the six days, he will check out of the resort in perfect condition and return to work having had a most enjoyable weekend.

•

Many may like the direction in which we seem to be travelling. They may not agree that super-consumption is the goal of our journey. But they will undoubtedly agree about the fact that today the factory is in the saddle.

The census of manufacturers makes it plain that the factory is steadily increasing its production while domestic and workshop production is steadily declining. New factory industries, like bread baking, are developing and taking from the home the remaining productive activities of the individual family. In addition, the census reveals a significant tendency toward concentration of production in larger establishments and a corresponding decrease in the volume of production in the smaller factories. We are evidently moving at an accelerating rate of speed toward production in large factories in which the technique of mass production will be of maximum efficiency. As this tendency develops the aggregate profits of the surviving manufacturing corporations will steadily increase even though mass production will probably have been carried beyond the point of optimum efficiency. Percentages of profit on sales, for instance, will decline but the total profits of manufacturers will increase because of the increased volume of production. The large aggregate profits will make possible constantly larger corporate stock and bond structures. To pay dividend and interest upon all these securities, constantly more difficult problems in production, distribution and finance will have to be solved. The responsibilities of those who manage and direct the factories will increase by arithmetical and geometrical progressions. Overhead will increase because the units of production will have become larger. Production will tend to be continuous and to conform to the ideal of twenty-four hours operation per day. Markets will have to be forced to absorb more and more goods. Consumption will be stimulated, prices made lower, goods made more and more enticing. Obsolescence, sufficient to offset improvements and inventions which tend to make goods last longer, will have to be built into the goods.

To evaluate this inevitable prospect, we shall consider four aspects of the factory's influence upon mankind.

First, the factory's influence upon the quality of the "goods, wares and utensils" mankind uses. Second, the factory's influence upon those engaged in doing the work of the world. Third, the factory's influence upon the public as consumer. Fourth, the factory's influence upon that quality-minded minority which has always occupied itself with the reduction of the chaos of life to some significant form in morals, in reason and in appearance. The discussion of these first three aspects of the influence of the factory involves mainly a study of the sociology and economics of production but the discussion of this fourth aspect demands the consideration of philosophic questions usually overlooked by the conventional apologists for the factory.

•

A brief summary of what the factory has already contributed and may yet contribute to the general welfare is advisable in order to anticipate many of the objections which are certain to be made to the unconventional position here taken. Such a summary will make it clear that consideration has been given to the most important propositions which the proponents of our factory economy adduce in its favor.

The factory has admittedly greatly increased the creature comfort of mankind. Innumerable articles now in general use were luxuries enjoyed only by the gentry and quite above the aspirations of common folk before the factory system was established. The factory has enabled the masses to live under conditions, and to consume "goods, wares and utensils," which otherwise they could not have afforded. Rich and poor both have been enabled to purchase more goods and more kinds of goods and to consume and destroy them more freely than was previously possible.

It is, of course, difficult to determine how much of the credit for all this is really due to the factory itself and how much to the fact that scientists and inventors directed their efforts to the development of factory machinery and factory methods to the neglect of improvements in domestic production. We have always to bear in mind that the well-being we credit to the factory is based upon comparison between the low prices and high consumption made possible by the factory after it has had the advantage of all the inventions and the increases in scientific knowledge of the past century and a half, and the high prices and low consumption which prevailed under a relatively primitive system of individual production.

Even if much is subtracted on this account from the credit due the factory for the diffusion of material well-being, there is still a very considerable residue of credit due the factory for providing, in large quantities and at low prices, all sorts of things ranging from such varied products as matches to electric light bulbs. The factory-begotten products which form this residue of credit justify our toleration of what might be called the essential factory—the factory manufacturing products which are essential to the maintenance of our present standards of living.

In addition to credit for its contributions to creature comfort, the factory has to be given credit for increasing the political freedom of men and women. It must be given credit for the present economic independence and mobility of the classes which furnish us our factory labor. The worker has now a voice in government. It is not much of a voice, but it is no doubt more than he had before he became a recognized part of the sovereignty of the state. The worker now has the right to quit his job. He is reasonably certain that he can change to a new job whenever he wishes, and support himself in the condition to which he had been accustomed without any long apprenticeship. The factory has, of course, destroyed the old relation of master and servant between employer and employee. It has made the worker his own master, subject only to the general state of business—to whether times are "good" or "bad."

Above all, the factory, certainly in its present form, has to be credited with both raising the wages and reducing the hours of labor of the average man. The average worker now finds it easier to live in accordance with the prevailing standards of the class in which he is born than ever before. By every definition of the term wages—money wages, hourly wages, yearly wages, real wages the factory has increased the income of the vast majority of men. By every definition of the term hours of labor—yearly, weekly, daily time at labor—the factory has reduced the hours at which the vast majority find it necessary to engage in productive labor. Both these things have tended to add to the material well-being for which the factory must be given credit. Higher wages have enabled the worker to buy more—to consume more, use more, and enjoy more of the things a factory-dominated civilization provides, and shorter hours have given him more leisure for consumption, for entertainment, and for what the herd-minded masses call education.

What is more, nothing on the horizon seems to preclude the realization of more and more material well-being of this sort; nothing can be seen which promises to check the present tendency toward lower prices, higher wages, shorter hours; nothing is visible that threatens to interfere with a standard of even more leisure and greater consumption.

The factory promises us in the future even more riches than we enjoy today. It seems to offer us a veritable golden age.

•

We shall see, however, that all is not gold that glitters.

CHAPTER V
THE FACTORY'S PRODUCTS

To what extent are the factory's products necessary to the maintenance of our present standards of living? When are the factory's products desirable? When are they undesirable?

Let us try to answer these questions.

•

The factory's products are of three kinds.

The first are products, of which copper wire is one example, which can best be made, or made most economically, by the factory. They *are desirable products* because they are essential to the maintenance of our present standards of material well-being.

The second are products, of which a can of tomatoes furnishes a good example, which are just as desirable as the first, but which differ from the first because they can be made just as well, and often more economically, outside of the factory.

The third *are undesirable products,* of which patent medicines are typical, which are undesirable because they are not essential and may actually interfere with the maintenance of a high standard of living. They are products which it would be better not to make at all.

•

Since the first kind of products, often not only factory-made but factory-begotten, so to speak, are essential to the maintenance of our present standards of living, it follows that the factories making them are essential factories. Ugly though all factories may be, and ugly though the factories making these products are, society will have to tolerate them because they furnish it products which really add to mankind's comfort.

But products of the second kind—products equally as necessary to material well-being as the first kind—we can provide for ourselves by other methods than that of factory production. The products of this class are essential, but the factories making them are not.

There are therefore two kinds of factories:

Essential factories making desirable products which can best be made by the factory.

Non-essential factories manufacturing either the desirable products which can be made just as well or even better outside of the factory, or the undesirable products which it would be wisest not to make at all.

A famous dandruff cure, which cures dandruff no more than it cures bad breath (for which it is also highly recommended by the manufacturer) furnishes a good example of an undesirable product, and the factory making it is, therefore, an equally good example of a non-essential and undesirable factory.

The ubiquitous canned tomato is a good example of a product of the second kind and the cannery which packs it is a good example of a non-essential factory. Desirable as are canned tomatoes as a product, the cannery itself is neither desirable nor essential because practically every household in the nation may can its own tomatoes.

The essential factory finds its justification in the making of the first kind of products—desirable products which can only be made or made most economically by the factory. These desirable products include most of our machinery—electric dynamos and motors, gasoline engines, tractors, automobiles and tools of all kinds—hammers, saws, planes and drills. They include all kinds of "intermediate" products and materials, (intermediate in the sense that they are used in the making of other things, as in the erection of houses), such as wire nails, copper wire and iron pipe. They include raw materials such as iron and coal, oil and cement. And of course they include factory-begotten products like automobiles which could hardly be made economically at all except by the factory.

There isn't the slightest doubt about the fact that the factory can and does furnish this type of product of better quality and lower in price than it would be possible to produce it without the factory. It is necessary explicitly to call attention to my full recognition of the useful part which the essential factories play in supplying us a plenitude of these things at low prices so as to anticipate the charge, certain to be made, that I see no good in any factories at all.

If factory production were confined to the making of these desirable products and if the public were to abandon the buying of the product of the non-essential factories, more than half the factories of the country would be eliminated. There would even be a reduction in the number of factories making desirable products, because a drastic reduction in the number of non-essential factories would greatly reduce the demand for the products of the "essential" factories now engaged in making supplies for the myriads of non-essential factories.

Copper wire and iron pipe are desirable products which can best be made in factories. The factories making them are certainly essential factories. But enormous quantities of copper wire and iron pipe are used by non-essential factories. If any considerable number of the non-essential factories in the country are eliminated, some of the factories making copper wire and iron pipe, and some of the mills making raw materials for these essential factories, would also disappear.

Furthermore, since every factory, essential and non-essential, is a large consumer not only of supplies and equipment of all kinds but also of transportation, elimination of the non-essential factories would be followed, first by a reduction in the number of essential factories making supplies for them, and secondly by a reduction in the number of factories, both essential and non essential, which furnish equipment and transportation to the essential factories. Once the process of reducing the number of factories were to begin with the elimination of the non-essential factories, the repercussion in the form of smaller demands for the products of other factories would mean a drastic reduction in the number of factories of all kinds.

•

The two largest of our manufacturing industries are the industries producing foods and kindred products and those producing textiles and their products. The products of these two great industries fall overwhelmingly into the class of desirable products which are essential to the maintenance of our present standards of living but which could be produced, just as well, outside of factories. A considerable part of the products of these industries, especially of the textile industry, consists of desirable products which are produced most economically in the factory. The factories making them are therefore essential. However, a very large part of the production of both industries (especially of the food industry) consists of goods which are undesirable and non essential and which it would be better not to make at all.

These two industries employ nearly thirty percent of the men, women and children over ten years of age gainfully employed in manufacturing in this country—manufacturing having been taken to include every productive occupation except agriculture and fisheries—and include over forty percent of all the factories listed by the census of 1920.

Since a very large part of the factories in these two industries are, in my opinion, undesirable and non-essential, it is quite possible that the number of desirable and essential factories in the two industries might equal in numbers the undesirable and non essential factories in all the remaining industries. On this as sumption over forty percent of all our factories are undesirable and non-essential. If this estimate errs at all, it errs in my estimation on the side of over-conservatism. I am using it merely for the purposes of making it possible to form a very rough idea as to the magnitude of the industrial counter-revolution which is involved in my proposal that *all these undesirable and non-essential factories should be eliminated.*

•

If we include the superfluous essential factories—those which supply the undesirable and non-essential factories with their supplies and equipment—at least a hundred thousand factories in the United States would be closed by such an industrial counter-revolution.

If we include all the persons who are supported by the activities of this hundred thousand factories, including not only the wage earners but also the owners and salaried employees, at least three and a half million persons now gainfully occupied in them would have to find other means of supporting themselves. While this is nearly thirty percent of the total number of persons gain fully engaged in industry, it is only ten percent of the total number of all persons gainfully occupied if we include agricultural, professional and domestic workers.

Baldly set down in this fashion, this industrial counter-revolution seems at first blush a ruthless proposal to destroy economic forces and instruments of colossal magnitude—perhaps the greatest for good or ill which man has yet evoked. But mankind's instinctive recoil from so startling an idea will be very brief. It will console itself with the conviction that the industrial counter revolution is too visionary, too utopian, too chimerical ever to become a reality.

But while the counter-revolution may be improbable, it is not impossible and it certainly is not impractical. Nor will mankind shrink from it once a sufficient number of people find it to their interest to bring it about. For men deliberately began a revolution of even greater magnitude about two hundred years ago.

The industrial revolution closed hundreds of thousands of workshops and community mills. It destroyed the value of incalculable investments of capital in domestic and workshop manufacturing equipment.

It destroyed the trades and livelihoods of millions of workers. It precipitated misery, ruin, and rioting. It was responsible for an amount of suffering that it is impossible for the human mind to fully visualize.

Criticism, therefore, of my proposed counter-revolution on humanitarian grounds—on the basis of the suffering which it might inflict—is equally criticism of the original industrial revolution. Mankind did not shrink from the industrial revolution why should it shrink from the counter-revolution?

If, however, one enlightened family here and another one there adopts scientific domestic production, the transition from the factory-system will be so gradual that the counter-revolution will come peacefully and without adding to the misery and suffering which already exists in our factory-dominated civilization.

As to the charge of utopianism, certain to be made by practical men because of the drastic and destructive nature of the proposed change, this cannot be made consistently unless the self same critics are willing to assert that Arkwright, Watt and Stephenson were equally impractical and utopian because they at one time proposed, and brought about, an even more drastic economic revolution. Their revolution has been justified on the ground that it improved the conditions of mankind and added to the wealth of the nations of the world. That is precisely the ground on which I shall justify the industrial counter-revolution—for I propose to show that the elimination of the non-essential and undesirable factory will add to the real comfort and true wealth of mankind.

A study of the products of some of the most important of the non-essential and undesirable factories of the country is all that is necessary in order to do this. Such a study requires a candid, and I am afraid a disillusioning examination of food products, for instance, and their production in our great mills, packing houses and canneries. It requires us to make a comparison of factory products and factory production with the products which we might consume and the conditions under which we could produce them if we turned to scientific domestic production.

•

White flour is a typical factory product. It has replaced the "rye and injun meal" of the American colonial era as the principal American breadstuff. That the flour of the American pioneers was a wholesome foodstuff is more than probable because on a devitalized dietary they could hardly have survived the hardships to which they were subjected. It would therefore be a brash man who would say that there was any dietetic justification for the substitution of factory-made white flour for the old American whole grain meals. Yet there are plenty of apologists for the modern milling industry who will be quick to assert that the modern product is superior to the product which it has almost entirely displaced.

The modern flour mill takes wheat, one of the oldest and perhaps one of the best of the cereals, and converts it into white flour, middlings and bran. The bulk of the middlings and bran is sold for poultry and cattle feed. Both, however, are also sold, in one form or another, for human consumption. The flour itself is sold for cake and bread making. The middlings, after being bleached and packaged, are advertised as the cream of the wheat and sold for breakfast food. While the bran, generally sweetened and flavored to overcome its natural woodiness, is also packaged and then sold for its laxative properties.

The white flour, which under our present scheme of factory production has become the principal breadstuff of America, (whole wheat flour being a negligible part of the total present day production), is hardly fit for human consumption. It is pale and pasty in appearance; to the palate it is flat and flavorless. The public demand for it represents an acquired and not a natural taste. But it is not only unappetizing to the normal palate; it is a nutritive atrocity. Essential parts of the wheat berry—the vitamins, the mineral salts, the natural laxative elements—are absent from white flour, because they are mainly found in those parts of the wheat berry which are milled into middlings and bran. Consumers of white flour who happen to eat middlings and bran bring about a sort of metabolic reunion of the three parts of the wheat; but unfortunately much of the virtue of each of the parts is destroyed before the reunion by the processes to which the mill has subjected them.

What is most unfortunate, only a small portion of the missing elements of wheat is consumed by this white flour eating nation. Most of the middlings and bran are sold to dairymen and poutrymen for cattle and chicken feeds. The cows and chickens thrive upon what we are too stupid to eat! The white flour—that part of the wheat which is most anemic and which contributes most to the well-nigh universal constipation of Americans—is used exclusively for human consumption.

There isn't a single good reason, from the standpoint of physiology, why wheat should be milled into white flour, middlings and bran. But there are many reasons from the standpoint of the factory system of production, distribution and consumption.

There are first of all the profits that grow out of the fact that white flour does not spoil quite so readily as does whole wheat flour. It can be shipped greater distances and stored for longer periods of time. It therefore lends itself to nation-wide distribution and makes it much easier for the larger mills to invade the local area of distribution of the smaller mills. Whole wheat flour, which is a complete and practically natural organic substance, decomposes more rapidly than white four which milling transforms into an almost inert material. Like fresh eggs and fresh milk, whole wheat flour is a product little adapted to large scale factory production because it has to be comparatively fresh in order to be marketable.

Secondly, there are the profits which grow out of the fact that milling the wheat into its constituent parts creates three profits, where otherwise only one would have existed. Aggregate sales and aggregate profits of flour mills are thus made larger. We are first persuaded, by the national advertising of the mills, that white flour is more genteel, and that it is tastier and healthier than the plebeian dark flour. A high price is then secured from us by the mills for the white flour. We are then persuaded that bleached middlings make a breakfast food superior to whole grain cereals. A high price is then secured for this part of the wheat as well. Finally we are persuaded that bran is an essential medicinal agent (for curing the constipation caused by eating the white flour from which the bran had been extracted) and thus the mills secure a fancy price from us for this last constituent of the original whole wheat.

These factory-begotten products—white flour, bleached middlings, and parched bran—are undesirable forms of a most desirable foodstuffs. We are not eating a superior foodstuff, be cause factories have taken over the milling of the wheat. But neither are we being furnished wheat products at a lower price than we could produce them for ourselves. And certainly the flour mills themselves are not objects of such beauty as to justify their being solely on esthetic grounds.

The great mills of which the nation is so proud are on all counts undesirable. And most of them are non-essential as well.

For we are not without practical alternatives to which we can turn in order to supply ourselves with flour—and four of a better quality at a lower price.

•

A small flour mill can be purchased from almost any mail order house. A suitable one is listed in the Sears, Roebuck & Co.,

1927-28 catalog for $10.35. It can be used to make whole wheat flour, cornmeal and oatmeal for table use, as well as coarse feeds for cattle and poultry. The mill uses self-aligning burrs for the actual grinding, instead of the great, clumsy mill-stones which were in use before the modern roller mill took over the matter of producing flour and cereals. The burrs are easy to replace and they can be changed so as to mill flour varying from fine to coarse in a very few minutes. The extra burrs cost only 87 cents. The mill can be operated with a one-horsepower motor or engine. Yet it has a capacity of from five to fifteen bushels per hour, depending on the fineness of grinding, condition of grain and the power used. With one of these mills we are independent of the flour factory; we get the finest flour, because it is whole and unbleached, at the cost of a little time, a little electricity or gasoline and the bare cost of the grain itself.

It will, of course, be objected that this is an alternative which cannot be adopted in the millions of homes located in our great cities. Such a mill has a capacity far in excess of the needs of the average city home. It is essentially a piece of machinery designed for the farm or country estate. But this particular piece of machinery, which is a relatively large domestic flour mill, does not by any means exhaust the existing possibilities for domestic milling even though this is an age in which the needs of domestic production are so terribly neglected. The same catalog lists a series of hand grist mills, ranging in price up from $2.65. The smallest size grinds about two pounds of grain every five minutes. Each mill is provided with steel burrs which grind coarse, medium and fine. It will grind everything which the larger mills will grind. If hand-power grinding is too tedious, quarter horse-power motors are listed in the same catalog at $9.75. One of these motors could be used to drive the mill through a friction pulley placed against the fly-wheel much as electric motors are used to drive sewing machines. At a total cost of less than $15.00 including freight, delivery and fittings, this equipment would enable even a small family to cut down its flour and cereal bill to one-fifth its present dimensions.

None of the mills now on the market, of which I know, is really an ideal domestic machine. While the two described above are serviceable, their designing shows nothing like the ingenuity which has been built into the machines used in our great flour mills. If human ingenuity were really put to work upon the development of domestic machinery, a mill would be produced no larger than an ordinary coffee grinder, driven by a tiny electric motor, with fittings for attaching it to any wall, the whole apparatus weighing a few pounds and costing not much more than five dollars. In a large family it would pay for itself within sixty days. In a small family, within three or four months. It should last, except for an occasional renewal of burrs, brushes and armatures, a lifetime. It would earn bigger dividends upon its cost than any other type of investment which we might make and would furnish us flours and cereals superior to those we now buy from the stand-point of flavor, nutrition and purity.

But the domestic mill would not only earn money for those of us who use it. It would forever free us from the menace and meanness of adulteration. Factories today are in business to make money. Many flour mills have not hesitated to use poisonous bleaches in order to whiten flour, as is shown by the history of the movement to enact and administer pure food laws. They have not hesitated to doctor spoiled and discolored flours with chemicals which made them look "like what they ain't." They have not hesitated to debase fine, hard wheat with an admixture of inferior grades and to palm off the resulting mediocre, though uniform, product as the finest flour it is possible to produce.

•

The average family in the United States consumes 4.6 barrels of flour per year. Every domestic mill put into use in an American family would reduce the demand for factory made four by 4.6 barrels per year. Every 6,529 families who turned to the domestic production of flour would put one flour mill out of business.

Twenty-five millions of these domestic mills would destroy factory milling. The 5,232 mills of all kinds in this country would be eliminated and the 35,194 persons engaged in them released for other work.

The incredible folly of concentrating huge armies of workers, salaried employees, and executives in the centers where these large mills are now located; of shipping both the grain and the flour, middlings and bran back and forth across the whole country; of trying to support all of these non-essential mills with million-dollar advertising campaigns to persuade us "to eat more bread," would be ended.

Instead we would have a few factories making these domestic mills and supplying parts and replacements for them, all of them engaged in the work of making machinery into a servant and not a master of men. We should not, as a matter of fact, increase the number of factories making machinery very much because factories making factory milling machinery would be replaced by factories making domestic mills. The decrease in mills making factory machines would offset the increase in mills making domestic machines.

In addition, if demand for devitalized grain products such as white flour ended, not only would the non-essential mills disappear, but many of our patent medicine factories would also disappear. For fifty percent of the stock remedies in modern drug stores consists of patent medicines for the alleviation of constipation—laxatives, cathartics and purgatives in liquid, powdered and pill form. These products, which are absolutely essential in this white flour age, would become more or less non-essential if one of the principal dietetic causes of constipation were eliminated.

•

It is to be hoped that social historians will not underestimate the part which advertising has played in creating the folkways of the period through which mankind is at present passing. For the placing of a social stigma upon home-baking, one of the most important activities of woman in the past, has been largely accomplished by advertising. In creating the new social attitude toward home-baking, advertising has served to increase the number of factories baking bread precisely as it has increased the number of factories generally.

Home-baking used to have the social standing of a useful art, an applied science, a means of self-expression. It was a contribution to the comfort and well-being of society quite within the capacities of most women. As a means of self-expression it is certainly not to be rated inferior to ironing shirts in a steam laundry or typing letters in a factory office.

The modern woman looks upon the rapid development of the commercial baking industry, (the factory system applied to the baking of bread and other bakery products), as a blessing and looks forward hopefully to the day when all baking will be done in factories and none in homes. In spite of what modern kitchen ranges and modern kitchen implements have done to reduce the labor involved in home-baking, the advertising of the baking industry, with the cumulative repetition of one idea millions of times, has made her feel that home-baking is drudgery. In this way advertising has built into the mental habits of women one of those great transvaluations of values which profoundly change the social history of mankind.

One does not need to be very old to remember when an altogether different set of values governed the attitude of women to ward baking. A report such as that of the Federal Trade Commission on the bread industry, in which it was stated that half of the bread of the country was no longer being baked in homes, would have been regarded by the women of the last generation as a calamity. The woman of those days who abandoned this particular household art would have been considered shiftless, without pride in her occupation as homemaker, and indifferent to the welfare of her family.

It is not necessary to be wholly in favor of a return to a state of mind and a set of values which, in spite of some compensations, tended to overload women with heavy work. The modern woman's demand for comfort is thoroughly justified but this does not justify abandonment of domestic production, especially when comfort can be attained without necessarily turning to the factory to provide the home with its breadstuffs.

There are two methods, both of which might be used by the modern woman, to provide her family with breadstuffs superior in quality and lower in price than those provided by the baking industry. Yet neither involves labor as arduous as that performed by the women who work in factories, stores and offices. If a large number of these women were to turn to these methods of supplying their families with breadstuffs, 18,739 large bakeries—the numerous small bakeries doing less than $5,000 worth of business per year are not included—would be put out of business and 202, 142 persons engaged in the factory production of bakery products would be released for other work.

•

First, machinery can be used to make home bread-baking very much less burdensome than it has been in the past. There are dough mixers now on the market which very largely reduce the labor of preparation for baking in spite of the fact that they are still relatively primitive in design. What is needed is inexpensive equipment and machinery, electrically driven, which will do for the home-baker what the elaborate and ingenious labor-saving machinery in the bread factory does for the commercial baker. The housewife who uses existing equipment, utensils, mixers, ranges, can bake bread with an ease that would have seemed quite marvelous to the colonial housewife. If, however, our inventors were really to put their minds to the task of developing machines for domestic use equal in ingenuity to those already developed for factory use, home bread-baking would experience a renaissance of portentous import to the commercial baking industry.

•

The second method by which the housewife can solve the problem of greater ease in home production of breadstuffs is even more simple.

Let her give up bread-baking altogether. Or let her at least greatly reduce the family consumption of yeast bread because of the relatively great labor its production entails. The art of bread baking, of making a dough, of putting in a yeast or ferment and then of baking the loaf, is an old one. But mankind throve before the art was developed, and could thrive just as much even if it were to be abandoned.

Abandonment of bread-baking itself is easy, as the modern housewife has already demonstrated, but breaking old habits of eating as I now suggest is not. But the temporary discomfort involved in abandoning the bread platter at all meals would be amply compensated for by the permanent comfort of eating a greater variety of breadstuffs.

A household mill, such as was previously described, is desirable though not essential to the adoption of this proposal. The domestic mill would provide whole wheat flour, whole rye flour, whole cornmeal, whole cracked oats, in fact the cereals generally, in the freshest, the healthiest, the most nutritious and the most appetizing condition and at a lower cost than the factory product into the bargain. Without a mill in the home it is difficult today to procure the cereals as nature, so to speak, made them to be eaten. But whether the various flours be home produced or purchased from dealers, they make it possible for the housewife to furnish her family with an endless variety of breadstuffs without once baking bread.

There is, for one thing, "johnnycake." Let a family once eat cornbread made from whole cornmeal—not from the pale, dessicated product that the factories are now turning out and miscalling cornmeal; not from the cornmeal of ordinary commerce, from which the toothsome germ of the kernel has been extracted, but made from the whole corn which includes the starch, the gluten, and the fibrous part of the kernel, and the universal popularity of johnnycake before the factory came along and destroyed the tastiness of the meal out of which it was originally made is understandable.

Then there are biscuits, pancakes and waffles. In the South to this day the hot biscuit is called bread. It is made from dough that is quickly and easily mixed. The baking is a part of the work of preparing the meal and the "bread" comes hot to the table. There is no more reason for our fear of hot bread than for fear about hot meat, or hot potatoes, or hot vegetables. Unfortunately, Southern hot bread today is generally made of white flour. If made of whole grain flour it would furnish an admirable, nutritions and palatable breadstuff without all the labor of making yeast bread.

But the waffle offers an even more appetizing breadstuff and involves an even less laborious process of production. Waffle batters can be mixed in a few minutes before a meal. If the fat is put into the batter while it is being mixed and an electric waffle iron used, the waffle can be baked right on the table—at breakfast, luncheon and dinner—without the annoyance of greasing the iron or of forcing the housewife to stand over a hot stove turning the old fashioned waffle irons while the rest of the family ate at the table. An infinite variety of waffles can be made. A single meal of whole wheat flour waffles will make the soggy, mushy white flour waffle distasteful to the average person. The whole wheat waffle is crisp, where the other is tough. It has flavor, the natural flavor of the wheat, where the other has none. It nourishes the whole body where the other merely furnishes heat. It is healthy, where the other is constipating.

In addition all sorts of waffle batters can be made. "The waffling family" does not have to rely upon a monotonous repetition of the same breadstuff. Mixtures of wheat flour and cornmeal are delightful. The waffle makes it possible to serve an infinite variety of breadstuffs without having to mix yeast dough and bake bread at home or abandoning home baking to the commercial bread bakery.

•

Let us now turn to another branch of the food industry and consider canned goods.

The canned goods industry is largely founded upon two self delusions of the American people: one delusion, that factory canned goods are cheaper than the goods which are canned and preserved at home—that if they are not actually cheaper the possible saving is not worth the labor and annoyance involved in home canning; and another delusion, that factory canned foods are a very desirable type of foodstuff.

Before discussing these delusions, which are largely responsible for the failure of American inventive brains to function upon the problem of how to make it possible for the home to preserve foodstuffs efficiently and economically, a bird's eye view of the canned goods consumed by the American people will be helpful.

The following table is divided into two sections, one of them listing the "natives" among canned foods and the other the "exotics." Native canned goods are manufactured primarily for sale in sections where similar fruits, vegetables and other foods are produced. Exotics are canned primarily for sale in sections where the exotics are not capable of being grown. When the place of production and the place of consumption is the same, the product is native; when the two places are not the same, the product is exotic. Canned grapefruit is an exotic in most parts of the country although a native in Florida and California. Canned fish, crabs and shrimp while exotics in most parts of the country, are native in most of the coastal states. Canned tomatoes, on the other hand are natives in practically every state of the union.

If we locate ourselves in the state of Indiana, which is very nearly the geographical center of the country, we get a table of natives and exotics something like this:

Native Canned Goods	*Exotic Canned Goods*
VEGETABLES:	VEGETABLES:
Peas	Olives
Corn	Fruits:
Tomatoes	Grapefruit
Baked beans	Pineapple
Beans, other than baked	FISH, ETC.:
Asparagus	Clams
Spinach	Clam chowder
Kraut	Herring
Tomato pulp	Oysters
Tomato paste	Salmon
Beets	Sardines
Canned soup	Shrimp
FRUITS:	Tuna
Peaches	MISCELLANEOUS:
Cherries	Peanut butter
Berries	
Pears	
Apples	
Apricots	
Fruit salad	
Prunes	
Plums	
MISCELLANEOUS:	
Sausages and other meats	
Condensed and evaporated milk	
Syrup	
Preserves, jellies, jams, etc.	
Pickles, sauces, etc.	

A glance at this table makes it very clear that native canned goods constitute the great bulk of the canned goods consumed in Indiana homes—canned goods which could be, but are not, produced and canned by Hoosier households for their own consumption. Yet with an unholy ingenuity, the factory has persuaded most of the families of Indiana to buy factory canned goods rather than to consume home canned goods even though they have to pay a higher price for an inferior product in doing so.

I can see little advantage, and less from the standpoint of the palate than from the standpoint of economics, in the canning of many of the exotics. But even though the desirability of enabling the Hoosier household to buy canned pineapple be conceded, there is no possible desirability in enabling the Hoosier household to buy canned sweet corn. In Indiana canned pineapple is an exotic; in Hawaii where the fresh pineapple can be secured and canned at home, canned pineapple is a native. It is in my opinion just as silly for the Hoosier to eat factory canned corn or peas or tomatoes, as it is for the Hawaiian to eat factory canned pineapple.

Whatever sense there may be in the eating of factory canned goods is confined to the eating of what I have called the exotics.

The exotics, of course, come to Indiana from "elsewhere." They are produced and canned abroad or in some one geographical section of the country adapted to their production. If not canned in that particular section, and shipped to Indiana where they are not produced, the people of Indiana might not be able to secure them at all. Thus the exotics may be said to lend themselves rationally and logically to canning in factories. Factory canning, so far as it is essential and desirable in a rational scheme of life, should be confined to the exotics. It should be limited to those foodstuffs which furnish the variety and the spice in our dietary. It should include only those products which would be too expensive for the average family if they had to be brought in the fresh state clear from a distant place of production to the point of consumption.

But the exotics represent a relatively small part of the pack of the canneries of the country. The great bulk of our canned goods production consists of condensed and evaporated milk, of vegetables like tomatoes, corn and peas, and fruits like peaches and cherries, native in practically every section of the country, and which can be grown in nearly every backyard garden in the nation. It seems to be folly of the rankest kind for us to buy the factory-made product when it is possible to can and preserve the same commodities so much more tastily at home.

Canning, preserving and pickling by the old-fashioned methods which generally prevailed fifty or more years ago was one of the most arduous of the tasks of our homemakers. The equipment was primitive in the extreme. The use of the appliances then available, including the use of the all-important apparatus for boiling and heating, was laborious in the extreme. Water, for instance, which was so necessary for the various boiling processes, had to be drawn from wells by hand, and this laborious work was typical of the hard labor involved in every stage of the work. Hours of standing and working in a steaming hot kitchen and of stirring boiling pots and kettles over a broiling hot stove was a part of the drudgery of the preserving season.

The packer and canner came along and relieved most of the women of the country of this labor. Grocery stores began to blossom out with every variety imaginable of canned goods—canned milk, canned fruit, canned vegetables and canned meat. During the harvest time, the canneries worked day and night, stacking up in cases the foodstuffs which consumers were to eat the year following. Home preservation of food stuffs began to shrink in volume. National advertising, brightly colored labels, new and ingenious ways of flavoring and cooking the products, and also adulterating them, all combined to persuade women to abandon the hard work of canning.

As a result most of us today have little idea of the extent to which modern methods of home canning and preserving have eliminated the drudgery of the old methods. We have little notion of the extent to which modern appliances reduce labor, improve quality and save money in the home preserving of foods. Domestic canning and preserving offer the average home-making woman the opportunity to "earn" more money for her family, per hour, than she could possibly earn in a factory or office and at the same time enable her to serve products far superior to all except the best canned goods now on the market.

Let us consider some of the modern appliances which have made this reduction in the labor of home canning possible. They are by no means as efficient as they should be, and as they will be if the ingenuity of America ever really directs itself to the solution of the problems involved. Yet the available appliances have already cut down the time involved in canning by one-third. Or, to put it in another way, with the best of the existing methods the homemaker can preserve three times as much in the same length of time, as was possible twenty years ago.

Sears, Roebuck & Co. list in their 1927-28 catalog a variety of steam pressure cookers. The best type made from heavy aluminum costs from $11.85 to $21.90 depending upon the size. This particular cooker is an improvement upon the original models of the same type. It has a new and greatly simplified locking device—a single quick-tightening screw instead of the four screws with wing nuts which were formerly used. Some of that ingenuity, of which so much more is needed in the field of domestic machinery, has evidently been put upon the problem of eliminating what used to be the most undesirable feature of this very efficient appliance. Yet the improved cooker costs less than half as much as the old style cooker cost ten years ago.

The smallest of these cookers will hold five pint jars or three quart jars. (Incidentally, the old-fashioned screw-top Mason jar has in recent years been replaced by a very much better clamp-type glass-top jar which makes the opening of a tin can even with the most ingenious can openers a difficult labor by comparison). The largest of these steam pressure cookers will hold eighteen pint glass jars or seven quart jars.

The same catalog lists less efficient devices, steam cookers which cost from $2.75 to $3.95, and a cold pack canner, including the boiler, for only $2.80. I mention these less efficient devices merely to make it very clear that the equipment for canning is not beyond the purse of even the poorest of families.

The best part of the story of what the steam pressure cooker has done to home canning can be told in the following tables, taken from Extension Bulletin 56 and 64 of the New Jersey State College of Agriculture.*

Time Tables for Canning

Fruits:	**In Boiling Water 212°F (Old Method)**	**Pressure Cooker 5lbs (New Method)**
Apples	20 minutes	10 minutes
Apricots	16 minutes	8 minutes
Blackberries	12 minutes	6 minutes
Blueberries	12 minutes	6 minutes
Cherries	12 minutes	6 minutes
Gooseberries	16 minutes	8 minutes
Grapes	16 minutes	8 minutes
Peaches & Pluma	16 minutes	8 minutes
Pears	20 minutes	10 minutes
Pineapple	30 minutes	15 minutes
Quince	30 minutes	15 minutes
Raspberries	8-10 minutes	4 minutes
Rhubarb	12 minutes	8 minutes
Strawberries	10-12 minutes	6 minutes
Vegetables:		**5-10 lbs. pressure**
Asparagus	1¾ hours	45 minutes
Beans, lima	1¾ hours	45-60 minutes
Beans, string	1¾ hours	45 minutes
Cauliflower	1¾ hours	45 minutes
Celery	1¾ hours	45 minutes
Corn	3 hours	1-1½ hours
Kohlrabi	1¾ hours	45 minutes
Mushrooms	1¾ hours	45 minutes
Onions	1¾ hours	45 minutes
Peas	1¾ -2¼ hours	45 min. - 1 hour
Pumpkin	1¾ hours	45 minutes
Salsify	1¾ hours	45 minutes
Squash	1¾ hours	45 minutes
Sweet potato	1¾ hours	45 minutes
Turnip	1¾ hours	45 minutes

* The editor recommends referencing materials produced by trustworthy sources within the last few decades. A great deal has been learned about food preservation and safety since these charts and information gathered. One trustoworthy and comprehensive source is *Preservation: The Art and Science of Canning, Fermentation and Dehydration* by Christina Ward (Process Media, 2017).

Beets	1¾ hours	45 minutes
Brussels sprouts	1¾ hours	45 minutes
Cabbage	1¾ hours	45 minutes
Carrots	1¾ hours	45 minutes
Parsnips	1¾ hours	45 minutes
Peppers	1¾ hours	45 minutes
Tomatoes	1¾ hours	8 minutes
Meats:		
Poultry and game	3 hours	1 hour
Beef, lamb, mutton,veal and pork	3 hours	1 hour
Soup stock	1½ hours	45 minutes

These tables make clear what so simple and inexpensive a piece of machinery as the steam pressure cooker can do to redress the balance of economy and comfort between domestic production and factory production. There is a clean saving of from one-half to one-third the time in processing. Sweet corn, which used to take three hours to process, can be finished in one hour. The saving, if the cooker is used for everyday cooking, is equally large. A ham which it takes three hours ordinarily to cook, can be done to a turn in 45 minutes.

In the competition between the cannery and the open fireplace and the old brick oven of colonial days, the cannery deserved to win on the score of comfort, labor-saving, and economy. But in the competition between the cannery and the modern kitchen—equipped with modern appliances and a modern wood or coal range or an efficient on stove, gas range or electric stove—domestic production deserves to win because it makes cooking as pleasant as any other kind of highly skilled manual labor in which human beings can engage.

According to the claims of one of the manufacturers, a half million steam pressure cookers have already been sold in cannery ridden America. If, instead of this pitifully small number, twenty five million were to be sold, one to every family in the country, and every family began to use them, most of the 2,177 packers and canners doing a minimum business of at least $5,000 a year would be put out of business and the 106,492 persons working for them would turn to some more useful work.

This ugly civilization, I believe, would be made less ugly by the change.

•

There is, however, little chance of this renaissance of domestic canning and preserving until the two delusions of which mention has been previously made are somehow or other exorcised: namely, the delusion that factory canned foods represent a very desirable type of foodstuff, and the delusion that the factory product is so economical that the labor and trouble of domestic canning is not worthwhile.

Upon the second of these delusions let me quote from Frederick Frye Rockwell's book entitled *Save It for Winter.*

> To anyone who has had much experience with the real modern methods of keeping food for future use there can be no doubt that it does pay, and pay handsomely. The new methods require very much less time and involve much less work than those which have been in general use up to the present time. The practice of both canning and drying has been practically revolutionized within the last few years. The new methods compared with those formerly in vogue are so simple that many persons have been inclined to doubt their efficacy until they become convinced by actual trial. The saving of food by these methods does pay even those who are located in cities and have not the facilities for producing the vegetables and fruit they can easily save for winter.
>
> Saving food for winter pays because it prevents waste. The surplus from the home garden, or cheap products of a glutted summer market, may be kept for the time when vegetable food is scarce and high in price.
>
> Saving food for winter pays because it enables you to make use of your garden, if you have one, to help support your family during twelve months of the year instead of only six or seven. The commonly held idea that these methods of saving foodstuffs apply wholly or chiefly to surplus garden products is erroneous. To take full advantage of the benefits which food-saving makes available one should grow crops especially for this purpose. This not only makes the work easier but permits making the most profitable second use of the ground occupied by the summer garden and allows one to plan sys-

tematically for the winter's requirements instead of just having what is left over from the summer garden.

Saving food for winter pays because it furnishes a healthier diet. Home saved products, if carefully prepared, will be better than those which you are liable to buy, and so much cheaper that a greater proportion of them in the daily menu will be used. We Americans have been, next to the Australians, the greatest meat eaters in the world—not because so much meat constituted a healthy diet, but because, owing to our prairie ranges and other cheap sources of production, meat was more inexpensive to get and easier to produce and prepare than vegetables. Times have changed; meat in America, in comparison with vegetable products, will never be so cheap again. Those who prepare to take advantage of the cheap vegetable supplies of summer, will be on the road to more hygienic as well as more economical living.

Saving food for winter pays because the actual expense for preparing and keeping vegetable food for this purpose has been greatly decreased by the new method, in spite of the higher prices of many things used. Dehydrated vegetables of many kinds will largely take the place of canned vegetables. This means a tremendous saving in the cost of containers and in the amount of space required to keep products. Improved utensils have cut down the labor required in preparing and putting up the food. The percentage of food lost by "spoiling" has been cut from a very considerable amount to almost nothing.

•

As to the delusion about the superior quality of cannery and packing house products, it would be easiest to dispel it by a little historical review of the hygienic practices of the packing industries, were such a method necessary. Upton Sinclair, in his unforgettable novel *The Jungle*, gave a vivid picture twenty years ago of this aspect of the packing industries. The records of the administration of the pure food laws by the federal government, and the records of state and municipal boards of health show that the conditions which *The Jungle* described are by no means entirely eradicated. "The less the public knows about candy making the better," said the manager of one of New York City's largest candy factories during the course of an investigation made by the Consumers League of New York early in 1928. Public delusion about the desirability of factory foodstuffs can, however, be dispelled upon the ground of palatability alone.

Mass production of foodstuffs is essentially an outrage upon the human stomach. Upon the theory that the common and ordinary occupations of life should yield all the satisfactions which it is possible by art and science to secure from them, eating ought to be a pleasure. The palate should be cultivated for the sake of enjoyment in eating just as the hearing is cultivated for the sake of enjoyment of music. But cultivation involves appreciation of fine distinctions. With mass production, of course, fine distinctions are impossible. When foods are prepared in the mass, they are prepared for a mythical average taste—for the least common denominator of taste. Not only that, but the methods used in mass production tend to destroy those fine bouquets in foodstuffs which ought at all hazards to be preserved if the most is to be secured in the way of enjoyment from eating. Factory canning and preserving tends to destroy these fine flavors, and to that extent cheats us of what should be a part of the joy of living.

Furthermore, mass production, which cannot cater to the individuality and personality of each consumer, robs us of one of the attributes that make life significant and less tragic than nature itself has made it. The food prepared in the home expresses the housewife's personality and caters to the personality of each member of the family. Personality is inextricably entangled in every dish and every meal. The very atmosphere of a real home gives to the meals eaten there values which cannot be duplicated in meals eaten in restaurants where the food is prepared in the mass and eaten in the mass. Those who habitually eat at home and who eat at restaurants occasionally, certainly do enjoy the novelty of a restaurant meal. But those who eat regularly in restaurants, who live perhaps altogether in hotels, very soon lose the ability to secure from their eating this kind of enjoyment. No matter how varied the bill of fare, a perpetual round of restaurant meals sooner or later ends in making all meals monotonous. The diners-out are a restless folk, shifting from one restaurant to another, seeking what is not to be found in the product of even the most skillful restaurant kitchen—the personal atmosphere of the home.

•

The possibilities of scientific domestic production have been indicated with, regard to only a few foodstuffs. The branches of our premier industry which we have been discussing—those making flour and cereals, baked goods and canned goods—are among the largest in the industry. Yet to them can be added many others if the production of every foodstuff that is adaptable to domestic production were to be discussed.

Domestic production is possible in milk, butter and cheese. In every branch of the dairy industry there are gains to society to be won by eliminating the non-essential factory, and re-establishing with new methods and modern equipment the domestic production of this group of immensely important foodstuffs.

Domestic production is possible in the packing of meat products. What a blessing it would be if all the stockyards and packing houses could be removed from the sight and from the nose of mankind! By concentrating the preparation and packing of much of the meat supply for twenty-five millions of families in Chicago and a few other packing house centers, a series of concentrated stenches are produced that make a farce out of our pretentions to being a really civilized people. If the stenches were resolved into their component parts in the twenty-five million homes of the country, each would become so small that it could be liberated without offense to the countryside. Chicago, Omaha, Kansas City, (Kan.), and other packing house centers would then become fit for the habitation of a really civilized people.

•

A glimpse at the probable future of factory production of foodstuffs may be worthwhile before we turn to the products of the textile industry, the next largest of our industries.

No Daniel is needed to read that future. The handwriting, already on the wall, is plainly to be read. The days of the farmer are numbered. Agricultural production of foodstuffs has been weighed in the balance by factory science and found wanting. The food factory of the future will make its products synthetically. It will soon cease to be a mere processor and packer of foodstuffs.

The factories are already making semi-synthetic foods of many kinds. For instance, they are making various vegetable "fats." These are semi-synthetic substitutes for lard. They look like lard, serve the same purpose as lard, and for all the purposes of business are lard. Lard, however, is after all an organic food—while the semi-synthetic fats, after having undergone chemical treatment in the factory, are an inert, if not an inorganic substance, of doubtful value to organic creatures.

What the factories have done with the fats, they have also done with the syrups. Enormous quantities of starchy cereals such as corn are now being chemically transformed into syrup. The semi-synthetic syrups, such as corn syrup, taste like molasses or like maple sugar, especially when suitably flavored with synthetic ex-tracts; they can be used for the same purposes on our tables, and they have most of the qualities of natural syrups except, of course, the quality of being natural—of being, in short, organic substances, and therefore, without question suitable for the consumption of organic beings.

In the future we shall erect factories that will go one step further.

Sugar, the factory-obsessed scientists have determined, is nothing but carbon dioxide and water, irradiated by sunlight. Professor E. C. C. Baly of Liverpool University is now producing sugar in his laboratory synthetically, Professor Baly turns the chemically powerful ultra-violet rays of a lamp on quartz vessels of water in which carbon dioxide is dissolved and which contains either iron or aluminium compounds—catalysts that provide a large active surface—and he obtains sugar. The proceeding is not entirely new. Daniel Berthelot was the first to synthesize sugar thus. Professor Baly's achievement is notable because he has mimicked nature with greater fidelity; for in some of his experiments he used colored catalysts as substitutes for the green chlorophyll of plants.

On the strength of his own success Berthelot argued that "theoretically there is no reason why we should not conceive of a day when we shall produce some of our cereals and vegetables in ultra violet ray factories and manufacture foodstuffs out of nothing but the gases of the air." And J. B. S. Haldane predicts that in the next century "sugar and starch will be about as cheap as saw dust" and foresees us making protein in the factory out of coal and atmospheric nitrogen, so that "agriculture will become a luxury and mankind will be completely urbanized."

What a prospect!

•

Before the era of factory spinning and factory weaving which began with the first Arkwright mill in Nottingham in 1768, fabrics and clothing were made in the homes and the workshops of each community. Men raised the flax and wool and then did the weaving. Women did the spinning and later sewed and knitted the yarns and fabrics into garments of all kinds. The music of the spinning wheel and the rhythm of the loom filled the land. Perhaps one third of the time of men and women—one-third of the total labor of the nation—was devoted to producing the yarns and fabrics which they consumed.

In America and industrialized Europe this is all gone. Only in India and in the Orient is the song of the spinning wheel and the weaver's loom still heard. Slowly but surely the mills took over this work from the protesting and embattled spinners and weavers. As late as 1810, for every yard of cotton woven in a factory in the United States, 112 yards were fabricated by families.[9]

In place of the loom rooms in its homes, America now has 7,816 factories employing 1,164,638 wage earners, not including owners and salaried employees. Many of the wage earners in these textile mills are children. And the wages paid by these mills are notoriously the lowest which prevail in any industry in the country. Yet in numbers gainfully employed, the manufacture of cotton, wool, silk and other fabrics is the leading industry in the United States.

A trifle over a third of the production of the cotton industry is used for industrial purposes. It is used in the fabrication of tires, car-bodies, etc. Two-thirds of the production of cotton and nearly all of the production of other branches of the industry goes to the consumer either as piece-goods or cut-up into wearing apparel by clothing manufacturers. This means that probably from ten to fifteen percent of the total number of factories and workers in the entire industry are engaged in producing for the needs of other industries. All the rest are doing work which used to be done in the home and much of which might still be done there.

•

Experiments with weaving in my own home show that if looms were equipped with flying-shuttles and modernized warping-beams, there would be no drudgery in the home weaving of most of the fabrics used by the average family today; there would be a substantial saving between the time needed for weaving and that now needed for earning the money to buy fabrics, and at the same time vast numbers of men and women without high talents for the fine arts would have the opportunity to express their creative spirit in a functional art.

Rugs, blankets, linens, draperies, and fabrics for dresses, coats, and men's suits, can be woven at home. With good equipment, it is possible for an inexperienced weaver to produce a yard of cloth an hour, while a rapid weaver can produce more. Enough cloth for a man's suit can readily be woven in one day. All the fibers can be used—wool, cotton, flax, silk, and an infinite variety of types of weaves produced on the same loom—satins, serges, herringbones, plaids, and plain weaves.

If antiquarian and "arty" worship of handicraft methods is avoided, and weaving undertaken with the same determination to be efficient which we take for granted in sewing or cooking or gardening, domestic weaving would not only prove practical and economical; it would furnish a liberal education in color and design to every member of the family. Eventually our homes would become filled with textiles of charm and beauty, and we ourselves would begin to wear costumes of a quality and durability well-nigh unknown today.

It is easy to make glowing claims and to demand excessive credit for the modern factory product. Modern designs, modern constructions, modern colorings and finishings, afford an amazing and entrancing variety. But how much of this credit is due to the factory and the factory system itself, and how much to the progress of the arts and sciences, which would have resulted in an equal improvement in domestic and handicraft yarns and fabrics, it is difficult to say.

•

The myriads of improvements which the factory has introduced into this branch of production have not been without some offsetting disadvantages. Recent developments in fabrics illustrate one of the disadvantages to which the pressure for continuous production subjects textile products as it does all other factory products. A certain poverty of invention is reflected in these new fabrics. Cotton has for many years been made to imitate silk by mercerizing, or to imitate woolen fabrics by fluffing the nap. But this was done largely in order to persuade the consumer to use a cheaper product instead of the dearer one—not infrequently in order to make it possible to sell the cheaper product as the dearer and secure a silk price for cotton goods. Such practices are not unknown in business. But this modern development is of a different order. It is a new form of factory art. Silk fabrics are now being produced which can hardly be distinguished by the eye, from woolens, and woolens which look exactly like silks. The wool is spun finely. It is woven into a sheer fabric, and then finished so as to have the luster that comes naturally to silk. Silk, on the other hand, is spun so as to be bulky and fluffy, and finished dull instead of lustrous, so that it looks like a wool fabric, feels like one, and is used in place of a wool fabric—in fact, it is in all ordinary respects a wool fabric but for the humor of the fact that it is not. Instead of the manufacturer striving to develop the natural characteristics of the fiber with which he is working into as beautiful a form as possible, he exerts all his ingenuity into making his fiber masquerade as another. Silk masquerades as wool; wool as silk; cotton as silk or wool; and rayon, invented by the chemists as an artificial silk, is made to masquerade not only as silk, but as the much less expensive wool.

Why this invasion of each other's natural fields? Why, in other words, does the manufacturer of wool raid the region of demand for silk, and vice versa? Partly, perhaps, as an outlet for the exercise of his ingenuity and a means of escape from the endless monotony of uniformity; mainly as a means of enabling the manufacturer of woolens, for instance, to keep his looms operating all the time by securing some of the normal demand for silk, and vice versa.

What this means esthetically can be better appreciated if the tendency is transferred to another field—to the realm of architecture and the building material industries. Its absurdities and incongruities are then more easily recognized. It is as though the steel men were to fabricate their building material into an imitation of lumber, brick, granite, and concrete; the lumber mills to fabricate lumber to imitate steel, brick, and stone, and all building material made to simulate competing building materials entirely unlike them in their natural appearance, in their composition, in their strength, in fact, in all their architectural qualities. Does this sound absurd? It is absurd, but that hasn't prevented the manufacturers of these materials from actually doing these things. Steel mouldings, columns, and sheets can be purchased that look like carved wooden mouldings, carved stone columns, and plaster cast imitations of carved ceilings. Wooden mouldings and columns are made that look like stone, and composition materials that imitate every imaginable other building material. This, of course, merely proves that when one turns to other products to illustrate the absurdity of what is now being done in textiles, the fact that the other products are equally the produce of the factory and factory system makes it almost certain that one will find similar absurdities in that product as well. The factory influence upon products evidently produces similar progeny no matter what the industry in which it is exerted.

In foodstuffs this masquerade of one product as another takes the sinister form, in many cases, of ingenious substitutions and adulterations. Molasses, maple sugar, and honey are made of corn. Flavors, extracts, spices are made by chemical factories—not food factories—out of inert substances. Preserves, jams, and jellies, which contain none of the fruits of which they are supposed to be made, are evolved out of concoctions consisting of glucose, apple pulp and hayseed and made to imitate genuine foodstuffs with the aid of artificial coloring matter, artificial flavor and artificial pectin. Manufacturers in one branch of an industry are not satisfied with the gross profit or the total volume of business that they can secure by selling what they apparently erected their factories to make: they try to add to their profits by imitating the products of other branches of industry with the aid of chemists who are disgraces to their profession.

That the sugar refiner should persuade the public to substitute what he makes in his factory for other sweets, such as molasses, is natural. If the public prefers the sugar, the fact that the business of the molasses maker is transferred to the sugar refiner is sound in both economics and ethics.

But when the sugar refiner inverts his sugar and flavors it so as to make it indistinguishable from honey in order to keep his factory busy, he poaches on the demand for the genuine product of our apiaries. What he thus does is bad ethics and bad economics no matter how profitable it may be to him.

Unfortunately there is a sort of Gresham's law operating in inter-industrial competition. Just as poor money tends to drive good money out of circulation, so *poor products tend to drive good products out of the market.*

•

The hope of any renaissance of domestic spinning and weaving in factory-ridden America and Europe seems slender indeed. The arts upon which this most fascinating and expressive of all economic activities is based are almost as dead as the arts of the temple and pyramid builders of Egypt. Spinning and weaving were the first of the domestic activities to feel the crushing competition of the factory system; they will probably be the last to experience a revival.

But that a revival is not impossible is indicated by two developments of recent times, one in the realm of industry and the other that of politics. One has to do with the rise of the electric power industry. Here is something which our non-essential factories will do well to consider prayerfully: *the electric power industry is beginning to discover that domestic production furnishes an almost unlimited market for its product.* The other is the fascinating page in history which Mohandas Karamchand Gandhi is engaged in writing in India.

In India domestic and craft production of textiles is not yet extinct. The village is still the chief industrial unit in India. The villages still contain workers whose chief occupations are, or were until very recently, weaving, pottery-making, iron-working and oil-pressing, nearly always in connection with the working of a piece of land. The highly specialized spinning of yarn and weaving of fabrics which existed in the larger towns of India at the time of the conquest by Great Britain, the making of muslin in Dacca and of calico at Calicut, has, of course, been destroyed. It was destroyed by the competition of British factories and the competition of factories which in recent years have been erected in India itself.

In the villages, however, spinners and weavers still are to be found. The tradition is still alive. And while the tradition survives, it is still possible to produce a revival. In the Indian village, too, the pre-industrial family is still to be found. Relatives still live together as members of the family in a communal organization. Income from the farm or workshop is collective—the joint income of the family. It is only when mills and factories appear upon the scene that this type of family begins to break down. Wages are then earned individually, and when wage-earning begins, jealousies, dissensions and differences in earning powers rend apart the group upon which the old system of domestic or workshop economy was erected.

Gandhi's searching analysis of the technique by which a relatively small number of Britishers were able to seize political power in the whole Indian peninsula and to keep under their dominion three hundred million human beings enjoying a very high state of civilization reveals the fact that the real British strategy was not martial but commercial and industrial.

The cheap and flashy cotton goods introduced by the British tradesmen destroyed the occupation of practically one-third the population of India. India was "persuaded" to consume imported fabrics even though importation of factory-made textiles deprived a third of the Indians of their means of livelihood. The British factories forced the greater part of the population of India to devote itself exclusively to agriculture. Indians were made to engage in the production of raw materials. Ex-spinners and ex weavers were forced to become growers of opium, indigo, and other agricultural products, or they were forced into the cities where they helped to form the reservoirs of unemployed labor, which made it so much easier for the factory system to establish itself,

Gandhi and his followers may meet defeat. A gallant group of patriotic men may suffer a crucifixion at the hands of quantity minded business men who are determined that the whole world shall be made safe for the factory. They will certainly be defeated if they rely too much upon the nationalistic interests of the Indians, and too little upon their economic interests. Patriotism and religion are able to move large masses of men and women to heroic and seemingly impossible achievements, it is true, but they cannot indefinitely suspend the normal economic life of any people. Christianity became powerful only after it recognized this fact. During the Middle Ages Catholicism was accepted in large part because its policy of land appropriation and monastic production made it easy for all classes to do so. The spirit of the church may have been religious, but its activities were economic. If Gandhi is to succeed he will have to rely less upon emotion and more upon economics, He will have to inspire his followers to solve the technical and mechanical problems involved in domestic production, to evolve superior styles both in design and in fabric construction, and finally, to build a distribution system that will make it possible for the Indian spinners and weavers to out-produce, out-design, and out-sell the best businessmen in the world.

"Slowly but surely," says Gandhi, "the music of perhaps the most ancient machine of India is once more permeating society."

Evidently the stage is being set in India for a pitched battle between individual production of yarn and fabrics and factory production. All the odds are in favor of the factory—ample capital, government support, accumulated technical skill, a distribution system built for the factory and not the individual producer; above all, direction by experienced, ruthless, and sometimes desperate business men. All the odds are against the individual producer—lack of capital, government opposition, his own hostility toward new methods and techniques; above all, a tendency to appeal to sentiment rather than self-interest in approaching the consumer. If better domestic machinery were introduced, if design and quality were improved, and if the economic and marketing problems were solved even in a rudimentary fashion, the basic sound ness of domestic production is so great that it is not beyond the possibilities that it would fully re-establish itself.

•

If all the resources of modern science and industry were to be tapped for the purpose of making the spindle, the reel, and the loom really efficient domestic machines—as efficient, relatively, as is the average domestic sewing machine—the number of textile mills which could survive the competition of the domestic producer would be insignificant. What is needed, if the industrial counter-revolution is to take place in the production of fabrics, of draperies, of rugs, of tapestries, is the development of electric-motor driven spindles, reels and looms, which would occupy relatively little space and make the loom room practicable in every home.

If the music of the spinning wheel is again to become a factor in the economic life of the world, the spinning wheel must be improved. In some of the Indian schools of spinning and weaving this is already recognized. Improvements, such as the change from the thick spindle to the thin spindle, are indicative of what is needed. This one improvement increases the number of revolutions of the spindle by from 50 to 100 for every revolution of the driving wheel, and correspondingly increases the amount of yarn spun with the same labor and in the same amount of time. A really "modern" domestic spinning machine should be no larger than a sewing machine. The motor should be started and stopped as the sewing machine motor now is, by a rheostat operated by the foot, leaving both hands free to manipulate the fiber and the yarn. The yarn produced would then cost the family hardly much more than the cost of the raw material.

If there is to be a renaissance of weaving, as craft and as art, and the craft woven textile is to compete in value with the mill woven product, the "hand" loom must undergo a similar series of improvements. It must cease to be a clumsy, labor-wasting piece of machinery. It should be smaller. It should be attractive enough to serve as a piece of "furniture" and so fit naturally into a room in the home as the easel of a painter fits into a studio.

If the human ingenuity which has built automatic machinery for our factories were to be directed to the development of simple tools and machines for knitting, or if the old-fashioned habit of carrying knitting around were to be revived among women, the battle between the knitting needle and the shuttle would be staged upon another plane, and no matter which won, the factory would lose.

If the non-essential textile mills of the country were to be subjected to domestic competition in which the individual producer used machines and equipment as efficient as those I have sought to describe a large number of our textile mills would be eliminated. Perhaps 4000 factories would disappear from the American landscape. New England mill towns would receive their final and well deserved quietus, while southern mill towns would cease to make the cotton regions hideous,

•

Now let us turn to the production of clothing.

In the sewing machine we have a piece of machinery which is ideally adapted for domestic production—a piece of machinery which represents the application to domestic machinery of some of that ingenuity and persistence in the solution of mechanical problems which has usually been devoted to the development of factory machinery. Howe and Singer, Wilcox and Gibbs, did for the housewife and her sewing what Arkwright, Crompton, Hargreaves and those who developed spinning machinery and power looms did for the factory and factory production.

It is no coincidence that the relationship of the actual invention of the sewing machine and the business men who saw fortunes in its production and sale almost exactly paralleled that of the inventors and the exploiters of the power-driven spindle. Howe, the real inventor of the sewing machine, had his invention filched from him by capable business men like Singer. More fortunately than Wyatt, Paul, Kay and Highs, upon the adaptation of whose ideas Arkwright built his fortune, Howe finally was able to vindicate his patent right and thus force Singer and the various manufacturers of sewing machines to pay him royalties during the life of his patent.

•

There are 16,904 establishments engaged in manufacturing wearing apparel from purchased fabrics according to the Census of Manufacturers for 1923. There are 499,413 wage earners employed in these factories. If the domestic production of the clothes that men, women and children wear were to be really inaugurated, most of these factories would disappear and most of the workers in them freed to lead more rational existences. The gain to society would be incalculable.

A modern sewing machine equipped with a small electric motor, a good dress form and a supply of paper patterns, enable the house wife to produce garments that are superior to those that are produced in factories, and at a lower cost. A sewing room thus equipped affords a complete demonstration of the proposition which I have been arguing: that the factory cannot meet the competition of the home producer if both are equipped with modern machinery and both use modern methods, Upon this point let me quote from an interview with Mr. Hubert M. Greist, Executive Secretary of the National Costume Art Association:

> Home sewing enables women whose expenditures are limited to obtain four things in combination which they cannot secure in any other way. The first of these is individuality—smart, distinctive styles and fabrics, interpreted in the exact lines, colors and textures which best suit their types and tastes. This demand is real even when it is inarticulate.
>
> The second thing, quality, is in growing demand. This means not only good material but painstaking workmanship, as distinguished from garments "thrown together," relying for their sale on a smart first appearance. Imitation of the better thing is rejected by many a woman of a type it would pay the merchant to cultivate. Her self-respect and refinement of taste prompt her to refuse a ready-made imitation of the real thing and to buy, within her means, piece goods of quality, good trimmings, findings and accessories and to fashion a garment which will accord with her own critical judgment and that of others with whom she has contact.
>
> A better fit is the third consideration. Skimpy dresses, or garments often shapeless where proper cut and line are important, frequently offend.
>
> The fourth objective is economy. Practically all women, when purchasing clothes, have that in mind. Ninety percent of all the women who sew at home, according to a recent Government survey, sew to save. When we consider that 85 percent of the families of the United States have incomes of less than $2,500 a year, we can appraise the possibilities of a well directed stimulation of interest in home dressmaking.[10]

Here is an occupation for the homemaker that has fallen steadily into disuse as the factories which comprise the "needle trades" have multiplied in numbers and increased in size. In a factory-dominated civilization, countless numbers of women take jobs of all kinds, both in factories and offices, in order to earn money over and above that which they receive from their parents or their husbands, to buy factory-made clothing. They buy an inferior product, skimpily cut and often ill-fitting; made of the cheapest fabrics which the manufacturer can buy and still keep his garments in the price-class at which he aims; exactly duplicating millions of other garments, and for it they often pay an outrageously high price into the bargain, That they could make the garments themselves, of better quality and at a great saving of money, and without the need of abandoning homemaking in order to do so, does not, of course, enter the heads of the great majority of them, If it did, the "needle trades" would perish. With them would disappear the industrial maladjustments of these trades. Hundreds of thousands of garment workers would no longer suffer from alternations of seasonable overwork and lack of work; they would cease to live under uncivilized conditions in congested centers like New York and Chicago; they would no longer endure packing like sardines in the subways and street cars which take them back and forth to their work. They would no longer be the slaves of the sewing machine.

For whenever men domesticate the machine, the machine ceases to be their master. The machine is made their slave—a labor saving device to be used when they need it, and to be laid aside when they are through with it.

•

Not all of the products of the "needle trades" lend themselves to domestic production. The making of coats and suits, both for men and women, requires a degree of skill beyond the powers of the average homemaker. In a sensibly ordered civilization this work would be done by craftsmen in innumerable shops in every community of the land. If the custom tailor and the custom dressmaker were to realize the possibilities of their crafts, the factories could not compete with them. They cannot, however, hope for a revival of craftsmanship until their customers are re-educated to the niceties of the art; niceties to which consumers are made insensitive by the factory product; niceties which the factory system makes it easy for the public to ignore. If domestic sewing was a part of the life of every home; if custom tailoring was the rule in every part of the country, opportunities for direct observation of workmanship and for contact with actual tailors would be frequent. Men and women would automatically receive an education in quality of materials and workmanship which would make them reject the tawdry product with which the factory now is able to satisfy them. This is by no means the least of the many advantages which flow from domestic and craft production—the education of the consumer.

It is a pathetic commentary upon the pass to which the factory has brought us, that modern pedagogy has had to discover the crippling effect upon the mind of this ignorance about the production of the goods we consume. The progressive schools furnish our children a substitute education for the direct education which the factory has taken from them. They grind grain so that their pupils may know something about the flour and cereals they eat; they make paper, spin yarn, weave rugs and cloth, work in wood and iron all in order that their pupils may have some understanding of the myriad of things which the factory sets before them and about the production of which they otherwise would know absolutely nothing. The factory having cheated the children of the factory age of any normal education in the crafts, the school is stepping into the breach and trying to reintegrate their personalities with a school-made substitute.

•

It is hardly necessary to further pursue the subject in detail, The results of this rather sketchy analysis of some of the most important products of our two largest industries—foods and textiles—and of the possibilities of supplying ourselves with them through domestic and custom production can be duplicated in most of the other industries of the country.

Most of the factory products which are desirable can be made just as well, and sometimes better, outside of the factory while large quantities of the products which we consume are actually undesirable. All of the factories making these products, and all of the factories making supplies and equipment for these non essential factories, could be eliminated without any lessening in our standards of material well-being.

Add to these products all those which it were better for society not to make at all, and the conclusion is irresistible: *factory production is in large part unnecessary.*

•

If we might develop a more beautiful and more comfortable civilization by producing things we need and desire outside of the factory, and if it is possible to use domestic machinery to furnish us a sufficiency of equally desirable and perhaps superior commodities to those which we now make in the factory, why should we hesitate to abandon the buying of undesirable and non-essential factory products? To answer this question conclusively we shall have to ask ourselves about the influence of the factory upon the quality and quantity of the "goods, wares, and utensils" which we now consume.

In what respects are factory products better; in what respects worse than the products which might be produced under a non-factory system of production? Would the non-factory product be as satisfying, as enduring, as beautiful as the existing state of science and art makes it possible for the factory product to be?

What about the enormous increase in the quantity of things which the factory makes it possible, and almost requires, that we consume today?

Finally, is the price which consumers have paid, now pay and will pay for the advantage which the factory confers upon them worth while?

•

First, the factory has substituted uniformity for variability in the commodities we use, and wear, and consume. It has not only produced for us a greater number of things of all sorts, but it has produced them of a uniform quality in material, workmanship, and size.

Uniformity, however, except in the case of machinery where interchangeability of parts is of great practical importance, and of course in the case of raw materials and products for refabrication, is a doubtful virtue. The factory has so accustomed us to this absolute uniformity that most people now attach a ludicrous importance to it. We have tended to transfer the unquestioned desirability of quantitative and qualitative standardization—that is, uniformity in sizes, materials, and workmanship—to the very questionable desirability of absolute uniformity in the execution of every detail of the product. There are good reasons why the collars men wear should be absolutely uniform in size. Variations in collars presumably of the same size would be a first rate nuisance since the collars must fit the collar-bands of the shirts to which they are to be attached. But there is no good reason why every collar that a man buys should be absolutely uniform in every detail of its design and fabrication. Small variations in height, in the peaks, and in the openings may be accounted virtues, since they not only relieve the monotony of absolute uniformity, but make possible more delicate discrimination in dress. What is true of the collar, is true of nearly everything that is purchased on esthetic grounds. Variety, not uniformity, is the real good. This tends to explain the present vogue for the hand-made product. The very imperfections in hand-made products and in the antiquities with which our homes are being furnished are accounted charming, intriguing, delightful, beautiful.

The factory, however, with its system of serial production can operate most efficiently only on the basis of absolute uniformity in the execution of every detail of fabrication, "No plant is big enough to make two articles," says Henry Ford, "Departures from uniformity create problems not only in production but also in marketing which can only be solved by abandoning most of the economies of the factory system.There is a certain Spartan beauty in the factory-made product when it does not purport to be anything but factory-made. Beauty of a certain sort undoubtedly is created by the skillful development of the sheer economy of line and form that is natural to the factory-made product. Unfortunately, beauty of this sort does not add to the costliness of the product. It tends to lessen costs—to strip off all extraneous ornamentation, especially any simulation of the ornamentation that is natural to the handicraft product. This acts as a very severe check upon the possibilities of profit for the factory. The factory, therefore, is under the strongest temptation to conceal the fact that the product is factory-made, and to use the factory-made product mainly as a skeleton which can be loaded down with an appliqué of imitation hand-decoration, because it is then possible to secure a higher price and a greater gross profit for it. Factory-made furniture is ornamented with imitation hand carvings. Textile designs are made to show systematically variations that are natural only to the handicraft fabric. Factory-made pottery and glassware, lamps and lighting fixtures, pictures and picture frames, carpets and rugs, all show in innumerable details of their design and execution the fact that the factory is deliberately sacrificing the beauty that may be said to be natural to the factory-made product in order that it may be sold at the higher price which imitations of the handmade product command.

•

Secondly, the factory influence upon the products we consume is responsible for the fact that goods have now to be designed for sale rather than for use. The factory's products are designed to be made as cheaply as possible instead of as finely as possible. The real objective of the factory is not to make goods, but to sell enough so as to maintain the volume of production upon which its profits are dependent. Decisions as to the quality and quantity of material and labor put into the product, and the amount of ornamentation placed upon it, do not develop spontaneously out of the creative instinct and craft pride of the maker—although that is never entirely destroyed—but develop out of the marketing needs of the factory. The salesman and the advertising man thus tend to usurp the functions of the designer and the maker. The vulgar taste is imposed upon the actual design of the product. This tends to restrict the scope of the designer. Instead of the designer being given full opportunity to educate the public to the standards which intimate study of the factory-made product would enable him to evolve, he is forced to create on the plane which may be called the least common denominator of the taste of the consumers of his product,

The same force—the necessity of designing and making the product *en masse* and selling it at a low price—is responsible for the fact that the quality and quantity of material and labor used is reduced to a minimum, while the amount and kind of ornamentation is rigidly restricted to that which can be applied mechanically and therefore cheaply. There is no inconsistency in the apparent contradiction between this tendency and the tendency to over-ornament previously discussed. The manufacturer tends to over-ornament and to use wastefully material and labor in an effort to raise his product to the highest price-class in which he can sell it in profit able quantities. But within the price-class in which he operates there is the counter-tendency, to reduce and cheapen material and labor, ornamentation and design.

•

Third comes the very nearly absolute waste of labor and material which results from the factory's inescapable tendency to continuous production. Only in the home can the owner of a machine afford the luxury of using it only when he has need of it. The housewife uses her washing machine only an hour or two per week. The laundry has to operate its washing machine continuously. Whether operating or not operating all of its machines, the factory has to earn enough to cover depreciation and obsolescence on them, office overhead, too, must be earned, whether the factory operates on full time or only on part time. Finally, continuous operation is necessary to enable the average factory to maintain a steady labor supply.

But with continuous operation of its machinery, much larger quantities of its products must be sold to the public. The public buys normally only as fast as it consumes the product. The factory is therefore confronted by a dilemma; if it makes things well, its products will be consumed but slowly, while if it makes them poorly, its products will be consumed rapidly.

It naturally makes its products as poorly as it dares.

It encourages premature depreciation. If a household heating plant depreciates at the rate of five percent per year, the house holder is in the market once every twenty years. If the walls of the boiler are thinned by half, depreciation is increased to ten percent per year. Cost to the factory is reduced at the same time that the householder is forced to buy a new boiler within ten years to replace his boiler twice as often as before.

The factory encourages premature obsolescence. It changes models and styles as often as it can and sets in motion an elaborate propaganda to persuade the public to replace still serviceable and still enjoyable types of its product with the new types which are presumably better because they are at least newer. The average life of the automobile of today is seven years. If the car lasted seven years in the hands of the original customer, we have been told, there wouldn't be a market for the 5,000,000 cars now being produced annually. So the social pressure for the new models must be made so great that all the models become obsolete yearly.

Finally, it encourages the absolute waste by the consumer of products it makes in order to stimulate more frequent purchases and premature replacements. If the product can be packaged so that a considerable part of it is lost in the process of using it, (as is the case with toothpaste in tubes), or if the public can be encouraged to use it in ways that waste considerable parts of it, there is created what is called by advertising men "plus-consumption" with consequent increase of sales for the factory.

Plus-depreciation, plus-obsolescence and plus-consumption these there factors are built—as far as manufacturers dare, into the factory product. They constitute a sheer waste of the material used and the time put into fabricating the factory products for which sales are thus made.

•

The factory furnishes us products which are uniform by making us sacrifice the advantages of variety.

It furnishes us products which are cheap by depriving us of the advantages of quality.

It furnishes products which are plentiful by making us abandon the advantages of conserving labor and natural resources.

Plainly there are obverse aspects to every advantage which may be claimed for the factory product. Mankind may turn to non-factory production without losing as much as may at first appear.

•

So much for the factory products and their production. So much for the possibilities of replacing them with better products and better methods of producing them. These random notes make it sufficiently clear that many of the advantages claimed for factory-made products of general consumption are factitious and fictitious; that domestic and workshop production could furnish us superior products in many respects at a lower cost, and at the same time eliminate the social, political and economic problems that go with factories and factory production,

Now let us see whether the factory furnishes superior conditions for the worker; whether men and women and children are better off laboring in factories and offices than they would be producing under their own rooftrees or in their own workshops.

CHAPTER VI
THE FACTORY WORKERS

THE factory found the masses of men living upon the land. It has herded most of them into cities, and has left a dwindling remnant to work in the country.

It found the forbears of our present vast armies of factory workers not much better than serfs. It has made peasants, domestics and artisans into wage earners.

It found the artisans still free men. It has destroyed their guilds, wrecked their crafts and driven their descendants into factories and stores and offices.

It found the intellectuals living upon the bounty of wealthy and powerful patrons. It has evolved from them a class of men living by their ability to capitalize their wits; their willingness to commercialize their talents, or to engage in work that conforms to the bounds set for them by modern business.

It found an hereditary aristocracy astride like a pack of vampires upon the whole of mankind. It has replaced these exploiters of mankind with an equally ruthless and more impersonal tribe of capitalists.

This is how the coming of the factory transformed the generality of mankind.

Now let us see what it has done for and to the masses it has transformed into factory workers.

•

There are four things which the factory and the factory system have done *for* the worker which the protagonists of industrialism seem to feel an adequate recompense for the things which they have done *to* him and which will be later discussed.

First, it has shortened his hours of gainful labor.

Instead of beginning work at sunrise and quitting at dark, and maintaining a jog-trot pace relieved by social interruptions of all sorts, he starts with the whistle and quits with the whistle, working at a pace set by the machine which he tends. Instead of working an average of at least seventy hours per week, with frequent festivals and holidays to relieve the monotony of his labors, he now works from forty-four to forty-eight hours per week, relieved by strikes, hard-times and lay-offs. He has more leisure each day, but, as we shall see, he has been deprived of the opportunity of developing the internal discipline necessary really to enjoy it.

But the factory did not produce the blessing of shorter hours very quickly. And very rarely were shorter hours voluntarily granted by the factory owners. High profits were the first fruits of the factory. Then came lower prices. Finally, shorter hours and higher wages. In 1815, the cotton mills were run on single shifts of fourteen, fifteen, and even sixteen hours per day. Robert Owen in his writings records the ghastly facts about the employment of eight and ten-year old children for these long hours with only a half-hour respite at noon. As late as 1860, hours of labor averaged sixty-six per week. Twenty-seven years later, by 1887, they were sixty hours per week. By 1907, they had dropped to fifty-seven. The drop has been steady ever since. At the present time, they aver age forty-eight, while in many highly unionized and highly organized industries, they are as low as forty-four and even forty hours.

This decline in the worker's hours of daily labor must not be confused with the reduction in his annual time at labor. There are good grounds for believing that we actually spend more time at labor today than we did in the days before the factory put in an appearance. During the Middle Ages, and during the even less complicated and more primitive ages that preceded that period, the time devoted to leisure was much greater than today. During the Dark Ages more than one-third of the year was devoted to the celebration of various festivals and holidays.

Men worked in those benighted ages in order to live.

In this enlightened age, we seem to live merely in order that we may work.

•

The second thing which the factory has done for the worker

has been to raise his real wages. For the work he does, he now is paid at a rate that would have seemed incredible to the pre-factory worker. He has money with which to buy things, but as we shall see when we study the matter, he, along with the general body of consumers, has been deprived of the education that would make it possible for him to spend that money intelligently.

We have no precise figures as to the average wages in this country earlier than the year 1840. By that time wages had already risen markedly. With further and further industrialization, they continued to rise. Fifty years later, in 1890, they were nearly double the wages prevailing in 1840. By 1920, they had doubled again, and were approximately four times as high as they were in 1840. They are still going higher. Of course these are gold wages, and not real wages, which would reduce the rise materially. And they apply to the United States only, which for the past decade has been in an exceptional position because it benefited materially from the World War while other highly industrialized nations were injured. But these wages are nevertheless indicative of what the factory does for the worker so far as wages are concerned.

•

The third thing which the factory has done for the worker has been to lower the prices which he pays for the things he buys. While this affects the worker as consumer rather than as producer, it is necessary to mention it here, because the lower prices which the factory has made possible were very early in the history of the factory an agency of great importance in improving the worker's material well-being.

At first the manufacturers lowered prices only enough to under sell the custom-made and the work-shop product, retaining an enormous profit for themselves because the buying-public was accustomed to the prices established for the products of manual labor. But when the factory-made goods had taken possession of the market, competition between rival factories brought prices down to a level which gave the public a considerable share of the reduced costs of production.

•

Yarn of a quality which in 1815 was sold for 3 shillings per pound,

> brought in the infancy of manufacture as high as 30 shillings. The British mulled muslins which when first manufactured, were eagerly bought up by the rich at $2.50 a yard, are now offered to the poor of less durable quality, however—for six cents a yard.[12]

•

The fourth thing which the factory has done for the worker has been to improve his social and political status. He is no longer a serf. He is no longer a member of a disfranchised class. He is no longer hemmed in by a thousand legal restrictions and regulations profoundly affecting the conditions under which he works and lives. The factory must be credited with giving the vote first to men and then to women.

But it has changed the legal and social status of woman even more than it has that of man. In the factory-dominated world, men, women, and children work outside of the home.

> Industry transferred the work of women and children from the home to the factory. The workingman's wife and children perforce forsook their home in order to obtain employment. To the extent to which women and children were drawn from domestic industry to factories it is accordingly fair to say that (factory) machinery entered and broke the circle of the workingman's home.[13]

In changing the economic foundation of the family from a domestic production to a factory production basis, the factory changed the entire social status of women and children.

The center of the woman worker's economic, political, and social life is, as a result of these changes, no longer in a home. It is outside the home.

Home is merely the place where men, women, and children of the factory age "bed and board," although it is becoming less and less even the place where they board. It is a dormitory—a mere place from which the workers go to work and the children too young to work, go to school, and from which all severally go to be entertained. It is not the place where they really live. It is no longer the place where they take root, and which nourishes the self-respect of every member of the family because it expresses their conceptions of life. The factory has made them into individuals who express themselves in what their jobs enable them to buy; individuals who devote themselves to spending rather than to the work of creating homes.

A shrinking, but still large number of women largely confined to our farms, have remained "homemakers" in spite of the factory. The minority of able women have become "careerists," while the fortunate group who marry well have become "shoppers." But the overwhelming masses of the women of the country have been made into "job-holders." For in our industrialized economy men can no longer support their families from their own earnings. According to Professor Irving Fisher, it requires two wage earners for a family of five to attain the family standard set by the Department of Labor.

In 1920, the continental population of the United States was 105,000,000. In that year, it is estimated that there were 24,351,000 familles in the country. The number of persons gainfully employed was 41,641,000. This gives 1.7 income producers per family of 4.3 persons. For up-state New York, which is highly industrialized, the indicated wage earners were 1.8 per family. For New York City, entirely urbanized and industrialized, the wage earners were 1.9 per family.

Women furnished almost entirely the increased number of wage earners per family. In 1880, the gainfully employed males over the age of 10 were 78.7 percent of the total number. By 1920, there had been an actual drop of 78.2 percent. In the same period the females gainfully employed rose from 14.7 percent of the entire female population over the age of ten, to 21.1 percent. In forty years, the number of women in industry, relative to the population, had increased by 50 percent. There is no reason for expecting that this invasion of industry by an equally emancipated, equally enfranchised, equally educated, but of course also equally uneducated, womankind will cease.

It must not be forgotten that the inevitable corollary of making the woman economically independent was to make men as well as women economically independent of each other. Slowly but surely, the law is taking cognizance of this change. Property law, marriage and divorce law, law as it relates to children, to sex-life, to Tabor, is adjusting itself to the new economic status of men and women.

To the extent to which this transformation of the political, social, and economic status of the male and female worker is an improvement, to that extent the factory should be credited with an improvement in the condition of the worker.

The change in status, however, has been accompanied by a change in the relationship of men and women and children to each other. In this factory-dominated world, with its indifference to whether the workers who keep its machinery in operation are single or married, men or women, adults or children, the home has disappeared as the economic unit of society; the individual has taken its place. The enforced cooperation of all the members of the family in producing the necessaries of life, has been replaced by competition between them for jobs. Individual competes with individual, regardless of sex or age, in the impersonal arena of the labor market. Men and women, whom nature intended to be partners, have become economic rivals. They seek each other out only in response to nature's imperious biological mandate.

The economic individualism introduced by the factory has reuced marriage to the status of a sexual adventure. Children endanger the adventure. To support themselves as they desire both husband and wife tend to work. Children interfere with this routine of working outside of the home, lower the scale of living and so endanger the continuance of marriage. The rise in divorce and desertion is a neural consequence. Present day criticism of marriage as an institution is an indication of the fact that mankind is beginning to fully accept woman's and man's economic independence. This independence is something which the factory bas produced for the worker. Under it the home has lost; perhaps the individual worker has gained.

So much for what the factory has done for the worker.

Now what has the factory done to the worker, and what is it continuing to do to him?

1. It relentlessly mechanizes the workman and reduces all workers, except the few "blessed with administrative genius," to mere cogs in a gigantic industrial machine.

2. It decreases the number of workers engaged in productive and creative labor by reducing the number of workers required to produce things and by condemning the remaining workers to elaborate methods of flunkeying for one another.

3. It arrays worker against employer, separating capital and labor into two independent and mutually antagonistic interests, and inflicts upon society an unending succession of foolish and often bloody strikes.

4. It makes it almost impossible for individual workmen to be self-sufficient enough to develop their own personalities.

5. It destroys the skilled craftsman to whom work is a means of self-expression as well as a means of livelihood, by offering work only for machine feeders and machine tenders, thus making it more and more difficult for skilled workmen to find employment.

6. It creates workers without initiative and self-reliance, and fins the state with citizens who lack a sustained interest in public affairs and good government.

7. It transfers the satisfying of the economic needs of the worker from the home to the factory, robbing the worker, his wife and his children, of their contact with the soil; depriving them of intimacy with growing things—with growing animals, birds, vegetables, trees, flowers; and destroying their capacity for fabricating things for themselves and of entertaining and educating themselves.

8. It condemns not only the natural robot, but those capable of creative effort in the crafts, the arts and the professions, to repetitive work, because it leaves open no field in which they may exercise their talents and earn a livelihood.

•

It is impossible, within the limitations of a single chapter to do much more than direct attention to the evidence for these conclusions. But an analysis of the most significant aspects of the influence exerted by the factory upon the workers of the world, is sufficient to justify all the conclusions. A glimpse of the worker, while he was still, presumably, a human being and before he became, in the expressive language of Adam Smith, "a manufacturing animal," furnishes a good point of departure.

The conditions under which the goods were produced which the world consumed prior to the introduction of the factory seem to have been much alike everywhere. The situation in New England was much like the situation in old England, and it is amazing how similar to the pre-industrial conditions in those sections are present-day conditions in those regions of Russia and India where industrialism is still in its infancy.

Farming was then generally accepted and treated as a part-time occupation. The seasons not having been abolished by industrialism, it is still in essence a part-time occupation. We have simply ceased to recognize the fact because specialization has begotten the monstrous superstition that no man can profitably devote himself to more than one occupation. Today we are so accustomed to the sharp separation of the occupations represented by farming and manufacturing that it is difficult to realize how abnormal this separation really is. There are seasons when the farmer has little to do. Those are the seasons when he is free to devote his time to manufacturing.

Henry Ford says:

> The real problem of farming is to find something in addition to farming for the farmer to earn a living at.

This is the situation today. But it was not the situation before the coming of the factory. Practically the entire working population devoted itself to part-time farming and part-time manufacturing.

In colonial New England, the villages in which the first steps toward industrialism developed, consisted of the homes of artisans and tradesmen who were also farmers. Each villager had a plot of land.

> These and the tradesmen and manufacturers who live in the country generally reside on small lots and farms, from one acre to 20.[14]

The weaving, blacksmithing, tanning, cobbling, milling, pottery-making, grist-milling in which these New Englanders were engaged were essentially part-time occupations. Tench Cox discusses this aspect of their life in some detail:

> Union of manufactures and farming is found to be convenient on the grain farina; but it is still more convenient on the grazing and grass farms, where part of almost every day and a great part of the year can be spared from the business of the farm and employed in some mechanical handicraft or business. Those persons often make domestic and farming carriages, implements and utensils, build houses and barns, tan leather and manufacture hats, shoes, hosiery, cabinet work, and other articles of clothing and furniture, to the great convenience of the neighborhood. In like manner some of the farmers, at leisure times and proper seasons, manufacture nails, potash, pearl ash, staves and heading, hoops and hand pikes, ax-handles, maple sugar, etc.[15]

Some quotations from the diary of Thomas B. Hazard, known as "Nailer Tom," who was a famous mechanic in those days, give a good idea of what this combination of many kinds of work meant to the skilled artisan before the coming of the factory:

> Making bridle bits, worked a garden, dug a woodchuck out of a hole, made stone wall for cousin, planted corn, cleaned cellar, made hoe handle of bass wood, sold a kettle, brought Sister Tanner in a fish boat, made hay, went for coal, made nails at night, went huckleberrying, raked oats, plowed turnip lot, went to monthly meeting and carried Sister Tanner behind me, bought a goose, went to see town, put on new shoes, made a shingle nail tool, helped George mend a spindle for the mill, went to harbor mouth gunning, killed a Rover, hooped tubs, caught a weasel, made nails, made a shovel, went swimming, staid at home, made rudder irons, went eeling.[16]

The notable fact in connection with all these varied activities is the admixture of work and play. If the worker "played" during the day, he labored at nail making or something else, at night. The day was not divided by the dock into mutually exclusive periods of work and non-work. Most of the play had an admixture of productive labor in it—it produced game or fish, for instance, while much of the work had elements of play in it.

Compare this record with the one which a modern factory mechanic would produce if he had kept a diary of his activities:

> Worked in the factory, home and listened to the radio. Worked in the factory, went to the movies in the evening. Worked in the factory, listened to the radio; worked in the factory, went to the movies; and so on, ad infinitum.

This would be his record, perhaps varied with an occasional marriage and funeral, or a dance or an outing under the auspices of his church, his union or his political ward leader.

The modern worker is a creature of routines. The general life of a highly industrialized country, which may seem full of interest and color to the traveller from another country, who is not a party to its routines, has no existence for the worker. As he goes through the daily routine which his factory imposes upon him he has neither time nor inclination to see it as a whole. He is a slave to a routine which changes hardly at all from day to day and from year to year. He knows nothing of what might be called the normal routine of life which changes from season to season with the grand cycle of the year, and which used to be broken up into an infinite variety of occupations by the need of solving the myriad of individual problems which develop as summer changes into winter and winter into summer.

The work of the colonial villager was physically harder than is that of the modern factory worker. His life was full of discomforts and privations unknown today. But his life was plainly not without many compensations for the hardships involved in producing for himself what he needed and desired without any of the tools and machines which science has since made it possible for the home producer to use.

•

Industrialism came and began by putting, as some of the early protagonists of the factory proudly proclaimed, the idle elements of the population to work. The first factory workers were not artisans, who happened to be unemployed—modern unemployment did not yet exist. Neither were they farmers or farm workers who preferred factory work to a landless existence. The first factory workers were the women and children of the villages and the countryside. These were the "idle elements" of the population which were to be put to useful work.

As soon, however, as the competition of factory products began to disorganize the existing economy based upon agricultural and handicraft production, and to create unemployment, the factories found it easy to recruit workers. The growth of the factories was so rapid, however, that shortages of workers developed in spite of these sources of labor. Armies of the unemployed had to be deliberately created in order to make more rapid development of the factory possible.

Artisans, peasants, and domestics were therefore deliberately driven by political, social and economic pressure into the factories. The craftsmen and their families were already being forced into the factories by the destructive competition of the cheaply produced factory goods. In addition, the peasantry, wherever feudal or semi-feudal conditions prevailed, were driven into the factories by shutting off their access to the common lands on which from time immemorial they had grazed their animais, and by rack-renting those foolish enough to stick to the land. Only domestic servants did not have to be forced into the factories. Changing social standards made force unnecessary in their case. The domestic was robbed of self-respect by the decline in the economic utility of the home. So long as the home was creative and productive, everyone in it could feel that they were contributing usefully to the life of society. But with the coming of the factory, the manor-houses and the houses of the rich and powerful ceased to be the economic centers of their districts. They became mere show places. They were used by the wealthy merely for competition in "conspicuous waste." The domestics in them were reduced to the status of pure parasites. To this day, domestics find the factory a welcome relief from the social ignominy and the social tyranny of domestic service.

In America, the factories relied upon the apparently unending stream of immigrants for their supplies of workers, and when the stream did not come fast enough, agents were sent to Europe to increase the labor supply of the textile villages of New England, the steel regions about Pittsburgh, and the packing-house centers like Chicago.

•

Degradation of both labor and laborers was one of the first results of the transfer of work and workers from the home-shop and the workshop to the factory. The factory with its labor-saving machinery can be considered a social gain only if its effect upon the worker is ignored.

With the coming of the factory, the worker found that the skill which he had already acquired was no longer a marketable product. Factory machines could be operated by unskilled workers—untrained women and often children were sufficiently strong and intelligent. Since the factory took over the work of the craft which had formerly given him employment and it was difficult for a skilled mechanic to change his calling to one equally as skillful and remunerative, the market value of his labor was reduced to that of unskilled workers who operated the factory machines.

This consequence of the coming of the factory is well described by Professor Dexter S. Kimball:

> The new methods of production have enabled many unskilled people to take an important part in many industrial fields formerly occupied solely by skilled workers. Today in nearly every large manufacturing industry the unskilled or semi-skilled labor greatly outnumbers the skilled, and a product of great accuracy and high finish is turned out by such organizations. This principle of extension of the field of labor is a broad one. As more and more skill and thought have been transferred to hand and machine tools it has become increasingly easy for men and women to take part in what was formerly entirely skilled industry. The *actual* production of shoes, watches, typewriters, etc., is conducted almost entirely by semi-skilled labor.[17]

Professor Kimball labors mightily to justify this process in discussing what he calls the factory's extension of the field of labor and its elevation of labor. Let me quote him further on this point:

> Manifestly these new methods have multiplied man's productive power many fold, enabling him to produce more per unit of time,

with a corresponding reduction in the cost of production. This feature, and the principles of the elevation of labor and the extension of the field of labor more than compensate in the long run for the effects of degradation of labor, though as before noted the many benefit at the expense of the few. Human progress apparently cannot take place without someone suffering. *Theoretically* all should be greatly benefited by these improved methods, and the reason why such has not always been the case is not because of the processes themselves, but because their net result is to *increase* production solely. They do not carry with them inherently any influences tending to rearrange the *distribution* of the increased profits derived from them, nor to offset the effects of the fierce competition rendered possible because of this increase in productive capacity. Invention and its result always act quickly; social and political changes move more slowly. The natural law of supply and demand operated quickly under the older and simpler methods. The complexity of modern methods tends to make these laws act much more sluggishly. It is only after a struggle lasting over a hundred years that there is hope, even of instituting reforms that will in a measure restore the equilibrium of distributive methods so badly distorted by the results of the great inventions. * * *[18]

While the introduction of these new methods may degrade certain classes of labor, they may, on the other hand, elevate others. The skilled mechanic who has been engaged in drilling plates is not necessarily degraded by the introduction of the drilling jig, because his skill can be utilized to make such tools; and this class of labor, namely, the skilled workers in the metal trades, has, on the whole, usually benefited radier than otherwise, by the new methods, though at times trying periods of readjustment have ensued upon the introduction of labor-saving machinery into their own industry.

Again the unskilled worker who is taken from low-paid menial employment and taught to operate a semi-automatic machine can usually earn more money than formerly and be elevated to a higher plane. The history of manufacturing in New England shows very clearly the absorption into the manufacturing industries of the successive waves of immigration of unskilled labor that have from time to time moved into these states.[19]

Unfortunately it is necessary to call attention to the great probability that the coming of the factory has actually reduced the relative proportion of skilled to semi-skilled workers. Professor

Kimball himself has already admitted that the factory has enabled unskilled workers to take an important place in many industries formerly occupied *solely* by skilled workers. But in addition, he is almost certainly wrong on almost every point he makes about the elevation of labor. He is under the impression that "low-paid menials" (What does he mean by "menials"? Does he include skilled domestic servants—cooks, seamstresses, butlers in the class of "menials"?) are elevated to a higher plane when they are taught to operate a semi-automatic machine? In what respect are they higher? He mentions only their pay for their work. But is he right about the fact that the ex-menials who have gone into the factories are higher paid? Taking wages, board, lodging, washing, medical tare, etc., into consideration, the average domestic servant is much higher paid than the unskilled or semi-skilled factory worker.

He is entirely wrong when he says the "waves of immigrants" to this country consisted of unskilled labor. If he thinks an Italian peasant is an unskilled laborer, then he has never discovered how much skill it takes to raise a garden. The vast majority of these immigrants were skilled workers—highly skilled workers: they were farm workers, stonemasons, basket weavers, tailors, domestics, for whose skill, however, the factory had no use.

But Professor Kimball is most wrong in failing to distinguish between the degradation of labor, and the degradation of the laborer. The distinction between the two is of the utmost importance. If it is kept in mind, it becomes plain that as far as the great masses of workers are concerned, the question is whether it is possible for the factory to degrade the labor which it requires them to do without ultimately degrading the laborer himself.

If we omit the casualties which involve degradation, but which are due to those periods of readjustment caused by inventions to which Professor Kimball referred, we can make what has taken place clear by simplifying the issue. At all times, we have a certain proportion of potentially skilled laborers. Whether or not they find skilled labor at which they can work and earn a living is determined by conditions over which, in an industrialized world, they have no control. Limited numbers of them will find skilled work to do, and if they find employment at such labor as tool-making, they may enjoy an elevation of labor. But Professor Kimball has shown that in many industries the proportion of skilled workers has gone down; that in many of the new industries only unskilled and semi-skilled workers are employed, and there is no evidence furnished that the tool-making necessary for these industries offers sufficient employment for the skilled workers who are excluded from the industries which might formerly have employed them. On the contrary, there is a considerable body of evidence that large numbers of potentially skilled laborers never do find employment that really utilizes their capacities. They are forced to work as semi-skilled or unskilled laborers—perhaps never have the opportunity to learn a skilled craft because of that. For them, as compared to their forebears, there has been a real degradation not only of labor, but also of the laborer. The potential journeyman machinist finds himself compelled to be a mere machine-operative and to live upon the relatively lower scale of existence which that involves.

The higher productivity which industrialization makes possible —the higher wages and the lower prices which follow—cannot really compensate the laborer for the loss of satisfaction involved when the work he has to do is constantly degraded. They are a form of compensation which in effect means that in return for accepting the mechanization of his working life, he should devote himself to extracting happiness only from the time he devotes to consumption.

If each new invention, if each new automatic machine, if each new factory means a degradation of a particular type of labor, then cumulative inventions, cumulative labor-saving machinery, cumulative industrialization must involve a cumulative degradation of labor. With the perfection of factory production, the degradation would reach its apex. The work he did would express nothing of the worker's own capacities. The worker would become an automaton. He would have to compensate himself for his dehumanized labor by the increased joy which he would get out of the consumption of the things which greater production and lower prices would enable him to buy. Having been cheated out of all chance to get happiness out of his work, he would have to be satisfied with the happiness he could extract from an ever-increasing consumption of factory-made products.

•

The modern factory has use for three types of workers, says Mr. John C. Duncan in his *Principles of Industrial Management.*

First, unskilled workers, mere manual laborers, of which it uses many especially in the continuons industries. According to Mr. Duncan, improvements in the technique of these industries tend to reduce the numbers of these workers, but they can hardly become, as he hopes, extinct, as long as there are inefficient—marginal—factories in existence.

Secondly, semi-skilled workers, an intermediate grade of labor between the unskilled manual laborer and the highly skilled mechanic. The semi-skilled worker, according to Mr. Duncan, is the ideal type for the efficient factory. He is already the most numerous of the three types and should become universal in the future. According to Mr. Duncan the semi-skilled worker's qualifications are as follows:

> In addition to regularity and good health [he] must have: (1) Ability to learn to handle machinery of a more or less semi-automatic type without injury to himself. (2) A willingness to attend closely to such machinery, seeing that it is constantly running properly, and is always supplied with material to keep it producing. (3) Ability to keep the machinery in his charge in good running order.

These qualifications are modest in the extreme. By comparison, "Nailer" Tom Hazard was a veritable genius.

Thirdly, the factory has use for skilled workers, the most highly intelligent and best educated non-professional class in the country, often earning wages which compare favorably with the incomes of teachers, lawyers, doctors, and other professional men.

In the interest of efficiency, and of course in response to the economic pressure exerted by efficient competitors, each factory is driven to increase the proportion of serai-skilled workers and to reduce the proportions both of skilled and unskilled workers which it employs. Mr. Duncan says:

> The great problem of a manager in any place is to introduce machinery and so arrange the work that the unskilled worker will be unnecessary, and the call for the highly skilled man will be small. . . . An organization which must have a large number of the third class of workman, the highly skilled man, is likewise undesirable, not be cause his services are not valuable, but because so much depends upon him. His grade is so high that it is difficult to obtain him. . . . It is highly desirable to get machinery to do as much of his work as possible.
>
> The second class of worker is most desirable. The advantages of this class are: (1) A short apprenticeship makes the mari valuable to the employer. (2) The employee with his limited capacity feels his dependence on the employer, and is likely to be a faithful and attentive workman because he receives a larger income than ordinary laborers, and could in most cases obtain employment only as a less valuable man in another place. (3) The employee becomes proficient in doing one thing, and is thus able to turn out a large product.[20]

Machiavelli could not have stated the reasons for the factory's warfare upon the skilled worker more cogently.

•

But if modern industrialization is therefore credited with elevating the status of the unskilled workers, it must be debited with degrading the status of the skilled laborer and the craftsman.

In the great Ford factories few of the operations require much training in order to make the workers proficient, and there are very few jobs for highly skilled workers, as Henry Ford himself makes abundantly clear:

> The length of time required to become proficient in the various occupations is about as follows: 43 percent of all the jobs require not over one day of training; 36 percent require from one day to one week; 6 percent require from one to two weeks; 14 percent require from one month to one year; one percent require from one to six years. The last jobs require a great skill—as in tool making and the sinking.[21]

By reducing practically all the workers to the status of machine feeders and machine tenders, taking from them all initiative and responsibility, and dividing and sub-dividing the work, all kinds of human material can be used equally well. Cripples and morons can do much of the work just as well as whole-bodied and whole-minded men. In the Ford factories no one is refused work on account of physical condition. The crippled are paid the same minimum wages as able-bodied men who may be doing the same work. Out of 7,882 kinds of jobs in the factory, at the time of which Mr. Ford writes, 4,034 did not require full physical capacity. In fact, 3,595 could be performed by the slightest, weakest sort of men and most of them could be satisfactorily performed by women and children. Of the lightest jobs 670 could be filled by legless men; 2,637 by one-legged men, 2 by armless men, 715 by one-armed men, and 10 by men entirely blind. At the time of the analysis the factory used 9,563 sub-standard men-123 had crippled or amputated arms, forearms, or hands; one had both hands off; 4 were totally blind; 207 blind in one eye; 37 deaf and dumb; 60 epileptics; 4 with both legs missing; 234 with one foot or leg missing. The others had minor deficiencies.

This is magnificent! Especially if we shut our eyes to the fact that many of these cripples are produced by the factory system which thus prides itself on finding useful work for them. But to appraise judiciously the combination of good-will and ingenuity displayed in this achievement we must consider the conclusion which Mr. Ford draws from his efforts along this line:

> Developed industry can provide wage work for a higher average of standard men than are ordinarily included in any normal community.[22]

This is at first sight rather ambiguous because it does not state clearly what Mr. Ford meant by the expression "average of standard men." The context, however, makes it clear that Mr. Ford really meant almost the exact opposite of what the statement seems to say. What he meant to say, and what his statistics proved, was that the division and sub-division of labor as he practiced it, made it possible to employ more sub-standard men than the community provided. What he proved and should have said was: Developed industry can provide wage work for more men of certain types—

physically or crippled types of various kinds—than are ordinarily included in modern communities. He should have added: it therefore provides less wage work for men of other types those capable of highly skilled work—than are ordinarily produced in the average community.

The factory in which scientific management has divided and sub-divided labor and introduced the most efficient and powerful machinery not only reduces the opportunities for work for skilled workers, but makes it possible to use more sub-standard men than mankind provides! With the community furnishing, as yet, an insufficiency of cripples and morons for the needs of the efficient factory, normal men and women must be impressed into jobs far below their true capacities. They must, however, be compensated for the sacrifice of their personalities upon the altar of the moloch of factory production. For implicit obedience to the rules and formulæ established by the management and the surrender of all individual judgment and initiative, they get what all factory workers get, if everything works perfectly: higher wages and shorter hours than they would have received under a non-factory regime.

•

The ingenuity of the devices in the modern factory, which make it possible to use low-grade workers for dangerous tasks and to make their movements automatically synchronize with the needs of the machines they operate, is amazing.

In the automobile factories, large numbers of men have to stand all day before presses which punch sheet steel. The operation of inserting and withdrawing the material requires no skill at all, but it does require that the worker withdraw his fingers and hands before the press, which rises and falls automatically, cuts them off. In spite of screen guards of various kinds, a steady stream of accidents nevertheless used to come from these punch presses. The workers, in moments of carelessness, perhaps due to the fatigue of monotony, or the indifference which repetitive familiarity breeds, left their fingers and hands in the presses. The problem before the management, if accident costs were to be kept down, was automatically to insure that the worker withdrew his hands before his press descended. The problem was finally solved by the simple expedient of handcuffing the worker's hands to a lever which pulled his hands away from the machine at the moment that the press descended.

Go to the press rooms today and you will see the lines of workers standing before their presses, their hands jerking away each time the presses move. As the individual workers do not control the movement of the presses, which are started and stopped by the foreman, once they are handcuffed to the machines their hands are jerked automatically backward until they are released. Even though they may be out of material, they have to stand before the press, their hands jerking back and forth. There they work, chained to their machines, as the galley slaves were chained to their oars. They cannot leave even to attend to the needs of nature until they attract the foreman's eye and he unlocks their handcuffs and releases them.

The process of making the low grade worker measure up to the necessities of the factory machine can hardly go much farther.

•

Is it necessary to point out in further detail how the necessities of the factory relentlessly mechanize the worker, decrease the number of workers engaged in creative labor, and produce workers without initiative and self-reliance? In factory work no means are afforded the worker for self-expression. There is no possibility of joy in work without it. Indeed, no joy is permitted or sought. As the greatest factory genius America has produced says:

> When we are at work we ought to be at work. When we are at play we ought to be at play. There is no use trying to mix the two. The sole object ought to be to get the work done and to get paid for it. When the work is done, then the play can come, but not before.[23]

This compensation is logical enough in a system of production in which repetitive labor, "the doing of one thing over and over again and always in the same way," is an essential factor.

The protagonists of the factory justify this repetitive labor on the theory that the great majority of workers prefer it and that most of them are incapable of any other. Henry Ford makes the flat assertion that he has not been able to discover that repetitive labor injures a man in any way. And he gives a number of specific illustrations to prove his assertion. He goes further. "Scarcely more than five percent of those who work for wages, while they have the desire to receive more money, have also the willingness to accept the additional responsibility and the additional work which goes with the higher places," he says on page 99 of his book. On page 103 he says: "The average worker, I am sorry to say, wants a job in which he does not have to put forth much physical exertion—above all, he wants a job in which he does not have to think."

There are, however, good grounds for suspecting a major in consistency in the arguments of the proponents of industrialization on this point. If it is true that most men prefer the repetitive work which the modern factory offers them, how explain the dislike of their jobs which is indicated by the high turnover of labor in most factories, and the almost universal prevalence of "soldiering" in our factories? Frederick Winslow Taylor, in the *Principles of Scientific Management*, calls attention to the contrast between the energy an American workman will put into a game of baseball and the energy he puts the very next day into his job. Taylor asserted that deliberate "soldiering" in many instances cuts down by more than one-third to one-half what should be a proper day's work and maintains that this constitutes the greatest evil with which the working-people of both England and America are now afflicted. In the packing-houses and the automobile factories and in all factories in which the speed of the worker's operations are determined for him by a continuously moving platform, "soldiering" may be eliminated. But the dislike of the work remains even though this particular consequence of the dislike be eradicated. As a matter of fact, it is not repetitive labor that is the damning fact; for there is repetition in labor of all kinds. It is the fact that the repetitive labor is without significance: that it is an isolated operation, and not a process with a beginning, a middle, and an end.

Mr. Marlen E. Pew relates a story which illustrates how dreary human life may become through the humdrum of factory life. Years ago, Robert Hunter met a stew-bum on the Bowery and questioned him. He told this story:

"I was born in a New England shoe manufacturing town and as a child went to work in a factory. My parents were poor and needed the two or three dollars I could earn by sweeping floors. There was a road through the town that led to the country and I used to yearn to follow that road to some country-ride where boys could lie and dream under the trees or play in the brook, but I kept on sweeping from early morning till late at night. As a youth I was put onto a machine. It was necessary for me to make a certain number of motions to operate the machine. Once I counted those motions. There were only nine. This was my life, making those motions. All day, six days a week, fifty-two weeks per year, I repeated those nine motions. As a man I got a larger machine and it required of the operative fourteen motions. Day in and out for ten years I fed my life into that machine. In the meantime I had married a girl who operated a machine in the same shop. We had some glimpses at happiness, but after all, existence for us both came down to those fourteen motions. Because I felt nothing was ahead for me I became ugly and on occasion would seek relief in booze. All the time the road was calling to me—'come out and play, lie under the trees and dream and bathe in the babbling brook.' One day I saw red and started to walk on that road. I have tramped over the country. I have been hungry and cold and thread bare a thousand times. I have been in jails, slept in flop-houses and box-cars, panhandled on the streets, drunk when I could get the price of booze and now I am a Bowery bum."

Mr. Hunter said: "Well, was it a mistake?"

"Mistake?" snapped the hobo. "I will say it was no mistake. I'd rather freeze and starve than go back to those fourteen motions; no sir, I'm still on the road and on the way out." [24]

•

Henry Ford has recognized the fact that factory workers can not be kept to their work unless they are given some relief from it in the shape of shorter hours and fewer days of work per week. The fact that the factory has made work more and more monotonous and more and more mechanical has been an influence in shortening the hours of labor. This is clearly recognized in the report of Industrial Conference called by the President.

The problem of hours has undergone a fundamental change through the introduction of large scale factory production and the growing concentration of our population in cities. Men and women can work

> relatively long hours at work which is interesting, which calls upon their various energies, which gives some opportunity for creative self-expression. Work which is repetitious, monotonous, and conducted under the confining indoor conditions of even the best industrial plant, especially where the plant is located at a distance from the homes of the workers, makes much more exacting physical and nervous demands. If the inevitable conditions of modern industry do not offer variety and continuing interest, the worker should have hours short enough for more recreation and for greater contact with his fellow workmen outside of working hours.[25]

•

Henry Ford thinks that men should work fewer hours per day and fewer days per week in order to have leisure in which to consume what the factories produce for them. If a man works only five days per week, instead of six, he will have two days per week in which to use his automobile instead of only one day. He will wear out his automobile twice as fast, thus enlarging the capacity of the market to absorb the products of the automobile factories; he will use up twice as much gasoline; wear out twice as many tires, in short, double his ability to consume while cutting down the time he devotes to production.

Gainful work, even in the most efficient industries, absorbs more than fifty percent of the worker's waking hours. It is, however, so tedious, so uninteresting, in the modern factory, that it can be said truly that the worker is required to yield half of his life to boredom in order that he might devote the other half to eating more than is good for himself; wearing out more things than is rational; and destroying the natural resources of the earth faster than real comfort and true enjoyment make necessary!

•

One of the most interesting consequences of the great development of our factories is referred to in the brief extract from the report of the Industrial Conference called by the President, above quoted—the fact that factories tend more and more to be located at considerable distances from the homes of workers. With domestic production and with workshop production, home and the place of work were generally one and the same. With the factory, they are never the same. In our factory-dominated civilization there seems to be a tendency for the home and the place of work to move farther and farther apart.

Most often the factory is located in a large city because among other advantages, the city furnishes it an ample reservoir of labor. It is not easy for the factory to get away from city congestion because even the factory located in the suburbs of a city, or even in a rural region, tends only too quickly to build city conditions around itself.

Time must therefore be spent by the workers in going to and from work. Lunches have to be eaten away from home. And in the larger cities, much of what is gained by the shorter hours of work in the factory, is lost by long trips back and forth in crowded street cars, elevated trains, subways, and suburban commutation trains. The worker flatters himself that he works only eight hours a day, while his grandfather worked ten or twelve. He forgets that he often spends from one hour to as high as four hours each day going to and from work, and that he dissipates some of the increased wages of which he is so proud for luncheons and transportation expenses. The luncheon restaurants multiply in every city in direct ratio to the increase in its streetcar systems and its suburban population.

•

But surely the very worst of the influences of the factory upon the worker has been the extent to which it has added to the in security of his economic life. It would be absurd to say that the worker of the pre-industrial age was without fears that are comparable to those of the modern factory worker. But while comparable, they were often ameliorable. He was dependent upon the favor of the lord of the manor, if a farm worker, or upon that of his journeyman master, if an indentured apprentice. But in neither case was there any insecurity about his "job." That he might suffer injustices from those for whom he worked was true, but at least he was face to face with his employer. It was the coming of absentee and corporate ownership which made appeal from injustice so difficult and unsatisfactory for the worker.

Today he often finds himself unemployed as a result of conditions which neither he, nor the impersonal corporation for which he works, may be able to control. As W. L. Chenery says, "Unemployment and the fear of unemployment are twin evils created by the factory system." These are among the gravest of the disadvantages from which the modern worker suffers that he may at other times enjoy the material well-being with which the factory system justifies itself. Chenery presents an excellent picture of what this means to the worker:

> The possibility of being workless and without income hangs over the great majority of wage earners. The factory worker of today knows little else that he could turn to account. He must live by his trade or not at all. In order to obtain employment he must ordinarily reside in congested cities, where the possibilities of subsidiary means of support are denied him. Usually he does not own the house or the tenement he lives in. He neither cultivates nor harvests the vegetables and fruits which his family consumes. If he is able to eat eggs, or to drink milk, he obtains these articles from dealers who are themselves far removed from the scene of actual production. His clothes are bought, not made at home. The modern factory worker must retain his job if he wishes to continue alive, and yet he knows that at recurrent intervals, regardless of zeal or fitness, many men and women will not be employed.[26]

"At recurrent intervals!" When business is bad; if there is overproduction in his particular industry; when he engages in one of his periodic strikes, or if some change in industry, such as the introduction of a new product, or movement of the factory to a new section, results in throwing out of work those in particular factories or particular regions—at these recurrent intervals he is unemployed. Is it any wonder that the fear of unemployment robs the factory worker of the security which is essential to any orderly economic, social, biologie life?

•

We have had about a hundred years of the factory in America. What has it done to the workers of America? The World War revealed the facts: Our workers are neither physically nor mentally creatures of which America might be proud, of which she might say, "These are my sons, in whom I take great delight!" Lewis Mumford describes the situation aptly:

> It is no special cause for grief or wonder that the Army Intelligence Tests finally rated the product of these depleted agricultural regions or of this standardized education, this standardized factory regime, this standardized daily routine as below the human norm in intelligence: the wonder would rather have been if any large part of the population had achieved a full human development. The pioneer, at worst, had only been a savage; but the new American had fallen a whole abyss below this: he was becoming an automaton.[27]

But the factory worker is not merely an automaton. He is a joyless automaton.

There is no song on his lips; no laughter in his heart.

Gone are the spring songs, the harvesting songs, the chanteys and the lays.

The factory worker at the top works grimly to accumulate profits; the factory worker in the ranks, grimly to remain on the payroll. The strain numbs nerves, sears spirits, and imprints it self indelibly on the expressions of the faces of the workers from top to bottom.

Go where men whose faces are marked like that are to be found; there you will find the factory.

CHAPTER VII
THE FACTORY'S CUSTOMERS

Adam Smith called man a manufacturing animal. But Adam Smith published *The Wealth of Nations* in 1776. He never saw a copy of a daily newspaper filled with hundreds of advertisements urging people to buy every conceivable article and commodity. He never saw a popular magazine with a circulation in the millions of copies and containing hundreds of pages of advertising urging the people of the entire nation to buy the various products which our factories are producing. And of course he never saw a self-service grocery store, nor a chain store, nor a modern department store, and above all, he never saw a modern bargain sale. Had he lived to see these things; had he lived to see the serried ranks of women whose daily occupation it is to descend on the shopping districts; had he lived to see the dawn of the distribution age when selling and not manufacturing was becoming the principal occupation of men, he would have called man a buying and not a manufacturing animal.

When he wrote, he saw the factory as an instrument devised by man as an instrumentality for manufacturing. He did not foresee that the factory would ultimately turn upon its creators. He did not foresee that the factory would force manufacturers to devote themselves to creating buyers to consume what industry produced. He did not, therefore, see that the factory would ultimately bisect humanity by making one-half of it into earning animals and one-half of it into spending animals.

Add the stimulus of profits, to the ever present fear of bankruptcy, and modern industry's preoccupation with the process of creating buyers is readily understood. For the manufacturer, the creation of buyers for his products is vital if he is to maintain his sales volume. He must keep his factories producing enough to pay an adequate return upon the investment in them. For the factory worker, and indeed for everybody dependent for their livelihood upon the operation of the factory, the failure to create enough buyers for the products of their factory means unemployment and hard times.

Fortunately for the sales department of the factory, the coming of factory production and the consequent decline in domestic production destroyed the self-sufficiency of men and forced them to supply their wants and desires by buying what formerly they had produced and fashioned for themselves. Men ceased to devote their time and thought to making and producing things for themselves, and devoted them to earning the money essential to the buying of what they needed and wanted. The money economy which was thus thrust upon man forced him to go to work for wages; to go into business to earn profits, to adopt professions which commanded cash returns. Within a hundred years of the time that Adam Smith called attention to the fact that man was a manufacturing animal, men had become creatures expected and trained to devote themselves to bringing home money; women creatures expected and trained to spend the money which their men brought home. By a perfectly natural course of evolution a folkway has developed in which the man plays the part of an earning-animal and the woman that of a buying-animal. Both are expected to be consumers of factory products, but the modern woman, rather than the modern man, has become the factory's actual customer.

•

The pre-eminent position of women as the purchasing agents for the home in these days is made evident in the following table from *What About Advertising?*[28] The table is based upon a recent survey of retail stores in New York City. In only two of the twelve classes of retail establishments were men more numerous than women as customers. These two classes sold hardware and automobiles.

The table shows the percentages of purchases made by men and by women in twelve classifications.

Type of store:	Percent of Purchases: By Men	By Women
Silks	2	98
Jewelry	10	90
Department store	18	82
Grocery store	18	81
Electrical supplies	20	80
Drug store	22	78
Pianos	22	78
Men's socks	25	75
Leather goods	33	67
Men's neckwear	37	63
Hardware	51	49
Automobiles	59	41

With buying the primary economic function of the modern woman, she ceases to be a domestic producer. The dominant type of woman today is no longer a homemaker. Indeed there is no dominant type. The modern woman may be a shopper, a job-holder, a careerist, or a homemaker. The difference between these four readily distinguishable types of women in respect to economic function is one only of degree. Not even the modern homemakers are consciously domestic producers. All types of women today are customers of the factory—even the homemakers who are slowly disappearing because the men who direct factories know what they want while the homemakers do not.

•

In industrialized America there are still considerable numbers of homemakers—women to whom homemaking is still a career and motherhood life's great adventure. Mostly they are to be found on the farms of the country, although a dwindling but gallant minority of urban homes can still boast of them.

Because of the glamour of adventure which has been thrown about the woman who earns a living outside of the home, we tend to forget that the making of a home is not only a career but a creative career of the highest order.

Homemaking is an art.

All art is self-expression. But art is also discipline. The artist expresses himself, but he expresses himself within the discipline which the art he practices imposes upon him. The painter has to master the technique of placing lines, shadows, and colors upon a plane surface before he can produce a really beautiful painting. The number of different elements with which he has to contend are actually few in number. Yet everybody recognizes that what he produces out of these elements is the product of his creative ability —ability which varies in different painters from zero to that of the highest genius.

In precisely the same way, the creative ability of the homemaker can vary from zero to that of veritable genius. But the elements with which the homemaker has to produce her work of art are far more numerous than those which the painter uses, and the technique she has to master far more difficult. She has to work with living beings: husband, children, friends, relatives, acquaintances. She has to work with inanimate materials which include nearly everything that mankind produces: food, clothing, shelter, furnishings. Finally, she has to work with the intangibles of life which include practically all of mankind's cultural activities: society, religion, literature, music and art. Out of these diverse elements—human beings, inanimate materials, cultural interests—the homemaker creates a home as truly as an artist creates a painting. He works in a studio—in effect a laboratory in which he evokes his painting. She works in a whole series of laboratories—in a garden, in a kitchen, in a nursery, in a sewing room, in a dining room, in a living room. And in these she creates what should be, as it is in some cases, the most beautiful thing which mankind has up to the present time created: a desirable environment in which to rear children, a comfortable place for herself and her mate, and a center of the good life for those who are within the social circle of which her home is a center. The time may come when the difficulty of the task will be recognized, and when the highest degrees of the colleges of the world will be reserved for the woman who has equipped herself for a career as homemaker.

Against the dwindling remnant of homemakers in America the factory is waging a relentless war of extermination. The factory extends itself by taking over the homemakers' creative activities. One by one it has taken away from them the household crafts and the household arts that furnished them the means to creative self-expression. The true crafts have all gone. Sewing is going; cookery is threatened; only furnishing the home may survive. The wonder is that there are still so many aspiring homemakers left. The wonder is that all women have not yet turned away from the task of creating homes, and despairingly accepted conditions which they see no way to alter—conditions which force them to rent homes and to buy everything to put in them; conditions which not only make them buy their family's clothes, food, furnishings, but also to buy education, culture and entertainment for them.

Today, in our factory-dominated civilization, only the farming class can still boast of homemakers in large numbers. The greater self-sufficiency of farm life explains their survival in rural America. But the automobile, and the good roads which the automobile has brought into existence, are fast thinning even their ranks. Closer contact with the city and the prestige it accords to the factory-made product, instead of stimulating farm housewives to a higher type of homemaking, is leading them to abandon many of the things they still do of a productive and creative nature. Reading daily newspapers, seeing movies, hearing radio programs, shopping in stylish stores, make the farm family want to wear factory clothes, to eat factory foods, to use factory furniture. The time may come when the farm homemakers of the country will cease all individual home production and join the urban women in their devotion to the factory product and their dependence upon factory production.

In urban America the homemakers are fast becoming extinct. Neither among the really rich, nor among the great masses of wage earners and office and store workers are there any considerable number of women of the homemaking type to be found. The instinct for homemaking does not seem able to survive the temptations of hotel and resort life in one case, nor the pressure of flat and tenement life in the other. The homes of the rich and of the poor tend to become dormitories: the places in which the members of the family sleep but not the places in which they live.

As for Suburbia: it can boast of some homemakers who use the land and the room available in the suburban home for a relatively productive domestic life, but they are being daily reduced in number. Suburbia does not furnish a social life which encourages housewives to make homemaking a creative occupation. On the contrary, suburban women are expected to devote their time to "keeping up with the Joneses." They become increasingly women to whom a home in the fashionable section of the town, membership in the fashionable church, and patronage of the town's fashionable doctor are the great values in life.

Suburban housewives hide their economies and parade their extravagances. They patronize the fashionable tradesmen of their town, and shop in the most expensive city stores so that high class delivery wagons may stop at their door—because it is the thing to do. The battle for social prestige is won by the amounts they dare to spend.

In Suburbia it is a social handicap to contribute to family welfare by creative and productive work in the home.

•

Within a very short time after the coming of the factory, careerist women appeared. Women of wealth; women of ability and personality; women of education and of intelligence were among the first to revolt at the desiccated homemaking into which church, state and factory were thrusting them. Yet they were the very women who could least be spared from homemaking. They were the women who should have discovered that woman's real task was, as Ellen Key said, "to ennoble woman's sphere, not necessarily to enlarge it."

While the factory was busily engaged in making it unnecessary for these women to devote themselves to homemaking as a career, they themselves were busily engaged in proving that they could do equally well everything which had been formerly considered exclusively the work of men or believed exclusively a masculine prerogative. They devoted themselves first to the winning of the various equalities with men which go under the name of women's rights; the right to academic education; the right to engage in the same professions and occupations; the right to vote; finally, the right to sexual freedom.

Perhaps no other single movement in all history was fraught

with so much in the way of good for the future of the race as was this assertion of the rights of womankind. Many of the rights for which the women who led the movement struggled have so far proved of trifling importance, but taking them as a whole, they had a tendency to free woman for a voluntary contribution to the life of mankind. They were a direct attack upon the involuntary contribution which the state, church and society had up to that time demanded of women. They had a tendency to make her entrance upon wifehood and motherhood voluntary and so to make a mutual undertaking of the vital activities which have to be conducted by men and women in common. But the struggle had a most unfortunate effect upon the women who made the work of winning these rights the basis of their careers.

The ablest among them set themselves up in opposition to everything that savored of compromise with men. Their rebellion against the age-old conditions which the men had complacently accepted, made them react against any normal relationships with the opposite sex at all. These spirited, independent women formed the habit of looking upon homemaking and motherhood as a sort of treason to the cause to which they were devoted. Work outside of the home seemed a heaven-sent outlet for their energies. They devoted themselves to reform, to law, to medicine, to journalism and finally to business. By comparison with careers in these fields, partnership with men in the creation of homes and the continuance of the race seemed submission to a lifetime of drudgery. Home making and motherhood seemed to offer them no scope for the expression of ability, no opportunity for adventurous activity and no hope for recognition and reward of genius.

Of the institutions which evolved out of the woman's rights movement, the women's colleges probably contributed most to setting up an abnormal appreciation of careers and an equally abnormal depreciation of marriages. A dean of one woman's college once made the significant remark that three-quarters of the women who graduated from her college were failures. Asked what type of graduates she considered the failures she answered: "Why, those who wasted their educations by marrying." Only of late is it beginning to dawn upon these teachers of women that partnership in the creation of a home and a family is woman's true career in life, precisely and exactly as it is man's. The awakening has probably come too late both for the women and the men. The factory has in the meantime taken over so many of the functions of the home that the graduates from the euthenics courses, now being added to the curriculum of these colleges, will probably find as little to do in their homes as do the men.

In turning their backs on homemaking, the careerists wholeheartedly embrace the earn-and-buy theory of living. They are buyers of everything that they consume, and generally very poor buyers as well. Lacking all training and lacking all interest in the homely activities of life, they are almost certain to be poor judges both of values and of merchandise. The more completely they devote themselves to their careers, the more ignorant they are certain to be about the things that they have to buy. But this is a burden of which they are generally unconscious.

Theirs is a life above mundane things. The careerists have managed to evolve a folkway—a pattern of life—that shields them from these grosser aspects of life. Most of them live intensively in their work, associate only with their own kind, know nothing of the possibilities of life in partnership with the complementary sex. Most of them live an abnormal sex-life—one ranging from complete sex-starvation to the partial sex-life of unions without home or children. For few of them marry, and fewer still have children. Thus they invite the life-long frustration which nature inflicts upon all those who flout her mandate of fecundity.

The excessive specialization which careerists impose upon them selves, however excusable to great genius, is no more good for normal women than it is for normal men. If anything this specialization is more harmful to women than it is to men, because the penalty exacted by nature from women who refuse motherhood is greater than that exacted from men who refuse fatherhood. For the majority of women, even for the women who have the ability to attain a considerable measure of success in careers outside of the home, the chance for achieving happiness in marriage and partnership with the right man—even if it is necessary to try marriage a number of times in order to find the right one—is better than the chance of achieving it in even the most successful of specialized careers. Specialization is bad for men—it is worse for women. Women's careers, even more than men's, ought, therefore, to be complementary to homemaking.

Unfortunately the factory system interposes every kind of obstacle to the development of homes which can enlist the talents of able women. It destroys the economic utility of women's work in the home. It cheats the women in the home of opportunity for self-expression in what they do. It deprives them of their husband's assistance in building real homes, because the men are forced to be away most of their days. And at the same time that it thus lessens the significance of all work in the home, it opens innumerable alternative careers for them. The careerists are there fore going to increase in number. As they increase in numbers, they will increase in prestige and inflict an ever more galling feeling of inferiority upon those women who strive to make home making their careers. Women of spirit will shrink more and more from homemaking and motherhood, and leave both increasingly to the less desirable types of women.

•

The vast majority of women whom the factory has driven out of the home, however, are not careerists. They are mere job holders. It is necessity which has driven them out of the home to earn money. Ambition for a career is a minor motive if it is prescrit at all. Our factories and offices are full of women job holders—women who are there because they have to earn money, and whose interest is not in the work they do, but in the pay which they get for it.

According to Miss Mary Anderson, head of the Women's Bureau of the United States Department of Labor, these women are in American industry to stay.

> They take employment young—when they leave school, and if they stop work to get married, it is only a short time before circumstances force them back to their tasks again. Failure of husbands to make adequate incomes is the cause.
>
> Too many people, however, blame the married woman who goes out of the home in this fashion, failing to realize it is dire necessity

> that is making her do it. The women themselves suffer, as well as the families and society. A whole new set of social problems—not really new in age, but unique in this generation—is the result.

For some time to come fortunate job-holders may still find in marriage and housekeeping a means of escape from their "jobs," but as the nation becomes more and more urbanized, and the home of less and less economic utility, this will become an escape more and more difficult to achieve. One quarter of all the women gainfully employed in the United States are already married women. Vast numbers of men find it impossible to support wives, much less families, on the money which they alone earn. When they marry their wives have to continue working outside the home, and have to postpone motherhood as long as possible.

The training for buying of these job-holders who form the vast majority of the factory's customers is pitifully inadequate for the task with which they are confronted. For buy they must when they marry, whether they retain their jobs or leave them to start a home. If they remain at work, the cooking, sewing and washing which they do at home must be done evenings after work or Saturday afternoons and Sundays. Naturally the amount of this work is reduced to a minimum. They cannot afford, as can their more able or more wealthy fellow-workers, the careerists, to go to restaurants very much, so they become what may be called without exaggeration, tin-can cooks. It is quite surprising how complete a meal they can prepare once they have learned to use a can opener with ease and precision, and it is quite amazing how elaborate some of these can openers have to be so as to reduce the dangers and the fatigue of this part of their housekeeping to a minimum.

They know little or nothing about the actual contents of the cans and packages which they buy. The manufacturers' advertising gives them a vague feeling that the advertised brands are the best, but they buy very largely whatever the retail clerks, who know as little as the women themselves, hand out to them.

They know nothing about the textiles which they buy. How should they? The different fibers are very largely just names to them. They know nothing about the construction of the goods and of their relative utility or durability. How can they? They have never seen the different fibers grown; never seen them spun into yarn; probably do not know what a loom is at all.

Their ignorance about the nature and the value of foods and textiles is duplicated in almost every class of product which they are called upon to buy. They probably abandon even the most elementary kinds of home sewing. They believe that the factories, in which they work or have worked and with which they are more or less familiar, make things so much more efficiently than they can be made in a home, and at so much lower costs, that it is foolish to make anything themselves. It is astonishing how often even thoughtful people fail to distinguish between the low costs for which the factory can make things and the high price at which they have to be sold by the time all the costs of distribution are added to the bare factory cost.

If these job-holding types of women devote all their time to their homes, it is usually because the coming of children forces them to do so. But even if they spend all of their time at home, there is no assurance that, with so much more of their time free to shop, they will do their marketing more intelligently than their non housekeeping sisters. They expend large drafts of their energy in haunting the stores advertising bargain sales, and in shopping from store to store so as to save small sums on individual items. They do not realize that the amount of energy which they expend in order to save a cent or two per can on the soup they buy, would enable them to make a better soup at home, at practically no cost at all. They so proudly buy with the herd that it is pitiful to see how gloriously they save at the spigot and waste at the bunghole. They buy from hand to mouth partly because their earnings do not permit them to buy in economical quantities and partly because the small flats or houses in which they live give them little room in which to accumulate any considerable quantity of supplies. This type of woman in ever increasing numbers furnishes the mass of actual customers for factory products. To reduce all the women of the country to the job-holders' complete dependence upon the factory product, the vast majority of factories are bending all their energies.

•

Finally we come to the shoppers—a type of women especially important because they are free to devote themselves entirely to buying things: clothes for themselves, furnishings for their homes, and food for their table. The shoppers live in hotels, in apartment houses, in boarding houses and occasionally in those suburban houses which demand the minimum of labor from the mistress of the house. After their husbands go off to work—the husbands of shoppers are generally salesmen, minor executives, well-paid office workers of some kind, and not infrequently small manufacturers or tradesmen—they have a little work in their houses, including the getting of the children, if any, off to school, the whole taking up not more than two or three hours. They are then ready for an exhausting day of shopping.

Shoppers devote an extraordinary amount of thought to the matter of what they buy, where they buy it, and how much their friends will think they have paid for it. The latest styles in cloth ing, the redecorating of their rooms, the buying of refreshments for their bridge parties—these are the problems upon which they concentrate their minds. If they have some spark of creative urge not otherwise sublimated, it takes the form of learning the new "arts"—decorating lamp shades, painting china, dyeing batiks, making hooked rugs—in which they are given the opportunity to dabble by department stores. These furnish new outlets for buying: strange things to buy for which otherwise they would have no use.

Shoppers are great patrons of the cuits: of which the beauty cuit is the prime favorite. They buy all sorts of cosmetics and perfumes; patronize beauty parlors, and devote a very large part of their time to buying whatever the advertisements tell them is helpful in warding off old age.

At a recent convention of large dry goods merchants, a woman speaker contrasted the shoppers of today with the shoppers of the nineties—a contrast covering a relatively short period of time, but still indicative of the change in women because no further back than the eighteen-nineties women even among the well-to-do classes could be homemakers without loss of caste. The women of the nineties, the speaker said, went to the stores with lists of things which they needed, and they bought them as promptly as possible. Today, this speaker said, the shopping lists are gone. modern shoppers do not go out to buy what they need—they go out to "shop." The principal by-product of this aimless buying, as far as the modern store goes, is an alarming increase of what is called in the trade the "return goods evil." Things are bought, delivered, and then returned. A large part of the merchandise which many American department stores sell has to be sold twice before it stays sold. Shoppers are thus enabled to make a triple in road upon the leisure which the factory furnishes them: the first, the lime devoted to the original buying; the second, the time devoted to returning what was first purchased; and the third, the time devoted to buying something which is actually kept. This is the ultimate in shopping. It furnishes the shoppers with a triple justification for their existence.

Unfortunate women, forever seeking to utilize a leisure for which they lack the necessary educational equipment, and pre vented by their husband's prosperity from the job-holding to which necessity drives their poorer sisters! But veritably perfect consumers of the factory's products: consumers who waste large portions of what they buy; who use what they buy so carelessly that it depreciates much more rapidly than is normal; who discard what is still serviceable because some newer thing has rendered it old fashioned.

•

The solicitude of the factory for its woman customers is touch ing in the extreme.

Let me quote upon this point one of the country's ablest apologists for modern industrialism. Writing in *The Nation's Business*, for July 1928, a magazine read by nearly 300,000 business men and published as the official organ of the United States Chamber of Commerce, Mr. Roy S. Durstine, Secretary-Treasurer of the advertising agency of Barton, Durstine & Osborne, Inc., New York City, said:

> Not so many years ago most American women were pretty busy doing the things that manufacturers are doing for them today. Women

> were old at forty and soon passed on, while their hardier husbands chose younger, stronger helpmates to take up the burden. "Why did you get married again so soon?" someone asked a middle-western farmer a month after his first wife died forty years ago. "Well," was the answer, "it was either that or get a hired girl."
>
> No wonder women on farms and in small towns and in Louisville and Atlanta and Seattle said to American industry: "We are tired of growing everything we eat and making everything we wear and use. Why can't we go into the nearest store and buy what we need when we need it?"

There are certain comments to be made upon this, most of them bearing upon the question of whether the facts presented are true and the inference based upon them justified. Let us take the first part of the statement, which includes a gross libel upon the average farmer of forty years ago, that "not so many years ago women were old at forty and soon passed on *because* most American women were pretty busy doing things that manufacturers are doing for them today." Even the alleged fact in this statement can be accepted by us only provisionally, while the assumption about the relationship of manufacturing to longevity is based upon one of those half-truths in which uncritical minds delight. Mr. Durstine breezily waves aside all that modern medicine, hygiene, dietetics, obstetrics, have done to add to the longevity of women and blandly gives the factory the whole credit.

It is true that years ago most women were old at forty, but so were the men, as the statistics of the life insurance companies show. Both men and women do not grow old so quickly today. In the case of the women, he ignores the special burden which aged the women of the past much more quickly than the women of today and from which the men of all times have been exempt. The women of the past, thanks to the superstitions of the church, were condemned to a life of incubation. It was the annual procession of babies, accompanied by the burden of carrying the pre-natal child, of blood-letting at parturition, of obstetrical ignorance, of nursing at the breast, and the strain of the slaughter of innocents in the first year of their life, that made the women of the past prematurely old. This was the burden, as if they did not have enough without it, which kept American women "pretty busy," and the carrying of this burden is not something which modern "manufacturers are doing for them." When American women began to cut down the birth rate; when the number of pregnancies per woman began to shrink from the traditional four surviving births, four deaths in infancy, and four miscarriages, to a total of probably less than four, including abortions, (which are not so serious with modern methods of curettage), women ceased to grow old at forty. This reduction in the pregnancy rate is something for which even advertising men will hardly have the hardihood to give the factories credit. Eliminate the burden which the annual procession of pregnancies imposed upon women, and the other work of women forty years ago aged them hardly much more than men's work at that time aged men.

Mr. Durstine's argument is no more reliable when he asserts, figuratively, that the women of the country became so tired of producing things for themselves that they asked the factories to lift the burden off their shoulders. Where is his evidence for such a statement? Go back as far as he will, even to the time of the building of the first factories, (which were built, according to Mr. Durstine, in order to lift the burden of spinning and weaving off the backs of laboring men and women), and what do we find? We find that far from having asked the factories to undertake this work, both the men and women of that time showed great hostility to the factory system and great reluctance at being forced to give up the "burden" of home spinning and craft weaving.

In the Middle Ages, women were identified with their spindles as men with their spears. While the spears did their own work, the spindles were busy, making the yarn for clothing, for curtains and tapestries, for soft wrappings for wounds, for banners, and in the Orient, for the rugs which are the envy and despair of modern manufacturers. Mr. Durstine may think that women are better off because the factories have deprived them of this labor, but the women themselves made no pleas to have this work taken from them and transferred to a caste of factory hands.

I can recall practically no instance in the early years of the factory in which women took the initiative in welcoming the factory. Even today, there are practically no organizations of women formed for the purpose of encouraging the growth of factories, and I can recall no convention of women which passed resolutions requesting manufacturers to take over the spinning, weaving, sewing, knitting, bread making, preserving, sugar making, soap making, which at one time occupied them. The initiative in taking over these activities always came from the factory—as advertising men like Mr. Durstine well know.

The reason that women generally showed such reluctance to abandoning home-work was not because they were so stupid as to refuse "to raise living standards and to gain leisure for recreation." They did not see a higher standard of living in what the factory offered them until the factory dominated the world and evolved a folkway which made the women see it as higher. The factory offered them a different canon of values: the women refused to see any superiority in it until advertising made them do so.

To the poorer classes of women the factory offered release from home-work in return for factory and office work. In the beginning these women saw no gain in exchanging long hours of work at home for equally long hours in mills, sweat shops, and stores. At first job-holding was an unavoidable interlude in a life that was ultimately to mean marriage and homemaking. Today, labor laws prevent the old exploitation of working women. The factory and office day is much shorter. Conditions for women workers are much better. Job-holding still seems to most women an undesirable alternative to homemaking, but many have now come to recognize it as an unavoidable one. Slowly but surely the women are accepting the new folkway. And in the new folkway, job-holding by women is strictly in the nature of things.

As for the more prosperous classes of women, avid acceptance of the leisure the buying of factory products made possible became general only after the factory had come to dominate our civilization and after the invention of such meretriciously attractive uses for the time no longer needed for housework as bridge parties and daily movies. Then women began to transform themselves from producers into purchasing agents. They proved intelligent purchasing agents, however, only as long as they retained the knowledge absorbed from the days of productive homeworking. The second and third generation no longer have such knowledge to help them to buy intelligently. They have leisure to shop—they even have the leisure for recreation of which Mr. Durstine speaks—but they have neither the knowledge necessary for intelligent buying nor the cultural disciplines which enable them to use their leisure intelligently.

•

It is precisely with regard to this matter of leisure that the factory has led women into a blind alley. It is the folkway today to consider leisure, and of course leisure for recreation, a sort of good-in-itself. Whereas the goodness or badness of leisure is precisely and exactly the same as the goodness or badness of labor. The virtue resides no more in the length of time devoted to leisure, than in the length of time devoted to labor. It is dependent wholly upon what is expressed and what is extracted from time.

As a matter of fact there can be no such thing as leisure, certainly physiologically, while human beings are alive. What protagonists of the factory like Mr. Durstine call leisure is the cessation of directly remunerative or actually productive activity. It is the substitution of one kind of activity for activity of another kind. Among these women customers of the factory, most of whom lack not only training but often capacity for education, leisure means time devoted to play. And it means largely vicarious play. For most of modern play is purchased. These women buy their amusements just as they buy food, clothing and shelter. Their leisure, therefore, is really time devoted to activities which involve the consumption of what has been bought, as contrasted to the time devoted to earning money in order to pay for what they want to consume.

The use of time for energetic consumption and for passive spectatorship of play, scarcely represents an improvement over the use which women made of their time in the past. On the contrary, a long enough period of devotion to this kind of leisure is certain to end by transforming women into inappreciative barbarians.

Those who think that a mere release from useful activity of all kinds will produce comfort are mistaken.

The factory's customers are on the wrong road.

What is needed is not a reduction of the time devoted to productive activities but the substitution of more intelligent activities for less intelligent activities.

That the process of making factory customers out of the women who, Mr. Durstine says, are tired of growing everything they eat and of making everything they wear and use, constitutes such a substitution of more intelligent for less intelligent activity, I utterly deny.

The road to comfort leads in an altogether different direction. It leads to more and more domestic production and less and less factory production. It requires the integration of production and consumption, not their disintegration.

•

The factory has robbed men and women of their occupations as producers of the family's needs and desires and forced them into the factory in order to procure the money to pay for them.

Before the coming of the factory, producer and consumer were one. Before the coming of the great Chicago packing houses, nearly every American home used to raise at least one pig, and to supply itself with its own fresh pork, smoked ham and bacon, sausage and lard. Today pigs are raised by hog farmers, often by factory methods; they are taken to market instead of being slaughtered at home; a packing house slaughters them, cures them and converts them into pork, ham, bacon and lard. The consumer has nothing to do but buy these products—and to work in factories in order to get the money with which to pay for them.

As factory products increase in number and variety, the warfare upon domestic production continues until no phase of home making can be carried on without the competition of factory products. With enormous accretions of capital to be invested, factories are constantly expanded and new ones built. The capital which went into the erection of flour mills first deprived the home makers of custom and home-milled flours. Then it went into the erection of bread bakeries, and began to make worthless the home makers' opportunity to make bread at home. Still later, it went into biscuit bakeries, cake bakeries, and pastry bakeries, and now the homemakers have this competition to meet, handicapped by the fact that social prestige is to be won, not by the skill which is put into home baking, but by the amount which the family can spend.

When the process reaches perfection, homemakers will completely disappear, and with them will disappear not only the home as a few still know it, but the home as it might be if the thought and ingenuity of man were really devoted to developing all its possible contributions to the mental and physical health, happiness, and comfort of mankind. The process has, however, gone far enough so that great numbers of women have already ceased to be homemakers. They have abandoned homemaking as a career because the factory makes it so difficult for the modern home to furnish them the opportunity to gratify and satisfy their intellectual, economic, and social aspirations. Most of the women have become mere buyers of what the factories produce to satisfy their own and their family's necessities and desires, and if they devote themselves to production at all, it is to producing that one thing which seems to command all things and to open all doors today: money!

•

It is difficult to disentangle the influence upon the family of the change from the home's preoccupation with productive activities to its present preoccupation with consumptive activities, from all the other influences which have come with the factory. The influence of more democratic forms of government; the influence of speedy and cheap forms of transportation and communication; the influence of periodical literature and more general literacy—all these act and react upon the family at the same time that the factory profoundly alters the home's contribution to the economic life of the individual and to society. As a result of all these influences the family is smaller; it lacks continuity throughout the generations; it is notoriously unstable, as the rising tide of divorce and newer forms of marriage clearly indicate. Of one thing there is little doubt: the destruction of the creative and productive home has destroyed an almost essential element in the cement which used to hold the family together.

At one time practically every economic activity of the home involved family activity: father, mother, grandparents and children all did their several parts in contributing to family production. In the production of textiles, for instance, the father grew the flax or cared for and sheared the sheep; the very young and the very old members of the family spun the yarn and reeled it; the fathers and mothers wove it into cloth. Today the only economic function in which the various members of the average family participate as a unit is that of sharing a common lodging. Not every family even eats together; fewer still cook together.

Now the family, we are told, is for the first time dependent wholly upon mutual affection for its cementing medium—presumably a great advance over the old compulsions of religion, of law, of custom. But it is easy to overlook the fact that lasting affections do not survive in a vacuum. Affection is most often produced as a result of experiences shared in common. Men who have endured perils together are often made fast friends by their experiences. In fact, any kind of activity together tends to set up an emotional tie. The greater the volume of common activities, the stouter the emotional tie. The homemaking family of the past, in spite of the compulsions which handicapped it, probably produced just as many happy lives as does the modern family.

•

It is not so difficult to determine the effect of the divorce between consumption and production on the masses of consumers. The factory has made the individual, as producer, shift his interest from making to earning; from craftsmanship to the wages paid for his time. It has made the individual, as consumer, dependent upon his skill and his ability in buying, rather than upon his ability to make things for himself. It has transformed him from a self-helpful individual into a self-helpless individual.

To a constantly increasing extent, men and women have become dependent for their shelter, their food, their clothing, their entertainment, upon what they can buy with money. Neither the necessities nor the luxuries which they desire are today gratified by their own craft and their own artistry. They are gratified to the extent to which they can procure money with which to buy things. They consume what others have produced, and are dependent for existence and happiness upon things about the making of which they know nothing.

Myriads of human beings in our cities are consuming canned peas without ever having in their life had the opportunity to discover whether peas grow on trees, on bushes, or in the ground. The factory's customers are spectators of economic life, not actual participators in it. Not even in the work in their own factories are they full participators. Division and subdivision of labor deprives them generally of any sight of the ends of their labor and confines them to the narrow field of the particular operations which they repeat endlessly throughout their productive days.

•

To cap the climax, the very system of production which has brought about the present superabundance of material well-being is responsible for destroying the factory customer's sense of values.

Perhaps the most appaling account of what this has led to is that devastating analysis of the merits of industrialized America's factory-made products by Stuart Chase and F. J. Schlink in *Your Money's Worth*. No one can read their arraignment without being impressed with the ingenuity with which the factory fools its customers and with the ignorance of the factory's customers which makes this fooling possible.

The factory, in the beginning, was able to prove to the buying public conclusively that it was furnishing similar products at a much lower price than craft production could furnish them. Now, having deprived consumers of the old basis for comparison, it leaves them helpless to insure full receipt of the savings which mass production theoretically produces. The things they buy all come to them from stores. They can only compare one factory's products with another factory's. And when they do so, they are handicapped by their ignorance about the materials out of which they are made, and the processes involved in fabricating them. When in the store, they are confronted with factory-made products the qualities of which are influenced by their needs and desires only in the most indirect fashion. A bewildering variety of products and brands and prices are submitted to them. The very abundance which the factory makes possible confuses them, disarms them, and leaves them almost entirely at the mercy of the manufacturer's propaganda. Naturally credulous, ignorance makes them gullible to an unbelievable extent. They are influenced by advertisement and sales arguments pitched in a key to appeal to intelligences whose average is that of twelve to fourteen-year old children. They judge the things they buy by the amount of prestige the products have acquired and in the last analysis mainly by the price asked for them. What is highest in price is presumably best. In their ignorance, they put a premium upon features of the product which frequently add to cost without really adding to utility or beauty. They know so little about the intrinsic merits of the products themselves that they are without a particle of judgment upon the question of whether the higher priced products represent commensurate increases in value.

As the head of one of New York's largest department stores put the matter, echoing Oscar Wilde: "Nowadays, people know the price of everything and the value of nothing."

CHAPTER VIII
THE CONQUERING FACTORY SYSTEM

FACTORIES, factory products, factory workers, factory customers —and a race dependent upon factories and factory goods—these are some of the fruits of the application of the factory system to the production of the things mankind needs and desires.

But they are not the factory's only fruits.

The factory has not been able to keep the factory system within the limits of its four ugly walls.

•

What is the factory system?

It is the group of methods used in manufacturing of which the most conspicuous are (a) systematic production; (b) standardization to insure uniformity of product; (c) division and sub-division of labor. These represent the application of the principles of efficiency to the work of producing the necessaries and luxuries of modern civilization.

Harrington Emerson, who has been called by an admirer [29] the "High Priest of the New Science of Efficiency," defines efficiency as "the elimination of all needless waste in material, in labor, and in equipment, so as to reduce costs, increase profits, and raise wages." This definition should at once make clear the legitimate field of the factory system and also the limited sphere of activities in which its application is desirable. In a factory, which has its justification only in its capacity for producing the largest possible quantity of commodities at the lowest possible cost, the elimination of every waste is most desirable. But outside of a factory, in all the activities of man which have their justification primarily in the extent to which they enrich life, the quantitative criterion which efficiency enjoins becomes absurd. Life, if man is to dignify it by the way he lives, must be lived artistically. Not quantitative but qualitative criterions apply in home life, in education, in social activities, in literature, painting, sculpture. Yet the apostles of efficiency have not been content to limit its application to the factory. They have made efficiency a philosophy of life and are now busily engaged in applying the factory system to the regulation of every activity of civilized man.

In his introduction to his epoch making volume on *The Principles of Scientific Management,* the late Frederick Winslow Taylor, the founder of the efficiency movement, said of the principles of which he was so ardent an advocate:

> The same principles can be applied with equal force to all social activities: to the management of our homes; the management of our farms; the management of the business of our tradesmen, large and small; of our churches, our philanthropie institutions, our universities, and our government departments.[30]

What was merely the distant vision of Taylor in 1911 is today in process of becoming an accomplished fact. As we shall see, we are now in the process of fulfilling in every activity of life Taylor's prophetic words: *"In the past the man has been first; in the future the system must be first."*

•

In order to understand why the factory system has spread from the factory to every aspect of American life a careful examination of the factory system in its original "habitat" is essential.

When the first manufacturers discovered that wealth could be accumulated much more rapidly by applying power to the making of one thing in one place instead of making many different things in one place, the first step in the development of the factory system had been taken. On the heels of this discovery came lower prices, made possible by economies in labor and economies in material, and a ruthless war of extermination upon the guild, the custom, and the domestic systems of production.

The ubiquitous village smithy, where horses and oxen were shod and where practically everything which the neighborhood needed in the way of iron work was made: agricultural implements—plowshares, bog-hoes, stone hooks, garden forks; carpenter's tools—broad-axes, pod-augers, beetles and frows; building hardware—hinges, latches, and locks; fireplace utensils, andirons, gridirons, cranes, tongs, and shovels; cooking utensils, cutlery and hundreds of other things, disappeared. The smithy's place was taken by mills and machine shops in each of which only one article or one commodity was made, or if a number of allied products were made, each was produced serially instead of on custom order.

The spinning wheels, the combs and cards, the reels and the looms and the loom rooms disappeared from the craftsman's shops and from the homes of rich and poor. These were replaced by mills in each of which only one process in the making of fabrics was carried on. One mill spun yarn. Another wove gray goods. A third dyed and finished them. Or mills confined themselves to only one fiber, to linen, to wool, to cotton, or to silk, and performed the various processes of manufacture in separate departments each of which made possible systematic factory production.

Much of the cooking and preserving disappeared from the home. Homes with kitchens, pantries, vegetable cellars, smoke-houses and milk houses in which foods were cooked, smoked, pickled and preserved by the joint effort of the entire family were replaced by packing houses and canneries, in which foodstuffs were systematically packed and canned and bottled by the most approved factory techniques.

•

Serial production in the factory destroyed the very foundations of individual production. The factory owners, by concentrating systematically on one product, were able not only to outsell the craftsmen but to paralyze most of the productive activities in the home. The factory product, eventually, sold so cheaply that the workshop producers could not hope to meet its competition. It became so cheap that it did not even seem worthwhile for individuals to continue its production for their own consumption.

Yet in spite of the competitive advantage of very low costs of production, the early manufacturers found it difficult to put the craftsmen out of their misery. It took generations for the mills and factories to establish their present supremacy. It was only after the manufacturer discovered that concentration of production upon a single kind of goods made it possible to support systematic salesmanship that the old craft production really began to succumb. Systematic salesmanship made possible the profitable operation of the factory because it enabled the manufacturer to sell at a profit in territory where handicraft competition had been destroyed while selling at a loss in territory where it still survived. The factory was thus enabled to extend itself into new territory, selling if necessary at a loss until all neighborhood production ceased and then recouping its initial losses after the sale of its product had become firmly established.

•

Home and workshop products tended to vary not only in response to the moods and creative urge of the maker, but often in accordance with the needs, desires and idiosyncrasies of the consumer. Under such conditions eccentricity was no luxury. Personality could be catered to because individual taste was not penalized. Being made individually and not serially, the products could be varied in size, in quality and in design to suit the maker or consumer without materially affecting the actual cost of production. But none of the economies of mass production, mass distribution and mass consumption is possible if the finished product is permitted to vary in this manner. Serial production in the factory is dependent at all stages upon uniformities: uniformities of design, material and workmanship. Each article exactly duplicates every other, not only because uniformity is essential for economical mass production, but because it is essential to the creation of mass consumption.

If the cooks in the canneries were permitted to vary each batch of soup as the spirit moved them, some of the cans of soup would contain more salt, other less; some would contain onions, others would have none; some would be thin, others would be thick. It would be obviously impossible to create a mass demand for the soup. Mass production is dependent upon mass consumption. The consumer must know beforehand just about what the soup is going to contain. The recipe, therefore, has to be a compromise which appeals to all kinds of demand. Taste has to be standardized, not only in soup, but in nearly everything that is consumed, or factory production becomes impossible.

The factory system involves an apotheosis of the mediocre. The least common denominator of taste is made the standard to which, on the score of efficiency, everything must conform.

With serial production and with uniformity in the product, division and sub-division of labor make possible revolutionary reductions in the amount of human labor which have to be used per unit of production. Special machines can be devised for each operation, and the worker instead of having to be able to perform all the operations involved in making the product from beginning to end can be confined to the endless repetition of a few simple operations. Amazing economies, as Henry Ford has shown, become possible.When one workman assembled the fly-wheel magneto for the Model T Ford automobile complete, it took about twenty minutes. By dividing the work of assembly into twenty-nine operations performed by twenty-nine men, the total time for the assembling was finally cut to five minutes; one man was able to do somewhat more than four men were able to do before.

In the assembling of the Ford motor, the work was at first done completely by one man. The Ford engineers divided this task into eighty-four operations. Eighty-four men operating the new way assembled three times as many motors as the same number were able to assemble before. They did the same amount of work per day as one hundred and thirty-two men did under the previous method.

Originally the assembling of the chassis took twelve hours and twenty-eight minutes. This operation was finally cut down by the same principle of division and sub-division of labor to one hour and thirty-three minutes. The sub-division of operations in the Ford factory is almost incredibly fine; the man who places a part does not fasten it—the part may not be fully in place until after several operations later; the man who puts on the bolts, does not put on the nuts; the man who puts on the nuts does not tighten them.

Thus division and sub-division of labor go on, in the factories and in the offices, not only in the automobile industry, but in all industries, and thus the economies of the factory system are fully realized.

•

The application of the three techniques which comprise the factory system to the production of the goods we consume has revolutionized life. It has enabled this civilization to realize the goal of increased profits, higher wages, lower prices. Material well-being has been increased; life in many obvious respects has been made less uncomfortable. Man has more shelter, more clothing, more creature comforts of all sorts than before.

It is only natural that those who have brought all this to pass should feel that the application of the factory system to all the activities of life, often under the *nom de plume* of "business methods," would result in equally startling improvements in every aspect of living. The factory system applied to the home should make the family happier; applied to the farm it should make the farmer more prosperous and farm products less expensive; applied to the business of our tradesmen it should add to their profits and make them serve their customers better; applied to the school it should produce a better educated citizen; applied to the church it should make our spiritual life richer; applied to philanthropy it should decrease the sum total of human suffering and make men more unselfish; applied to politics it should make government function more justly, more benignantly, more intelligently--above all more economically.

And this is precisely what we have in recent years begun to do. For better or worse, we have been systematizing all the activities of life; we have been transferring the "mechanizing" of life which began in the factory to the office, to the church, to the school, and to the home.

•

It is perhaps not correct to say that the application of the factory system to administrative and clerical work in offices of all kinds is an invasion of regions outside of the factory. The modern office should be considered a part of the factory, or at least of the industry with which it concerns itself even though it may be located in a city hundreds of miles from the place where manufacturing is actually carried on. And yet the invasion of administration by the factory system is worth mentioning because office workers generally, especially those occupying executive positions which correspond to the position of foreman and superintendents in factories, are fooled by their white collars and their more genteel clothes into total blindness to the fact that they are just as truly cogs in the industrial machine as are the men who work in overalls in the factory itself. Modern offices contain an increasing number of workers who are expected to perform their work well, just as are the machine operators in the factory, but who, like the laborers, are not expected to rise higher.

Because the schooling of the modern child must equip it for the sort of work it will have to do as an adult, the application of factory and mass production methods to office work is profoundly affecting our school curriculums. The Y.M.C.A. and the Y.W.C.A. educational classes which are primarily vocational, have above all else to reflect existing business conditions. This also is true of many of the high schools and colleges of the country. They are, however, a little slower to respond to changing conditions. In 1928 the National Board of the Y.W.C.A. considered the tendency toward systematizing office work so important that they made a survey of conditions in offices and their influence upon workers. A striking example of the length to which factory methods are superseding old ways in business offices is described in the report of this survey:

> Orders are passed along by means of a belt from a chief clerk to a series of checkers and typists. Each one does only one operation. One interprets the order, indicates the trade discount; the second prices the order, takes of discount, adds carriage charges and totals. The third girl gives the order a number and makes a daily record. The fourth girl puts this information on the alphabetical index. The fifth girl stamps it. The sixth girl makes a copy in septuplicate and puts on address labels. The seventh girl checks it and sends it to the storeroom. Measurement of production by various methods, by the square inch, line, by a cyclometer or by the number of pieces produced, is being done in some offices that are under scientific management.

But with the progressive mechanization of the work in the office, the one thing that made office work endurable to a really civilized man is disappearing. The most cherished aspect of office work used to be the fact that it could be utilized as a stepping stone to executive positions. Every office boy was supposed to carry the "baton" of a partnership in his knapsack. But this is fast disappearing. Both office clerks and office executives today get their positions on the strength of their training in school and college, and they tend to stay in the positions in which they first find employment.

•

But the invasion of fine arts by the factory system! Here indeed is an invasion of a sphere of activity which ought to be sacredly preserved for the creative expression of the individual.

Consider how modern literature—if we dare call much modern writing literature—is standardized by the demands of mass publishing. Author *A* has written an interesting short story about New York's East Side Jews. It has made a distinct hit. He must therefore fill book after book with stories devoted to the identical theme, or cease to be an author with a marketable commodity. Author *B* has written a dashing novel of the West and its cow-boys. He must therefore endlessly repeat himself on the same locale and characters. The more uniform their stories, the more ideally they fit into the scheme of modern, factory methods of magazine and book publishing.

Of course, the factory system dominates the production of the American newspaper. The local news, unavoidably, must be written to fit local conditions, but aside from that, editorials, cartoons, "columns," comic strips, short stories, fashions, pictures, magazine sections, all are fabricated and syndicated by factory methods. You may move from New York to San Francisco—traverse the whole continent—and never for a day stop in a city in which some paper does not publish your favorite "column," your favorite comic strips, and your favorite poet's effusions.

A quotation from *Editor and Publisher* (the leading magazine devoted to newspaper publishing) of March 3, 1928, shows that the "craft" is beginning to recognize the situation:

> The one department of newspaper production in which consolidation and modern methods have reduced the number of employees has been the editorial, in which machinery plays a small part. The

> syndicates have made available to the smallest publisher at prices within reach of the thinnest purse, the best that the big city newspapers create and enjoy. This means of economy can be and has been abused, and it bears seeds of danger both to the individual publisher and the craft in general. The profession and business of gathering and selling news and commercial information to the public is one that requires direct contact between man and man. The press is one machine to which the deus is indispensable.

The writer in *Editor and Publisher* is probably whistling to keep up his courage when he says that the individual is indispensable to the press. Our factory civilization has repeatedly produced machines and methods which placed in the ranks of false prophets those who said the individual was indispensable.

•

The factory system has been applied in a most masterly fashion to the task of entertaining the masses. A populace bored to the point of inanity by the monotony of its work in office and factory, and supplied with ample leisure by the process of taking from the family most of the occupations which might make home making interesting and important, has to be entertained. Entertainment is therefore provided which is quite as thoroughly standardized, as easy to assimilate, as little disturbing to the mind as is the work which they do while earning their daily bread. The movies, with standardized tragedies, comedies and news features, with standardized actors and actresses and standardized show houses, furnish a splendid means of escape into a world of adventure and apparent life. If the movies do not satisfy the masses every night in the week, there is the alternative of standardized vaudeville and standardized burlesque, and even without leaving the home to be entertained, there is the standardized entertainment of the radio, the phonograph and the piano player. There is plenty of music, but it is mainly vicarious music, not music that is the product of personal effort. There is less of that kind of music and that kind of singing in the lives of the men and women of our factory-dominated civilization than in that of the African negroes in the forests. Family dancing and folk singing has gone the way of family and craft production:

it has been systematized out of existence.

We buy our music today; we do not produce it ourselves. Perhaps the time will come when it can neither be produced or enjoyed by us.

Says Waldo Frank:

> Art cannot become a language, hence an experience, unless it is practiced. To the man who plays, a mechanical reproduction of music may mean much, since he already has the experience to assimilate it. But where reproduction becomes the norm, the few music-makers will grow more isolate and sterile, and the ability to experience music will disappear. The same is true with cinema, dance and even sport. Only when the theatre for instance, is an ennobled symbolization of common social practice (as it was in Athens and in Medieval Europe) can it become an experience for the onlooker.[31]

•

In this country where industrialization has gone so far and where leisure is more abundant than in any other nation, more money is spent for commercialized amusement than for anything else except food, and more money invested in the "factories" which produce it than in anything else except land. As Dr. George B. Cutten, President of Colgate University, said, we seem to have become "amusement mad." He says:

> We have more than 20,000,000 daily admissions to the moving-picture exhibitions and more than 100,000,000 admissions to sporting events yearly. Three million dollars is spent in admissions to see a prizefight, and far more than that in traveling and hotel expenses in connection with it. Probably the 80,000 people who witness a Yale-Harvard football game pay in admissions and expenses more than $1,000,000, and the great Yale Bowl can barely accommodate one fifth of those who desire to see this contest. The gate receipts of a world's baseball series are more than $1,000,000; $30,000,000 is spent annually on admissions to circuses, and probably more than $100,000,000 is paid every year to jazz orchestras. The space given to sporting events in daily newspapers shows the demands of the public for this form of amusement.
>
> Our great national game, baseball, is following along the line of college football—more and more we are showing our interest in

it, not by playing but by watching contests. Playing games by proxy is becoming more popular, and has in it the seeds of degeneration. On the other hand, there are 3,000,000 golfers in this country, and factories that formerly manufactured baseball gonds are now manufacturing golf clubs. Half a million boys are caddying on golf links; twenty years ago boys of similar age were playing baseball on vacant lots. Golf links are becoming more numerous and vacant lots are disappearing.

There are worse uses for our leisure than play, but too much play tends to weakness. Passive amusement, moreover, such as watching others play or being entertained in other ways, even if the amusement is not morally objectionable, tends to soften the fiber and to weaken the moral structure. The race came to its present lofty position through struggle and strife, and it is not likely that it can maintain its position by any program of passivity and inactivity.

Leisure has increased to such an extent that we must think of something besides amusement with which to occupy it. There are some individuals and some groups in every community to whom this matter of leisure is never a problem. By training and planning, the spare hours are cared for in a way that is profitable to them individually, while at the same time a relief from business or professional toil. But these individuals and groups are not numerous; to most persons leisure is a problem, and to the country as a whole it is a menace.

The various fads—those which spring up suddenly, capture the attention of the people, become the topic of conversation and the chief occupation of the masses for a season, and suddenly decline and are forgotten—show the necessity of some more lasting program and a more purposeful scheme for the occupation of the spare hours of the general public. One has only to mention turkey trotting, mahjong, and cross-word puzzles to call to mind a much longer list of harmless, inane, and valueless modes of wasting time, which like Jonah's gourd have sprung up in the night and faded before the rising sun.

It is not what these things were in themselves, but more especially what they indicate, which is important. They were seized upon by people who had excess time at their disposal, were not vicious, and were looking for some innocent way to spend it. Most of these had neither the ability nor the initiative to work at their own programs, and waited for someone else to suggest means to occupy their leisure.

The suggestion was not a program but a temporary expedient which from its very nature must be ephemeral.[32]

•

The factory system dominates modern methods of education. The system begins in the nursery school. It ends in the university. As more and more of the work of education is taken over by the school and less and less left to the home, schools become bigger and bigger institutions; the army of teachers becomes larger and larger; the educational system, more and more efficient. The modern school becomes more and more like a modern factory. It becomes an institution notable for its efficient equipment, efficient methods, and efficient personnel. The pupils go through the school in standardized classes; study a standardized curriculum; pass standardized examinations; and emerge with standardized educations.

The work of teaching is divided and sub-divided among specialists much as the work of making an automobile is divided and sub-divided among trained laborers in the automobile factory.

Mathematics is taught by one teacher; history by another. There are plenty of teachers of mathematics who, though they probably did know enough history to graduate when they went to school, have forgotten all that they know of that subject and yet build splendid reputations in their specialty. True, the school can never hope to attain the degree of specialization which enables the automobile factory to train its workers for their tasks in a single day. But it can specialize to a point which will make it easy to use stupider and stupider types to perform each minute task in pedagogy; to shoot the teachers through normal schools more rapidly than before; to standardize systems and teaching techniques; in short, to apply the principles of efficiency to the whole task of running itself and of preparing the young for their factory dominated futures.

Scholars may be as various in temperament and background as they can well be, but they must nevertheless be educated by a system in which they are treated as mere units in a carefully graded class of like units. They enter school as raw material in the kindergarten. The kindergarten prepares them for their primary work. They pass from one class to another; from the grammar school to the high school; from the high school to the college, and exit at various convenient stopping points along the route into the factory-world, much as raw cotton enters a mill at one point and finally emerges at another as finished cotton goods. Each individual yard is the same as every other yard. Each individual scholar tends to be the same as every other—educated for a place in the factory world, with the same identical range of reactions to factory, office, religion, politics, as the school and college boards consider it best for them to possess. They may, for instance, react either to Republicanism or to Democracy, but to Socialism, never!

From the moment the child is able to leave the home, he is expected to do what all of his fellows do. Not only in school, but out of school as well. The boys join the Boy Scouts and the girls the Campfire Girls, the Girl Reserve, or the Junior League.

They go to school *en masse*, they play *en masse*, they think *en masse*. Modern mass education makes them memorize more abstract facts, infinitely more than the child of the pre-factory age, but they probably do not understand their environment as well.

This is the factory system applied to education.

•

Where has this factory system not gone? It has been applied to the most elementary aspects of life—to the feeding and sheltering of mankind. We eat in restaurant and lunchrooms dishes produced by factory methods out of foods which all came from factories, and we sleep in apartment houses and hotels in which every detail of living is as meticulously standardized as is every step in the making of a Ford car.

Strange as it may seem, some of the most acute students of civilization are completely blind to the deadening effect upon us of this systemization of all the ordinary activities of our lives. Havelock Ellis, who is not afraid to advocate the most revolutionary changes in our sexual customs, is yet willing to accept, with an amusing fatalism, the existing factory systemization of life as part of the solution of the problem of domestic happiness. He would make homes happy by destroying their every function except that of being dormitories for the couples who inhabit them. In an essay he urges mankind to replace the wasteful, extravagant, and often inefficient home cookery by meals cooked outside; "to facilitate the growing social habit of taking meals in spacious public restaurants, under more attractive, economical and wholesome conditions than can usually be secured within the narrow confines of the home," and "to contract with specially trained workers from outside for all those routines of domestic drudgery which are inefficiently and laboriously carried on by the household worker, whether mistress or servant." [33]

Is it really desirable to give up home cookery and to substitute for it mass cookery and mass service in restaurants? Wouldn't it be wiser to utilize our scientific knowledge for the purpose of making home cookery more attractive, more economical, more wholesome and to make homemaking a creative art rather than to abandon one of the few remaining economic functions of the home?

In our American cities we seem to be acting upon Mr. Ellis's prescription, according to Charles Laube, President of the National Restaurant Association.

> Apartments have been largely responsible for the decline of the domestic kitchen. They are small and they aggravate modern wives who don't like to cook, anyway. The restaurateur has competed successfully against the home kitchen in the past because he has made money through labor-saving machines, electric dishwashers and patented potato peelers. From now on success will lie in making his place more attractive, in dispensing atmosphere as well as good food. The restaurant will be decorated more artistically and a new type of waitress will appear—one who is prettier, more congenial and dressed becomingly.[34]

This is probably as it should be in a factory-dominated world. The "atmosphere," the artistic decorations, the prettily dressed homemakers are obsolete. All these must be transferred from the inefficient privacy of the home to a "spacious public restaurant" where they can be enjoyed *en masse* and in public.

•

In a civilization reflecting at every point the conquering factory system it is fitting to find that we have applied the factory system to the business of being born, of being sick, and in the end of dying and being buried. We now have maternity hospitals, nurseries, and nursery schools, sanitariums and even funeral churches, all of them efficient—and hard.

The modern mother is merely maternity case number 8,434; her infant after being finger and foot printed, becomes infant number 8,003.

By virtue of the same mania for system, a modern corpse be cornes number 2,432; while a modern funeral becomes one of a series scheduled for parlor 4B for a certain day at a certain hour, with preacher number fourteen, singer number 87, rendering music number 174, and flowers and decorations class B.

Thus the factory system begins and finishes the citizen of the factory-dominated world.

It introduces him to his world in a systematized hospital, furnished him a standardized education, supports him in a scientifically managed factory, and finishes him off with a final factory flourish, by giving him a perfectly efficient funeral and a perfectly scientific entrance into the regions of eternal bliss.

PART III

THE PERSONS IN THE DRAMA: The Great Men and the Small

Naked have I seen both of them, the greatest man and the smallest man, All-too-similar are they still to each other. Verily, even the greatest found I all-too-human.

—*Thus Spake Zarathustra.*

CHAPTER IX
THE PERSONS IN THE DRAMA

THE quest of comfort is a drama. It might be called the tragedy of civilized man. The whole earth is the stage upon which it is being played. The history of civilization records the acts of the play. The accumulated wealth of mankind forms the properties being used by the players.

Three types of actors have played parts in it and still tread the boards:

Herd-minded types;
Quantity-minded types;
Quality-minded types.

An analysis of their characters and their relations one to another is necessary to an understanding of the plot.

•

In speaking of "Americans," or of "business men," or of "artists," we have in mind the characteristics which Americans, businessmen, and artists each have in common. Each of these types of men lives a life similar in its essentials to that of his fellows of the same type. Each has like environments, like interests, like problems. Each has like mental characteristics in part because their common mental bent determines their choice of a common life-work and in part because their life-work determines their mentalities. Americans thrill at the sight of the stars and stripes, rise when they hear "The Star Spangled Banner," revere the Declaration of Independence and the Constitution even though they pay no attention to them, speak English, write the Roman alphabet, use Arabic numerals. These American characteristics are common to Americans just as business men's characteristics are common to business men and artistic characteristics common to artists.

This is the reason that makes it possible to say that in every age and in every region of the globe men have always consisted of three types of individuals: an immense majority of herd-minded men who have the characteristics common to average men; a small minority of quantity-minded men who have the characteristics which predatory, acquisitive, power-seeking, ruthless men have in common, and a still smaller minority of quality-minded men.

The beauty or ugliness of a civilization—the condition of its culture, the state of its society, and the richness or poverty of the life of the individuals in it—is determined by the parts played in that civilization by these three types of individuals—by the position accorded to quality-minded individuals and the extent to which they are able to impose their ideas upon it. Where the quality-minded play the leading part you have a beautiful civilization. Where the quantity-minded play the leading part you have an ugly civilization. Where the herd-minded play the leading part you have no civilization at all.

•

Mr. Everett Dean Martin has very aptly observed that "society is a wave; the wave moves forward, but the water of which it is composed does not."

Society does change—it moves forward, if you will—from age to age. But the parts played in the drama of civilization by the various types of individual who make up society seem never to change.

The relationship of the three types of players in the drama to one another and their respective contributions to civilization seem to be unchanging.

•

It is almost impossible to say of a particular individual that he is in every respect a herd-minded, a quantity-minded, or a quality-minded type. Human beings do not lend themselves to such rigid classification. Most of them are mixtures of two and even three of these types. The most ambitious, the most predatory, the most acquisitive specimen of the quantity-minded type may be average in every respect except the direction in which his appetite seems to have been abnormally developed. John D. Rockefeller, for instance, may be a devout Baptist, a convinced Republican, a sincere patriot. Upon everything other than money-making his reactions may be precisely the same as John Doe's and every other member of the herd-minded mass. On the other hand, herd-minded individuals may be sensitive to line, to form, to color, to sound; may in some fields be skilled workers of a high order; they may lack only that qualitative attitude toward all the aspects of life which cornes from high sensitivity and profound understanding.

Yet it is possible in spite of these self-evident limitations of classification to throw a flood of light upon the forces that move our civilization by assuming that practically all human beings do belong in one or the other of these categories. The dominant characteristics, the general behavior, the outstanding activities, the values that motivate individuals are sufficiently distinctive to determine the category in which each belongs. And for our purposes it is possible to ignore those who are so definitely on the border-line as to resist all classification.

Fortunately, the theory here set forth rests upon so many inductive analyses of individuals that it cannot be upset by the differences of opinion which may develop as to the class in which historical personages and particular persons of the present period should be assigned. A concordance of circumstances puts John Doe in one class, John D. Rockefeller in the second, and Charles W. Eliot in the third. They remain in the class to which circumstances assign them only as long as they are characteristically unchanged. No man, of course, is "born" to one of these three classes. And no title of nobility, no fiat of government, no amount of wealth, no university degrees can keep him in one of these classes after changes in him or in his circumstances have developed which have actually transferred him to another. The same individual may at one time belong to the herd-minded class; later to the quantity-minded class, and at a still later time, to the quality-minded class.

Take a thousand human beings, and 997 will be herd-minded like John Doe and his fellows; two will be quantity-minded like John D. Rockefeller; and one quality-minded, like Charles W. Eliot. I cannot, unfortunately, vouch for the statistical accuracy of this formula, but it is at least suggestive of the actual state of affairs. Everyday observation makes it very probable that individuals of these three types exist in society in the ratio of 997 to 2 to 1.

And in most of mankind's tragic history, the two quantity-minded individuals have been busily engaged in quarreling to see which one would exploit the remaining 997, and in forcing the one quality-minded soul in the thousand either to entertain them or to assist them in the business of exploitation. Yet, as we shall see, there are good grounds for concluding that whatever we have of civilization has come into being because the quality-minded, exploited though they have been by the quantity-minded possessors of power, and hated by the unthinking masses, have always been able, after an often heart-breaking lapse of time, to impose their ideas upon mankind.

•

Programs for the improvement or the reformation of society which do not take these differences in the types of man into account are doomed to inevitable failure. Democratic, humanitarian, equalitarian programs, when strongly charged with political or religious emotionalism, create interesting and dramatic pages in history, but they do not produce a stable and satisfying social life for mankind. Indeed, history is largely the long record of the futile efforts to better society predicated upon false theories of the equality of man and of equally disappointing efforts based upon equally false theories of the inequality of man.

The time has come for the abandonment of programs based upon fictions about man and for the formulation of a program based upon facts.

•

Men are neither physically nor mentally equal. They are not equal though every politician in the land proclaim the fiction that law has conferred equality upon them, and every church endlessly proclaim the fiction that religion makes all men equally precious to God. General acceptance of the fact that some men are superior to others and that some are, by the same token, inferior, is important because of the check it would furnish upon the social and political fallacies which abound today.

The plain fact is that individuals are unequal physically and mentally by reason of inexplicable and ineradicable accidents of breed, rearing, and experience. Some are just average because they were born that way, and some are made average by education and circumstances. Some are predatory and acquisitive and others creative, and in all cases what any individual is at any given moment is the end-product of a set of equally incalculable accidents. There are no hard and fast lines of demarcation between the various types of individuals. The range is from complete idiocy to absolute genius, and from an almost perfect purity of type to every combination of types. Every individual is a miracle. Every individual is a law unto himself because each individual is the product of a sequence of events which are not exactly duplicated in the life of any other.

•

It is the fact of the inequality of the individual man that is most important. It is the "clinical history" of the individual; his heredity, environment and experience, and not that of his race, nation or family that determines whether he is to be a member of the herd-minded masses, whether he is to be one of its quantity-minded masters, or its quality-minded leaders. For genius, like stupidity, falls "like the gentle dew from heaven" upon those born and brought up Frenchmen and Germans; upon those of the Nordic and the Slav races; upon those coming from families "to the manor born" and those from the "poor white trash." Genius is not the exclusive prerogative of any of these divisions of mankind perhaps because stupidity seems to be no respecter of even the finest of families, the most progressive of nations, the most superior of races.

Individual men are first of all unequal because they do not come from one race, one nationality, one family. They are unequal by reason of the differences in the blood, history, culture, environment of their races, their nationalities, and their families. The men of one race are not equal to those of another; of one nationality to other nationalities; of one family to other families. No two individuals can ever be equal because the sum total of all the factors of heredity, environment and experience can never be the same in any two individuals.

Even if two individuals were in every controllable respect identical—identical in parentage, identical in education, identical in experience, identical in age—they would still not be equal. No possible combination of all the controllable equalities—equality of income, of education, of feeding; of shelter—is sufficient to produce two really equal individuals.

Two men may have the same father and mother and yet the heritage with which one began was different from the heritage of the other. Even though born twins, the biological material in the cells from which each developed would not have been the same; their development during gestation different, and their history from the moment of delivery, of course, unlike. And from birth onward, every minute difference in rearing and experience would have heightened the early differences in them. They would not have eaten the same food, even though served at the same table; worn the same clothes, received the same treatment from relatives and acquaintances, occupied themselves always alike. They would not have read the same books, met the same persons, taken away from them and from their reading the same set of ideas, nor encountered the same experiences. They could not be exactly alike.

Variation is a basic fact in nature.

Only man is a standardizer.

Variation must therefore be accepted in any really practical plan for producing a beautiful civilization.

With men so different from one another, it is absurd to generalize about man. There is no such thing as "man." There are only individuals. It is dangerous enough to generalize after we have divided men into types of various kinds. We can say that all men have certain conspicuous physical and mental characteristics in common: they walk on legs, for instance; they talk; they eat. But we cannot say that all men are equally entitled to a voice in the counsels of the state.

It is childish to make anything except the most obvious of generalizations about man. Sound generalizations can only be made after full acceptance of the fact of difference, of variation, of inequality in mankind, and generalizations should be qualified with many reservations even then.

•

In trying to outline a really beautiful civilization, not only must this inequality of individuals be accepted, but the inexorability of this inequality must be likewise accepted.

> The moving finger writes; and, having writ,
> Moves on; nor all your Piety nor Wit
>   Shall lure it back to cancel half a line,
> Nor all your Tears wash out a Word of it.

Men may be likened to a race of runners who started to race from some dim and distant mark in the unrecorded past. At any given moment of time, some of the runners are old and some are young; some are rich and some are poor; some are intelligent and some are stupid; some are weak and some are strong. Onward they run, leaving the dead and dying behind them, pressing into the dim and distant future toward some perhaps non-existent goal. As each individual enters the race he finds that there are runners ahead of him, far behind him, and all around him. He enters into the struggle, quite without regard to the fact that he does not start on an equality with, nor even at the same time as the others, helped and hindered in his own running by various advantages and various handicaps which perhaps no other individual in the race exactly duplicates.

The runners in the race of life are not equals.

It is impossible for them to be made equal physically and mentally by fiat no matter how exalted the source from which the decree might emanate.

It is the vainest of vain hope to believe that religion or politics or science can cancel, now that the race is on, any jot or tittle of the existing inequalities among the racers.

Nor can what we call progress change the relative position of the racers. Progress may help the rank and file of plodders to move faster, but it helps the leaders in the race equally as much and sometimes it helps them to move relatively still faster than before. The difference between the Attic helot of ancient Greece and a Plato is not a whit greater than the difference between the average comic-strip reader of a modern New York newspaper and a Charles W. Eliot. All of what is generally called progress—a republican form of government, rapid and cheap transportation, factory production—has contributed in combination all that it could to the development of the average modern New Yorker. Progress may have made the New Yorker a superior being to the Attic helot, although the evidence upon this point is by no means conclusive, but it has not brought him nearer to an equality mentally with a Charles W. Eliot. It has not even brought him to an equality physically with a prize fighter and of course it has not brought him to an equality financially with a John D. Rockefeller. The future may, if we continue to progress, do as much more for the average New Yorker as the past has done for him since his forbears were serfs and slaves. But it cannot bring him to a parity with the predatory men who boss him, nor with the cultured men who civilize him. Progress may increase the speed at which all in the race run: it may substitute wheels for the legs which nature provided for the racers in the beginning of the race, but it cannot bring the racers to an equality.

Men are not equal.

Their inequality is inexorable.

And that they should be equal is undesirable.

•

Man is the end product of a long evolutionary process. Everything that he is today, mentally and physically, has been slowly developed by a process which seems like adaptation to his environment, but which has been in reality a process of natural selection of those most fitted to survive from countless millions of variations throughout all time. The varieties best adapted survived. The varieties ill adapted to survival have disappeared because of the handicaps under which they labored in the struggle to maintain themselves and to reproduce their kind.

There is little doubt that man today is superior to his ancestors: that the genus homo sapiens is superior to the primates from which he sprang. That superiority, however, could not have developed had every individual primate been exactly equal to every other primate—had there not been inferior and superior specimens among them—inferior and superior at least in their survival aptitude. Progress, therefore, to the stage of development to which man has now attained has been dependent upon the fact that the primitive stock out of which the present race developed did not consist of identical nor "equal" individuals. It has been dependent upon the inequality of the individuals, and on the consequent ability of the superior among them to be selected as the breeders and nurturers of their successors.

Unless we are, therefore, to argue that no further progress is desirable, it is plain that there must be in the future a continuance of this inequality. If we are to progress from our present state; if we are to produce a race superior to the present and a state of society superior to that which we now enjoy, indeed even if man is to survive at all, the continuance of this selective process is absolutely essential. And since the process involves not only a selection of the superior types from among the whole group of individuals for survival, but also the imposition of their ways of life upon their fellows, it is eminently desirable that men should not be equal.

Social obstacles to the increase in the varieties of human types are most undesirable.

Individuality, and not uniformity, should be encouraged.

•

What has probably prevented a general acceptance of the desirability of inequality has been a mistaken assumption that it involves idealization of mere brute strength. But this is an assumption which grows out of a complete misreading of the history of man. Man triumphed over every other animate creature, not because he was the stronger brute, but because he was the more intelligent. Indeed, his physical handicaps may have played a considerable part in forcing upon him a discipline and training which helped him to his present eminence in the animal kingdom.

What is true of man in competition with other animals, is also true of the individual man in competition with his fellows. Not the man who is strongest physically, but the man who is strongest mentally tends to prevail, and tends to reproduce his kind.

It is the race which invented guns and gunpowder which has vanquished the physically superior races of primitives wherever they came into conflict. It is the individual who is intelligent enough to invent some better method of adapting himself to his environment who survives in competition with other individuals. The fact that it is the predatory and not the intellectual types of individuals who generally exercise immediate power does not vitiate the rule. The rulers who survive in the contest with their fellow power-seekers are those intelligent enough to apply to their problems what the intellectuals have to teach them. Ultimately, therefore, it is intelligence which determines survival. In a society of which the cardinal principle was that every encouragement should be given to the individuals best fitted to survive, not brute strength, but intelligence would triumph. Such a society would produce real supermen. Not super-brutes, but super-rational men. They would be healthy in body as in mind, but they would not be muscular giants. They would be notable, not for their ability ruthlessly to sate their appetites, but for their sensitivity to what it is desirable to do with life.

In such a society the things which today are supposed to be in the interests of the masses would be subordinated to things in the interests of the superior individuals. All customs and institutions would be organized so as to encourage the superior individuals in every way, not only to reproduce their kind, but to impose their methods of living, their ideas about life, and their tastes upon the masses of mankind.

They would be the acknowledged teachers of mankind, the accepted architects of its culture patterns.

And in such a society, the general level of the comfort of the great masses of men would be far higher than in one in which no such recognition of the importance of inequality prevailed.

•

In spite of "Liberty, Equality, Fraternity!", in spite of the ring ing dogma from our own charter of liberty: "All men are created free and equal," the nineteenth century has not succeeded in producing a really beautiful civilization. Western society has been largely relieved of the incubus of a medieval priesthood. American society has been freed of the exactions of kings and nobles. Society generally has made some revolutionary steps toward economic freedom. But it is the great tragedy of the age of revolution that so many of its experiments in remoulding society were based upon democratic theories of the equality of man. Political, economic, social, educational programs which begin with the proposition that men are equal are predicated upon a foundation of fiction. Societies based upon them contain within themselves the seeds of their own futility and failure.

The democratic theory will always fail to produce a really desirable society because it ignores the patent fact that some men are superior and others inferior; because it assumes that the inferior are capable of selecting those who are best fitted to guide and rule, and because it romantically fancies that power-seeking individuals will accept the dictation of those who lack their own ruthless determination to gratify gargantuan appetites.

Democracy seems to confer power upon the masses. But it can no more prevent the masses from being preyed upon by predatory individuals than a herd of sheep can themselves prevent the wolves from preying upon them. Power cannot be conferred upon those who are incapable of exercising it.

What is probably the greatest evil inherent in democratic forms of society is the fact that they encourage the masses to think themselves equally as good as the superior types of man. Instead of encouraging the superior individuals; instead of giving them every opportunity to act as the fashioners of the average man's habits of life; of being the artificer of society's folkways, democracy handicaps the activities of intelligent individuals by the way democracy organizes its social, economic, and political institutions. It tries to force superior individuals to conform to what is normal for the mediocrities and nonentities of whom mankind is so largely composed.

Democracy makes conformity the greatest good in the world.

•

But the aristocratic theory, which has been largely destroyed by the rising tide of democracy, furnishes no better basis for a really beautiful civilization. True, it involves a recognition of inequality in mankind. But the inequality it recognizes is a false one. It is one based upon the single accident of birth. The classes into which aristocratic societies are divided have little or no correspondence to the superiority or inferiority of the individuals of which it is composed.

Aristocratic society imposes an artificial inequality upon mankind; it imposes a false test of superiority and an equally false test of inferiority.

The aristocrat is not necessarily a superior individual. For superiority is not merely a matter of birth and breeding. It is these things only in part. There is as yet little real knowledge about the part heredity and the part environment play in the production of superior individuals, and the wise society must therefore make provision for the leadership of those superior individuals who come out of classes and from environments which normally seem to produce only inferior types.

What mankind needs if it is to produce a really desirable state of society is an aristocracy of truly superior persons. The inequality in such a society would be based upon the actual differences among individuals and not upon differences due to the accident of race, nationality, or family.

•

In such a society there would be no arbitrary leaderships.

Really superior individuals cannot be selected by examinations any more than they can be selected by elections. The most desirable attributes of the superior individuals neither lend themselves to the pedantry essential in selection by civil service commissions, nor to the demagogery necessary in selection by some form of election.

Whenever there is a general acceptance of the idea that it is in the high self-interest of every individual and of society as a whole to try to recognize intelligence and to give it every opportunity to develop, superior individuals will be recognized merely because they are superior. When it becomes the fashion for the masses to imitate the ways of life of really superior individuals; when it becomes a folkway to make heroes out of quality-minded and not out of quantity-minded individuals, the speed with which quality-minded individuals will impose their ideas, first upon the quantity-minded and then upon society as a whole, will be greatly increased.

The lag in time, between the *conception* of a better way of life or a better method of doing something or a better idea and the *final acceptance* of it, which now disgraces civilization would begin to shorten.

In such a society, every activity would be subjected to the scrutiny of its critical intellectual social leaders.

Government would be rationalized and secularized. The divinity which used to hedge about the king and the priest and which modern nationalism has transformed into patriotism, would wither under the ridicule visited upon every effort to impart a sacred character to anything or anybody having to do with government. With this would go much of the emotionalism and mass hysteria with which all political activities are now permeated. Most of the sacred principles, which are supposed to justify the fervor and the fanaticism of present day political leaders, do not bear critical examination. The differences between Republicans, Democrats, and Socialists do not stand factual examination. If it ever becomes the habit to follow those who turn first to fact-finding on controversial questions, politicians will find it difficult to excite themselves, and the multitudes who follow them, with the sort of political questions which now go by the name of paramount issues. With politics thus deflated, the issues between nations which now develop wars could not develop enough hatred to make men kill each other. Armies and navies would go to the scrap heap with the sectionalism and the nationalism which now make them necessary.

Government would be restricted to the barest minimum necessary for the restraint of stupid and vicious individuals, and for the conduct of community enterprises which cannot be more effectively carried on by individual initiative or voluntary cooperation.

•

In such a society the necessity for hospitals and jails would be very considerably reduced. In a state of society such as we now enjoy both of these institutions have to be larger than the normal state of mankind requires.

Just as we shall always have super-normal individuals, we shall always have sub-normal individuals. It is necessary to accept this fact and to accept the consequences which flow from it. But it is not necessary to assume that the number of sub-normal and anti social individuals must be as great as that with which society has to struggle today.

Today the erection of insane asylums of one kind or another is one of the principal activities of society. Our insane population seems to multiply itself at a terrific rate. There is no real necessity for all these institutions. They are the inevitable consequence of the resolute refusal of society to apply to all the important questions of life even a modicum of uncommon sense.

It is today the folkway of society, a folkway encouraged by all the churches, not to control the instinct of reproduction. Men and women are not only encouraged to get married and rear large families, regardless of their own fitness for fatherhood and motherhood and their own ability to rear their children properly, but they are forbidden by Federal, State, and Municipal law to acquire information about methods of controlling and restricting birth. It is difficult to picture how much crime, disease, and insanity this one unintelligent custom injects into society. Not only does it encourage a prolific multiplication of undesirables through birth; it fills hospitals and asylums with the victims of abortions; it fills jails with those who violate laws having to do with "illegal" operations and appliances and teachings.

With one hand society manufactures the necessity for these institutions; with the other it devotes itself to building them.

No wonder laws, officials, and public institutions multiply endlessly.

If society would acquire the habit of listening very carefully to the studied conclusions of its intellectual leaders about the innumerable prohibitions which it now inflicts upon itself, it would cease manufacturing so many idiots and criminals, and would find that the true sub-normals would shrink to such a small percentage of the total population that provision for their care would cease to be an increasing social burden and an increasing social problem.

•

In such a society the church would become an anachronism. With the masses of men following the pattern of living set for them by the most intelligent of their fellows, the hope of heaven and the fear of hell would not be necessary in order to make society function cooperatively. The waste of precious materials and of more precious human effort in dotting the landscape with churches—most of them ugly as sin—would be ended. The colossal amount of human energy now put into maintaining them—the energy which is organized in committees, boards, and conventions—would be released for more intelligent purposes, and the hundreds of thousands of preachers drooling superstitious rubbish about the virgin birth, the resurrection, the life everlasting, would be forced to engage in more useful and edifying occupations.

Churches, preachers, and religions have merely an ethnological interest for intelligent people. If the masses of mankind were to follow their more intelligent fellows in so regarding them, the gain to social health would be incalculable.

•

In such a society the factory, and all that the factory implies —mass-production, mass-distribution, and mass-consumption would be restricted to those products which intelligent men, by the example which they would set in their buying, would determine as desirable for the material well-being and comfort of man.

Man would produce in order that he might live comfortably; he would not live in order that he might produce.

•

Finally, in such a society, art would at last come into its own.

Science, which has been subverted into a mere accessory to factory-production, would begin to devote itself to the problem of how man might live more beautifully and how he might produce more beautiful things.

In such an atmosphere, art would not be an interloper. It would not be a mere excrescence upon a civilization devoted to production. It would become the real objective of existence; the necessary protest of every individual against the mundane and ordinary necessities which nature imposes upon man if he is to live.

In such a society all men might, in their due degrees, be artists. Every individual man would be alternately artist and audience: artist to the extent to which he himself produced beautiful things —even though what he produced might be only the product of his vegetable gardens—and audience to the extent to which he was able to show a discriminating enjoyment of what others produced. For the world to be a tolerable place for a really civilized people, this duality must be developed to a high degree. Great art flourishes only where there is a great, discriminating, intelligent patronage of it. And a beautiful life is only possible where the masses of men imitate their superior fellows in their appreciation of the beautiful.

•

In such a society!

Why continue to describe what is for the present merely the figment of a dream?

For no such society is as yet within the realm of the probable. Perhaps it is not even in the realm of the possible.

But this is possible—in spite of the fact that the quantity-minded types of men will probably always dominate society, at least in the immediate moment—that individuals who desire to live the superior life shall erect enclaves of their own, enclaves in which they and their families and friends may live without dependence upon the patronage of the quantity-minded and in which they may enjoy such comfort and attain to such understanding as the limitations of life make possible.

Enclaves of this sort—little islands of intelligence and beauty amidst the chaotic seas of human stupidity and ugliness—would not only free the quality-minded from exploitation by the quantity minded, but they would furnish to the rest of mankind the pattern for a more comfortable and more intelligent existence. Mankind being what it is, the tendency of the average man, whether quantity-minded or just herd-minded, to imitate the ways of life of superior persons would be irresistible.

Enclaves of this sort, whenever they became numerous enough, would begin to lessen the ugliness of this civilization.

•

Social changes find their genesis in three forces: (1) the forces set in motion by great natural convulsions—changes in climate such as those caused by the movement of the glacial ices—and which are independent of man; (2) the forces set in motion by the efforts of ambitious individuals to sate their appetites for pelf or power—the forces set in motion by an Alexander, a Cæsar, a Napoleon, and to come up to date, by the forces set in motion by the activities of a John D. Rockefeller, an Andrew Carnegie, a J. Pierpont Morgan; (3) the launching of new ideas, as for instance, the forces set in motion among men by the idea that the world is round; by the idea of immortality; by the idea of equality; by the idea of democracy.

Nature's convulsions may be dismissed from consideration because they are beyond the control of man. Man cannot produce an ice-age—yet; he can only adapt himself to those produced by nature.

It is the operation of the second of these forces that explains most of our social, economic, and political history. Quantity minded men, in their struggles to sate their ambitions, have been able to impose their wishes upon mankind because of their domination of the herd-minded masses and the dependence upon them of the quality-minded individuals. An Alexander the Great could remake Greece and the regions which he conquered as he wished because he dominated the Macedonian and Greek masses and the Aristotles of his time were so dependent upon him that they could do little on their own initiative. So it is today: the quantity-minded businessmen who direct the General Electric Company remake America as they wish because they dominate the American masses and because quality-minded geniuses like Steinmetz—an idealist, socialist, and humanitarian—are so dependent upon them that the idealists aid them in actually hindering society from adopting the reforms in which the idealists believe.

Let the quality-minded individuals free themselves from this dependence upon the quantity-minded and the civilization of the future will be built upon the basis of intelligent ideas of what changes are desirable in society and how it is most desirable to bring the changes about.

CHAPTER X
JOHN DOE, AVERAGE MAN: The Herd-Minded Type

In a brilliant discussion of what they call "The Sea of Humanity," the authors of *What About Advertising*, Kenneth M. Goode and Harford Powel, Jr., paint an admirable portrait of the average man—the herd-minded type which forms the overwhelming majority of mankind. I am taking the liberty of selecting a very few of the most illuminating items from their compendium of evidence upon this subject, adding some which they were probably constrained to omit out of respect to prevailing orthodoxies.

First, as to John Doe's academic education. Taking the method of Dr. Brigham and following the schooling of one thousand typical American men, all of whom began their education in the first grade of our public school systems, Goode and Powel record that:

1,000 boys enter 1st grade
970 of them enter 2nd grade
940 of them enter 3rd grade
905 of them enter 4th grade
830 of them enter 5th grade
735 of them enter 6th grade
630 of them enter 7th grade
490 of them enter 8th grade

Of our original one thousand boys:
230 boys enter 1st year high school
170 of them finish 2nd year high school
120 of them finish 3rd year high school
95 of them graduate from high school.

Of our original one thousand boys:
50 boys enter lst year college

40 of them finish 2nd year college
20 of them finish 3rd year college
10 of them remain in college to be graduated.

The academic development of John Doe ends with his schooling. When he leaves school, he reads, writes, and has a smattering of arithmetic, history, and geography, and he considers himself educated. Thereafter his intellectual life is paralyzed by a regular reading of newspapers, popular magazines and church attendance.

What kind of mentality has this schooling produced? A few years ago 700,000 typical American young men and women who were members of the Epworth League, voted that the greatest men in history were as follows:

1. Thomas Edison
2. Theodore Roosevelt
3. William Shakespeare
4. Henry W. Longfellow
5. Alfred Tennyson
6. Herbert Hoover
7. Charles Dickens
8. General Pershing
9. Lloyd George
10. Andrew J. Volstead

This collective judgment was plainly a product of conventional education through the public schools, the churches, and the daily newspapers. The selection of Shakespeare, Longfellow, Tennyson, and Dickens, was influenced by the schooling of these 700,000 young Americans; the selection of Edison, Roosevelt, Hoover, Pershing, and Lloyd George, by their reading of the newspapers; and the selection of Volstead, the author of the Federal Prohibition Enforcement Law, by their church attendance.

•

John Doe goes to Sunday School. North America boasts of 195, 343 Sunday Schools with 2,459,799 officers and teachers and 17,510,830 pupils—a total membership of 19,970,629. The Bible, which is the foundation of the teaching in these schools, is a compilation of some of the sacred books of a barbaric Semitic people and the writings of the followers of a possibly mythical Jewish messiah. Yet its pronouncements upon the most difficult ethical, social, and political problems are accepted in all seriousness by John Doe and the millions of his fellows who make up the "sea of humanity."

John Doe gets his philosophy of life from his church. His church-going makes him understand clearly, both by precept and example, that virtue demands credulity and conformity; that skepticism and nonconformity endanger his future felicity, and that departures from the herd judgment involve business, social, and political handicaps in his present life. His priest, minister, or rabbi iterates and reiterates the glories of conventionality to him fifty-two times per year. He is one of the 18,604,000 Roman Catholics, 4,516,806 Methodists, 4,087,000 Jews, 2,546,127 Lutherans, 3,061,576 regular Baptists, 2,450,574 Presbyterians, 1,173,679 Episcopalians, and the other 200 religions in the United States which are listed in the Census of Religious Bodies in 1926. Of course, a few of the sects, of which the Unitarian church is typical, (but which numbers only 60,152 members all told), are hardly more than masks which shield their members from some of the contumely which the average man and woman visits upon avowed rationalists and "free thinkers." These liberal church goers, as is to be expected, represent only a very small part of the total church membership of 55,000,000. They shrink into even a smaller part of the total mass of conformers and are rendered doubly insignificant because most of the millions of John Doe's non-church-going fellows accept the superstitions of the prevailing religions even though they do not actually belong to any church.

•

John Doe is not a book reader. The *New York Daily News* and the New York Evening Journal are the sort of newspapers which he likes to read. The Saturday Evening Post, and The American Magazine" are most popular with him in the field of magazine literature. In addition to this reading, he feeds his mind through frequent attendance at the movies, and many hours daily of "listening in" on the radio. Goode and Powel say that there are 6,000,000 radio sets in America in use from one to two hours every day in the year. They estimate the movie audience at an average of 10,000,000 people per day.

The popular literature, the movies, and the radio, in order to secure the volume and circulation which is essential to profitable mass production, are of course keyed by the astute publishers, movie magnates, and radio broadcasters, (who know their public), to appeal to an intelligence no higher than that of normal twelve to fourteen year old children. It is easy for John Doe to enjoy what they offer him.

•

As Goode and Powel summarize the situation:

> The average American, broadly speaking, celebrates his twenty-fifth birthday by shutting shop mentally and refusing to accept any new ideas. He has then the literate capacity of a twelve- or fourteen-year old child.

Then, addressing themselves to the problem of manufacturers who have to write advertisements that will move these morons into action, they say:

> Many an advertiser may be discouraged to realize that copy aimed anywhere above the comprehension of an eighth-grade schoolboy cuts his audience in half, while any argument over the head of a college freshman misses nine out of ten of his possible prospects.... Your average audiences—which means any American audience as soon as you reach into the hundred thousands—is like that: $8-, $10-, $12-a day workers; thirteen- or fourteen-year-old minds scarcely equal to second-year high school. Each gets a book every four months where public libraries reach them; four out of five haven't even this service. And one out of three families have no books in their home. They like Tosti's *Good-Bye*, *David Copperfield*, *The Big Parade*, *Abie's Irish Rose*. They all go to the movies every other week; and about one in four listens to the radio perhaps an hour a day. They like dark blue as a color and lilac as a scent. Writing themselves, they use a vocabulary generally of fewer than a thousand words although each can understand, in reading, maybe six times that many. In their aggregate action the element of intellect is practically negligible.

This is the mind of the unthinking majority in America after more than a century of public school education, with compulsory attendance in most states, and after an expenditure of public funds for popular education that is not equalled in any other nation nor in any period of recorded history.

•

The predatory individual has a set of bigger though not necessarily better aspirations than John Doe. The values which he cherishes are often the values of John Doe, swollen to heroic proportions. Both want automobiles, but he wants really gorgeous ones. Both want homes, but he wants mansions. The predatory man sees himself an heroic individual. He takes what he can, and rationalizes his taking on the ground of "service" to the state, "service" to the church, or "service" to society. Partly because of this conventional justification of his conduct, and partly because John Doe can understand such aspirations, the leadership and dictation of the quantity-minded man are accepted by John Doe and the great masses of average men and women.

Because it is impossible to justify the tastes and interests and activities of the superior man by conventional standards, the average man and woman distrust and fear him. John Doe envies the millionaire, but he dislikes or hates the philosopher. The peculiar relish of the intellectual for new and apparently bizarre ideas; his preoccupation with ideas generally in preference to things; his tarte in music, in literature, in art, is incomprehensible to the generality of mankind. John Doe lacks the psychical equipment to perceive the values that motivate the cultured man and woman. Since he cannot recognize any superiority in their values, he denies their existence, and naturally hates the "high-brow" who he thinks is seeking to impress him with a mythical superiority.

It is possible to say that the great masses of Americans, like the great masses of peoples everywhere and at all times, are herd minded like John Doe for the very good reason that all the evidence of history and all the evidence of contemporary life prove that they are. From birth to death John Doe is a follower of custom and convention. He permits others to make his thoughts for him, his emotions for him, his decisions for him. He cherishes the delusion that he does his own thinking, feeling, and deciding merely because he thinks, feels, and acts in accordance with tradition, custom, and fashion, or as he is told to think, feel, and act by business men, clergymen, politicians and propagandists. He is not acquisitive and predatory enough to rise above the rut in which he lives. He is not sensitive, not intelligent enough, not aspiring enough to develop tastes and interests above that of the group to which he belongs. He distrusts, when he does not hate, the really learned man. He is born to his politics—Republican or Democratic. He is patriotic; he is industrious; he is honest; he is credulous. He has conventional likes and dislikes in music, literature, art. He has an essentially traditional set of taboos and sins, and a largely conventional adherence to the ethical principles he professes. Here in America his values are generally those of whites, Protestants, and 100 percenters.

A vulgar scoundrel like D. C. Stephenson, a Grand Dragon of the Ku Klux Klan, by exploiting the myth of Nordic superiority and the hatred of John Doe for the negro, the Catholic, and the Jew, was able to persuade the state of Indiana to vote the Knights of the K.K.K. into political power—to put his henchmen into nearly every office in the state from that of Governor down to that of the village constable. Had he not made the mistake of committing rape and murder, he would still be master of the commonwealth.

No wonder it was possible for the Emperor Constantine to make the European masses embrace Christianity *en bloc*; for a tough old goat like Henry VIII to make the masses of England accept a special kind of Protestantism by a kingly ukase; and, to bring the historical illustrations up-to-date, no wonder it was possible for Woodrow Wilson, who had had himself re-elected to the presidency by persuading the American people that "he kept them out of the war," in less than a year after his election, to make John Doe enlist apparently wholeheartedly in a war "to make the world safe for democracy!"

Is there any doubt that those who look to the education and improvement of the masses of herd-minded individuals as the hope for the building of a more beautiful civilization, suffer from a foolish delusion?

CHAPTER XI

JOHN D. ROCKEFELLER: The Quantity-Minded Type

AMONG the captains of industry with which factory-dotted America has added to the Chamber of Horrors of history, hardly a single one has fired the ambitions of more Americans than has John D. Rockefeller. Too successful to be typical of modern quantity-minded men generally and very different in outer appearance, he is yet worth studying because the very greatness of his success makes him the arch-type of the class to which he belongs.

Andrew Carnegie radiated a rather dour self-satisfaction. Charles M. Schwab a cheerful, steady conceit. Thomas F. Ryan a contented rapacity. But John D. Rockefeller never gave any impression of happiness. Yet he was happy, probably in the same way that all of these men were happy. Alfred Henry Lewis[35] relates a story which a bookish neighbor of Rockefeller in Cleveland told about him. Rockefeller had a habit of dropping in to see him. One evening Rockefeller asked him, "You get pleasure out of your books, Judge?"

"Yes," responded the bookworm.

"Do you know the only thing that gives me pleasure?" queried Rockefeller. "It is to see my dividends coming; just to see my dividends coming in."

•

John D. Rockefeller was a huge-boned bulk of a man. At the heyday of his career the Rockefeller eyes were small and glittering, an unflattering student of him said, and added, "like the eyes of a rat," while the contours of the Rockefeller mouth—a thin, long slit, which drew down at the corners—further suggested the cutting, gnawing rodent.

His father was a swashbuckling country sport, peddler, and horse trader. To his son the father gave only the sort of education which the country districts afforded at that time. At sixteen the son left school and started to work. At eighteen he was a bookkeeper in Cleveland, Ohio. At twenty-one he formed a partnership, and under the firm name of Clark and Rockefeller went into the produce commission business. The Civil War came along. The war, with its opportunities for profitable trading, made them both moderately rich.

•

The first American to vision the possibilities of petroleum, according to Ida M. Tarbell,[36] was not Rockefeller nor any of his associates. It was George H. Bissell, a graduate of Dartmouth College, a journalist and teacher, who sent a quantity of coal oil, as it was then called, to Professor B. Silliman, Jr., Professor of Chemistry in Yale College. The Silliman report contained all the facts that were essential to fire the cupidity of the Rockefellers. The report analyzed the oil and pointed out the value of the oil as lubricant, as gas, and as illuminant. A horde of pioneers and adventurous business men then laid the foundation of the industry.

In 1862, when Rockefeller was only twenty-three years of age, an Englishman, Samuel Andrews, who was anxious to establish a refinery in Cleveland, gave him his first insight into the on business. A $4,000 investment by the produce partnership backing Andrews, who became the ablest mechanical superintendent of the early history of the industry, set Rockefeller on the road that enabled him in 1870 to incorporate the Standard Oil Company for a million dollars, and later to become one of the few billionaires the world has produced. The period of eight years between twenty three and thirty-one, which culminated in the formation of the first American trust, was one of intense preparation for the golden future. Alliances were formed, reformed, and rejected. The interest in the original refinery he sold to his partner Clark. He bought a share in a larger refinery for $72,500 and formed a new partnership with Andrews. Rockefeller and Andrews absorbed a refinery started by his brother William, and Henry M. Flagler was at that time added to the partnership. At the end of this period of preparation, John D. Rockefeller, his brother William, Flagler, Andrews, and a refiner named Stephen V. Harkness, formed the Standard Oil Company of which John D. Rockefeller was made President.

It was in 1870, when he was thirty-one, that Rockefeller began the far reaching campaign which not only established the Standard Oil Company as the first American trust, but made him personally the master of the industry.

Railroad rebates were the weapons with which he struck down his competitors though he used with equal effectiveness other weapons when rebates failed him. The weapons with which he fought for the conquests of business were different from those with which Cæsar and Napoleon fought for the conquests of empire, but they were, if anything, more effective. Within three months after he had frightened the railroads into giving him rebates and drawbacks on both what he paid them for freight and out of what his competitors paid as well, twenty-one out of twenty six refiners in Cleveland were bought in by him at about fifty cents on the dollar. The fury and hatred which this inspired in those whom he was crushing was like that with which the rising tide of Christians inspired the Apennine Romans. The hatred of the relatively decent men in the oil industry was so great that for a time all those who dealt with the Standard Oil Company and its allies were ostracised. Men who sold crude oil to the trust were sent to coventry. Lifetime associates cut them on the streets; they would not drink with them—in an age when social drinking had the character of tribal ritual; they tried in every way to ruin them for deserting the cause of free trade. As the truth about the operations of the trust became public, the sympathy of the entire nation went out to those whom he was ruthlessly stripping of their wealth.

•

An average man would have been thwarted by the popular contempt which was inspired by the exposure in 1872 of the methods by which he and his associates were ruining their competitors and stealing their business.

But Rockefeller was no average man. He had the average man's appetite for money, but swollen to colossal proportions. He had the foresight which the average man lacks, and saw the enormous profits to be realized if he could control the oil industry. He had the cunning which enabled him to formulate the schemes that would give him that control. Above all, he had the one essential ingredient of the true quantity-minded man—the indomitable will necessary to make other men do what he wished them to do in order that he might get that control. The oil regions might rage and try to boycott him; the railroads be forced to repudiate their agreements with him; legislatures and congresses investigate and excoriate him; grand juries indict him; competitors sue him; the public hate and fear him. He kept on undisturbed.

"The oil business belongs to us," he said. It has a familiar sound. Did not a quantity-minded king say: "The state? I am the state." And a quantity-minded Pope of Rome equally sure of his title to rule, proclaim himself the vicar of God over all the earth?

•

After he was fifty, Rockefeller discovered other realms than that of business. He had always remained a pious member of the Baptist church, a church which in his formative years was even more devoted than it is today to the folkway of which tithes, alms-giving, and charity are the symbols. When Rockefeller had become many times a millionaire, he naturally became a philanthropist. In 1892, when he was fifty-three, he began the series of philanthropies on the grand scale which quantitatively dwarfed those of all contemporary millionaires. He discovered education in that year something to which Charles W. Eliot had at a corresponding age already given more than thirty years of productive and creative time as teacher, scientist, author, publicist, reformer, and university administrator. Between 1892 and 1910, he gave to the "University of Chicago founded by John D. Rockefeller" twenty five million dollars; to The Education Board he gave during the same period forty-three million dollars. He gave millions to the Rockefeller Institute for Medical Research in New York City; to the Rush Medical College in Chicago, to Johns Hopkins Hospital in Baltimore, to Barnard College in New York City. His gifts to the various branches of the Baptist church, notably the Baptist Missionary Society, dwarfed all similar gifts to the churches of America.

If we measure the contributions of men to the development of education, to medicine, and to religion, quantitatively and not qualitatively then it is possible to construct a very ingenious argument to justify Rockefeller's whole career of aggrandizement. It is possible to argue that the net result of his cupidity, his political debaucheries, his ruining of other men, his exploitation of the consumers of oil, was a concentration of wealth which resulted in great gifts to education, to medicine, and to religion. On the theory that the end justifies the means, it may be argued that good having come out of evil, the evil has been justified. This is, however, a very superficial view of this whole matter.

First, the qualitative contributions to these aspects of civilization are more important than the quantitative. Pestalozzi and Froebel contributed more to education, Pasteur and Lister more to medicine, and Cardinal Newman and Theodore Parker more to religion than did Rockefeller. It is not number of buildings, amount of equipment, or size of staffs that is most important; it is the ideas that are contributed which go marching down the ages and which make for the real forward movement of mankind. And these ideas are not contributed by the men who devote their lives to quantitative acquisition.

Secondly, it is a complete mistake to assume that without philanthropies of the Rockefeller type, the world would have been without the educational, medical, and religious institutions and activities which their gifts brought into being. On the contrary, it is quite probable that, had wealth not been so concentrated, support of these institutions by the state, and contributions from individuals who had been deprived of wealth by the Rockefellers, would have exceeded their relatively niggardly philanthropies to them. The institutions might not have become such grandiose projects in point of size, but they might have permitted a much greater degree of freedom to those who really created and conducted them. The present stranglehold which "big business" has upon all our eleemosynary institutions would have hardly developed had the part played by educators, by scientists, and by artists in their development been better recognized, and the part played by the contributors of money been minimized.

Finally, had these various projects not been centralized, as sheer "bigness" required, there would have been less regimentation, less standardization, less conformity in American life. For quantity-minded men always build so as to make mankind amenable to centralized control. The empire builders, the church builders, the business builders must have great multitudes who respond alike to patriotism, to religion, to consumption. Multitudes must thrill to one flag, to one creed, to one trademark. And it is not a mere coincidence that the institutions which the Napoleons, the Pope Gregorys, the John D. Rockefellers create and develop, all tend to make mankind conform to things as the quantity-minded like to have them.

The Rockefellers of today "give" colleges, hospitals, foundations, just as the medieval barons used to "give" monasteries, nunneries, chapels, and the Roman senators used to "give" baths and amphitheatres. But in reality they "give" nothing. They merely return a part of what they were acquisitive and powerful enough to seize. Unfortunately they return these parts of their accumulations in forms and on conditions which lessen if they do not completely destroy their value to the public.

•

History is a record of mankind's leadership by its John D. Rockefellers. Now and then mankind has turned for a time to a more sensitive type to be led, or to be entertained, or to be instructed. In religion it has sometimes followed a Zoroaster, a Buddha, a Christ. In ethics, it has sometimes followed a Confucius, a Socrates, a Spinoza. Even in political leadership, it has sometimes followed a Pericles, a Danton, a Lincoln. But it has usually followed such men for a short time only. It generally ends their leadership by crucifying them. It always ends by perverting their ideas. Generally, and naturally enough, and perhaps properly as well, the herd-minded masses are turned from their leadership and from devotion to their ideas by the quantity-minded men—men more interested in extending the sway of the church than in the practice of its teachings; men more interested in enlarging the territories of the state, than in making it the instrument for carrying out ethical ideas; men more interested in acquiring the wealth to be secured from the entertaining and exploiting of the multitude, than in enriching life—these types of men seize power by a superficial appearance of carrying out the ideas of the leaders they pretend to follow.

•

The quantity-minded individual may or may not begin his career with a better intellectual endowment than the herd-minded majority of his fellows. The opportunities which wealth and the exercise of power confer naturally affect the quantity-minded man and place him in an environment that tends to raise him above the intellectual level of the masses. John D. Rockefeller began his career with no more in the way of schooling and intelligence perhaps even less—than the average man. Success created the environment that enabled him to rise far above the John Does from whom he sprang.

The peculiar toughness of mental fiber and unusual strength of appetite which make the quantity-minded man are no respecters of family, of nationality, of race. They put in an appearance in the peasant's hut, just as readily as in the king's palace; in the person of a laborer digging in a trench, just as readily as in an educated and intelligent individual. Quantity-minded John D. Rockefeller and herd-minded John Doe may be alike in their tastes, in their preoccupation with the material aspects of life, but the predatory man has what the average man lacks: the superb appetite for pelf and power and the indomitable will without which it is impossible to secure and retain great wealth and great power. He is fascinated by the value of the things which he possesses; the amount of power that he can wield. What counts are millions of dollars—not how they are secured; the hundreds of factories he owns and thousands of workers he exploits, not the quality of the things he makes; the size of his houses, the value of his paintings, the amount of his philanthropies, and not the design of the houses, the taste in the paintings, the wisdom of the philanthropies. He is merely objectified personal will, much as is the barbarian, the child, and the brute. The quantity-minded man can always be recognized by either of two qualities: the ability to get wealth and power, or the ability to hold on to the wealth and power he already possesses.

What amazing forms the type has taken throughout the history of mankind: the priests, Torquemada, Loyola, Gregory, Luther, Calvin, Knox; the warriors, Genghis Kahn, Tamerlane, Alexander, Cæsar, Napoleon, Constantine, Charlemagne; the business men, Arkwright, Goodyear, Boothe, Vanderbilt, Daniel Drew, Jay Gould, Carnegie, Morgan, Patterson. But no matter what the outward form of activity, the quantity-minded man has always been in pursuit of more of whatever it is the "thing" to acquire by the conventional standards of his times: more converts, more subjects, more territory, more business, more wealth. The things he accumulates are merely outer expressions of an inner psychosis. They vary from age to age. Henry Adams calls attention to the way in which Constantine the Great used Christianity:

> Good taste forbids saying that Constantine the Great speculated as audaciously as a modern stockbroker on values of which he knew at the utmost only the volume; or that he merged all uncertain forces into a single trust, which he enormously overcapitalized, and forced on the market; but this is the substance of what Constantine himself said in his Edict of Milan in the year 313, which admitted Christianity into the Trust of State Religions. Regarded as an act of Congress, it runs:
>
> "We have resolved to grant to Christian as well as all others the liberty to practice the religion they prefer, in order that whatever ex ists of divinity or celestial power may help and favor us and all who are under our government." The empire pursued power—not merely spiritual but physical—in the sense in which Constantine issued his army order the year before, at the battle of the Milvian Bridge: *In hoc signo vinces!* using the Cross as a train of artillery, which, to his mind, it was. Society accepted it in the same character. Eighty years afterwards, Theodosius marched against his rival Eugene with the Cross for physical champion; and Eugene raised the image of Hercules to fight for the pagans; while society on both sides looked on, as though it were a boxing match, to decide a final test of force between the divine powers.[37]

The quantity-minded man, being practical, conforms to the taboos, the virtues, and the traditions to which he finds it necessary to conform in getting whatever it is that he wants. Even when he seizes upon a fanatical idea, he remains, like Constantine, practical enough to secure results. Since he cannot gratify his passion for imposing his will upon the rest of his fellows unless he is an adept at compromise, he conforms in substance even when engaged in changing the outer appearance. He has a genius for recognizing the fundamental conventions.

Where valor is the ruling convention, an Alexander out-valors all others.

Where piety is the ruling convention, a Loyola out-pieties all others.

Where wealth is the ruling convention—a Rockefeller out wealths all others.

The quantity-minded founders of the Christian church, for instance, imposed a religion invented by fanatics upon the hostile masses of Europe by adopting one after another of the essential superstitions of the pagans and barbarians whom they sought to convert. The "unknown god" of the Ephesians became the Christian Jehovah; the Saturnalia, the birthday of Christ; the hierarchy of gods and godesses, the college of patron saints.

Times change, but the formula seems unchanging: 997 to 2 to 1. The predatory individuals simply adapt themselves to their times, and use equally well armies, or churches, or factories, in their struggle for pelf and power.

The tragedy of mankind, as it is the tragedy for the quantity minded themselves, is the fact that the values that inspire their activities offer no clue to what is a really superior way of life. Accumulation is set up as the supreme value in life. Accumulation becomes the most desirable activity in which man can engage. Unfortunately, devotion to accumulation contributes nothing to life, unless the purely negative virtue of acting as horrible examples is accounted a contribution.

The quantity-minded man today finds in business, as Lewis Mumford points out, "love, adventure, worship, art, and every sort of ideality," with the consequence that "to withdraw from industry was to become incapacitated for any further life."[38] The mighty wills, which in the past built great empires and great churches and which today build great fortunes, find themselves palsied when confronted by the yearning, not entirely to be killed in any man, to live a really superior life.

There is something tragic in even the best-lived life. There is something doubly tragic, grotesquely tragic, in the life of an Andrew Carnegie—fifty years of successes achieved by the ruthless extinction of competitors in the race for wealth and power—frustrated in the end because the mind that achieved miracles of acquisition in business could not perform an equal miracle in re-education.

CHAPTER XII
CHARLES W. ELIOT: The Quality-Minded Type

A MEMORANDUM by Charles W. Eliot, from 1869 to 1909 President of Harvard University, containing notes for a lecture on what equipment a student should take from college for success in after life, was recently found.

> 1. An available body. Not necessarily the muscle of an athlete. Good circulation, digestion, power to sleep, and alert, steady nerves.
> 2. Power of sustained mental labor.
> 3. The habit of independent thinking on books, prevailing customs, current events. University training, the opposite of military or industrial.
> 4. The habit of quiet, unobtrusive, self-regulated conduct, not accepted from others or influenced by the vulgar breath.
> 5. Reticent, reserved, not many acquaintances, but a few intimate friends. Belonging to no societies perhaps. Carrying in his face the character so plainly to be seen there by the most casual observer, that nobody ever makes to him a dishonorable proposal.[39]

This is an excellent concise statement of the values to which men of superior qualities attach importance. But it is most interesting as a revelation of what Eliot himself considered the "durable satisfactions of life."

This was a matter much on the mind of Charles W. Eliot. To it he devoted many of his writings and public addresses. His preoccupation with this problem furnishes a significant point of contrast with the devotion of men like John D. Rockefeller to money making.

•

Some idea of Eliot's writings can be gleaned from the following list: *The Happy Life* (1896); *Five American Contributions to Civilization, and other Essays and Addresses* (1897); *Educational Reform, Essays and Addresses 1869-1897* (1898); *More Money for the Public Schools* (1903); *Four American Leaders—Franklin, Washington, Channing, and Emerson* (1906); "University Administration" (1908); and with F. H. Storer, a *Compendious Manual of Qualitative Chemical Analysis* (Boston, 1869; many times reissued and revised).

Rockefeller's writings were, with one exception, confined to business documents, of which the infamous "letter to Mrs. F. N. Backus," a widow whose lubricating oil company valued at $200,000 he "took over" for $79,000, furnishes an interesting example, (November 13, 1878). Most of his writings consisted of contracts such as that dictated by him for freight rebates between The South Improvement Company, (a Rockefeller masquerade), and the Pennsylvania Railroad (January 18, 1872) ; and corporation charters such as the "Act of Incorporation of the Standard Oil Company" (January 10, 1870). The volume of *Random Reminiscences* (1909) was Rockefeller's one contribution to literature. It does him no injustice to place a higher value on his other writings.

•

At twenty-four, an age when Rockefeller was already successfully launched in th produce business, Eliot was an assistant professor of chemistry at Harvard University, and at a miserable salary compared to the earnings of the quantity-minded monster with whom I am comparing him.

By the time he was thirty-five, Eliot had studied chemistry and foreign educational methods in Europe, served as professor of analytical chemistry in the newly established Massachusetts Institute of Technology, and been elected President of Harvard University. During the same period of his life, Rockefeller had laid the foundations for the first American trust. The methods of the feudal barons of old having been rendered obsolete by the changes which industrialism and democracy imposed upon quantity minded men, Rockefeller showed the captains of industry how to prey with even more efficiency upon an entire nation.

At thirty-five Eliot began that career of educational reform and university administration which so largely occupied the next forty years of his life. With Johns Hopkins, Harvard under Eliot led in the work of making graduate schools efficient educational instruments. The Harvard elective system was thoroughly established by him. The raising of entrance requirements, which led to a corresponding raising of the standards of the secondary schools, and the introduction of an element of choice in these requirements, which allowed a limited election of studies to secondary pupils, became national influences as a result of his advocacy of these measures. He urged the abandonment of brief disconnected "in formation" courses and the correlation of the subjects taught; the equal rank in college requirements of subjects in which equal time, consecutiveness and concentration were demanded, and a more thorough study of English composition. He worked to unify the entire educational system, minimize prescription, eliminate monotony, and introduce freedom and enthusiasm and to insure special training for special work. He was the first to suggest co-operation by colleges in holding common entrance examinations throughout the country, and it was largely through his efforts that standards for entrance were established which made this possible. He contended that secondary schools maintained by public funds should shape their courses for the benefit of students whose education goes no further than such high schools, and not be mere training schools for the universities—a contention which shows that he clearly recognized the different capacities for the acquisition of education in various types of human beings. His success as administrator and man of affairs and as educational reformer made him one of the great figures of his time. What he said on any topic was a subject of deep interest among thoughtful people throughout the country, while his annal reports as President of Harvard were accepted as contributions to the literature of education rather than routine reports to a Board of Trustees.

During the corresponding period of his life, Rockefeller made himself a billionaire. The Standard Oil Company was made to bestride American finance like a Colossus of Rhodes. Frenzied finance under his ægis produced a crop of millionaires, and an even larger crop of bankruptcies and suicides. He was indicted for conspiracy but not convicted. One of his companies was fined twenty-nine million dollars, which of course, the government never collected. The original oil trust he had formed was finally dissolved for violating the Sherman Anti-Trust Law, but its parts were promptly re-organized by Rockefeller so that their activities made him even wealthier than he was before.

•

While Eliot was busy with his life work, he was public spirited enough to take an active interest in civil service reform and private spirited enough to be a successful husband and father and to produce a son who became one of the country's ablest landscape architects.

Rockefeller's public side-line was to debauch legislators, and his private contribution to posterity a son notable for the fact that he became the greatest Baptist layman of the world. Only after the years produced some realization in him that there were other things in the world besides money-making did he begin that series of contributions to philanthropy which in quantity outshone the philanthropies of all contemporaneous captains of industry, much as the robber barons of the Middle Ages felt that a worthy end to a lifetime of rapacity required a series of imposing contributions to the Church which should if possible outshine those of their hated rivals.

I have compared Charles W. Eliot to John D. Rockefeller in order to make plainer by contrast what I mean by the qualityminded man and what I mean by the quantity-minded man. It is not possible, however, to make a similar comparison between Eliot and John Doe—between the quality-minded man and the herdminded man—for John is unfortunately a mere effort to personalize an abstraction. But a memorable coincidence makes such a comparison quite superfluous.

Charles W. Eliot died on August 22, 1926.

On August 23, 1926, Rudolph Valentino, the movie actor, the great "lover" of the screen, the idol of the masses, died. The death of Valentino was a first page sensation in the daily newspapers. The death of Eliot won obscure paragraphs hidden in the body of the paper.

The reports about the illness of the movie actor were as full and complete as those of a President of the United States. They were telegraphed to every newspaper in the United States. The entire nation knew that Valentino was fatally ill. But few, except those personally interested, knew that Eliot was also ill. There was no "human interest" in the illness of this great educator; no appeal to the masses in the end of his career, and there was therefore no newspaper forewarning of his death.

While the crowds streamed in an endless hysterical procession past the hier of Valentino; while the mobs broke the decorum of the "funeral church" in which he lay in state by shattering the great plate glass windows, and policemen worked strenuously to maintain order; while special trains brought hysterical Hollywood actresses clear from the Pacific Coast to New York, and the newspapers published pages about their antics at the funeral, Eliot was buried without benefit of the masses and with practically no publicity from the newspapers upon which John Doe relies for so much of his intellectual fodder.

It is, in view of this, unnecessary to point out that the world in which John Doe and his herd-minded fellows exist is a totally different planet from that in which Charles W. Eliot and quality-minded men generally have their being.

•

Why does the quality-minded man feel that the life he would live constitutes the really superior life? There is no answer to be found to this question in the infinite variety of ways in which he earns his living. He may be a creative artist or writer; he may be a professional man; he may be a mechanic; he may be a farmer. It is not what he does so much as how and why he does it that makes it clear that his is the really superior life. He extracts beauty, truth, and goodness from the common stuff of life, no matter what his vocation, much as a miner extracts gold from crude ore, and thus he enables himself and those about him to understand more and to see more, to feel more, and know more than they would otherwise apprehend.

In biographical notes the achievements of the quality-minded man are usually summarized, if he is an author, by a list of his writings, with the years in which they appeared following each contribution in parenthesis, and similar lists of paintings, if an artist, buildings, if an architect, discoveries and researches, if a scientist. It is possible to summarize the life of the quantity-minded man in the same way. Such a summary of a Rockefeller might read: worth one hundred dollars (16); 12,000 dollars (21); 1 1/2 million dollars (23); 12 million dollars (31); 122 million dollars (44); over one billion dollars (57). Change dollars to countries, duchies, nations, and the summary would describe the life of a quantity-minded conqueror of the past, or to converts or churches or monasteries, and it would describe the life of any of the quantity-minded fathers of the church.

The quantity-minded man lives a life inferior to that of the quality-minded man—the life of a John D. Rockefeller is an inferior life to that of a Charles W. Eliot—because he values too much the mere possession of things that seem to him tangible: land, money, buildings, soldiers, policemen, laws, facts. These things because they seem so real, interest and fascinate men of ordinary minds. They are important to him, and their acquisition motivates his activities. Naturally he is objective, rather than subjective; to use William James's expression, tough-minded rather than tender-minded, and in the language of the man on the street, "hard-boiled" and not "sissified." The desire to win—to win more territory, more converts, more subjects, more money—dominates the thought of the quantity-minded man. This desire to win, this pre-occupation with the means of winning, precludes objective consideration of his own activities. It leaves him no time for the development of an intellectual attitude. Money is his final measure of his business achievement. Every moment of his time must be made to pay, and to produce a tangible return as promptly as possible. He has no time to waste upon investigation; upon weighing evidence; upon considered decisions, much less upon effort at understanding and creating superior values.

In their reaction to the things which this civilization produces; the things which are the object of its economic activities; the things which are made to be bought and sold, and the services which are rendered for money by one individual or group to other individuals or groups, is to be found a very significant difference between the quantity-minded and the quality-minded.

The quantity-minded react to how many; how large; how expensive.

The quality-minded react to how fine; how unique; how beautiful.

The one is interested in magnitudes; the other in forms.

•

The quantity-minded man likes to think, and endlessly proclaim, that he is a practical man. The quality-minded man is, as a matter of fact, generally an even greater respecter of facts than the so-called practical man. In many respects, what he calls the intellectual's theoretical notions are actually much more practical, much better adapted to achieve the ends that the intellectual has in view than are the methods which seem so practical to him. The essential difference between the quality-minded man and the acquisitive, power-seeking man lies in the considered thought the intellectual puts into his activities, and the great value he attaches to ideas—ethical ideas, intellectual ideas, esthetic ideas. Tangible things acquire their value to him only as they promote in some way the ideas which interest him and which he values.

To illustrate. Consider the tubes of oil-paint which an artist uses in painting. To the artist, the tubes of paint have a value that is related to the purpose for which he uses them. If the tubes he has can be used in his painting, they are useful; if not, they are useless. To him the tubes of paints are mere vehicles for the expression of his ideas in color. They acquire value for him, at any given time, by virtue of their qualities as colors. Because it helps him to paint well, he probably knows something about the pigments, the oils, and the driers of which they are composed. From his standpoint all knowledge is practical in the extreme which may help him to express his ideas in his painting.

But to the quantity-minded business man, these tubes of paint are something altogether different. They are a measurable number of items of merchandise, having certain money values, and useful to the extent to which they enable him directly and indirectly to get what he wants out of life—usually money. To him the artist's fascination in the work of using them to express his ideas seems a sort of mental aberration. He can to some extent make allowance for it, on the assumption that the artist is foolish enough to believe that he will be lucky enough to find some equally foolish buyer who will make him famous and pay him a lot of money for his pictures. But he cannot understand why it is that, while the artist is often interested in the fame and the money, he is often more interested in the idea he is trying to express that money and fame lose their savor for him if they are procured at the sacrifice of freedom to express himself. It is easy to understand why the business man more or less despises a man who devotes his time to the pursuit of apparently intangible values such as this instead of devoting himself to enriching himself from his activities, and why the quality-minded man is doubly despised when the business man succeeds in using for his own enrichment ideas of the artist's which he happens to grasp and is able to exploit.

•

The great masses of average men and women, on the other hand, hate and despise the intellectual individual because they cannot understand the ideas in which he is interested; cannot grasp the abstractions which seem so important to him; doubt whether the values to which he devotes himself have any reality at all. Mr. Everett Dean Martin tells of an occasion when it was announced to a crowd in a New York theatre that only twelve men in the world could understand Einstein's theory of relativity. *The crowd hissed.*

The masses are confirmed in this hatred of the sensitive and the learned man because the "practical" men who rule and lead them and who are intent upon accumulating things which they can see and feel and taste and which they too would like to possess, confirm them in their belief in the value of things as they are.

All leadership of the masses requires the practice of demagogy. The leaders of the masses tend to subscribe to cant and buncumbe in public, even when they are intelligent enough to scorn it in private. Even when they do not need to flatter the masses in this way in order to attain power or wealth—when they are born to these things and inherit them—they still employ it in order to retain the positions which they already have. The Tzar of Russia, born to autocratic power, was of necessity a demagogue; he had to placate the stupid muzhiks in his dominions with the pomp and piety of Orthodox Greek Catholicism. A fortuitous concordance of accidents—the ambitions of Stephen Douglas, the fears of the Southern Democrats, the split in the Democratic party, the impotence of the Whigs—made possible the election of Abraham Lincoln in 1860. But he had to turn demagogue in order to keep the tired populace fighting for an idea—for an abstraction—the preservation of the Union.

Is it any wonder that the masses fear the intellectual? Even if they could be made to grasp the ideas in which the intellectual is interested, they cannot become interested in them, because their leaders, whether a Tzar or a Lincoln, insulate them against novel ideas.

•

But this process of insulating the masses against exceptional men is true not only of their political leaders—it is true of their leaders in the pulpit and in the press. Let me quote from a very popular writer for the masses, Albert Payson Terhune. In an article which was entitled, "A Roughneck's Religion," published in a magazine which has a circulation of 2,200,000, he said:

> Not from the Roughneck has come the horde of sneers at religion, either now or in the past. The Roughneck has ever been sound, to the core. He has left doubts and atheism and higher criticism and the like to the Intelligentsia ("the Highbrow Bunch," as he would call them); and to the Parlor Intellectuals who go smugly on, thinking 44-caliber thoughts with 22-caliber brains, and seeking to lead the Roughneck unleadables.
>
> I like the Roughneck. Perhaps I like and understand him because I am one of him; and because, off and on, for a half-century, I have associated much with him. It is he who is the backbone of religion—not of dogma nor of quibble, but of the terribly simple and irresistible religion which made him stand in silent prayer at a prize fight.
>
> So it was, nearly two thousand years ago, when Christ walked

> the earth. The Bible tells us: THE COMMON PEOPLE HEARD HIM, GLADLY, and that the Scribes and Pharisees did not. Even in that day, you see, the Roughneck and the Intelligentsia were arrayed in opposite religions camps.[40]

•

"There is no expedient," says Sir Joshua Reynolds, "to which men will not resort to avoid the necessity of thinking." Relatively few men enjoy thinking. This is the quality-minded man's greatest departure from the mass. He is "sicklied o'er with the pale cast of thought." He is never satisfied with things as they are, but constantly striving to live life as he thinks it should be lived; to devote his time to occupations to which it is worthwhile devoting life; to produce during it the things that will really increase the sum total of beauty and understanding. Is it any wonder that the masses ridicule him; sometimes persecute him, and when incited to it by their leaders, actually crucify the man who really under takes to make them think?

•

Henry Adams said about some of the ideas of the scientists of the nineties that they "were occult, supersensual, irrational; they were a revelation of mysterious energy like that of the Cross; they were what, in terms of mediæval science, were called immediate modes of the divine substance." This can be said equally truly of all ideas, the understanding and creation of which the quality minded man imposes upon himself and for which he is so often penalized under the present state of affairs.

It is simply impossible to measure the power of ideas. By comparison with them, all the other powers with which man plays are infantile. Ideas make economic power seem insubstantial. Political power seems even less substantial than economic. Physical power, whether mechanical as in a dynamo or animal as in an athlete, seems the least substantial of all. All these forms of power last hardly a few generations. But ideas have endured, some of them, throughout the centuries of recorded history. Some which go back to prehistoric periods are still with us, sometimes in their original form, and sometimes in reincarnations. There are such hardy and enduring ideas as those of personal immortality, and of the existence of a god. Though false as the devil (who symbolizes another enduring idea) they will probably in one form or another endure forever. There are such ideas as those of the Buddha—the idea of Nirvana; there is the Christian idea of the vicarious atonement; and there are the ideas of Confucius about the supreme value of wisdom. These ideas have not only the power to endure, but the power to spread from person to person, nation to nation, continent to continent by channels as mysterious, when viewed from a distant perspective, as that in which electricity and magnetism travel. So it is with ideas which are embodied in philosophy, in art, in music, in science; in comparison the powers which the quantity-minded man is able to seize and for which the average man hopes, are mère ephemeral toys.

The child thinks that the toys for which it longs and which it manages to acquire are far more desirable than the strange, and to it incomprehensible things, which adults prize.

Knowing the superiority of ideas—their greater "dynamic" and "kinetic" power, and the superiority both as occupation and entertainment of the understanding and creation of ideas—the quality-minded man can look, if he is free, at the activities of the rest of mankind, its preoccupation with money, political office, with automobiles, and similarly apparently substantial things, much as an adult looks at a child's preoccupation with its toys.

•

We come now to the question of the effect upon the quality-minded type of man of the domination of human activities by the factory and by the needs of a factory civilization.

The factory has changed but little the fundamental relationship of the quality-minded man, the quantity-minded man, and the average man to one another. With one hand it has increased the opportunities of the three types of individuals into which we have resolved mankind to make life itself more dignified and the individual life richer and more comfortable, and with the other it has decreased them. In our industrial democracies the intellectual is generally politically and economically freer than he was under the agricultural feudalism which preceded it.

The intellectual of the aristocratic class, it is true, enjoyed a considerable degree of freedom, suffering only the handicaps which his kings and his priests imposed upon him. The intellectual of non-aristocratic lineage, however, was dependent for the opportunity to live an expressive life upon the patronage of nobles and churchmen. Industrial society such as we now know has replaced the former variety of dispensers of patronage with a new variety. There has been an exchange of patronage by aristocrats to patronage by capitalists and politicians. If the exchange has made it possible for quality-minded men to enjoy a greater measure of personal freedom, it has been secured by the sacrifice of the patronage of the much more discriminating aristocratic class.

Unfortunately, the factory tends to an increasing extent to destroy the value of this greater freedom by forcing the modern intellectual to engage in the production of trivia. In this way it is actually hindering the quality-minded man from occupying himself with the work of contributing to the beauty of civilization and to the understanding of life.

Our factory economy restricts the freedom of the quality-minded man by forcing him to devote himself to the satisfaction of the tangible desires of the masses. It exerts a pressure upon him through his economic needs; he finds that he must serve the factory directly, or compromise on some sort of service for it, in order to live.

The service is sometimes direct and sometimes indirect. If he engages in some sort of work for a factory, then of course he is yielding to this pressure by serving it directly. If he tries to devote himself to work which apparently has no relationship to the factory—as for instance, to teaching—he finds that the whole institution of education is oriented toward the needs of the factory. He finds that he is yielding to the same pressure and serving the factory indirectly. The business men who form the boards of trustees of modern schools and colleges are as effective curbs upon the teachers of today, as the aristocrats and the churchmen were in the period before the Darwinian era.

The factory concerns itself with multiplying our tangible wants and these are made so engrossing that no one is given time, even if he has the inclination, to supply the world with desirable ideas.

Ideas must still be smuggled into the world precisely as they had to be smuggled in during the past. Until the man who is interested in ideas and who produces new ideas is really free to do so—free economically, socially, and politically—neither he himself, nor the world at large will really be able to live in mental and physical comfort.

•

It is true that what the really superior man produces; what he extracts out of his life, however circumscribed; what he expresses in his work and in his moral, political, economic and social philosophy, is ultimately accepted by mankind. But ultimately is generally a very long time. The bones of the pioneers are often bleached very white before their ideas are generally understood and before they are accepted by mankind as a whole. There is a lag—a tragic lag both for the quality-minded man and for mankind as a whole—between the time of the conception of new ideas and the time of their acceptance.

The lag between the time when the earth was first conceived as a globe by the Pythagorean philosophers and the time when the fact was accepted by Ferdinand and Isabella was a period of hundreds of years. The idea that the globe is round has not yet been accepted by the entire unthinking masses of Christendom, while the numbers in Africa and Asia who have not heard of it is staggering.

The quality-minded man sometimes consoles himself with the thought that the ideas which his contemporaries reject will be gratefully accepted by a distant posterity. But the consolation is hardly very great. He turns to this consolation not because he is indifferent to recognition of his work by his contemporaries, but because that is about all that he can find in order to justify his working at all.

What is very badly needed is to shorten the lag between the conception of new ideas and their acceptance by mankind. Today it is the needs of the factory that prevent further shortening of this lag, just as the church prevented any shortening of it in the immediate past. It may be impossible to eliminate the lag entirely. But even in our time it could be shortened if quality-minded men in considerable numbers were to make themselves independent of the factory. The factory's demands upon them mean either an abandonment of intellectual life or an interference with the spread of the ideas which come out of such a life. They must free themselves from the factory and the businessman, partly for mankind's sake and partly for their own.

Only by freeing themselves can they dictate to the quantity minded masters of the masses the terms upon which they will furnish the intellectual and artistic effort the world must have if society is to function well.

Only by freeing themselves can they insist that their ideas, and not the dead and decaying flotsam and jetsam of old ideas, of superstitions, of outworn values, of trivia of small minds—shall rule mankind.

Only by freeing themselves can they attain a position in which they can shorten the lag between the time that new ideas are produced by them and the time the new ideas are accepted by the world.

•

Factories operate profitably only when directed by men who are content to devote themselves to substantially the same task year after year; when directed by men who can for a whole lifetime devote themselves to the problem of making the same product, of hiring and firing those whom they employ to make and sell it, and of financing and earning profits from the marketing of one product. The men who are willing to devote their lives to this sort of work, to administering the factories, to creating markets for their products and to training in school and college those who can administer, and sell and advertise, are robots—sublimated robots it is true, but just as truly robots as the laborers who tend and feed the machines in their factories. Quality-minded men simply cannot do that sort of work. They are neither tough enough to stand the strain of the administrative and executive work in factories, nor thoughtless enough to be unconscious of the boredom of spending their lives at work of that sort.

Quality-minded men have something to say, something to express, something to contribute upon other aspects of life than that of production and distribution. But it is impossible for them to say it, even though it means life more abundantly for all, if they are harnessed in a treadmill in which production and distribution absorb the best that is in them.

•

In ages when quality-minded men are largely free to express themselves, the world enjoys a period of high civilization. In ages when they are prevented from doing so, we have a period of darkness.

A dark age is merely one in which the educational influence of intelligent men has in some manner been destroyed. It is the educational influence of the intellectual minority of quality minded men that makes for light. A dark age is one in which the normal functioning of this minority has in some manner been prevented.

The educational influence of quality-minded men is great when they are free to say what they think, and almost nil when they are constrained by church, government, or business to say what they do not really believe.

Quality-minded men are a sort of leavening in the lump of mankind. They produce ideas, create beauty, promote understanding. Willy nilly, mankind ultimately accepts what they prescribe. It accepts their ideas slowly, reluctantly, inappreciatively. There are long periods of time when mankind because of an obsession with such a thing as religion, or such a thing as feudalism, or such a thing as industrialism, abandons the whole cargo of things truly civilized; when it sinks into a dark age because it has forced its intellectuals into the cloisters, into the armies, or into the factories.

Between the Spartans and the Macedonians, the civilization created by the Greek intellectuals was destroyed.

Between the Goths and the Christians, the civilization which the intellectuals built in Rome was destroyed. Solon and Alexander, Alaric and Constantine were practical men. They knew what they wanted and proceeded to get it even though that involved driving the intellectuals into slavery, into war, or into the church.

The Renaissance was merely a re-emergence of the intellectuals —a period when the Catholic Church was forced by the humanists to permit them to function. Just as the age of science was merely a period which began when the Darwins, Huxleys, Tyndalls and

Haeckels were able to force the entire Christian world once again to permit the intellectuals to function.

•

There is little, if any, spontaneous progress in the ideas, the work, the life of the masses of average men. They are clay shaped from age to age by very small minorities of men.

And nothing much from within themselves makes for progress and culture in acquisitive, power seeking, quantity-minded individuals. Their very toughness enables them to maintain their leadership whether society be savage, barbarian, or civilized. And their preoccupation with accumulation prevents them from devoting time to the objective thinking which produces spontaneous changes and improvements.

Both the quantity-minded leaders and the herd-minded masses of average men suffer from inertia; sometimes the inertia of mass, and sometimes that of motion. In the Middle Ages it was a static inertia—today it is a dynamic inertia.

But quality-minded men are forever spontaneously progress ing: that is the thing that makes them different from their fellows.

Let anything happen which prevents them from functioning; let them cease to put forth ideas, and society ossifies at first and then collapses into darkness. The body lives on but its brain ceases to function. Darkness comes on for all; for the quality-minded, for the quantity-minded, and for the herd-minded masses.

•

I believe that the factory menaces the very existence of this leaven in the lump of mankind.

The factory, as it spreads, leaves quality-minded men no escape from the horror of doing one thing over and over again in exactly the same way once they have been forced to turn to it for a livelihood. The business men who operate factories do not have to escape from it because they are insensitive to its horrors. Henry Ford says:

> When you come right down to it most jobs are repetitive. A businessman has a routine that he follows with great exactness; the work of a bank president is nearly all routine; the work of under officers

> and clerks in a bank is purely routine. Indeed, for most purposes and most people, it is necessary to establish something in the way of a routine and to make motions purely repetitive—otherwise the individual will not get enough done to be able to live off his own exertions.[41]

It is only for repetitive workers—for the semi-skilled laborer, the "productive" salesman and the efficient business executive that there is real demand and real opportunity in our factory dominated civilization.

If the factory is permitted to continue forcing quality-minded individuals into its repetitive regime; if it continues to deprive them of the opportunity to earn their living in ways which enable them to express the best that is within them; if it ever succeeds in destroying completely their life as intellectuals—a task to which schools, colleges, and universities are to an increasing extent devoting themselves: making potential quality-minded men into quantity-minded salesmen, short story writers, advertising men, commercial artists—then we shall have a new dark age. We shall suffer a repetition of the disaster which the Catholic Church inflicted upon mankind when it forced every intelligent person into the cloisters by offering him the alternative of conformity or of excommunication and extinction.

•

There is no doubt that mankind has already made its choice. We are not at a cross-road. We are not confronted by two roads, one leading to a factory-dominated world and a socialistic civilization, and the other to an art-dominated world and an individualistic civilization. We have long since passed the cross-road. We are far along the road that leads to the goal of perfect industrialization.

It may be true, as Glenn Frank says, that it is too late to retrace our steps—that the real task before us is to adapt ourselves to what lies before us—to find silver linings in the clouds of encircling darkness. If it is too late for mankind to avoid what seems to me the abyss, then let those who prefer to drift with the tide no longer deceive themselves about what the present civilization in its ultimate perfection will become. Imaginative individuals are already describing it. The robots in *R.U.R.* are allegorical figures, it is true, but they are prophetic too.

Those who do not care to drift with that repetitive tide must free themselves from those who not only are willing to drift with it but insist that all shall do so. It may be too late to check the descent of mankind to the Avernus. But it is not too late for intellectuals to prevent their own plunge individually into it.

"Men of superior minds," says Confucius, "busy themselves first in getting at the root of things, and when they have succeeded in this, the right course is open to them."[42]

This is good gospel for quality-minded men. Let them place the problem of charting a right course for society in a secondary position, since society is doomed to go where the factory will lead it. Let them think first of the problem of how they should live their own lives.

The individual quality-minded man may not be able to prevent society from plunging into the indignity of a mechanized dark age.

But he may be able to save himself.

BOOK II

THE CONQUEST OF COMFORT

If the goal of humanity be still lacking, is there not also lacking—humanity itself?

—Thus Spake Zarathustra.

PART IV
THE MATERIAL ASPECT

Creating—That is the salvation from suffering, and life's alleviation.

—*Thus Spake Zarathustra*.

CHAPTER XIII
COMFORT

It is easy to see why we have come to believe that the unending increase in production which the factory makes possible must ultimately make all mankind comfortable.

Until the coming of the factory, population pressed upon subsistence. Malthus enunciated a law that seemed inexorable: mankind's capacity for populating the earth was greater than mankind's capacity for producing the means of subsistence. But with the coming of the factory, capacity for production began to overtake capacity for consumption. Today it has reached the point where aggregate production presses upon aggregate consumption.

Our captains of industry have actually turned to stimulating consumption in order to create a market for all that their factories can produce.

Is it any wonder that we have come to believe that the factory is destined not only to end the age of want but to usher in an era of golden plenty?

•

If we assume that an insufficiency of creature comforts is the principal cause of our discomfort, then the factory does seem the answer to our quest of comfort.

But comfort has qualitative as well as quantitative aspects. It is not enough that we should be able to secure a sufficiency of the necessities and luxuries we desire.

There is no conquest of comfort if the things that satisfy our wants are secured at the sacrifice of our capacity for enjoying them.

And the capacity for enjoyment seems inextricably interwoven with the methods by which we create what we consume.

•

It is not impossible for society to insure to all its members the essentials of normal living: food, shelter, clothing and other necessaries; self-expressive work; a normal sex-life including parentage; an education and a social environment in accord with its own aspirations.

Primitive societies often do it.

But the industrialized states, even with modern science to assist them, seem unable to do so. They fail because they have consecrated themselves to the production of wealth and not to the production of comfort.

That comfort is to be attained through an unending increase of production is a fallacy. It is more nearly true to say that it is to be secured not by producing as much as possible but as little as possible. Comfort really depends upon producing only as much as is compatible with enjoyment of the work of production itself.

It is because the factory production of food, clothing, shelter and the trivia of existence is being secured at a sacrifice of self-expression in labor, of a normal sex-life and parentage, and a desirable educational and social life that the quest of comfort through the factory is beginning to prove disappointing.

Mankind, by its too great devotion to the sheer increase in the production of creature comforts, is making it impossible to attain the comfort it has in view. It would be pathetic if it were not so tragic: mankind forever seeking to attain a comfort which it seems forever doomed to lose.

•

What is comfort?

Comfort is a condition of freedom from involuntary, unjust, or imposed pain, cold, hunger and other distresses of the body. Comfort is a state of moderate, temperate, stable physical well-being. It does not preclude activity—even strenuous and adventurous activity. Activity and intense exertion destroy comfort only when they become meaningless, purposeless and pointless.

But comfort is a condition of mental as well as material well being. We can hardly be comfortable when we are starving or shivering. But we may be warm and well fed and still uncomfortable if we are fearful, credulous, ignorant, insensitive and lack the capacity for discriminating use of the creature comforts which mankind has evolved.

Our present problem is: how can we secure the material essentials of comfort without, in the process of securing them, sacrificing our capacity for really enjoying them? And, is it possible for us to do so—to end our present slavish dependence upon the factory—in the face of the existing dominance of our economic life by the factory and the factory system?

•

Suppose that my contention be granted—that the abolition of all non-essential and undesirable factories would ultimately not only add to the real comfort of mankind but reduce the ugliness of civilization—isn't it a waste of time to discuss an idea that is entirely outside the realm of the possible? Wouldn't it be wiser to accept the inevitable and adapt ourselves to a state of affairs which cannot be changed? Wouldn't it, in short, be wiser to try to make factory production less ugly and factory products more satisfying than to waste time discussing their abolition?

I do not propose to shirk these questions, for while I am interested in the possibility of a civilization less ugly and more comfortable than the one in which we find ourselves, I am equally interested in the practical problems which must be solved to make that civilization a reality, and in the personal problem of individuals who have to live today, before that civilization has been achieved, and while they may have to try individually to achieve comfort. In short, I do not propose to ignore the question of what it may be possible for us to do immediately to free ourselves from the factory.

•

The ugliness and the discomfort that the factory has brought into being can lie almost entirely abolished by the simple expedient of refusing to buy the products of our undesirable and non essential factories. Factory domination of civilization would not very long survive a widespread refusal to patronize these factories. The ugliness inflicted upon civilization and the discomforts imposed upon mankind by factories would disappear with the factories themselves.

True, if a mere handful of individuals were to cease buying the products of these factories, as is all that can at first be hoped for, and very fortunately from a business standpoint, the factories would not be very quickly eliminated. But those who abandoned the buying of these factory products would be gainers in wealth, health and happiness.

As far as the individual is concerned, this is a program which does not have to wait upon a nation-wide "agitation" and "education" and "organization" of great masses of people. No legislation needs to be secured. No political parties need to be formed. It is dependent merely upon individual self-education and discipline. The men and women who enter upon this way to comfort begin the conquest of comfort for themselves even though they are too few in number to conquer comfort for all mankind. Nation-wide agitation, and organization—dangerous methods in the hands of narrow, fanatic, quantity-minded individuals to whom they make an irresistible appeal—might speed the day when the great masses would adopt this way to comfort. They might hasten the day when people in large numbers would stop buying factory products; when lack of patronage would begin to force non-essential factories to close their doors; when the number of factories in the nation would begin to shrink to a more tolerable total. The legions of rain and snow, heat and frost, rust and rot, fungi and vegetation would a little sooner begin the work of reabsorbing the buildings and machinery which the factory workers had been forced to leave.

The process of reducing abandoned factories to picturesque ruins and of returning them to the integral soil and landscape from which they should never have been evoked, might be hastened by the usual methods of organized reformers. But so far as the individual family is concerned it does not have to be.

•

The question is, how can we today abandon any of our buying of factory products and still live? Or, abandon factory products as I believe we can in large part, and live more comfortably than we do today—as we are certainly entitled to live in this age of scientifically possible abundance?

The buying of factory products can be reduced by us to the degree in which we equip and organize our homes to produce what we need and desire for ourselves.

The organized, creative and productive home can free us from our dependence upon the factory. The home of today, as the factory has fashioned it for the factory world's better functioning, cannot.

The home of today usually houses a "natural" family consisting of parents and their unmarried children. It is built around two individuals, often both working outside the home, whom an imperious biologic impulse has trapped into marriage. Because the home of this small family has come to function economically only as a consuming center it is an economic rudiment—a rudiment in the same sense that the os coccyx is a biological rudiment.

Like all rudiments, the modern home tends to shrink and shrivel. It persists in rudimentary form long after it no longer functions as it was originally designed to function.

To be able to abandon the buying of the products of our non essential and undesirable factories, and still be comfortable, the home must be reorganized—it must be made into an economically creative institution. It must cease being a mere consumption unit. It must become a production unit as well. It must be as nearly as possible an organic home—house, land, machines, materials and a group of individuals organized not for mere consumption but for creative and productive living.

To the degree in which families, large or small, and even single individuals organize homes of this sort, to that degree they can free themselves from the factory.

•

While all families today are consuming factory products, all of the families of the country are by no means equally dependent upon them. Rural and urban families both patronize the factory, but differ greatly in their degree of dependence upon it.

The urban family, confined in small space, and tending more and more to live in a kitchenette apartment, is wholly dependent upon the factory. Everything that enters the urban home must be bought. Most of the commodities consumed in it are subjected to factory processing of some sort. But the rural family still produces many of the things it consumes. It produces its own milk and butter, for instance, where the urban family buys canned milk and dairy-made butter. True, it is the tendency of the age for the rural family to imitate the urban family's habits of living more and more. But as long as the rural family remains close to the soil, its dependence upon the factory will be less than that of its city cousin's.

As industrialization progresses, the number of rural families declines, the number of urban families increases. In 1900 only 40 percent of the population of the United States was urban. By 1920 the urban population had become 51.4 percent. In twenty years the rural population—the population on farms or in towns of less than 2,500 population—had declined nearly one-fifth. The proportion of the population almost entirely dependent upon the functioning of the factory is constantly increasing; the proportion which can live independent of the factory, more or less, is constantly decreasing.

The rural family is generally a farming family. In 1920, 61.5 percent of the population classed as rural by the census lived on farms. The farm home, because it is equipped with large kitchens, barns, cellars, sheds and work rooms, and all sorts of tools and equipment, makes a large amount of domestic production practicable. But even when not farming, the rural family usually lives on a plot of land upon which vegetables, fruit and poultry may be raised. It lives nearly always in a house—not a flat. It therefore has much more in the way of storage room and space for domestic productive effort than the city family.

The urban family usually lives in rented quarters and to an increasing extent in flats and not in houses. Only 37.4 percent of the urban population owns homes; 62.6 percent consists of renters. Of the rural population the reverse is true; only 45.1 percent rents its home, and these rural renters live mainly in houses, while the urban renters tend to live in flats.

These facts make it plain that only the rural population of this industrialized country is capable of any wide-spread action upon my proposal that the public should refuse to patronize the non-essential and undesirable factories. The urban population, before it can act upon it to any considerable extent, will have to provide itself with some of the facilities for domestic production which the rural population already possesses.

But if a considerable number of the farmers, who form so large a part of the rural population of the country, acted upon my proposal, this would be sufficient to precipitate an industrial counter-revolution. The whole citadel of undesirable industrialism would collapse. A withdrawal of the buying power represented by this immense group of consumers would make it plain that present day over-industrialization is supported upon the flimsiest of economic foundations.

If farmers but knew it, they would realize that they have everything to gain, and little to lose by insuring that collapse.

•

The farmer of our pioneer period was economically as well as politically free. The land policy of the early republic, with its liberal homestead laws, served temporarily, at least, to destroy feudal land ownership, which had kept the agriculturists of previous epochs in a condition of slavery and serfdom and which is still the principal factor in keeping the farmers of most of the world in a condition of peasantry.

Land was free to the homesteader. The pioneers had only to occupy it, build houses upon it, fence it, cultivate it—they had, in short, only to use it and it was theirs. Free land made it possible for every pioneer family to be economically self-sufficient. For land furnished them nearly everything that they needed. It furnished them stone and lumber for their buildings; grain, fruit and meat for their table; wood for fuel; flax, wool, furs and hides for their clothing; while the trees, minerals, clay and stone of their neighborhood furnished them raw materials out of which they fashioned nearly every implement which they used.

Theirs was a hard and a primitive life, it is true. Yet hard as it was; primitive as it was; it still furnished something—perhaps a crude plenty combined with self-sufficiency—which made pioneering attractive to the great masses of the more settled sections of the country. In spite of the ample knowledge of the hardships, the privations, and the dangers of the life, men and women of all kinds answered the call of the free land.

It is not necessary to go over the process, step by step, by which the hard and crude life of the self-sufficient farmers of our pioneer period evolved into the hard but much less crude life of the utterly dependent farmers of today. The life of the pioneer farmer was little affected by the rise and fall of the prices in volatile produce markets. A bounteous crop, instead of bringing a small return for the greater labor involved in harvesting it, meant to the self sufficient pioneer farmers a winter of plenty and content. Today, the farmers are gamblers who may be ruined by a bounteous crop. They live well when the market quotations on cotton, corn, wheat, eggs, milk are high and live poorly when they are low. A sharp fall in prices wipes out their capital; reduces them to poverty; drives them to the city. It transforms them from dependent farmers into even more dependent urban factory workers.

•

The responsibility for the destruction of the independence of our American farmers can be attributed largely to the application of the factory system to our agriculture. Specialization upon the production of one crop destroyed the diversified agriculture of the past and replaced it with the factory agriculture of today. The diversified agriculture in which each farmer produced grain, fruit, and garden crops, livestock and animal products for his own use as well as for sale has been replaced by the present factory agriculture in which each farmer produces for the market one crop, such as cotton or wheat, or one kind of livestock (perhaps also raising feed for the stock) as in dairying and poultry farming. With farming by the factory system, farmers tend to sell all that they produce and to buy all that they consume.

Specialization enables the farmers to effect all the economies of factory production. But it involves their selling what they produce at wholesale in the primary market and their buying what they consume at retail in the consumer market.

The enormous quantities of each crop which have to be marketed yearly create distribution costs which the farmers themselves have to absorb because they are unable to shift them to the consuming public. Manufacturers can add freight, sales and advertising costs to the prices they receive for their manufactured products. But the freights, commissions, shrinkages and spoilages on the cotton, wheat, corn, hogs, cattle, fruit which farmers produce for the market are deducted from the prices which they secure. The farmers have to be content with what is left after these costs have been deducted from the market quotations. What they gain through factory methods in lower costs of production, they lose in the hazards of marketing and in the higher prices which they pay for what they buy.

But in making themselves into "manufacturing animals," to use the expressive phrase of Adam Smith, they have also had to make themselves into "selling animals" and "buying animals." Wheat farmers produce wheat, and often nothing else. They sell wheat, and with the money received for their wheat they buy flour, condensed milk, canned vegetables, packing-house meat and packaged cereals.

Cattlemen, producing steers for slaughter, though they must have herds of cows to produce their calves, milk none of them. They sell beef and they buy canned milk.

Dairymen, on the other hand, produce nothing but milk and cream. With the money received for their products they buy feed for their stock and beef for their table, both often raised thousands of miles away from the farms on which they are consumed.

Specialization, it is true, enables farmers to use machinery to lighten their labor, and to increase the total amount of their production. But it puts the farmers in the same unenviable position in which our manufacturers find themselves: able to produce much more than the market will absorb at a profit. Specialization tends to force them to go on producing without adequate return for the risk, the capital and the labor involved.

As a result farmers generally have been relegated to a situation in which they labor for a smaller return than that of the lowliest and poorest paid unskilled laborers. They get less than the unskilled laborers, yet they risk their capital, take grave responsibilities and assume the burden of solving difficult administrative problems. And in addition their work includes much manual labor more arduous than that of the average industrial laborer.

More specialization and more buying of factory products can only result in increasing the supply of what they have to sell and increasing the demand for what they buy. The prices they would receive for the wheat, corn, cotton, hogs and all the other produce they raise would be still further depressed; the prices on the products they buy would be still further raised.

•

There are 6,448,343 farms of all kinds in the United States. Of these 3,925,090 are operated by farmers who own their farms and 68,449 by managers who operate them for the owners. Approximately 2,454,804 are operated by tenant-farmers. Of the farm-owning farmers about 2,074,325 own their farms free from debt; 1,461,306 are mortgaged on an average for $3,356.

We have thus three classes of farmers, all of whom can take some steps toward economic freedom, but who are differently situated as to the extent to which they can do so.

First, the tenant-farmers who have to produce a cash crop large enough to pay the rental for the farm they occupy.

Second, the mortgaged farm-owners who have to produce a cash crop large enough to pay interest averaging from $200 to $250 per year and often something on the principal of their indebtedness.

Third, the free and clear farm-owners who are in position to reduce their cash crops to a size which will earn them just enough for taxes, and to pay for those things which they cannot make for themselves and which they must buy from the factories.

If any considerable proportion of these three classes of farmers were to make even a partial step toward economic freedom the industrial counter-revolution would cease to be a mere figure of speech. It would become an actuality.

•

Why shouldn't farmers reduce their production of cash crops to the barest minimum that will enable them to get enough cash for their fixed expenses and for the factory products they absolutely must buy? If great numbers of them were to cut down production in this way, there would be a reversal of the customary excess of supply over demand in the various farm produce markets. There would be smaller supplies of grain, of hogs, of steers, of eggs, of poultry, of vegetables and of fruit. Demand, however, would be the same. Prices would soar. The farmers might actually get a greater cash return for the little that they would produce than they now get for producing as bountifully as hard work and modern agricultural methods and machinery make it possible for them to produce.

That this would inevitably follow has been demonstrated over and over again.

Taking most of the important crops produced in the years 1926 and 1924 for comparative purposes because in those two years the purchasing power of the dollar was almost exactly equal, we find that the farmers generally received a larger return for the smaller of the crops they produced.

In 1926, the farmers produced 2,645,031 bushels of corn; in 1924, they produced 2,309,414 bushels—which is 335,617 bushels less than in 1926. Yet they received $2,266,771,000 for the smaller crop and only $1,703,430,000 for the larger one. They were paid $563,341,000 more for producing 335,617 bushels less of corn. When they brought a large crop of corn to market they received 64.4 cents for each bushel, but when they brought a small one, they received 98.2 cents! A comparison of yields and prices of twenty-three of the most important crops in these two years shows that in the case of twenty of them the farmers received a higher aggregate money return in the year in which they brought the smallest crop to market. But for the coincidence of a large wheat crop in the United States in the same year when all the other wheat growing countries produced small ones, the money return in 1926, when they raised the smaller wheat crop, would also have been larger than in 1924, when they raised a larger one.

Let farmers produce primarily for their own consumption and cease to produce bountiful surpluses which benefit only city dwellers, and each individual farm family will receive more for the little surplus it sells than if it had specialized on one crop and produced a superabundance of it.

•

Let the farmers of the country devote the time which the cutting down of cash crops would leave on their hands to the production on their own farms and in their own homes of everything for their own consumption that it is practicable for them to produce.

Let them raise everything that the regions in which they are located and the particular pieces of land they cultivate make it possible for them to raise for their own table, and store and preserve what they will need for winter when the growing season is over.

Let them frankly recognize that farming is naturally a part-time occupation. There are certain seasons of the year when it makes relatively little demand upon them. At such times the members of the farm family should turn to crafts of various kinds with which to earn the money to buy the products they feel necessary to their comfort which it is impractical for them to make themselves. They should be crafts which can be carried on at home or in its neighborhood.

Let them go back for their principles of operating to the pioneers though not back to the primitive methods which the pioneers used. For they can use the methods and the machines which the past century and a half of scientific progress have developed to make themselves as independent as were the pioneers while yet avoiding the heartbreaking and backbreaking hardships and hard work of pioneer life.

That they would cut down their buying of factory products is obvious. But in addition they would greatly lower the prices which they would have to pay for the factory products which they did buy. For while they were cutting down the total demand for factory products, the factory's production of them would go on for some time at the same pace, and for a long time at a pace far in excess of demand. Prices of factory products would go down, because supply would so greatly exceed demand.

If enough farmers did these things, or all farmers did them to some extent, they would bring about a farmers' millennium: high prices for the limited quantities of farm produce that they brought into the wholesale market, and low prices for the limited numbers of factory products that they bought in the retail market. Even if only a few farmers were to act upon these proposals, and the millennium did not for that reason develop, each of these independent souls and their families would be economically more free than they are today. They would live more comfortably than they do today, without a bit harder work, and without the risks and responsibilities of factory farming.

•

What a gorgeous prospect this possible declaration of independence by the farmers of the world presents to the speculative imagination!

For any considerable movement of this sort would produce far reaching dislocations in the delicate economic machinery of present day industrial civilization. Hard times would plague the cities: bankruptcies, financial panics and bread lines would become chronic.

The self-sufficient farmers could reciprocate the indifference with which their city cousins view the present plight of agriculture.

The railroads, confronted by the great shrinkage of freight, both of agricultural and industrial products, would be at their wits' ends to meet even essential operating expenses: they would have to raise freight rates over and over again in order to keep any trains running at all. This might prove a blessing in the long run. For with higher freight rates, neighborhood factories would have restored to them the natural economic advantages of location. The big factories would find it almost impossible to compete with them because of the freight differential which would be operating against them as distant producers. The neighborhood market would revive, and the farmers would again gain because the cost of the long hauls and of the complicated system of middlemen now needed to distribute their produce in distant markets would no longer be deducted from the prices paid them.

The machines in most of the factories would be stilled. The ugly factory buildings which house them would turn first into picturesque ruins and then dissolve into the elemental earth from which they were originally evoked. The great masses of laborers and white-collar workers now in them would be forced out of their city rabbit-warrens. They would be left with the alternative of going back to the land themselves and doing what the farmers were doing, or of submitting to a process of pauperization followed within a few generations by extinction. The subways, elevateds, street cars would no longer carry stifling, sweating crowds. The beautiful green grass would slowly reclaim the stone and concrete deserts of city streets.

There would be incidental suffering, of course. Unemployment on a vast scale spells starvation. Starvation on a vast scale spells revolution. But revolutions, fortunately, tend always to bring about a re-baptism through land and a re-birth through self-help.

This is a melancholy vision. It should not, however, agitate sensitive souls overmuch. There is little probability that enough farm families would ever make so sensible a change in their manners of life to really stay the conquering course of the factory and the factory system.

But some of the farm families might cut down what they bought of factory products by producing as much as is practicable for their own consumption. Some laborers and office workers' families might follow their example. Some business men's families might; some professional men's families, sick of their parlous position in a factory dominated world, might. Individually each family would gain by such a change in their manner of living. And collectively all would gain if a large enough proportion of the entire population joined in the movement.

•

Today the farm family is farming too much. The industrial, commercial and professional family is farming hardly at all. The farm family should cut down its farming to its own needs; the non-farming family should farm enough to supply itself with the essentials of life. This is the road to economic freedom and economic freedom is essential to the conquest of comfort. For the farmer this is still a comparatively easy road to follow. For the industrial laborer and the office worker, it is a difficult, though not entirely impossible road to follow. For the successful business man it is more difficult because there is no compelling need for him to follow it. But for the quality-minded individual, it is often the only road to comfort. And if he has some sort of craft or profession, it is almost as easy for him to follow as it is for the farmer.

Unfortunately for the millions of city dwellers, who need economic independence just as much as do the farmers, generations of dependence upon the factory have well nigh destroyed their ability to fend for themselves. Most city dwellers, even after years of schooling which includes all that pedagogy has to offer in the way of biology, botany, chemistry, physics and economics, can be put down in an uninhabited but fertile countryside and starve and freeze to death because they have been deprived of any access to dairies, bakeries, delicatessens and to all the stores which contain the factory products to which they are accustomed. They could be furnished with all the tools and implements which the Swiss Family Robinson providentially found, but before they could use them to provide themselves with shelter, clothing, and sustenance, they would the of exposure, of sickness, and of hunger. Their pathetic dependence upon the factory-made necessaries and luxuries of life; the superiority which they feel because they buy things "ready-made," and the sense of inferiority which they feel about what is "home-made"; the pride which many of them display in their inability to use tools—because of their inability "even to drive a nail straight"—renders very remote the prospect that many of them could make themselves economically free.

Generations of dependence upon factory work and factory made products have destroyed their ability to turn to self-sufficiency as a means to the conquest of comfort. The atrophy of the attributes which make man the supremely adaptable animal, makes a further and ever further specialization of their productive and home life both easy and necessary. Any effort to take a considerable step in the other direction, toward independence and individualism, would spell their doom. Only farmers and the more adaptable non-farmer would survive a movement toward individual economic freedom. The rest would all disappear, as did the Roman patricians and their parasitic clients, before the on-rush of the more adaptable Germanic tribes. They would disappear, not because there is not ample useful work in the world for them to do, but solely and simply because our industrial civilization has turned them into semi-automatons incapable of the readjustments which would make self-reliant beings of them.

There is arable land enough in the state of New York alone, and New York is by no means a banner agricultural region, to furnish real homes to all the workers in its undesirable factories, and to the city workers who are engaged in distributing their products. Yet New York probably has more undesirable factories, and more cities in proportion to available arable land, than any other state in the union. There is land enough to furnish each family in the state with gardens, orchards, yards for vegetables, for fruits, for chickens, for pigs, for goats.

The work on these small homesteads would not, of course, be

sufficient to occupy all their time, nor could they produce enough on them to furnish themselves with the domestic machinery and equipment which would be essential to their comfort. But there is work enough for the spare time of all of them in the building crafts alone, if the miserable painted wooden shacks which now house the greater part of the people of the state were to be replaced by beautiful and substantial structures of stone, brick, and concrete. In this one field alone, there is work enough to utilize all the time of the millions now engaged in producing and distributing the products of our undesirable and non-essential factories. Instead of devoting themselves to the semi-automatic labor in these factories, let them devote themselves to stone-cutting, masonry, bricklaying, carpentry, joining, iron-working, and all the other crafts essential in the building of beautiful and substantial homes. Let them support themselves partly on the produce of the land, and partly out of their earnings as craftsmen. They would then be able to work for less in the way of wages and yet live far more comfortably than they do today.

If even a small proportion of the workers now engaged by non-essential factories were really directed towards the huge task of housing the population comfortably and beautifully in individual homes, the collateral development of all sorts of neighborhood industries would bring about a revival of rural social life of revolutionary cultural significance. The villages would cease to be mere trading centers. They would become social and industrial centers, in which the sharp distinction between working in a factory and working on a farm, which is one of the worst aspects of our factory dominated civilization, would be absent.

•

A major change in the direction in which capital is invested is essential if such a transformation of our economic life is to become possible. Instead of the present ingenious and highly efficient system for directing capital into industrial channels, there must be developed an even more ingenious and more efficient system for directing capital into home-making and home-producing channels. Building and loan associations, land and agricultural banks, installment finance corporations must be developed so that ample capital is available for the building of substantial and beautiful homes, for equipping them with modern domestic machinery, and for purchasing whatever is needed to enable the home to shelter an independent unit of society comfortably and beautifully.

If existing agencies for procuring and furnishing capital for these purposes were developed, capital would be made available at reasonable rates of interest and on an amortization basis. It would become possible to build millions of homes of the best of materials and with the best workmanship, and to equip them with modern, scientific machinery for domestic production. A market would be created for the producers of building materials, of domestic machinery, of tools and equipment, of furniture and furnishings so much larger than the existing market that there need be no concern about what would have to be done with the millions of workers whom my proposal would seem to leave without the means for supporting themselves. They would be able to devote themselves, when not working their own homesteads, to useful instead of useless occupations. The notion that useless occupations are desirable and that more and more of them have to be invented in order to make it possible for the entire population to work, is a delusion.

Those who console themselves with the thought that the consumption of luxuries and the waste of necessities has a useful aspect because they thus "make" work are consoling themselves with an economic delusion. There are enough essential and desirable things to be done—of which the building of beautiful homes is only one—to furnish work to every person today engaged in the production and distribution of the goods made by our undesirable and non-essential factories. The trouble is that today society has accepted a pattern of living based upon a set of financial and economic ideas which makes the direction of labor into the factory and away from the home seem desirable and rational. The same ingenuity in organization and the same perseverance in operation which have filled the land with factories, can fill the land with beautiful homes and comfortable families.

What is needed is a more intelligent economic ideology.

The really superior types in society must impose new and better values upon the ruthless, acquisitive and powerful types which delight in forcing the masses to cater to their wishes. Just as Watt,

Stephenson, Faraday, Morse slowly imposed their ideas upon the whole of mankind by showing the quantity-minded minority the possibilities of power and profit in bringing about the industrial revolution, so this new economic ideology will have to be imposed upon society by showing the quantity-minded minority that domestic production furnishes great opportunities for power and profit to those who first exploit its possibilities.

In the eighteenth century an entirely new group of men acquired power by seizing upon the discoveries of science and exploiting them through the factory. They acquired wealth and climbed into the seats of power formerly reserved only for the landed aristocracy, the military, and the clergy, because they directed their ingenuity, their perseverance, and their ruthlessness to the development of the factory.

The self-same type of men exists today. Such men can be made to impose a better social and economic ideology upon the masses by the simple expedient of showing them how they can acquire wealth and power by developing installment credit, domestic machinery, and electrical power.

•

Fortunes are now being made out of the exploitation of electrical power. Slowly but surely the quantity-minded masters of the electrical industry are being driven by a small number of men who are doing some real thinking about electric power into the development of the latent possibilities of the industry. If the Duponts, the Mellons, the Insulls really begin to develop the industry they control, the stage will be set for a real battle between the two systems of production which we have been studying, and this battle domestic production will fend itself for the first time assisted by talent of a type which up to the present has been almost exclusively on the side of factory production.

Students of the electric industry like Mr. Morris L. Cooke, whose monograph *What Price Electricity for Our Homes?* makes the existing situation in the industry clear, are plainly aware of the social implications of a greater use of electricity in the home even though they do not dwell upon the revolutionary cultural potentialities of cheap, flexible, and small unit power.

Mr. Cooke's study was designed to show the fallacy, both from the standpoint of the consumers of electricity and the producers of electricity, of the present large differentials between home consumers' rates and industrial power rates. When the first electric companies were organized, electricity was used almost exclusively for lighting purposes. Current was wanted only when light was used. It was used in the evening and not the daytime. Equipment large enough to supply the maximum demand had to be installed and then had to remain idle most of the day. Lighting consumers naturally had to be charged the cost of producing current while it was being consumed and also the cost of maintaining the plant even when practically no current was being produced. The companies had to secure an ample return on the investment in their entire plant from the sale of lighting current only.

It was not long before the electric companies discovered that stimulating consumption of current during the daytime, even if it had to be sold without charging the day-time power user anything for the maintenance of the plant, produced an added clear profit. Factories were therefore persuaded to abandon the use of steam power by offering them electrical power at rates lower than they could produce power from steam. The process of stimulating the consumption of power in the "slack hours" in this way has been continued down to this day. Industrial rates are often only one-tenth of the domestic rates. As a matter of fact, the differential in favor of the factory seems to be increasing: in 1923, lighting consumers paid on the average 4.8 times as much as the power consumers, by 1926, this had been increased to 5.7 times as much.

The conditions which originally justified this discrepancy no longer exist. So much power is now used for industrial purposes that "slack hours" are practically non-existent and there is no longer any need of selling current to the factory at less than cost in order to create a market for current throughout the entire day. Yet the differential in favor of the factory is being continued, partly because of the stupidity and partly because of the cupidity of the electric companies.

On the subject of the social value of lower rates to domestic consumers, I can do nothing better than to quote rather fully what

Mr. Cooke says:

> It is not generally realized how important, from the standpoint of public welfare, the lowering of domestic electric rates really is. It is not so much that the lowering of electric rates would save the consumer money. The main gain would rise out of the increased use of electric current. The consumer may spend more for electricity at low rates than at high ones; but he will have gained the very material advantages which can be derived from an abondant use of low priced light, power, and heat.
>
> Our limited use of electricity in the home and on the farm constitutes a serious ground for national self-reproach. In the factory machinery has already largely displaced man power, and in the mine it is doing so rapidly. It has relieved men of heavy muscular strain, and it is constantly making inroads on the hard performance of monotonous and uninteresting jobs. It has shortened hours. But in the home, machinery has not as yet been generally introduced. In 1920, only 10 percent of the farms had running water in the house. Consider what this meant in the way of carrying water, as well as in the lack of sanitary conveniences. Urban homes are better equipped in this respect; but of more than 5,000,000 urban families for which the General Federation of Women's Clubs obtained reports in 1925-1926, only 35 percent had electric vacuum cleaners ; only 23 percent electric washing machines; only 4 percent electric sewing machines, and less than 2 percent electric flat work ironers. Only 2.1 percent had electric ranges and 1.3 percent electric refrigerators. Yet, of more than 7,000,000 families reported upon 80 percent had electricity in the house, as evidenced by the fact that they had electric lights. Sixty-four percent had electric irons. While some of the household equipment mentioned is expensive, evidence which has been submitted suggests that a very important factor in limiting its more general introduction and use is the cost of current. The housewife who would use additional electric current for operating a sweeper or ironing machine is charged five or ten times as much as is the factory where her husband works, this though the current is identical. It would seem that considerations of ordinary fairness and chivalry would condemn a rate discrimination which retards the introduction of mechanical equipment which would relieve the strain and save the time of the busy housekeeper and mother while the use of machinery is so encouraged in men's work. The importance of the

home in the whole scheme of national economy is hardly realized. In the not far distant future the homemaker will be listed and tabulated with other occupations by the Census. When we see the great numbers of individuals—mostly women, of course—so engaged we will recognize a national incentive for surrounding the occupation of home making with every possible facility for making it efficient.

Taking up specifically some of the lines along which more and more electricity can be used in the home as rates are lowered, the following table estimates the number of kilowatt hours of electricity which tend to be consumed by various types of electrical apparatus. The table is based on an analysis of energy consumption data made by the Home Economics Division of the Iowa State College. Although methods of manipulation, personal habits, and the individual abilities of electrical users vary, those who prepared these figures consider that they give a fair ides of the energy consumption under normal conditions.

Device	Kilowatt Hours per Month	
	Per Family	Per Person
Electric range	102	25
Refrigerator	28-45	11-15
Ironing machine	2.8	.46
Iron used with it	3	.5
Electric cooker	5.5	.9
Waffle iron	2	.5
Washing machine	2	.5
Percolator	6	1.5
Toaster	1.2	.3
Glow heater	5	.7
Water pumping (shallow)	795 gallons per kilowatt hour	
Water pumping (deep)	576 gallons per kilowatt hour	
Incubators (79% hatch)	370 watt hours per chicken	
Water heater (60-70 degrees inlet, 128 degrees outlet)	4.5 gallons per kilowatt hour	

The above tabulation does not include fans, vacuum cleaners, warming pads, or electrically operated farm machinery (except pumps); nor does it make much allowance for the use in spring and fall (or in winter in poorly heated corners of the house) of a number of electric heaters. If there are some homes where, as respects some uses, the cost of current is not considered, this is not true of other and potentially larger uses.

The use of electricity for lighting has by no means reached its maximum. Under lower rates the present 25- and 40-watt lamps will tend to give place to 50-, 60- and in parts of the house to 100-watt lamps; or the smaller powered lamps will be used in greater number. Houses will also be lighted more fully, and for longer periods. The generous lighting of stores, theatres, streets, and public monuments and buildings which is revolutionizing the appearance of our cities at night will have its counterpart in the illumination and beautification of the home, as reasonable rates make this possible.

In the rural areas present electric rates discriminate not only against the housekeeper but against the farmer. The following is a more extensive list of electrical appliances which may be used on the farm, including farm machinery as well as household equipment:

A. General Farm Applications

- Bone grinder
- Groomer
- Corn ear crusher
- Corn cracker
- Feed grinder
- Fodder cutter and crusher
- Ensilage cutter and blower
- Fertilizer mixer
- Feed mixer
- Wood splitter
- Wood saw
- Water pump
- Grindstone
- Grain elevator
- Grain separator
- Bench grinder
- Clipping machine
- Shearing machine
- Hay hoist
- Baler
- Oat crusher
- Silo filler
- Straw cutting
- Fodder-cake crusher
- Threshing
- Treatment of ensilage
- Electro-culture
- Plowing (Germany and Sweden)
- Meat curing
- Hay drying
- Wood preservation
- Root grinder
- Lathe
- Air compressor
- Burr mill
- Concrete mixer
- Potato grader
- Portable storage battery
- Lantern

A. Dairy Applications

- Ice breaker
- Ice cream freezer
- Ventilator
- Concentrator
- Filler and capper
- Forewarmer and mixer
- Churn
- Electropurification of milk

Electric milker	Separator	Churn and butter worker
Pipe line milker	Pasteurizer	
Babcock milk tester	Can dryer	
Homogenizer	Bottle washer	

A. Poultry Applications

Oyster shell crusher	Water heater	Electric lighted chicken house (to stimulate winter laying)
Poultry feed mixer	Grain cracker	Stimulation of growth
Egg tester	Feed grinder	
Brooder	Corn sheller	
Incubator		

A. Horticultural Applications

Fruit harvester	Dehydrator	Fruit press
Cider press	Fruit packer	Frost prevention
Cider mill	Spraying apparatus	Destruction of insects

A. Residence Applications

Clothes dryer, centrifugal	Dishwasher	Washing machine
Meat chopper	Vibrator	Range
Bread mixer	Rectifier	Vacuum cleaner
Bell ringing transformer	Piano, electric	Fan
Flatiron	Curling iron	Electric phonograph
Percolator	Warming pad	Grinder and buffer
Heater	Sewing machine motor	Soldering iron
Egg beater	Hair dryer	Portable motor
Immersion beater	Toaster	Mangle
Waffle iron	Grill	Ice cream freezer
Refrigerator	Ozonator	House lighting
	Humidifier	
	Siren	

Other uses might be added. For how many of these operations it will be worthwhile to have special equipment, and in how many cases electricity affords the best means of applying power, we do not as yet know. The whole development is in its infancy. That there are highly important uses for electricity on the farm cannot, however, be questioned.

Service to industry has been the main concern of the electrical industry for over thirty years. It has been a full sized undertaking involving not only the solution of innumerable technical problems and the development of public relations on an entirely new order but the creation of vast credits with which to pay for a stupendous construction program. No small part of the credit for our present industrial prosperity and supremacy must be given to the electrical industry for the part it has had in providing our mines and manufactures with cheap and plentiful and widely distributed power. It is pertinent to the discussion to recall that the result would never have been achieved if—especially in the early days—special consideration had not been shown, and even concessions made, to power customers. The thought is now beginning to grip the imagination of the leaders of the industry that in the home and on the farm is to be found the next big area of electrical development. The key to the solution of the problem lies in breaking the vicious circle of high rates and the restricted use which they induce. If, as every indication suggests, low rates—even rates so low as to be based on cost plus a reasonable profit—will bring about what amounts to a revolutionary increase in the normal use, then the quicker the industry gets to the new basis of charges the better it will be for all concerned.

Home life and especially life on the farm are after all fundamental to the well-being of the American State. Electricity can play a master rôle in their upbuilding. Therefore the question as to whether or not the electrical industry should inaugurate rate schedules designed to bring about the largest possible domestic use of electricity becomes one of national policy. In this matter happily the interest of the nation, of the consumer and of the security holders of the electrical industry are the same. We appear to be on the eve of a period of radical reductions in the charges for domestic current.

Plainly Mr. Cooke is very conservative in what he says about the social revolution which "radical reduction in the charges for domestic current" may bring about. Yet it is not unreasonable to assume that if cheap power and the application of power to factory machines helped the factory to destroy domestic production, the coming of cheap power in a form suitable for application to domestic machines may help to redress the present adverse balance between the home and the factory.

When we shall have become sufficiently civilized to create a demand for small generating plants driven by windmills and water-mills, they will be developed and placed on sale at even lower prices than the very ingenious plants driven by gasoline engines, which are now on the market. The domestic producer will then have power, heat, and light at no cost in money except for lubricants and maintenance.

In that day, no factory will be able to produce the essentials of comfort cheaply enough to compete with the productive home.

•

In all probability neither the farmers nor the great masses of non-farmers will try the road to the conquest of comfort which has been here outlined, even though modern science and modern machinery offer means to economic independence which do not entail the hard work and the harder deprivations of pioneer life. The masses of farmers have been led to believe that specialization, instead of diversification, offers them economic salvation. The masses of non-farmers, deprived of both the facilities and the personal attributes essential to domestic production, have been reduced to a state in which they dare not consider any such radical departures from their present ways of living.

Here and there individual families which have somehow managed to retain the initiative and fortitude that distinguished the pioneers, may take this road to the conquest of comfort. For them what follows may point the way to a richer life than that which they now lead. And if by some miracle a sufficient number of them were to try this way to comfort and so effectively boycott the products of our non-essential and undesirable factories, it would ultimately result in the creation of a much more beautiful civilization than the one in which we now find ourselves.

CHAPTER XIV
FOOD, CLOTHING AND SHELTER:
The Essentials Of Comfort

No conquest of comfort is possible if we have to procure the essentials of comfort—food, clothing and shelter up to the standard of living to which mankind's progress entitles us—by excessive labor or by inexpressive and uninteresting labor. Because it is possible in industrialized America to secure these essentials with relative ease, we overlook the fact that the way in which cure them is as important to our comfort as the food, clothing, and shelter are important to our survival.

What is more, we tend to believe that because America is producing creature comforts in greater quantities than ever before that the quest of comfort will end when it is impossible to further develop the system of production to which we now seem irretrievably committed. We have come to believe that comfort is increased to the degree in which production is increased. But when we increase production at the sacrifice of significance in our daily labor, then what we gain through the increase in the quantity of our so-called comforts is overbalanced by the decrease in our capacity for enjoying them.

We accept the sacrifice of comfort which our factory economy imposes upon us because it does not occur to us to ask whether some better method of procuring the necessaries of life might exist.

Yet a method does exist which makes it possible to attain a material well-being equal to that which we now enjoy with less unpleasant effort and greater security than is the rule today.

The necessaries of life can be procured not only without excessive and unpleasant labor but without fear and uncertainty. For no conquest of comfort is possible if we live fearful of our ability to secure these essentials of comfort; if we live menaced by the pervasive spectre of want; if unemployment, illness and old age mean not only misfortune but economic disaster.

We must feel as certain of our ability to procure the material essentials of comfort as we must feel certain that we shall inhale air when we breathe.

•

Under our factory economy the sequence by which those of us who have not inherited wealth* secure what we need and desire is as follows:

1. We sell our labor directly or indirectly in order to earn money; *we devote ourselves to production for sale.*
2. But as we cannot eat money, wear money, nor house ourselves *in* money, we buy everything we need and desire—shelter we buy from landlords; apparel from clothiers; food from grocers, butchers, and bakers; entertainment from theaters and clubs; culture from schools and newspapers.

Under the economic system which I am here advocating, the sequence would be as follows:

1. We would move on a homestead of our own; install a workshop and loom-room; equip the whole with efficient tools and machinery; develop a garden and orchard; stock the place with livestock.
2. We then raise and make all the things which we need or desire and which it is practicable and economical and pleasurable to produce for ourselves; *we devote ourselves to production for use.*
3. We work the remainder of our time at jobs or crafts or professions; with the money earned in this way we would pay taxes and interest and buy the factory-made products which we could not advantageously make for ourselves.

The change to this economic scheme would furnish three clear gains over the earn-and-buy system upon which most of us depend today:

1. The time we devoted to work would be spent more pleasantly.
2. We would reduce the time spent now in securing the things which are essential to our comfort.

---

* It should not be forgotten that we have developed a folkway which demands that even those who inherit wealth should work precisely the same as if they had to earn the necessaries of life.

3. We would become secure as to the basic necessaries of the good life.

•

Food, clothing and shelter absorb about sixty-five percent of the income of the average well-to-do American family of today. If we add fuel and light, approximately seventy percent of the budget of such a family is devoted to the purchase of essentials.

Sundries and savings absorb the remaining thirty percent. While this provides the family with its luxuries, many essential expenditures, such as those for medical treatment, would have to be deducted from the sundry expenditures and added to the seventy percent if the amount for producing the essentials of comfort were to be established.

Upon this basis the following table* is constructed. It gives a rough idea of how much of the time spent in gainful labor is devoted to earning money for a comfortable life.

	Items	*Days of labor per year*	
32.5	percent of income devoted to Food	91	days
17.5	percent of income devoted to Clothing	49	days
16	percent of income devoted to Shelter	44.8	days
4	percent of income devoted to Fuel and Light	11.2	days
70	percent of income devoted to Basic Essentials of Comfort	196	days
30	percent of income devoted to Sundries and Savings	84	days
	Total lime spent in gainful labor	280	days

If this table means anything,** it means that more than two

* If the reader will substitute his own actual budget for the budget used in this table, he will be able to better test the validity of the argument so far as his own situation is concerned.

** The figure of 280 labor-days per year was arrived at as follows: 365 days per year less 52 Sundays; 8 holidays—New Year's, Lincoln's Birthday, Washington's Birthday, Memorial Day, Independence Day, Labor Day, Columbus Day, Christmas and 12 days for vacation. Vacation in the type of family which we are trying to picture usually consisting of two weeks but from this the two Sundays which have already been counted have to be deducted. This thirds of the time which we spend earning money—more than four out of the six days of the working week—is really devoted to securing the basic necessaries of a comfortable existence.

The question which has now to be considered is whether we would save lime and enjoy equal or greater comfort if we were to substitute a large measure of making-and-consuming at home for much of our present well nigh complete dependence upon earning-and-buying.

In short, can we produce the material essentials of comfort for ourselves more economically than we can buy them?

That most of us, having become habituated to the present earning-and-buying economy may not like the proposed making and-consuming economy, does not prove its inferiority. Habit simply has perverted the modern taste and rendered the conventional judgment worthless. The fact that paupers cease to like work, does not prove that a life of pauperization is superior to a life of work.

•

Earning the money with which to buy food absorbs nearly two days of each week's work—approximately 91 days out of the entire year's labor. Yet there are good grounds for believing that much more than a third of this time could be freed for other activities by turning to a make-and-consume economy.

If we divide the food budget of today into its component parts, the fact that the great bulk of the foods we consume can be raised in an organic home at once becomes apparent.

---

makes the net result up to this time 293 labor days per year. This could be further reduced by 25 days to 268 if Saturdays were reckoned as half-days. But this figure would be a rank misrepresentation of the working lime of not only the vast majority of the population but even of the more prosperous classes. In very few states are all eight holidays actually observed; two-week vacations are by no means universal; neither are half-day Saturdays. On the whole, a figure midway between 268 and 293 would probably be a fair one. This makes the number of labor-days per year the 280 used in the table. It would no doubt be better to use labor-hours instead of labor-days. But to make a fair estimate of hours devoted to labor per year would be even more difficult. On a basis of labor-hours, the time spent earning a living would probably represent a greater proportion of the total year than on the basis of labor-days.

Percentage of Food Expenditures [43]

Meat, Fish, Eggs	31.3
Milk and Cheese	12.4
Bread and Cereals	14.7
Vegetables and Fruits	18.5
Fats	11.0
Sugar, etc.	3.7
Miscellaneous items	8.4

Meat, fish and eggs represent one-third of our food requirements. A poultry yard, a pig or two, and a herd of sheep and goats can furnish us the great bulk of our requirements for these proteid foodstuffs. The care and feeding of these animais, if proper houses, yards and equipment are used, would not take up more than a few hours per week of our time, since many of the tasks in connection with their care could be entrusted to the young and the members of the family too old to work outside of the home.

Producing the next largest item, vegetables and fruit, for ourselves is, if anything, an even easier task for us if we are anxious to procure the essentials of a comfortable existence with the minimum of labor-time. An adequate vegetable garden, which will furnish us all of our vegetables and small fruits, need not be very large, and it requires considerable time and attention only in the early spring. The garden tractor and the wheel hoe have so lightened the labor, that gardening when confined to the growing of our own needs only, requires nothing much more in the way of time than would furnish us the moderately vigorous exercise which every man needs. With a vegetable cellar for storage and the kitchen properly equipped to dehydrate and to can vegetables and fruits for the winter, a year-round supply can be produced in much less time than is needed to earn the money with which to buy them.

The bread and cereal bill can be materially lowered by domestic milling of cereals and flour, and by home-baking of bread and pastry, and can be almost entirely eliminated in the case of a large family where there are a considerable number of adults by undertaking grain farming on a modest scale. If the family is small, however, it would be better to buy wheat, corn and the other cereals and be content with the saving in labor-time which domestic milling and home-baking make possible.

Milk and cheese need hardly be purchased at all because they can be produced on a relatively small scale without excessive labor. The cow is the dairy animal for the large family only; the goat is better adapted to the needs of the small family. Goat's milk is richer in fat and easier to digest than cow's milk while the goat itself is cleaner and easier to care for than the cow. It is not, however, suitable for butter making. With either goat's or cow's milk, cheese, (which is one of the most nutritious and tasty items in the dietary), can be produced at a fraction of the time required to earn money for buying it.

Fats today consist mainly of two items: butter and lard, and their synthetic imitations—oleomargarine, crisco, cottolene, etc. If the family is large enough to have a cow, the butter problem is solved and if it has pigs the lard problem is solved. The fats are thus procured with smaller sacrifices of time than are necessary if they are purchased. The synthetic imitations so widely advertised are not only inferior in nutritive value to the organic fats, but sometimes positively harmful and we can therefore afford to dispense with them entirely.

There remains the sugar bill—white sugar, corn syrups, and similar sweets—the buying of which can be largely eliminated if we will use the products of the honey-bee, the sugar-maple and the sorghums as nature makes it easy to use them. Surely honey, maple sugar and genuine molasses, (not the dregs of sugar which now go by that name), furnish sugars which are superior to the desiccated products bought from the modern sugar refinery and glucose factory.

Such a program would not entirely eliminate the buying of factory-made foodstuffs, but it would reduce the time which had to be spent earning money to buy food to probably a quarter of that necessary at present. Instead of having to spend nearly two days a week earning money with which to pay the weekly food bill, only half a day of our time would be needed—the other one and one-half days would be freed for food production on the family homestead. But a day and a half per week would not be needed for this purpose—fifty days per year, an average of less than a day a week throughout the year, would suffice. And of these fifty days' time, a full third would be furnished by other members of the home.

This would mean that we, (speaking of the money-earning members of the home), would be called upon to contribute only 33 days per year to the domestic production of foodstuffs. Add the 23 days which we would spend earning money to buy foods not produced at home and we would be devoting a total of 56 days per year, instead of 91, to the task of providing ourselves with food. This is a clear gain of 35 days, in addition to the gain of spending the time at work which is far more healthful, more interesting, more expressive than that of most of the repetitive "jobs" open to us in this factory-dominated civilization.

•

We come now to housing, water, light, and fuel—both for heating and cooking. Today the work of securing these items absorbs about twenty percent of our time. For those who live in the city this figure is much too low. In New York City, and in many of the growing cities of the country, rent often represents more than twenty-five percent of the budget, with gas for cooking and electric current for lighting still to be added. In such cities, it is hardly an understatement of the situation to say that over one-quarter of the time we spend at work is devoted to earning the money for the sheer shell of existence.

The question is, can we furnish ourselves with shelter, fuel and light with less effort than these figures indicate? Taking the average figure, rather than the high New York figure, it now takes a little less than one day's time per week to earn the money for these necessities of life—about 44.7 days per year. Can they be provided at any reduction of this time?

If we assume that we have our own home; that the home is equipped with a well and an automatic water pumping system; that it has a hygienic sewage system; that it has a wood lot which can at least furnish fuel for that source of great joy in the home, an open fireplace, and that it has its own automatic electric lighting system; thus reducing to the minimum the necessity for buying shelter, fuel, light, water and sewage disposal facilities, then all that these things will cost us is the time we spend caring for the home plus the time we shall have to devote to earning money to buy what cannot be produced in the home itself. We shall have only to buy such supplies as oil and gasoline, and paint and varnish. The care of such a home with a "janitor" service fully equal to that of the average rented home today, will require less than one and one-half days' time per month. Add the time necessary to earn the money for maintenance, supplies, replacements, taxes, insurance and interest—probably a trifle more than one day per month—and the total time required to provide shelter and the shelter items will still be less by half than now has to be spent in earning the money for rent, fuel and light.

But with such a home we should be furnishing ourselves much more than the equivalent of rented and purchased shelter, fuel and light. We should cease to be cave dwellers in a city and would no longer crawl about in the canyons that are called streets. We should be abandoning the noisy, crowded, treeless, grassless cement desert of the city for the quiet, the privacy and the blue and green of the countryside. We should be furnishing ourselves not only a home but also a homestead—with land for flowers and vegetables, for shrubs and for fruit, for pets and for domestic animals. And time formerly necessary to earn money for rent would be released to be used productively, creatively, healthfully in the development of the homestead.

•

We come now to that very difficult subject, clothing. Clothing represents sixteen percent of the expenditures of the average American family. It requires forty-nine days of labor per year to earn the money to meet the cost of procuring this item of the average budget.

As long as men and women—but men especially—insist upon wearing the style of clothing which they wear today, domestic production can probably cut this item less than any other part of the budget. Men's clothing will have to be made by skilled tailors as long as they insist upon the hideous garments which they now wear.

Women's clothing, however, is fortunately still simple enough to lend itself to home sewing. A very material saving could be made in the time which now has to be devoted to earning money if, as far as possible, it were made in the home.

While no revolutionary savings are probable on clothing in the immediate future, a very great reduction in the economic "sacrifice" needed for clothing ourselves is possible if we were to take into our own hands the whole subject of costuming. Today this is in the hands of a caste of "designers"—designers working for textile mills which have to keep thousands of spindles and hundreds of looms busy, and designers working for the garment manufacturers who have to keep their serried ranks of sewing machines busy. Naturally the fabrics and garments they design have little relationship either to the physiological or the esthetic needs of human beings. Whether a new style is healthy or unhealthy, ugly or beautiful, is a matter of no consequence to the designer, provided it possesses the one essential virtue of persuading consumers to buy new garments and discard their old ones. New styles are produced not because they are more beautiful or more useful than the old but because they keep the wheels of industry turning.

If the designing of clothing were to be taken over by the wearers of clothing, the costumes would probably be simpler than they are today; they would probably exploit the sense of beauty more intelligently; they would attain a dignity entirely absent from the machine-dominated products of our factories. And it is quite possible that if the designing of clothes became an outlet for the creativity of the individual, a revival of home spinning and weaving might accompany the new interest in home garment making. A renaissance in sewing, embroidering, knitting and the kindred arts might mean a revival of weaving, the craft which furnishes a form for the expression of the creative abilities of every individual, from individuals of minimum artistic endowment to those endowed with real genius. This revival might be further helped by the fact that weaving, if it were developed into a domestic artistic craft, would have economic utility for other things than clothing. It would provide the home with fabrics for hangings and curtains, for robes and bedding, for rugs and carpets.

With scientifically designed domestic machines and equally scientific methods for operating them, we could provide ourselves more abundantly with more beautiful clothing, and supply the home with many of its textiles at an actual reduction of the time which now has to be spent earning the money with which to buy factory-made products. Without waiting for any revolutionary change of costume we could cut down the time now needed to earn money for clothing more than a third, especially since sewing time would be contributed largely by those not now engaged in working outside the home. Ultimately, by displacing the costume values which prevail today with a better set of values, and making our costumes and textiles both more beautiful and more durable, the time now devoted to securing them could be cut in half. Perhaps a quarter of the forty-nine days' time now needed would be devoted to earning money to buy what we cannot produce for ourselves, and another quarter to making clothing and textiles in the home.

We would be the gainers by fully twenty-four days' time per year.

•

We come now to the possibilities of economy in the eighty-four days we now devote to earning money for sundries and savings.

When we consider the vast number of things comprised in the category of "sundries" which the factories make for us but which we could make for ourselves, I am convinced that if I have erred in these estimates, I have erred wholly on the side of underestimating the net savings possible under such a making-and-consuming economy as is here proposed. Soaps, cleaners, floor wax, furniture polish, paints, medicines, germicides, cosmetics, baking powders, beverages of all kinds—both alcoholic and non alcoholic—are only a few of the innumerable things which we can make for ourselves of better qualities and at a large saving of time, if the time necessary to make them be compared with the time necessary to earn the money to buy them. A considerable part of the time now devoted to earning money for these "sundries" can therefore be saved.

When we come to the time devoted to earning money for saving and investment, a making-and-consuming economy would mean an even greater economy of time than is possible with regard to any of the items of the budget which we have up to the present time considered. For we save and invest today at the high rate here estimated—10 percent of the total time devoted to gainful labor—in large part because of the economic insecurity imposed upon us by our factory dominated civilization. We have to save, when saving has not become a pathological habit, because we must provide against illness, unemployment and old age. But under a regime such as that which I advocate this insecurity would almost entirely disappear. We should live with almost absolute security as to the basic essentials of life. We should be certain of food, clothing, and shelter so long as any of the members of the home were able to get about at all. Saving of money would not therefore be so urgent. The mere possession of a productive home and homestead doubly reduces the need of saving because it provides the essentials of comfort for dependents in case of our death. It is no accidental coincidence that the great growth of life insurance has been an accompaniment of the great growth of the factory. With the factory came insecurity, and with insecurity came life insurance.

With saving not nearly so urgent, it could be spread over fully twice the number of years now given to the task of providing against the future. And if we devoted five percent of our yearly time, instead of ten percent, to earning money for this purpose, there would be a clear gain of fourteen days' time per year.

Even if we disregard entirely the economies possible on the item classed as sundries, and add merely these fourteen days to the economies previously enumerated, it is plain that *more than one third of the time we now devote to gainful employment is unnecessary.*

At least four months of each year might be released for play, for education, for artistic, literary and scientific endeavor.

I say "of least" deliberately because the following table represents, I am sure, a very conservative statement of the possibilities of time-saving under a making-and-consuming economy.

Item	Time Needed Under Factory Economy		Time Needed Under New Economy			Net Saving Under New Economy
			For Domestic Production	For Earning Money	Total Time Needed	
Food		91	33	23	56	35
Shelter	44.8					
Fuel & Light	11.2	56	18	15	33	23
Clothing		49	13	12	25	24
Sundries		56	(*)	56	56	
Saving		28		14	14	14
		84				
Total		280	64	120	184	96

*Omitted because of the difficulty of making any estimate. The probable saving is very large—perhaps as much as one-third of the time at present devoted to earning the money for sundries.

•

If we can persuade ourselves to devote to the quest of comfort some of the concentrated energy which we now devote to the quest of wealth, we shall find that the domestic production of the essentials of comfort makes it possible to furnish ourselves with food, clothing and shelter not only in the qualities and the quantities to which we are now accustomed, but in qualities far superior to the factory products which we now consume, and in quantities so abundant that hospitality might again become one of the graces in which we could indulge our souls.

The thought and the time which we now give to the four factors which govern the production of wealth must be transferred to the four factors which govern the production of comfort.

For just as land, labor, capital and management are the factors which govern the production of wealth, so the homestead, time, machines and wisdom are the factors which govern the production of comfort.

The substitution of these four categories for the customary categories of classic political economy will make both the practicability and the desirability of the economy I advocate self evident.

CHAPTER XV
THE FACTORS IN THE QUEST OF COMFORT:
I. The Homestead

A HOME, says the dictionary, is the house in which one dwells, and a homestead, the home and the land immediately connected with it.

In this civilization of apartment hotels, kitchenette flats, and hall bedrooms it is being made easy for us to forget that there can be no conquest of comfort without both a home and a homestead. We can no more have real comfort in city flats than we can have children without mothers. In both cases the object sought cannot be attained if one of the means for attaining it is absent. For when we take the places in which we dwell away from the country; deprive our homes of intimate contact with the growth of the soil; shut off our access to sun and light on all sides, we do not merely deprive ourselves of fresh air and sunlight, green grass and majestic trees—we deprive ourselves of what is an elemental need of mankind: the inner discipline which comes from communion with the land.

•

Man is a land animal. He may fly in the air that is above the land; he may sail on the waters that surround the land, but to survive he must always return to the land—the land from which he comes, which sustains him as long as he lives, and which re-absorbs him when he finally dies.

That we are land animals is one of those very obvious truths which we tend to forget when we make the endless number of decisions about what we should do and how we should live. Yet a full acceptance of it and deliberate application of the logic of this fact to the practical problems of life are essential to freedom and to comfort.

As long as we have access to the land we remain free to labor as we wish and free to live as we please. The moment our access to it is conditioned, is limited in some way, our possible freedom is conditioned. And where freedom ends and servitude begins, there comfort ends and discomfort begins.

•

Out of the twenty-five million families in the United States, thirteen million are landless and homesteadless.

Under the system of land tenure prevailing at the present time, the freedom of those of us who belong to these thirteen million families is limited in innumerable ways. Much of our time has to be devoted to earning money to pay rent. In one way or another we have to support those who own land and from whom we have to rent homes that we may have even a limited access to land. What we pay as rent conditions our freedom. The two millions who occupy the Borough of Manhattan in New York City can work and play, eat and sleep, only after paying rent to the forty thousand landowners who hold title to the various plots of land into which Manhattan Island has been divided.

This system of land tenure, in which most of us supinely acquiesce, requires us to work nearly a quarter of the time we devote to gainful labor merely to shelter our families, or it compels us to pay money for rent which we would prefer to spend for other things. When we are homesteadless, we are thus compelled to devote a large part of our strictly limited time on earth to securing money to pay for the privilege of access to land; to land which nature really provides us but which our system of land tenure makes it easy for a limited number of landowners to own and exploit.

Land ownership makes us freer than landlessness because it releases labor-time which otherwise would have to be devoted to securing the money with which to pay rent. It is true that even with homestead ownership we are still conditioned under the existing system. We are conditioned by the interest we have to pay upon any mortgage upon our property and by the taxes which the state levies upon our homestead—grossly inequitable taxes under the existing system. Yet if we own our homestead free and clear, we are as free under the existing laws of the country as it is possible for us to be.

•

As long as America was mainly rural and agricultural, before it became industrialized and largely urban, the homesteadless family was a rarity. As long as there was an abundance of "free" land, free to any family which was willing to pay for it with no cost but the discomforts and privations of "homesteading," the economic sacrifice of the average individual family in providing itself with shelter was so slight that it could accept or refuse employment on a basis of practical equality with those who offered employment. Easy access to land furnished the average American an alternative to employment. For nearly half a century it was a major factor in keeping down the numbers in America who were willing to work for others. Only after the most desirable and most accessible land was no longer free did industrialization on a large scale become possible.

As the free land disappeared, the price of land rose. Rising land values made it more and more difficult for the increasing population, native-born and immigrant, to acquire land and to establish their own homes and homesteads. More and more men had to support themselves by working for others. They furnished the factories with large numbers of laborers who had to work in them in order to find work at all. They built up our cities and filled them with tenement homes. Millions of immigrants who had been agriculturists in Europe were forced to become factory hands and city dwellers in America. In addition, the factory, which was quicker than the farm to utilize machinery and power, offered farm workers more attractive conditions of labor, while to the more ambitious men engaged in farming it offered greater opportunities for advancement. The government encouraged manufacturers in every way. Tariffs were established to protect industry. The prices of manufactured products were raised. Manufacturing profits were made super-normally high, and because farm products could not be protected, farming profits were made sub-normally low.

So began the steady absorption of our population by the factory. The constant decline of the popularity of farming as an occupation for ambitious men, and the rise to favor of all the occupations which have to do with the products of the factory, have continued ever since.

Thus has industrialized America created its present disestablished population. In the beginning, the individuals disestablished by the factory included craftsmen and artisans, most of whom owned houses and shops and land which they cultivated when not at work in their shops. As fast as factory products came into the communities and replaced products made by the craftsmen, the local market upon which the craftsmen were dependent was destroyed. The textile mill destroyed the market for the services of the weaver; the iron mill for the old iron-worker and black smith; the patent flour mill for the work of the local grist-miller; the shoe factory for the cobbler; the clothing factory for the tailor and dressmaker. These craftsmen and the members of their families were forced to go to the cities in which factories located. Their shops were closed or replaced by stores in which factory products were sold; their homes and barns, fields and gardens were abandoned and exchanged for city homes.

They became home renters, most of them, at the same time that they were made into wage-earners.

•

Before the industrial revolution, the home was both the residence and the producing center of the craftsmen. After the coming of power and machines, home work by handicraft methods became unprofitable, while home work by factory methods became unbearable. With power, with division of labor, with specialization, and with serial production, work was transferred from the home to the factory. The disestablished workers had to earn their living in one place, and to spend their time living in another.

The separation was certainly justified on esthetic, if on no other grounds. For with the coming of the factory, the place of work became large, noisy, ugly, and generally dirty and unpleasant.

After the separation, the home naturally began to lose its importance. It shrank in size as rapidly as it began to lose its economic functions. Today it has dwindled in function until it is hardly much more than a place in which to sleep—where time is spent when it cannot very well be spent anywhere else. The smaller the number of rooms of which the home consists; the fewer the pieces of furniture it contains, and the smaller the quantity of household goods which need to be moved if a change of "jobs" makes a change of location desirable, the better. The more mobile the home, the better is it adapted to the exigencies of this civilization.

As a matter of fact, the apartment hotel furnishes the home which best meets the needs of a factory economy. Such a home makes the fewest demands upon the time of the various members of the family. It leaves the parents and older children free to go to work; the younger children free to go to school.

The apartment hotel is still too expensive for the masses. But it is being developed so amazingly that the time may not be far distant when it will be within the means of even unskilled workers. The so-called California apartment house, with beds which fold up and disappear into closets, and which do away with bedrooms, thus making it possible for a single room and a kitchenette to serve all the needs of a small family, is a step in the direction of bringing the apartment hotel down to a level which eventually will enable the masses to live in them.

When the apartment hotel becomes available to the entire population, disestablishment will be complete. People will be land less, houseless, bedless, and the only property with which they will burden themselves will be the clothes they have to wear.

•

For the masses with their relatively low standards of taste, the change from the farm to the city and from the shop to the factory had many sorts of compensations. In the city and its factories they did not work so hard. They did not work such long and irregular hours. They worked in large crowds amid a pleasant excitement. They earned more cash, and were able to buy things which under the old order they had either to make for themselves or go without.

That the disestablished masses should overlook the fact that the comforts which industrialism gave them with one hand, industrialism took away with the other, is understandable.

And it is also understandable why they should fail to ask themselves whether a redressing of the balance between the farm and shop on one side, and the city and factory on the other might not make it possible for them really to enjoy the abundance which mechanical progress has made possible.

But it is not easy to understand why we, who pretend to be intelligent, do not face the facts, and ask ourselves whether supine acceptance of the ugliness, the discomforts, and the servitude of industrialism is unavoidable.

I believe that it is possible for us to avoid these aspects of our civilization.

I believe that it is possible for us to make a conquest of comfort, at least so far as the ultimate tragedy of life permits us to do so, by turning to the production of the greater part of what we need and desire for our own consumption in our own homes and from our own homesteads.

It may even be possible for the masses to make a similar conquest of comfort, improbable though such a contingency certainly is.

For the individuals adventurous enough to repudiate completely the factory economy of today, the first step toward freedom is homestead ownership.

•

Here and there some of us may deliberately re-establish ourselves on homesteads.

But the great masses will never voluntarily do so.

History records almost no instance in which landless city dwellers abandoned city life until they were driven into the country by famine, pestilence or warfare. Not even pauperization will make the city-bred masses consider any kind of life in the country. The misery which they know in the city is as nothing to the abject terror which they feel at the prospect of having to fail, for fail the majority would, in trying to secure a living from the land. Once the masses of a nation begin to concentrate in cities, the qualities essential to the enjoyment of country life begin to atrophy. The city-raised individual is from childhood deprived of the training, the knowledge and the mental habits necessary to country life. He not only has none of the abilities required to live comfortably in the country; he has none of the values which make the countryman enjoy the country.

To the city dweller, whether from the slums with their tenements or the fashionable districts with their apartments, the country is a habitable place only in the extreme hot weather of the summer.

Country life is inferior to city life because there are no crowds. There are no crowded stores, theatres, streets.

Country people have to do a host of things for themselves things which are done for the city dwellers either by the hotel management, when they live in hotels, or by the janitor when they live in flats.

And of course, country families must think ahead. Since they cannot run around the corner to a store, they must put in a somewhat larger supply of the goods they need from day to day. They must think not only in terms of supplies covering their needs for weeks ahead, but in terms of whole seasons. If they are to secure vegetables from their gardens, they must plan early in the spring what they want to harvest late in the fall. Indeed, if they want tomatoes early in the summer, they must begin to acquire plants, or seedlings, the moment the snow begins to leave the ground. This becomes so much a part of the make-up of country people that it is second nature to them. It is difficult to picture how intolerable the effort to acquire this mentality is to the city dweller.

The average city family hardly thinks farther than from pay envelope to pay envelope. There are few transactions of vital importance to city people which require them to think months ahead. Only one important incident in life requires them to think as much as a month ahead, and this is the payment of their rent. The only other incidents affecting their economic life which dates farther ahead are installment payments on automobiles, furniture, pianos, radios. But these are broken down into weekly and monthly payments, and require no particular consideration of the future since they are really thought of in terms of the current pay envelope.

One of the great tests of intelligence is the extent to which the individual perceives the time value of future wants. The city dweller is losing this ability. Like a child he is concerned more and more only with present wants. And because of this unavoidable economic myopia, he is degenerating in judgment and discernment, socially and politically. In short, he is becoming as dependent upon the articulation of his city as was the Roman mob upon the tribute from the colonies during the decline of Rome.

The masses of city dwellers will therefore stay in the city. They are already anesthetized against the noise, the smoke and smell, the crowds and the strains of the city, and they are immunized against country life by their utter inability to acquire the wider mental horizon necessary to it.

The cities of our factory-dominated country will therefore tend to grow larger and larger. A myriad of refinements upon the existing devices for handling crowds in buildings, in streets, in stores, and in transportation systems will make it possible to accommodate crowds two, three and four times as large as are now accommodated within the limited areas of each city. Human ingenuity, scientific knowledge, scientific management will be concentrated upon the problem of enabling two human beings to dwell, work, and move about where only one could before.

And to almost none of the city dwellers will it occur that the dedication of all this thought and effort to overcoming the difficulties of crowding millions of people upon a few square miles of land represents the sublimest foolishness in all human history.

Without a complete collapse of civilization, of which there is no immediate indication, it is exceedingly improbable that the masses can be persuaded to adopt a normal country life. Only individual families can therefore be expected to adopt it. But those of us who will devote one-half the effort which we now put into winning a precarious success in business or professional life, into the solution of the problem of attaining the first step on the way to economic freedom will find that all the instrumentalities for achieving it are already in existence. If we can generate the necessary initiative, we will find that the agencies at hand, far from ideal though they may be, can be used by us to establish homes and homesteads.

If any considerable number of the quality-minded would begin in this way to free themselves, the quantity-minded drivers of mankind would become dependent upon and subservient to them. Then for the first time in history businessmen, politicians and soldiers, who rule this society as the quantity-minded have always ruled society, would find that they had to treat with artists, scientists, teachers, doctors, and professional men generally on a substantially equal basis.

Business men would not be able to say to them: "You must help me to make more goods and to sell more and more goods."

Politicians would no longer be able to say: "You must teach science as the ignorant religious masses demand."

Generals and admirals, and the imperialists who direct them, would no longer be able to say: "You must write histories to justify the wars the government proposes to wage."

The artist who wishes to paint what he believes beautiful would be in a position to refuse to do commercial work which he despises; the scientist who wishes to accumulate knowledge for its own sake could refuse to devote himself to cutting factory costs; learned men generally would be enabled to refuse to devote their lives to manufacturing, selling, financing and administrative routines.

Quality-minded types of men and women would possess an alternative to the acceptance of work on terms which the masters of industrialism dictate. They themselves, and not the quantity minded, would determine how they lived and what they did with their time.

A culture based upon significances and not upon magnitudes would be given the opportunity to acquire the social prestige now accorded only to sheer size, and a really superior model of living set for the imitation of the herd-minded multitudes of mankind.

•

As long as we have to devote from one-fifth to one-third of our time to earning money for rent, we are from one-fifth to one third dependent upon and subservient to the factory economy of today. If we eliminate rent entirely, we immediately become from one-fifth to one-third free.

We cannot, of course, entirely eliminate the expenses which the landlords have to pay out of their rentals. Whether the home is owned or rented, taxes, maintenance and depreciation have to be paid. At best, therefore, we can only become free to the extent to which we reduce our rent by eliminating what is from our standpoint the tribute to the landlord. This reduction alone is sufficient to justify home and homestead ownership.

Ownership, however, is able to free us from the necessity of paying tribute to other lords than landlords. Even a few acres of land can reduce by from one-third to one-half our dependency upon this factory-dominated civilization.

Ownership of a home frees us from dependence upon the factory for earning the money with which to pay the landlord. That alone is half of the possible reduction.

But ownership of a homestead frees us from dependence upon the factory to earn money to pay the butcher, the baker, the grocer, the milkman, the poultryman, and the vegetable and fruit dealer. That is the other half of the possible reduction.

If some of the ingenuity we now expend in business and professional life in order to secure the money to buy what we need and desire were expended upon the development of a few acres of land, our present abject dependence upon the functioning of modern business for an income, and upon the factory itself for goods, would be ended.

Over thirty percent of our income is spent for food—for meat, for milk and eggs, for groceries and vegetables and fruits. The factory furnishes these to us in neatly labeled packages, bottles and tin cans—at a price which seems to me excessive. The home and homestead can provide us with all that we wish of everything but the exotics of the table—the delicacies and luxuries which come from distant sections and from far countries. What is more, the homestead enables us to produce most of the native foodstuffs purer, cleaner, fresher, healthier and tastier than the factory furnishes them to us, for hardly much more in the way of investment than is needed for modern labor-saving gardening and kitchen equipment and for hardly much more in the way of labor than is necessary to our good health and good cheer.

The garden and the woodlot furnish an excellent substitute for the present day cult of physical culture. Exercise is a basic human need. Muscles must be brought into vigorous play; the blood sent coursing through the veins; the whole body stimulated, unless we are to become soft and flabby, sickly and uncomfortable. But exercise for the sake of exercise is an anachronism. Yet it is to an increasing extent a part of our factory-dominated life. At precisely seven o'clock in the morning, millions of us in America tune in our radios and go through our "daily dozen" of exercises. Most of us, under city conditions, ought to do so. But that fact doesn't make the whole procedure a bit less absurdly wasteful of human cnergy. Primitive man never exercised for the sake of exercise. Yet this is precisely what we moderns find it increasingly necessary to do. We waste energy in exercise which could be usefully and joyfully expended in a garden.

•

But if the homestead is to make its proper contribution to the production of the essentials of comfort, no attempt should be made to raise produce for the market. There must be no specializing in poultry, in fruit, in garden-truck—no effort to kick out the factory system at the front door and to reintroduce it at the back.

The garden must be just a family garden; not an intensive truck farm with its accompaniment of back-breaking labors and heart-breaking marketing problems. It must be confined to the production of vegetables we wish to eat fresh during the growing season and which we wish to store, to dehydrate, and to can in glass jars for winter.

The poultry yard must be a substitute for the dairy and meat market; not a poultry farm with its inevitable and inedible white Leghorn egg-machines which produce a great stream of eggs which have somehow or other to be marketed. It should provide the home with fresh eggs, with broilers, roast chickens, chickens for boiling, above all with the greatest delicacy the poultry yard can furnish—capons. It should provide the Thanksgiving and Christmas turkey. It should provide us with squabs and guineas, delicacies which only the wealthiest can today afford.

The orchard must be just large enough to provide summer, fall and winter apples and pears, peaches, plums and cherries for the family—a dozen and a half trees are ample. It should not be an orchard with hundreds of trees with their pruning and spraying problems, picking and packing problems, and shipping and marketing problems.

There should be bushes between the trees which furnish the small fruits—strawberries, blackberries, raspberries—all the berries the family can consume fresh, canned, and preserved.

There should be two or three hives of bees to provide honey the healthiest of all the sweets; nature's own sweet for which the white sugar of the factory is a tasteless and health-destroying substitute.

Perhaps a few nut trees to provide a supply of pecans and walnuts and so furnish the family the best of all the proteins which nature provides.

And milch goats with their cleaner, healthier, sweeter milk to take the place of canned cream and condensed milk and the A, B and C grades of boule milk with their varying degrees of germ laden cows' milk.

But in no case should the farming be to excess. Nothing should be done on a scale so large as to make the work monotonous or to create a marketing problem. Surplus crops, if large enough, might be sold, but they should first be used to enable the family to indulge in an abundant hospitality. For with pantries and cellars and storehouses full, hospitality ceases to be a luxury; it becomes a joyous rite.

A home, a few acres of land, machines and equipment which eliminate drudgery, and no more skill and application than most human beings possess, make all this possible.

•

But such a home provides us with much more than the means for producing shelter and food. It provides us with beauty as well. The flower garden, the grassy sward, the trees and shrubs and rocks minister to that within us for which no factory and no city provides a substitute. It is not only the fact that the homestead furnishes a beautiful background for family life; that it fills our homes with shrubs and flowers, (without our having to pay florists for them), that makes this esthetic content possible. It is the fact that planning and planting and cultivating on the homestead are creative and artistic activities for which the city offers no satisfactory alternatives.

New York, that prodigious jewel of modern civilization, boasted in 1928 of a new association—the Parks Association of New York City, Inc. Outlining the purposes of the organization, Nathan Straus, Jr., its president, said:

> No human being was ever intended to spend his or her entire existence in underground subways and artificially lit offices. The more

> the necessities of modern cities require such unnatural modes of living, the more urgent becomes the need for adequate park space, adequate outdoor breathing-spots full of sunshine and fresh air as an offset to those unnatural living conditions. The Parks Association of New York City has assumed as its task continual vigilance so that the City Government authorities will properly maintain and increase our city parks.[44]

It is a strange world: mankind abandoning the country to herd into cities and, once in the cities, moving heaven and earth to bring the country into it—as if light and darkness could occupy the same place at the same time! But no matter how efficiently the city dwellers may design their parks and how vigilant may be their parks associations, at best these only enable them to be spectators of grass, of trees, of shrubs and of flowers. To truly participate in the growth of the soil, the vicarious country life of the city park must be abandoned.

•

In abandoning the country for the city, and the productive home for the consuming home, not only we, but our children have become victims of the factory system.

So remote are the productive processes in the city that our children have to learn about them from pictures and books and from the advertisements of the manufacturers who tell them only what the manufacturers want the world to know. What our children should absorb at first hand from observation and practice they have to try to learn at second hand from advertisements colored by the self-interest of the manufacturers or from school teachers who have themselves in all probability never once been inside the factories about whose processes of production they are trying to inform their pupils.

Yet we plume ourselves upon the superiority of our modern systems of education! Because our children are able to read about fabrics in newspapers and magazines and to see them on display in attractively decorated stores, we think them better educated than the benighted children of a hundred years ago whose education about fabrics began when the flax grew in the fields or the wool was sheared in the spring. A hundred years ago children needed neither textbooks nor teachers to learn about the fabrics which were in use in those days. The cleaning and scouring of the wool; the spinning of the fibre into yarn; the weaving of the yarn into cloth; the dyeing and finishing and cutting and sewing of the cloth into garments were processes which they observed at first hand, and in which they participated as soon as they became old enough. Without scientific pedagogy, intelligence tests, modern psychology; without perfectly equipped, steam heated, automatically ventilated buildings; without specialists in mathematics, in history, in science; without modern texts and modern libraries, they learned infinitely more about the processes of production than our modern children.

The school of that age needed to furnish only what the home, in many cases, could not: instruction in reading, writing and arithmetic. In the better class homes, even this part of education was a home responsibility. Instead of leaving the education of their children to the tender mercies of great educational factories, full of teachers many of whom are working for hardly much more than wages, the education of the children was a matter for the personal supervision and constant discussion of the entire family. No wonder Henry Adams considered the time he spent in school largely wasted. He learned so much more at home.

The only productive activity which our children are apt to see in their homes is that of cooking. Home sewing, especially in the city, is vanishing. Both cooking and sewing are now practiced so little in the home that modern mothers are no longer able to instruct their daughters in these arts. The schools therefore have had to add cooking and sewing to their curriculums, in a probably vain effort to teach their pupils certain elementary facts in connection with housekeeping. But aside from these two occupations, nothing goes on in our homes which gives our children any insight into the amazingly complicated world into which they have been born.

Our children drink milk which cornes to the house in cans and bottles, and butter and cheese which comes in packages. What can they know about dairying?

They eat factory-made bread, cake, cereals, vegetables, jams, jellies, meats, sausages. What can they know of the work of first growing and rearing the material for these products and then processing them into the forms in which they are consumed?

They go to stores in which their clothing, their shoes, their hosiery, their hats are purchased ready-made. What can they know about the complicated economic activities of which these things are the final result?

The modern school tries to teach them about this complex world from printed books and pictures. And the very books in which that world is described are printed so far from the children that they cannot know anything about the fascinating industry which is called appropriately the "art preservative of all arts."

The modern school is just beginning to discover the nature of the handicap under which it labors. So-called "progressive" schools are being established to try to fill the gap in the life of our children.

Go into a progressive school. There you will find the pupils working in gardens, building houses, working with tools, making pottery, weaving cloth. The children are taught to spin, and to weave, on spindles and looms often as primitive as the instruments which savages use. Yet the most backward savage child knows much more about textiles and their production than the average modern child can hope to know.

The dye-pot having gone out of the home, the progressive school is re-introducing it so as to put back into the life of children the esthetic lessons it used to teach.

Elaborate curriculums and elaborate educational activities are built around similar productive projects; about the growing of vegetables and flowers; the building of model houses; the making of pottery, of paper, of flour. Ingenious educators are busily tying these projects into their teaching of reading, writing and arithmetic. Thus the progressive school lays a foundation for the education of the children of this factory-dominated civilization.

We flatter ourselves that all this is an evidence of real progress in education, and overlook the fact that much of it is superfluous if children are brought up in productive country homes which furnish to all the members of the family a liberal education in the various manual crafts. Life in the country is the ultimate of progressive education. Rearing and caring for growing things, animal and vegetable, is a "head and hand" educational process. Country life produces masters-of-all-trades. It produces human beings able to work with hammers and saws and chisels; to tinker with iron work and with machinery; to use spades and hoes and agricultural implements; to operate water pumps and plumbing systems, heating plants and lighting systems. These activities into which children in the country are naturally inducted, furnish real and not sham progressive educations. They furnish the conditions needed for a firm foundation for a liberal education. Life in the country furnishes opportunities for the study of biology in the raising of poultry; zoology in thc care of animals and birds; botany in the cultivation of gardens, flowers and trees. It furnishes opportunities to study hydraulics in the care of the water supply; electricity in securing light, heat and power; chemistry in cooking and preserving; mechanics in wood working and machine working. Above all, it furnishes children a foundation for a normal emotional life in the abounding panorama of nature, in the procession of the seasons, and in the all important facts of life and death which become less awe-inspiring and poignantly tragic when children are prepared for them by a life of intimacy with what we call the dumb animals.

We are rediscovering the educational value of these contacts with reality through the experiments of our progressive schools. That this latest development in pedagogy should consist so largely of a discovery by the school of the importance of the culture-medium of which the factory and the city have deprived mankind, is the most amazing of satires upon civilized society.

•

If the day ever comes when we devote to the organization of our homes and families the thought and interest which it is now believed should only be devoted to the organization of business, of religion, of education and of politics, we may develop true *organic homesteads—organic* in that they are consciously and with the maximum of intelligence organized to function not only biologically and socially but also economically. We shall then have homes which are economically creative and not merely economically consumptive.

The organized, perhaps incorporated, home may not be needed to assure the economic well-being of the very wealthy, but it is absolutely essential to the economic security of the average individual. For the poorer we are, the greater is the need of pooling individual resources and the greater is the benefit from the formation of an economic unit large enough to make it practicable for us to produce our own food, clothing and shelter. Such an economic organism, (which it is possible to establish without a preliminary lifetime devoted to accumulation, reform legislation, or social revolution), may be the only instrumentality through which those of us who are not wealthy and who aspire to a superior life even in this factory-dominated civilization—who seek conditions which will enable us to express ourselves in art, literature, science, philosophy—can achieve our hearts' desires.

The natural family seems to me the normal nucleus around which to build such a home. But an organic home might conceivably be established by a group of individuals unrelated to each other. Not marriage, not common blood, not even like tastes are essential. What is absolutely essential is that those who undertake to establish such a home shall be individuals with like values. To function with real effectiveness the group should be large enough to make division and rotation of the work of homemaking possible. The homestead must be organized so that it can continue to function uninterruptedly even when individual members are absent traveling or adventuring, or working and studying away from home. The "family," in short, should be large enough to enable the members to enjoy sabbatical leaves of absence; yet not so large as to preclude administration of its affairs by common consent based upon common understanding.

•

Perhaps the best method of suggesting the potentialities of such an organic homestead is an outline of a possible form for its constitution:

> Preamble— We, the members of this homestead, in order to form a more perfect home, establish justice, insure domestic tranquility, provide for the common interest, promote the general welfare and secure the blessings of liberty to ourselves and our posterity, do or

dain and establish this constitution.

1. Membership. Membership shall be of two kinds: Regular Membership and Auxiliary Membership.

(a) Regular Membership shall entitle the member to a vote at all meetings and to such an interest in the homestead as may be from time to time agreed upon. Regular Members are those either born of the regular members or those adopted into the home.

(b) Auxiliary Membership may be accorded to those from time to time employed on the homestead, and shall entitle the member to such privileges as the regular Membership may prescribe. Auxiliary Members shall have no vote.

(c) At the age of sixteen, the children of regular Members are entitled to half-votes at the meetings. At the age of nineteen full membership shall begin.

(d) Adoption into the home shall be by majority vote. Upon adoption, the member shall be provisionally admitted, with a half-vote if between the age of sixteen and nineteen. After each year of provisional membership, the family shall by majority vote decide whether or not to continue or end the provisional membership. At the end of their third year provisional membership shall end and full membership shall be accorded.

2. Resignation. Membership may be ended by resignation, by abstention and by expulsion.

(a) Resignation may be at any time, such resignation to be based upon a written agreement making all necessary provisions for the duties which may be owing by the member and for the member's equity in the homestead. All such resignations shall be provisional for a period of three years, during which time membership, at request, may again be accorded provided the resigned member discharge all obligations which may in fairness be exacted to cover the period for which he has failed to contribute to the support and development of the home.

(b) Absention from the home shall begin whenever by majority vote it has been decided that a member has wilfully absented himself from the home and failed to discharge home obligations. Such absention shall be considered provisional for three years, at which time it will become permanent expulsion, and readmission there after can only be as a result of application for adoption.

(c) Expulsion shall be by majority vote, and such expulsion shall be accompanied by a settlement of all interests which the expelled member may have in the home. Such expulsion shall, at the request of of the member, be provisional for three years, and if it be continued by majority vote for three successive years, shall then become permanent.

3. Meetings. There shall be a regular weekly meeting of the members of the home on Sunday morning of each week. There shall be an annual meeting on the first day of each year at which time an annual votes as to membership shall be made.

4. Officers. All the officers shall be elected by majority vote, and shall hold office for one year, or until their successors may be elected. In general, the principle of rotation of office shall be followed. Only regular members shall, however, be qualified to hold office.

The officers shall consist of a Chairman, a Vice-chairman, a Secretary and a Treasurer, who shall perform all the duties usually performed by such officers. In addition there shall be a Manager of the Household, a Manager of the Homestead, an Assistant Manager of the Landscape, and an Assistant Manager of the Gardens. The managerial offices may be combined in one person.

The Manager of the Household shall have complete charge of all the activities within the household itself.

The Manager of the Homestead shall have general charge of all the activities outside the household itself, including all machinery, buildings, etc., and general supervision of the three assistant managers whose sphere of activities are described by their titles.

Other managers may be from time to time appointed.

5. Property and Finances. (a) The property and financial interests of the home shall be kept separate from that of each individual member.

(b) When any of the home property is used by a member to the exclusion of others, such member shall pay into the homestead treasury a fair rental for its use.

(c) When the home receives from any member property or services in excess of that which is normally prescribed, the member shall be paid for it from the treasury.

(d) A complete financial statement shall be prepared once a year, and any divisible surplus disposed of at such times and in such ways as the membership shall direct.

(e) Each member shall have such pro rata interest in the entire property of the home as may be provided at the time of acceptance into membership.

(f) If an adopted member transfers no property to the home at the time of adoption, the member's interest shall be confined to the divisible surplus accumulated by the home after adoption. If the adopted member does transfer property to the home at the time of adoption, such transferences shall be added to that member's pro rata interest in the home.

(g) An appraisal of the value of the home shall be made once each year, and shall be used to determine the relative value of the contributions of those admitted to membership or the interests of those withdrawn from membership during that year.

(h) At the time of withdrawal, a member shall receive back a pro rata interest, more or less than at the time of admission, depending upon whether the property of the family has increased or decreased since admission, and in such form, if the family desires, as the member contributed property to the family.

(i) If necessary the family may issue notes or bonds in order to make payment of such pro rata interests possible.

6. AMENDMENTS. The Constitution may be amended at any time by majority vote, but if such amendment be not in accordance with the fundamental principles of this constitution, such amendments may on the request of one-third of the members be considered vital amendments, and shall then be binding only if they have been adopted for three successive years.

•

For quality-minded men and women, the economic independence which such a homestead would furnish would be of revolutionary consequence. For note this: while freedom from dependence upon the factory would prove a boon to all types of men, it has a distinctive value for this minority of mankind. In our factory-dominated civilization it would enable them to "sell" their talents without having to prostitute them. If the majority of our artists, writers, architects, engineers, teachers, musicians, scientists were in this way to secure the freedom to refuse to do work which outrages their tastes, life for everybody would undergo a radical change. The mere fact that businessmen would lose their power to dictate to the idealists of the world; that they would have to solicit the services of idealists rather than that idealists should beg them to utilize their services, would be sufficient to change a society in which emphasis is placed upon money into a society in which emphasis would be placed upon ideals.

But it would go farther. It would furnish a better pattern of how life should be lived because it would furnish mankind a more intelligent social leadership. Our plutocracy, which today furnishes society with its culture patterns, makes accumulation seem the most desirable thing in life. It stimulates all of mankind to a reckless race for material possession on the theory that wealth is the key to happiness. An economically independent, intellectual aristocracy would very quickly demonstrate the hollowness of a life of mere acquisition. The ancient Chinese long ago showed that it was possible to set up a civilization in which belief in the divine right of learning seemed just as natural to all classes as belief in the divine right of kings seemed to the people of the Middle Ages.

Confucius said:

> To learn, and then to practice opportunely what one has learnt—does not this bring with it a sense of satisfaction?
>
> To have associates in study coming to one from distant parts—does not this also mean pleasure in store?
>
> Are not those who, while not comprehending all that is said, still remain not unpleased to hear, men of the superior order? [45]

How can the quality-minded create such a society unless they fiée themselves from an economic servitude which makes them ridiculed and despised by their fellows? Today it is inevitable that they should be despised and hated by the generality of men; that they should be called "high-brow," "theorists," and less elegantly, "nuts." And why not? How can they win respect for the ideals about which they prate when everybody sees them prostituting their talents because they have to secure money with which to pay the butcher, the baker, and the landlord; when everybody hears them preaching what they cannot practice, and everybody observes them accepting the inferior position to which business men condemn them? Let them reverse the whole present scheme of things; practice what they preach, cultivate their talents, devote themselves to their own interests, and work only in ways that are compatible with their self-respect, and they will set up a new social order—an order in which the philosopher, the teacher, the student shall be first instead of last, and in which a marked shortening of the lag between the conception of ideas by the learned and their final adoption by the world will have lessened what has always been the greatest obstacle to the achievement of a beautiful civilization.

•

Certain practical objections may be raised to the economy here outlined by those who have solved the problem of supporting themselves along other lines. They may have large incomes—they may be saving and investing—they may not be manually skilled—they may have no taste for bucolic delights—they may need and crave the glitter that the city offers—they may have become dependent upon the organized menial service which the city store, the city restaurant, the city hotel render. Many of these objections are based upon a failure to grasp the distinction between what I propose and the sentimentalism of the return to "nature" which Rousseau proposed or the "back to the land" movement of twenty years ago. Some of the objections are based upon a set of values which are meretricious; values which cannot be transvalued without great effort but which those who still possess the possibility of basic re-education would certainly find worth transvaluing. The best answer to the objection that I tend to overlook the sacrifices involved and the practical difficulties of what I propose is the fact that I am no advocate of poverty and barrenness for the sake of its "beauty" and of hard manual labor for its "moral" value. I suggest an economy which begins with an organic homestead principally for two reasons: because it makes for economic independence, and because it makes for a richer and fuller life.

Let us consider some of these objections in detail, and we shall see that they are not nearly so formidable as at first sight they might seem:

(1) *You say you have already attained a large income, and so doubt the wisdom of sacrificing it?* But the sacrifice you fear is illusory. Life on a homestead of your own does not involve any sacrifice of real income. On the contrary, even when it reduces gross income, it increases net income. Cutting down rent and food bills does not involve a sacrifice of income; it produces a net gain of income. It releases income for books, for music, for art, for travel, for all of the luxuries of a cultured life.

But often such a life increases both gross and net income. What you command for your work, for your services, for your judgment at the hands of those for whom you work or who are your patrons or clients depends to a very considerable extent upon the relationship between you and them as seller and buyer. Economic independence immeasurably improves your position as a seller of services. It replaces the present "buyer's market" for your services, in which the buyer dictates terms with a "seller's market," in which you dictate terms. It enables you to pick and choose the jobs you wish to perform and to refuse to work if the terms, conditions, and the purposes do not suit you. The next time you have your services to sell, see if you cannot command a better price for them if you can make the prospective buyer believe that you are under no compulsion to deal with him.

(2) *You say that it is easier to achieve economic independence through saving and investment than it is to travel against the whole stream of events today under a make-and-consume economy?*

But even if it is easier to achieve economic independence in that way, you will not be equally equipped to take advantage of it when—and if—you achieve it.

For many years, and those the most vigorous ones of life, you have to endure a regime of self-denial so far as doing the work you might most like to do is concerned. You will have to postpone the time when you can enjoy your work until you may be too old to really enjoy it. In the meantime you will be working in one of the treadmills which must be kept moving if the factory economy of today is to function. When the time comes to release yourself, the years of routine will have played their part in making you prefer the certainties of your treadmill to the unknown dangers of the work and life to which you at one time aspired. Most tragic of all, the years may have killed the aspiration: you find yourself in the beginning of old age, economically free, but unprepared to use your freedom.

But observe the irony of it all: you may spend your whole life saving—investing in stocks and bonds—and by the very deficiencies of the economic system to which you pin your faith, fail to win the independence you seek. These things may cheat you:

1. The investments you make may fail. You may pick the wrong ones. You lose not only money, but the years of time which you spent saving it.

2. The value of money may decline. When you wish to retire, the original capital you thought ample may prove insufficient be cause in the meantime the dollar will have declined in purchasing power.

Of course the reverse may prove your good fortune. Instead of losing on your investments, a "bull" market may result in a great appreciation of it. While an appreciation of the value of the dollar is improbable, other changes, perhaps in the nature of industry itself, may greatly increase the yield on your investments. But to the degree in which you strive to make yourself independent through investments, to that degree you plunge into speculation, and to succeed at speculation, you, who are striving to be quality-minded, must become money- and quantity-minded. You will have to match your wits against those professionally engaged in money-making and in that game you, who have other aspirations, are almost certain to come out second best.

The more you try to escape this hazard; the more security you demand in your investments, the higher will be the institutional burden which will have to be borne by the securities you buy. By the time the yield upon them has been reduced to cover the costs of supervising them by conscientious and careful investment bankers, brokers, accountants and trust companies, the net yield is small indeed.

On the other hand, the acquisition of things which you can use to produce the essentials of comfort—houses and lands, machines and equipment—are not subject to these vicissitudes.

Land endures forever. Houses can be made to serve for generations. Machines and tools, with care and replacements, can be made to function indefinitely. These things may rise and fall in money-value, just as investments in stocks and bonds do. But unlike investments you do not acquire them for their money-value. You acquire land for gardening; houses for shelter; machines for saving labor. Money may rise and fall; science and invention change the method of production and industry; laws and governments come and go, but the land will continue to feed you; houses continue to shelter you, and machines will deliver power to you precisely the same year after year. For their economic utility is dependent upon yourself and is not subject to change by markets, by laws or by corporations which you do not control.

Above all you work and live as you aspire to work and live *all your life.* You do not have to postpone the good life into some indefinite future. You live it while establishing your homestead.

(3) *You say that you are not manually skillful—that you could not possibly master all the crafts which are essential in a home and homestead such as I have described?* You may be right, and therefore as unfortunately crippled mentally as you would be unfortunately crippled physically if you were armless, legless, or sightless. The man who cannot operate machines and use tools and the woman who cannot cook and sew are both cripples. They are dependent upon others much as cripples are. Practically every woman can learn to do household work well. Practically every man can learn how to handle tools with equal skill. Furthermore, a proper use of modern machinery—domestic machinery, however—the electric drill, the circular or band saw, the lathe, takes all the drudgery out of home mechanics. The garden tractor and the wheel hoe take the drudgery out of gardening, just as modern kitchen and sewing equipment take the drudgery out of house keeping. All the mysteries of which the carpenter, the machinist, the electrician, the plumber are master are like all mysteries: mysterious only to those who have never themselves made any effort to do what these mechanics do.

Any intelligent man who can study textbooks and follow instructions can learn enough of what is necessary about these crafts for life upon the land and so acquire a new delight in life because he has heightened his mastery of his environment.

(4) *You say you have no triste for bucolic delights and crave the glitter which the city offers?* Then you are indeed unfortunate. For then you are in need of a transvaluation of values exceptionally difficult of achievement. A steady diet of highly spiced foods destroys the palate's sensitivity to the fine bouquet of natural foods. Frosting is a good thing on a cake, but the man who eats nothing but the frosting develops a pathological appetite which does not make it possible for him to enjoy the cake itself. So it is with this matter of life on the land; it has a set of values all of its own. They are immeasurably important values: touching something very deep in the life of man. When we lose our capacity for enjoying them; when we are unable to take these basic cravings of the race and dignify and elevate them into a form of artistic expression, we lose a part of our inheritance as human beings, and we become mere flotsam and jetsam on the stream of consciousness, endlessly bruising ourselves as we live because we are rootless and adrift and hurtling against every snag and rock in the stream of life.

We have applied all our ingenuity to solving the problem of enabling hundreds of families to live in the same house—to cook in separate kitchens, to marry, to give birth to sons and daughters, and finally to die in absolute privacy. This achievement we call an apartment. With equal ingenuity we have made it possible for hundreds of perfectly strange individuals to eat together and sleep under the same roof. And we call this achievement a hotel. I refuse to believe that it is impossible for men and women of like tastes, like educations, like social backgrounds, to live together in such a home as I have described, the individual members securing the freedom to develop themselves by contributing a share of their time to the labor which furnishes the entire group the essentials of comfort.

Productive homes of this kind, by making us economically independent, would free us from the necessity of spending our time as the quantity-minded masters of the world now make us spend it and would make for that reintegration of work and play which is essential to a full conquest of comfort.

•

So much upon the subject of the homestead—the first factor in the quest of comfort.

We have now to consider the second factor—the factor which I have called time in order to emphasize the point that the question of labor should be approached not from the standpoint of how to increase productivity, but from the standpoint of how to wisely spend the years and days and hours of which life itself is composed.

CHAPTER XVI
THE FACTORS IN THE QUEST OF COMFORT:
II. Time

SAID the Lord God:

> In the sweat of thy face shalt thou eat Bread.
> Cursed is the ground for thy sake.
> In toil shalt thou eat of it all the days of thy life.

For untold centuries this judgment which the priestly rulers of Israel put into the mouth of their tribal deity has been quoted as a justification of the hardness of human labor and the unpleasantness of the time man has to devote to self-support.

A bigger lie was never sent echoing down the ages.

For although much of man's labor has been heavy and unpleasant, it was not necessary that it should be so either because Adam and Eve ate of the fruit of the Tree of the Knowledge of Good and Evil or for any other reason. It is only because the time spent of labor has so often meant working without playing; because it has meant sowing but not reaping; because it has meant endlessly toiling without expressing anything, that mankind has come to associate labor with heavy and unpleasant effort.

What the barbarian biblical authors set down as the reasoned judgment of the Lord God upon human labor, the institution of slavery made a reality in the past, and the institution which I call the factory makes a reality in the present. The Hebrews were a slave-minded race. They had been slaves in Egypt in the beginning. They were just escaping the Babylonian captivity when their priests began to formulate their philosophy of life for them. It was natural that their vision of paradise should be a Garden of Eden—a garden notable above all other of its delights for the fact that there man did not have to devote time to supporting himself.

Today we still believe the cessation of work is a prerequisite to happiness. How perfectly natural! For we can no more extract happiness out of our work, as mere cogs in great industrial machines, than could the enslaved Hebrews out of their work toiling for the Pharaohs in the parching sunlight of ancient Egypt.

Today, as in ancient Judea, work is still considered the greatest of all evils. The traditional reaction to labor of the oft-enslaved Hebrews of yesterday continues unbroken down to the present moment. One of the greatest blessings which the factory is supposed to have brought to mankind is a reduction in the time which men have to devote to work and an increase in the time which they can spend without labor.

•

The real genius of our age is engaged in thinking about how to abolish labor instead of how to ennoble it. Our efforts to ennoble work are confined to fulsome eulogies of the dignity of labor. But our conduct gives the lie to our words. We are constantly seeking to escape labor, as we naturally seek to escape from any thing which we think unpleasant.

The habit of thinking of work as something one has to do but dislikes and play as something one likes to do but cannot, is poisonous. It is a habit, however, which we cannot help forming in a civilization in which work is made monotonously exhausting and play meretriciously delightful.

If we are to spend our time wisely, we must destroy the present dichotomy between work and play.

Expressive, productive, creative, interesting work is the only thing to which we can devote much time without boredom. Only very exceptional individuals can use large quantities of leisure.

Much leisure merely releases men whose work does not interest them for a restless search of amusement. Excessive leisure turns them into creatures perpetually seeking escape from a boredom which they carry about, much as snails carry about their shells, wherever they go and whatever they do.

What we need is not fewer hours of labor at the wrong kind of work, but the substitution of work of the right kind for work of the wrong kind. Labor must be self-justifying. It must be both a means and an end—the means to life and the end of life. It is only when it ceases to be an end—when it becomes only a means to life—that it becomes a curse, and men seek to escape from it as they seek to escape from a plague.

The factory, with its degradation of labor, perpetuates the hatred of labor which had its origin when time devoted to work meant time devoted to drudgery. For the factory relieves the laborer of the indignity of hard labor only to replace it with the greater indignity of repetitive work. Under our factory economy it seems more necessary than ever before to escape from labor to cut down the hours of labor per day in spite of what machines may do to lighten work itself. It is factory work which furnishes the real justification for labor's struggle for the shorter day and the shorter week. Trade unionism is an effect of which factory work is the cause. The factory makes the trade union necessary to labor not merely because labor needs some such club to secure decent wages, but because it has to shorten hours of labor if life is to be made endurable at all.

Less and less labor—the eight-hour day, the five-day week, and as the socialists hope, the time when only two hours per day will have to be devoted to labor—is essential to the maintenance of a factory economy.

But less and less labor is not necessary to the conquest of comfort.

•

What is the logical part which labor should play in the really comfortable life? Why, in short, should we devote time to labor? To answer, "that we may support ourselves," is to state only half the truth. The full truth is: we should labor that we may live *and live more enjoyably.* We should labor to secure what we need and desire, but it should be labor which enables us to enjoy both the produce of our labor and the time spent in producing it.

Does the factory make this possible? Is a method which requires us to devote the greatest part of each day to labor which we do not enjoy necessary in order to furnish us the things we wish? Is it possible to intensify the enjoyment of the time left over from work sufficiently to compensate us for consecrating most of our waking time to boredom? I do not think so.

Man, as Alfred Korzybski points out in the *Manhood of Hu-*

manity, is a "time-binding" animal. He is different from other animals. The dog, for instance, while freely able to move in space, is unable to live in time. The dog is only a "space-binding" animal. It has no notion of time in a degree comparable to that possessed by man.

The unique fact of memory gives us a past, and the even more astounding fact of imagination, gives us a future. We find happiness a much more difficult achievement than do the beasts of the field and forest because we are burdened by our past and worried about our future.

We cannot live in the moment only, except by descending to the level of the beasts.

We cannot confine enjoyment to an isolated present moment without sacrificing our birthrights as humans.

We cannot, therefore, enjoy the creature comfort and the leisure which the factory bestows upon us, with utter disregard of what we have had to do in the past and what we shall have to do on the morrow.

When we spend the best hours of our days doing repetitive work which we do not enjoy in order to get the money with which to do what we think will make us happy in the remaining hours of the day, we destroy the very capacity for enjoyment itself.

•

The apologists for the factory reply to this in two ways.

First, they say, most men do not dislike repetitive work. The doing of one thing over and over again and always in the same way holds no terrors for them. On the contrary, it is actually the most pleasant kind of work to great numbers of men.

Secondly, they say, men generally are well justified in doing this alleged "unpleasant" work during their working time because it is only by devoting a certain amount of their time—eight hours per day at present—to factory work that they can produce enough to satisfy their wants during the remaining sixteen hours of each day.

The first argument can be dismissed on the ground that it is "immaterial, irrelevant, and incompetent." It is immaterial because the fact that the majority of men do not dislike repetitive labor has bearing on the matter only if repetitive work is unavoidable in the production of the goods necessary to their comfort, or be cause repetitive work itself is essential to their happiness.

Men do not do repetitive work as a matter of choice. They do it out of dire necessity. They can be driven to this sort of work only if they are deprived of access to the land. Our system of private property in land forces landless men to work for others; to work in factories, stores, and offices, whether they like it or not. wherever access to land is free, men work only to provide what they actually need or desire. Wherever the white man has come in contact with savage cultures this fact becomes apparent. There is for savages in their native state no such sharp distinction between "work" and "not working" as docks and factory whistles have accustomed the white man to accept. They cannot be made to work regularly at repetitive tasks in which they have no direct interest except by some sort of duress. Disestablishment from land, like slavery, is a form of duress. The white man, where slavery cannot be practiced, has found that he must first disestablish the savages from their land before he can force them to work steadily for him. Once they are disestablished, they are in effect starved into working for him and into working as he directs. Only after he has made it impossible for them to support themselves as they desire, does he find it possible to drive them to work for him according to approved factory techniques, with sharp distinctions between the time devoted to productive labor and the time devoted to rest or play.

The savages may, in time, become just as inured to repetitive labor as the so-called civilized factory worker. They may in time come to enjoy it, just as Henry Ford says that his workers enjoy it. But the fact that they have accommodated themselves to their predicament does not make them any less the victims of an economy in which they have to choose between the alternative of starvation or of submission to factory labor.

•

The second apology for repetitive labor needs more careful examination. Is it true that man can produce enough to satisfy his needs and desires only by working the best part of his waking day in a factory and under a factory regime? Henry Ford voices his convictions on this point in rhetorical fashion:

> If a man cannot earn his keep without the aid of machinery is it benefiting him to withhold that machinery because attendance upon it may be monotonous? And let him starve? Or, is it better to put him in the way of a good living? [46]

Mr. Ford is evidently not aware of the fact that his defense of factory work is based upon a very vague conception as to what constitutes "his keep" or what constitutes a "good living." And he shows no appreciation at all of the fact that what constitutes a good living is not measurable merely in economic terras.

A good living is not a mere matter of earning plenty of money. It is not merely the securing of enough money to buy all the components of what economists call the standard of living. When we talk about a "good living" we are dealing with our social ideals. A particular scale of living becomes "good" only after society accepts it and we have come to aspire to it. Mankind's aspirations change from age to age, and as they change the amount of money or the kind of things that have to be secured, change with them. What was a high standard of living two hundred years ago would mean a rather barren, Spartan poverty today. Yet those who lived then may have enjoyed a higher degree of satisfaction than we are able to extract from our life today. The realization of comfort is supposed to be higher today, thanks to the factory, but the expectations of comfort have changed just as much. It is, if anything, easier to fall short of expectations today than it was a hundred years ago.

It will not do to say that we are more comfortable today because our houses, our clothing, our foods are supposed to be superior. If the standard of living has risen, the standard of comfort has risen with it. It is in the degree to which we are able to live up to the standard that we recognize as desirable that we are really comfortable.

A good living, however, depends less upon the material produce of labor than upon the psychological life of the laborer. A social ideal such as "a good living" represents aspirations both as to what we should consume and how we should work and play. It is not how much we produce in the time devoted by us to labor so much as the nature of the work which we do that makes for the really comfortable life. A method of laboring such as that which prevails in the modern factory may enable us to produce things which the masses think more conducive to happiness than another method of laboring such as that which prevailed in the days of the handicrafts, and yet handicraft labor might have provided more comfort when it prevailed because it enabled the worker to extract happiness both out of the time spent in consumption and the time spent in production.

•

But if we are not to spend our time at the kind of labor demanded of us today, how should we spend it? We have to produce the material essentials of comfort. How should we produce them so as not to sacrifice the comfort which is our object while engaged in producing them?

Plainly we should not spend our time at work which disregards our deepest needs as workers. The system of production which we adopt should not neglect our needs as workers in order to favor our supposed likes as consumers. The factory system, with its atrophying of some of our qualities of mind and muscle in pursuit of an ideal of unlimited production, should as far as possible be abandoned.

There is a law: *Man must use all the faculties of mind and muscle with which he is endowed.* This is the law of comfort.

We receive premiums in well-being to the degree in which we observe the law, and we pay penalties of discomfort to the degree in which we dare to disregard it.

We are rewarded with mental and physical health when we obey the law. We are penalized by psychic frustration and physical atrophy when we fail to observe it.

Our factory-dominated civilization, with its minute specialization of tasks and vocations, has use for only a strictly limited number of our faculties. It has to ignore our need of using all the faculties we possess to the uttermost of our capacities. It furnishes us an abundance of creature comforts and of leisure for vicarious play, but these cannot compensate us for the frustration and degeneration caused by denial of our needs as workers.

The factory cannot, in any of its myriad of manifestations, furnish us with work which meets the deepest needs of our being. But the home can.

For in the factory-dominated world we must spend our time doing what machines require, while in a home-dominated economy we can devote our time to making machines do what we desire.

The more time we work at home and the less time we work in the factory, the more comfortable we shall be.

•

But can we secure from an organic homestead the essentials of a good living without drudgery?

I believe we can.

I believe that the drudgery we associate with home work and country life is avoidable.

We think of drudgery when we think of the farm and the home partly because industrialism has made farm work and home work profitless, adventureless, spiritless, and futureless, partly because it still is in very large part arduous, monotonous, repetitious, dirty, lonesome, endless, and partly because we have been told for so many years that it is unpleasant in the advertising of manufacturers who would have us abandon home production in order to buy what they have to sell.

Because we feel that the farm and home are futureless, we have failed to give real thought to the problem of home and country drudgery. But let us once recognize the infinite possibilities of the organic homestead, and we shall find that machines and methods have already been developed which prove that the drudgery is not ineradicable and certainly not inherent. We shall find, if we give serious thought to the matter, that it is already possible to (1) socialize, (2) mechanize, or (3) abolish most of the endless, hard, dirty tasks of housekeeping and homemaking.

Practically all the homework we consider unpleasant can be socialized. It can be performed by the family as a group, or it can be divided among the various members of the family, or rotated among them. This method of disposing of drudgery not only distributes the work but tends to destroy its unpleasantness by socializing it. Dishwashing, when one person has to do it meal after meal, day after day, year in and year out, is certainly not pleasant. Yet even such an essentially unpleasant task as dishwashing assumes a different character if it is performed by two or three people, one gathering up the dishes; one washing them, and one drying them and putting them away. The task is then disposed of in a few minutes in an atmosphere of pleasant activity and cheerful talk.

Nearly all the home work we consider unpleasant can be mechanized. The time which has to be devoted to unpleasant work can be reduced or changed into less unpleasant work or entirely transformed into pleasant work. Modern machines and efficient methods can be used to reduce the laboriousness, the dirtiness, and the time now devoted to such tasks. Such a laborious task as that of procuring water can be completely mechanized and the whole hygienic life of a country home transformed by the installation of an automatic air-pressure water pumping system. Water can then be secured by turning on a faucet instead of taking a bucket to a well and then carrying it full of water into the house. Country life can be made more pleasant not only by mechanizing the work of securing water but by making possible the luxury of using all the water one desires.

Finally, a surprising amount of the home work we consider unpleasant can be entirely eliminated. We fail to realize that the elimination of wasteful methods in the country and the home can be made to pay bigger dividends of comfort than their elimination in industry. Cultivating the garden with the old-fashioned hoe used to be one of the most tedious and unattractive of tasks in the country. But the battle with weeds and hard soil can not only be socialized by having a group cultivate the garden together, or greatly reduced by using a wheel-hoe or garden tractor—it can be entirely abolished by using mulching paper. With mulching paper, the ground is covered at the beginning of the season and once seeds and plants are set nothing needs to be done to the soil until harvest time. Cultivation is completely abolished.

If the home is located upon a proper homestead, if it is properly equipped with domestic machines, and if the time of those who live in it is properly organized, domestic production will not involve a return to what seems to us the drudgery of the pre-factory home. Scientific methods, domestic machinery, and the products of essential and desirable factories make it possible for us to turn to domestic production of most of the things we need and desire without at the same time returning to the simple life and the hard work of the past. We can use scientific methods to increase and improve what we produce in our homes; domestic machines to reduce the labor and time which we have to devote to the various processes necessary, and products made in essential factories to furnish us the things we cannot make so well for ourselves.

•

It is perhaps one of the gravest defects of the earn-and-buy economy which the factory has brought into being that it has made money the measure of all things economic.

We measure the things we consume by what they cost.

We measure men we know by what they earn.

We measure the life we have to spend in terms of money; we say that "time is money."

Time is not money at all.

Time is life itself.

To make life itself secondary to so trifling a thing as money is to make the ghastly mistake of confusing the means to life with the precious thing to which it should be a mere servant. Money should be a mere means to comfort. We should stop seeking it the moment it interferes with comfort—the moment we can better attain comfort through other instrumentalities.

The true economy is not of money but of *time,* just as the true waste is not of money but of the irreplaceable materials of nature.

Man has a habitable globe on which to spend his time—a veritable treasure trove and alchemist's laboratory full of useful raw materials with which to produce whatever his genius may lead him to design. Yet he burns the coal and the oil, cuts down and devastates the forest, pollutes and poisons the streams and lakes, and levels hills and mountains, not because this is the wisest use he can make of his time but merely in order that he may keep his factories busy and make the money with which to buy what they produce.

•

With our present earn-and-buy economy, the ratio of money

income to the size of the family fixes economic status. The large family is an economically handicapped family. Every additional child is merely an additional handicap. In the family of today the children, the aged, and the home-staying women are on the liability side of the family balance sheet; only the actual money makers are on the asset side. Hence the family of today tends to restrict the number of its children; to shift the responsibility for caring for its aged relatives and servants to public institutions; to drive even the wife and mother out of the home into money making, and to place its infirm and crippled members in hospitals of various kinds. Child nurseries, boarding schools, sanatoriums, hospitals and asylums of all kinds multiply in industrialized nations because the homes cannot afford to indulge in the luxury of caring for non-money-makers. The care of the young and the old, the sick and the crippled, is left to public institutions which at their worst are cruel, and at their best, indifferent.

But under such an economy as is here advocated, young and old, strong and weak, can all contribute time to the creation and production of what the home needs and desires—time which would be not merely a contribution to material well-being but which would furnish them the great joy of cultivating growing things, of making things with their own hands, of devising their own sport, play, and recreation. Homemakers would join the ranks of recognized producers. No member of a family would be a luxury. The available labor time would be increased with every addition to the number in the home. For children take a natural and inherent joy in doing creative and productive work, while the aged and crippled are rarely so old and infirm that they cannot enrich their own lives by sewing, knitting, preserving, gardening or otherwise satisfying the productive instinct by contributing to the hundreds of creative tasks in such a home.

Under such an economy the aggregate labor-time needed to provide food, clothing and shelter would be distributed among the various members of the family, each of whom would be assigned work for which their strength, ability and inclination fitted them.

Under such an economy time could be devoted to work and to play, to production and creation with none of the insecurity which haunts the myriads who can buy the necessaries of life only as long as they hold their "jobs." Fear would be banished. Except for fire, war and other "acts of God," everybody would be certain of the essentials of comfort.

Under such an economy there would be no need for excessive and exhaustive labor, for domestic machinery would not only eliminate undesirable heavy labor, but reduce drudgery of all kinds to a minimum. The great variety of tasks would furnish a first guarantee against boredom; the changing nature of work as the seasons progress would furnish a second guarantee, while the social atmosphere of a group working together to achieve common ends would furnish a third. But above all, the fact that the tasks are comprehensible and that they could be charged through and through with those creative and expressive touches which develop personality would prevent work from becoming flat and stade, uninteresting and abhorrent.

Finally, under such an economy no single task would be so large as to constitute a full-time task. No one would be compelled to take full-time jobs, to give to his craft or profession his full time except during the seasons when home-work permitted. Home-work would make it possible to make outside work a service instead of a servitude. Above all, the total time devoted to both home-work and outside work combined would be smaller. We would have more time for the leisure which creative and productive work had disciplined us to enjoy.

•

The method of saving over one-third of the time now needed to earn the money for food, clothing, shelter, fuel and light described in Chapter XIV would mean a release of the earnings of about four calendar months of the year for other purposes. Or it would mean the freeing of that much time for the pursuit of interests entirely different from those we call economic. A family which began its quest of comfort with nothing, would find it necessary to devote all the earnings of these four months to meeting the payments on the purchase of the home and its equipment. But each year would find it able to release more and more of its time for other than bread-and-butter activities.

Strangely enough, if mankind generally were to adopt this procedure it would result in what can be truly described as a recapture of a leisure lost to it since the coming of the factory. We may find that the greatest of all the advantages which would flow from a renaissance of domestic production, both to the individual and to society as a whole, would come from the release of our time for the cultivation of a more spacious life.

Deliberate failure to work and deliberate refusal to earn money are considered disgraceful today.

Before the coming of the factory there was no disgrace in failing to do so.

Our moral code has accommodated itself to the needs of a factory-dominated civilization and has made servitude to industry take on the character of a virtue.

For if we compare the aggregate time which was devoted to work before the coming of the factory with the time which we devote to work in the factory-dominated world of today, it is extremely doubtful whether we have actually reduced the total time we devote to labor. On the contrary, we may be actually devoting more hours per year to work than had to be devoted to it before the industrial revolution.

During the Middle Ages fully one-third of the year was devoted to holidays and festivals of various sorts. What we have gained in the reduction of the hours we work each day, we have lost by increasing the number of days we work during the year. Today, in spite of power, machines, division of labor, serial production, it is doubtful if we have effected any real saving of time at labor. We have failed to reduce the time we have to work partly, no doubt, because our standards of consumption have increased, but mainly because the savings made possible in manufacturing by the factory system have been so largely absorbed by the distribution costs which are its inescapable concomitants.

The progress toward leisure or which we boast may be entirely illusory.

It is only when we compare the time devoted to labor over comparatively recent intervals, the time men devote to labor today compared with the time devoted to labor fifty years ago, that we can credit the factory with shortening the time needed to earn the living to which we are by present standards entitled.

Eventually the factory may enable us to get back to the leisure of the Middle Ages.

Ultimately it may furnish us an even greater leisure.

•

But the leisure with which we may be ultimately endowed is almost certain to find us without the disciplines necessary to its enjoyment.

It will be a leisure rendered sterile for us by the conditioning to which youth, maturity, and old age are being subjected by this civilization.

Consider the conditioning of youth with regard to leisure in this factory-dominated civilization.

Year by year the number of states in which child labor is prohibited increases. Year by year the age at which we may begin working for a living is made later and later. It used to be 12, then 14, now 16 and ultimately it will be 18. By a sort of self-denying ordinance, the factory-dominated world is enforcing what might be called compulsory leisure upon childhood and youth. By fiat of law, working absorbs less and less of our time during youth and schooling absorbs more and more.

Naturally the school has had to take on the burden of educating youth in all directions—academically, vocationally, civically and domestically. And so we begin life conditioned by the canons of efficiency that prevail in the modern school. For the school not only trains our intellects; it trains our emotions and it trains our bodies. It equips us for our vocations; it equips us for citizenship; it equips us for home-life, it equips us for culture. And in each case it adjusts us to the patterns of living which a factory-dominated civilization has evolved. If it succeeds, it prepares us for our work as automatons and for our life as consumers.

How entirely logical are the pedagogues who are studying how to make it possible for the school to take over the full responsibility of equipping us for our places in the world! The factory having made the modern home incapable of playing a constructive part in our educations, isn't it natural that we should spend more and more of our childhood and youth in school, beginning with the nursery school and ending with the college, and less and less of that time at home? In the schools, at least, the disposition of our time is not left to rank amateurs at child training, such as parents, but to trained—though not necessarily skilled specialists.

Carping critics may complain about the intelligence, the initiative, and the versatility of the product, but certainly the product is more uniform, more interchangeable, more adaptable to the range of demands which will be made upon it in after life, than if it were left to spend too much of its time subject to the infinite variety of influences in the home.

If we turn from a factory economy and adopt domestic production, the present tendency to make us spend most of our childhood and youth in the school and less and less of our time at home would be reversed. Home, and not school, would have to be made the central factor in our educations. Parents would themselves have to devote time to the education of their children and incidentally to educating themselves. The school would be used only for academic instruction which could not be furnished us at home, and we would spend most of our time in childhood and youth in homes which abounded in opportunities for learning both from observation and from practice.

•

For youth, the school. For maturity, the factory. For old age, nothing.

The factory-dominated world is built around young men and young women. It demands vigor. It is a mechanism geared to operate at the optimum speed of the vigorous adult. Youth it can use even though youth is burned up. But old age it cannot use because it cannot afford to have its machines slowed down. Above the age of 35 women workers find it more and more difficult to spend their time at factory and office work. Above the age of 45 the same fate overtakes the men.

Leisure is made compulsory for the aged by the efficiency which is an inescapable necessity in our factory-dominated civilization.

Modern industry has no use for the aged. But neither has the modern home. In an industrialized civilization they are useless because they are functionless. They have to end their days in an enforced leisure for which neither their youth nor their maturity has equipped them. For the aged, the leisure with which the factory endows them means in reality the boredom of sheer idleness, the tragedy of compulsory uselessness, the frustration of life's only justification.

•

Enforced leisure no man wants.

Leisure for which we are unprepared is more evil than no leisure. To contribute to our true comfort, the leisure we all need should find us equipped intellectually, emotionally and physically for educating ourselves and our fellows and for creative work in the arts and sciences. In short, it should find us equipped to use our leisure for play in the all-embracing sense in which Havelock Ellis uses the word in his very beautiful essay on "The Play-Function of Sex."

Ellis describes in detail three kinds of play to which we may give the names of courtship, education and esthetic effort. Thought provoking as are his distinctions it is probably that they represent only different aspects of the same essential thing.

All sex-play should be courtship. It should be courtship, how ever, not necessarily pursuit. This aspect of play is important because courtship exerts a direct internal influence upon the whole organism. It stimulates all the faculties. It acts upon our whole being through our glands.

But play should also have the aspect of education. That we can make play out of reading we know, but that we can make play out of history, mathematics, and philosophy is not so generally recognized. We do not associate education with play because modern education is so largely cursed by compulsion and burdened by preparation for money-making. To be play, education must be pursued for its own sake.

Finally, play should have an esthetic content. Play should be made out of both "useless" activities such as singing and dancing and out of "useful" activities such as sewing, gardening, painting, cabinet-making by pursuing them not only for their utility but also with the intention of achieving esthetic forms. It is in creative work in the fine arts and in pure science, however, that play can be made to manifest itself in the production of the highest of human achievements.

Today we do not play—we only distract ourselves. We have neither the time nor the inclination for play in these threefold aspects. Yet real comfort is impossible without play in all these aspects.

Our activities need re-integration if we are to play in this high sense. We cannot put play in one tight compartment of our lives, and work in another. We play best when we work best. The two are really inseparable. For play is no passive thing. We must participate in play if we are to extract from it all that it is possible for us to secure from it. To the extent to which we indulge in vicarious play, we sacrifice the courtly, the educational, and the esthetic potentialities of play.

Today there is hardly a single aspect of play which has not been prostituted by a combination of exhibitionism and commercialism. Professional singing, for instance, is a manifest abnormality. Do not the over-developed bellows and the artificial facial action of a professional singer largely destroy the beauty of her performance? In order to really enjoy a professional singer one must either close the eyes or get far enough away so that it is impossible to see the contortions involved in the production of the beautiful tones of the song. No such feeling is invoked when one hears someone quite spontaneously break into song at work, or when there is singing within the circle of a friendly group.

There are practically no good grounds for believing that either the esthetic content or the educational value of play is being increased by the sort of leisure which the factory seems to be thrust ing upon us. Educational play today consists of extension courses, lecture courses and chautauquas. Esthetic play embraces art collecting, uplift work and that idiotic form of self-expression of which the tea-room and the antique shop are excellent symbols.

As to the play aspect of our sex-life there can be no doubt that the factory is taking the place of the church as the greatest prevention of courtliness in sex-life. Against the church, Havelock Ellis and his disciples, notably Judge Ben. B. Lindsey in the United States, may be winning; but against the factory they are almost certainly losing. The beauty which they are trying to infuse into sex-life by freeing us from the incubus of church dogmas is being withered by a factory-dominated civilization which turns us into irresponsible animals to whom sex means mere barbaric self-indulgence.

•

With the intensification of home life which would follow upon an adventure in domestic production, the home would become almost automatically the center of our social and play life. Youth, maturity, and old age would not only work at home but play at home as well.

In a factory-dominated civilization we spend our play time in watching baseball, tennis and football rather than in playing them.

The time we should devote to participating in sports we spend as spectators of professional players.

The time we should devote to singing and to playing on musical instruments we now spend listening to singers, orchestras and phonographs.

The time which we should spend, especially in youth, in court ing and dancing in our homes, we now devote to purchased entertainment in dance halls, movies and amusement resorts.

And the time which at one time was given to extending hospitality and to receiving it in homes has now been replaced by the more convenient and more fashionable custom of buying this hospitality from hotels and clubs which are in the business of manufacturing it for us.

Why shouldn't chess, checkers, cards and the legion of games which can be played within the family circle enliven our homes? Why shouldn't our homes contain libraries, tennis courts, billiard tables, swimming pools and rooms in which to dance? It costs much less to secure and maintain all these things in our homes than it costs us today to purchase their equivalent in minute installments from clubs, pool rooms, restaurants and theatres. In homes located, equipped and organized for play few would feel the present drive to spend time satisfying social instinct in theatres, hotels, roadhouses and country clubs. And in such homes hospitality could be dispensed with a lavish hand.

We must either provide play for ourselves or accept the ignominy of buying substitutes for it. And if we drift with the tide and spend our time upon the substitutes, we shall end by losing our ability to enjoy any kind of play. So far, in fact, have we already drifted that the schools find it necessary to provide instructors to teach our children how to play. Failure to play, to participate in play, evidently affects our habits precisely as failure to exercise affects our muscles. It is the law that faculties which are not used degenerate. Certainly this is the law with regard to the faculty for play. As we decrease the time devoted to real play and content ourselves more and more with vicarious play, we tend to lose not only the ability to participate in play, but even the capacity to enjoy play as a spectator.

The penalty exacted by nature for a lifetime of vicarious play is boredom.

•

For those of us who aspire to the cultivation of exceptional talents; who aspire to write, to paint, to sing, to teach, a saving of one-third of the time which we now have to devote to earning money for the basic essentials of life has revolutionary sociological implications. For it means much more than the release of four full months out of each year for work which we really love; it means also freedom from a servitude to the factory-dominated world which forces us to prostitute our talents in order to earn a living. We would no longer be compelled to routinize and commercialize work which should be a perennial joy to ourselves and our fellows.

A beautiful civilization needs more men and women to whom the work of their crafts and their professions is the expression of their own inner aspirations and fewer to whom it is merely a way of making a living. It is this deficiency in our civilization which would be corrected by a release of one-third of the time which quality-minded men and women now have to devote to earning a living. Such a release would free them for the practice of their professions in a genuinely amateur spirit.

The world needs amateur writers, painters, sculptors, dramatists, teachers and scientists. It needs men and women who can appreciate the great achievements of the arts and the sciences because they are themselves engaged in contributing to them. Many of the greatest achievements of the human race in the arts and sciences have been the work of amateurs—men and women who worked in many fields and brought to bear upon each of them that fresh point of view which the specialists and the technicians do not supply.

I do not mean incompetents when I speak of amateurs. The world does not need mere dilettantes who have neither the patience nor the stamina for the discipline which is necessary to the production of good work. The world needs able men who have such rounded personalities that they can express themselves in many fields with satisfaction to themselves and benefit to society generally. A Benjamin Franklin who is a printer, a writer, a scientist and a statesman; a Thomas Jefferson who is a farmer, a philosopher, a teacher, a statesman, a lawyer and a writer; a George Washington who is a military strategist, a statesman, a surveyor and a farmer: these are worth more to the world than dozens of one-track-minded specialists and technicians.

The versatility of these great men proves that it is possible for men to be masters of many trades, provided they are masters of their own time.

As long as we are forced to solve our basic economic problem solely by the practice of our professions, we cannot afford to experiment and adventure in any field that happens to interest us. And what is even more important, we are not free to refuse to do work which does violence to our inclinations and our ideals.

To this extent we can free ourselves if only we organize our economic life so that earning the money for the material essentials of comfort ceases to be the major problem of our lives.

•

Because of the pressure of our earn-and-buy regime, we have to measure our time by the money return we can secure for it. In the case of those of us who devote ourselves to the arts, the sciences and the professions, the consequence is tragic. Undue emphasis has to be placed upon the vocational aspect of our chosen work. The work therefore ceases to be a way of living. It becomes a way of *earning* a living. Willy nilly we tend to be warped in the direction of expressing ourselves in money-making rather than in the work we do. And we pay the inevitable penalty in self-frustration. Unable to use our work as the medium for the expression of our creative abilities, is it any wonder that artists, scientists, writers, lawyers, doctors, teachers—learned men of all kinds —lack self-respect?

The time which we devote to the practice of our chosen labors is infected by the same disease that infects the time which laborers spend at their work in the factory. It is lime devoted to a particular method of procuring money; not time devoted to self-expression in work.

And like the great, unlearned masses, we are condemned to find "happiness" in spending money, and not in the production of creative works.

•

The dedication of our time to the commercialization of our chosen work, something we can hardly avoid as long as we secure a living by contributing to the functioning of the factory, supplements our loss of self-respect by creating an actual contempt for us in the general public. The learned man is deprived both of self-respect and public respect.

Why should the businessman who is greedy for money respect doctors when he sees that the doctors all about him are just as completely absorbed in money-making as he is himself? If doctors make it plain that doctoring is to them no more than business is to the business man, a mere means to procuring wealth, why should the business man dignify the doctors?

Consider the significance of the present-day acceptance of this commercialization of the professions by our colleges and universities. At the same time that our institutions of higher learning place more and more emphasis upon the commercial aspects of the professions, the process of professionalizing even the most non professional of occupations goes on apace.

The doctors are losing prestige. The business men are gaining it.

Business in fact is being made into a so-called profession. Schools of business are graduating professional administrators, accountants, advertising men, and even salesmen. Degrees and doctorates are awarded for activities that answer to none of the requirements of professional life. The distinction between an occupation that is followed for its own sake and one which is followed for money's sake is thus obliterated.

•

Finally to accommodate ourselves to the circumstances in which this factory-dominated civilization has placed us, we have had to transfer all the techniques which make the factory efficient from the factory to the professions. Specialization, institutionalism, and expediency have to take the place of the wisdom which ought to be the major interest of the learned man. For our civilization has opportunities for expert technicians rather than for learned men.

Those of us who expose ourselves to all these influences by trying to earn a living out of some professional activity are subjecting ourselves to the most prolific incubator of malformed personalities which mankind has in all its history devised. For in order to support ourselves and those dependent upon us we are driven to devote our time to the cultivation of so narrow a sphere of activities that we are largely helpless and utterly useless outside of the field in which we make our living.

Unless we repudiate this regime; unless we free ourselves from the servitude to the factory which such a method of self-support imposes, the time we work and which should contribute most to the conquest of comfort will burden us with the heaviest of all discomforts.

Unless we do repudiate it, we acquiesce in an almost complete misuse of our time; in a thriftless waste of the most precious of the attributes of life.

•

For time unnecessarily spent in labor which we do not enjoy is a crime against ourselves and against civilization.

While we live we have only one thing to spend: time.

The way we spend our time; the activities to which we dedicate the days, hours, and minutes of our lives, these constitute the only stuff out of which we can create real comfort.

No amount of wealth and power; none of the creature comforts of which our factory-dominated civilization offers us such an abundance; no purchased sport, amusement, art, literature, music no matter how perfectly executed, is a sufficient compensation for the waste of precious time in work which destroys our very capacity for enjoying life.

•

And now let us become really "practical."

Let us consider the question of how we are to procure the capital with which to establish such homes as I have described and to equip them with the machines which will make it possible to devote our time to labor which we do enjoy.

CHAPTER XVII
THE FACTORS IN THE QUEST OF COMFORT:
III. Machines

If the home is to produce, it must contain the means of production. And if it is to produce comfortably, the "means of production" must include the machines which will make this possible.

But by far the largest number of families in this factory-dominated civilization have neither lands nor houses, tools nor machinery. Money enough to buy them is for these families an iridescent dream. They cannot seriously think about producing their own essentials of comfort nor of making themselves economically free until some practical plan is available which would enable them to secure the means for domestic production.

How can a family today, which may be without any real capital to begin with, secure a home and furnish it with the machines that are necessary to produce a standard of living as high as that to which it has been accustomed?

•

With rising land values; with higher wages for building labor and high prices of building materials; with tools, supplies, livestock, farm equipment, and above all machines, often outrageously high in price, (because of the selling extravagances of manufacturers and distributors), a sum of money of which few families can boast today is necessary to establish the creative home which I have been describing. The average disestablished family, even if it now has a large income, finds the cost of living so high that it is certain to shrink from the task of saving the money needed even for a modest first step toward acquiring its own means for domestic production. How is this family to go about securing the money to buy itself a homestead? How is it to buy all of the things over and above real estate which it will need if it is to produce for itself material comforts at least equal to those which it now enjoys? It is difficult enough now to save. How is the family to make the out lays required for establishing a productive home and for equipping it with a full complement of domestic machines?

Let us see whether these questions are not in reality much less difficult than they appear at first sight.

•

Capitalization makes it possible to take anything capitalizable which produces an income of $60 yearly and realize nearly $1,000 upon it even though its real cost be only $100. The formula is:

$$(I \div M) \times 100 = D$$

which gives us:

$$(\$60 \div \$6) \times 100 = \$1{,}000$$

I being the annual income from the property, *M* the prevailing cost of money, and *D* the dollars realized through capitalization.

Plainly, the process of capitalization makes it possible to borrow capital with relation to the income from an investment and not the cost of the investment itself. Capitalize any income-basis with a net income of $60 yearly, and you can sell a thousand dollars worth of securities to secure it, even though it may actually cost you only a small part of that sum.

If that is not magic, nothing is.

•

Provided we have something to capitalize, the means for buying a homestead, for buying domestic machinery and for buying all that may be necessary to make an organic homestead function, can readily be procured.

Strange as it may seem, we have only in recent years rediscovered that time, the one universal possession of all men, is capitalizable.

The ancient world knew it well. Even in America it was generally understood hardly more than half a century ago. Slavery was a system for capitalizing time. The slaves were merely unfortunate creatures whose time had been made into property by law. In abandoning slavery, and the system of indenturing all sorts of workers, from servants to ministers of the gospel, which is so similar to slavery, society lost sight of the fact that time was capitalizable. This was no light loss to society; for the failure to provide every man with some method of capitalizing time made wage-slavery possible. Disestablished workers of all kinds, the professional workers as well as proletarians, have had no access to the accumulated capital of society until in recent years a new technique was developed which made it possible for them to capitalize their time and so re-establish themselves.

Now the one thing which the change in the economics of the family and the home which is here proposed does is to release time. Let our homes cease to be merely a place for consumption; let them become places of production as well, and much of our time is freed to be used for other things than the buying of consumption goods.

Less time has to be devoted to earning the money for rent when we produce shelter for ourselves.

Less time has to be devoted to earning the money for food when we produce most of our own foodstuffs.

Less and less time has to be devoted to earning money to buy things which are to be immediately consumed as more and more of the essentials of life are produced in the home itself.

Time thus becomes available for earning money to buy the machines which make drudgeless domestic production possible.

But what is most important, the time saved is released for capitalization.

For the time which does not have to be used for procuring the necessaries of life is in effect an income-base and with an income base, the magic of capitalization is made available for us. If by domestic production we cut our food bill in half, we save at least one day's time per week. If we can earn $10 per day, the 52 days saved during the year create an income base of $520. Applying the formula, ($520÷$6) x 100, we get $8,666. This sum be comes theoretically available to us for investment as a result of domestic production of foodstuffs alone. But the $8,666 can be realized only if we are willing to pay interest for its use indefinitely. And also it demands of us a financial wizardry sufficient to secure money for 6%. In practice, money costs more than 6% and provision must be made for the amortization of the principal. This cuts down the dollars actually realized through capitalization. More than $5,000 may be realized if the money is wanted to build a home. Less than $500 may be realized if the money is wanted to purchase a tractor.

The saving of even one day's time per week through domestic production makes a capital of from $500 to $5,000 available to us.

And cutting down the food bill by no means exhausts the possibilities for saving time through domestic production.

•

If credit were to be defined as electricity has to be, by what it does rather than by what it is, the temptation to say that it is money would be irresistible.

With money we can go anywhere and buy almost everything. With credit too we can go anywhere and buy almost anything. In this crucial quality—as a medium for buying—money and credit are almost indistinguishable.

It is not necessary to have money when it is possible to secure credit.

The businessman who needs money with which to equip his factory can capitalize it and with the proceeds from the sale of stocks and bonds equip it as he desires. But with only time to capitalize we cannot adopt the complex expedient of issuing stocks and bonds. Nor do we need to do so. Not only can we equip our homes with domestic machinery; we can secure the homes themselves by taking full advantage of installment credit, probably without paying the finance corporation more for the credit we use than businessmen have to pay investment bankers for the money they put into their corporations.

In America we have only begun to capitalize time through the instrumentality of installment credit.

But already nearly ten percent of the national income is devoted to the purchase of goods and real estate in this way. Nearly ten percent of the time spent by the American people in earning money is now devoted to paying for what they have purchased on installment credit. On the average, thirty days out of the average man's working year is already capitalized by him through the instrumentality of installment credit. Yet the yearly purchase of real estate on the installment plan amounts to only $1,600,000,000. None of us need hesitate to take the first step toward the establishment of a productive home for lack of capital. Of course we have to show under the rules of the economic game as it is played today that we can earn money, save money, and pay money when we owe it. Yet if we prove these things by accumulating a nest egg, however small, a building and loan association will be glad to capitalize for us the time that we are willing to appropriate to acquiring a home.

•

Modern accountancy has made it plain that there is a great difference between expenditures for investments and expenditures for current expenses. If the treasurer of a corporation makes out two checks, each for one thousand dollars, and sends one of them to a manufacturer of machinery for new machines which have been installed in his factory, and the other to a banker for interest on bans, the two expenditures are clearly distinguished in his mind and on the books of his corporation. One represents investment—the other overhead expense. The $1,000 invested in machinery is expected to earn enough not only to enable him to pay interest on the investment, but the cost of the machinery it self. The $1,000 paid out for interest is an expense different in every respect. The treasurer finds it easy to distinguish between the two types of expenditures. But the self-same man may be very much surprised if he is told that identically the same distinctions exist with regard to many expenditures his wife makes for his home.

If she presents him during the same week with two bills each for $25—one for an improved fruit press, and the other for groceries, he is apt to think of them both as just $50 worth of household expenses. Yet the expenditure for the fruit press is distinctly investment, while the expenditure for groceries is distinctly current expense. The difference is practical, not academic. If the fruit press is properly used, it immediately begins to earn its own cost. It either reduces her expenditures for preserved fruits and for table beverages, or, if she is already making these at home it reduces the amount of labor expended in their production, and so frees her time for other activities. The saving made possible with domestic machinery is so large, often larger than that which is possible as a result of the installation of machinery in a factory, that the investment in an appliance such as a fruit press, is wiped out often in a single season. The equipment is then on hand to effect similar savings in the future and to make the purchase of other labor-saving machinery just so much easier.

•

If the investment in house, in gardens, in poultry yards, in fruit trees, in farm equipment, in machinery of all kinds is considered from this standpoint, no family should hesitate to use credit in order to purchase them. For, unlike expenditures for consumption goods, they cost nothing. They pay for themselves, for their maintenance, for their depreciation in precisely the same way that properly selected and properly operated machinery in the factory pays for itself. They are different only in that the net dividends upon the investment in them is so much larger than in factory machinery.

For with domestic machinery there is no cost of marketing the production, and little loss from improper balancing of production and consumption. The savings made possible by the use of machinery are not in large part wasted by costs of transportation, selling, advertising, wholesaling and retailing. Nor is the net dividend whittled away through the production of a greater supply than the market demands. Our own needs determine the amount produced and practically all that is produced is consumed.

Our real problem is therefore only the initial problem of securing the capital with which to purchase the machines which make domestic production practicable.

•

That problem vanishes when proper use is made of credit.

There is, it is true, no excuse for buying on credit if cash is available, or money can be borrowed on regular terms from a bank. Installment credit—the form most generally used—is rather expensive. But if due allowance is made for this fact, it still remains the part of wisdom to buy equipment for domestic production on this plan provided in each instance the saving which a particular purchase makes possible is greater than the cost of the installment credit. On most types of domestic machinery the savings justify the payment of even usurious "finance" charges. As a matter of fact, it is only because so very large a part of the installment buying of today consists of things that are productive in this sense that the whole edifice of installment buying has not already collapsed. The fact that so many of the things purchased on installments tend to pay for themselves is the explanation of the public's ability to meet excessive selling costs and financing charges. Some figures compiled by Mr. Milan V. Ayers which were published in *Advertising and Selling* for August 8, 1828, are here arranged in two columns, one representing the public's purchases of productive goods and the other of non-productive goods, for the purpose of demonstrating this fact.

	Productive	Non-Productive	Total
New passenger cars	778	1,556	2,334
New trucks	485		485
Used cars and trucks	400	561	961
Household furniture		789	789
Pianos		234	234
Phonographs		174	174
Sewing machines	106		106
Washing machines	104		104
Property improvements	108		108
Radio sets		181	181
Jewelry store goods		108	108
Clothing		282	282
Tractors	75		
Vacuum cleaners	56		
Other farm machinery	31		
Gas stoves	27		
Mechanical refrigeration	16		
Miscellaneous (not classified)			108
	2,186	3,885	6,179

The classification of the items as productive and non-productive in this table is open to much question. Furniture, to consider one type which I have classified as non-productive, might well be classified as productive on the assumption that the family which provides itself with furniture is producing for itself what a family in a hotel rents along with the shelter, laundry and maid service which the hotel furnishes. Pianos, phonographs and radio sets might also be classified as productive on the assumption that they enable the family to produce its own entertainment instead of paying for it in a club, theatre or movie. But even if these items are classified as non-productive, 36 percent of all the purchases of the American people on the installment plan are of a productive character. Add the purchases of real estate, which are estimated at more than four times the aggregate purchases of all the non-productive items, and it is plain that most of present day installment buying is self-liquidating in the same sense that investments in factories, factory machinery and real capital for business purposes generally are self-liquidating.

In spite of the high cost of commercial installment credit, in spite of the terrific burden of selling costs that are loaded upon many of the things sold on the installment plan, it is the part of wisdom for those of us who are without capital to buy and equip a productive home on the installment plan.

•

So long as our scientists, engineers, inventors, all those whose ideas predetermine the developments of this industrial age, continue to concern themselves with the development of factory machinery and factory techniques; so long as clever business men, advertising men and salesmen continue the development of mass production of consumption goods with distribution in the national market at the expense of the local production with local distribution, there is little hope for any great development in domestic production. But let them once begin to see the enormous market for household appliances which a general movement toward economic self-sufficiency would bring into existence, and captains of industry would begin the process of cramming domestic machinery down the throats of the masses, just as their prototypes have always crammed new ideas down the throats of the masses in every age.

Alexander crammed Greek ideas down the throats of all the populations he conquered. Cæsar crammed Roman ideas down the throats of most of Europe. Constantine crammed Christian ideas down the throats of the masses wherever his rule extended. Manufacturers with their factories have up to very recent times crammed the ideas of Smith and Mill concerning the production and distribution of wealth down the throats of most of the world. Between the industrially-minded big-businessmen of America, the Fascists of Italy and the Bolsheviks of Russia, mass-production under scientific management is being crammed down the throats of the modern world.

For the quantity-minded care nothing about the nature of ideas but only about how they can be turned to account for their own aggrandizement, their own power, their own glory, and how they can use a new idea for the purpose of winning in the competition with their fellows. The ideas which they impose on mankind vary from age to age. There is no consistency in them. They are perfectly willing to be pagan in one age and Christian in the next; competitive in one age and monopolistic in another.

For the past one hundred and fifty years they have been busily developing the factory, filling the world with smokestacks, and harnessing mankind to factory machinery. In the next fifty years they may turn around and undo all that they have recently done by decentralizing electric power and promoting the sale of domestic machinery.

Well, let them wheedle, flatter, frighten, even bully mankind into the idea of domestic production. Let them develop and manufacture domestic machinery, furnish the individual home with power, multiply the agencies for credit so that larger and larger sections of the population can buy the means of domestic production. Let them wax rich and powerful in the process—as those who pioneer in it surely will. They will at least make it possible to lessen the ugliness of civilization instead of, as today, making it almost impossible to do so. Above all, they will make it easier for the quality-minded to achieve the freedom to be themselves.

There will be fewer factories, less waste of precious raw materials, and more time for all of us to devote to expressive living if business men devoted themselves to making such a world. And certainly in a world filled with creating and producing homes there would be more comfort than prevails in the factory-dominated homes of today.

CHAPTER XVIII
THE FACTORS IN THE QUEST OF COMFORT:
IV. Wisdom

THREE of the factors in the quest of comfort have now been discussed.

A fourth yet remains to be considered.

•

At first, economists spoke only of three factors in the production of wealth: land, labor and capital.

Then they found it necessary to add a fourth: management. For it was soon discovered that administrative skill, courage to take risks, leadership and ideas were just as essential to the production of wealth as land, labor and capital.

So it is with regard to the factors in the production of comfort.

We may bring to the quest of comfort a productive homestead; we may provide the necessary time; we may acquire the machines, but to these three factors we must add a fourth which shall play, in our effort to produce comfort, a part similar to that which management plays in the production of wealth. This factor must, however, more than provide us with the creature comforts to which the existing state of art and science entitles us. It must make possible a spiritual* as well as a material conquest of comfort.

Man does not live by bread alone.

•

The factor in the quest of comfort which deals with both the material and the spiritual aspects of comfort, I call wisdom.

•

It is the factor in the quest of comfort which transcends the production of material well being.

For wisdom is not only a combination of enterprise, knowl-

* Whenever the term "spiritual" is used in connection with comfort it is used as an antonym for "material" and without any intent to suggest anything mystical or religious.

edge, experience. It is not only what economists call management. It is also understanding.

•

And understanding we must have, in part to enable us to achieve material comfort without sacrificing spiritual comfort in the process of securing it, but mainly to enable us to create a goal the human life less ugly than that with which we are satisfied today.

For thus spoke Zarathustra:

> If the goal of humanity is still lacking, is there not also lacking—humanity itself?

•

Whilst the whole world strives madly to become wise in the production of wealth, it is time for some of us to become wise in the production of comfort.

The consciously ignorant but inquiring man; the man to whom experience is a liberal education; the man who appreciates the importance of understanding, can acquire this wisdom if only he will abandon the herd-taboos, the herd-thinking and the herd-callousness of his factory-dominated fellow-beings.

•

For man, my friends, is a creature who functions between two planes of values; a low plane upon which he acts automatically and with the minimum of intelligence, and a high plane upon which he acts consciously and with the maximum of intelligence. Whether he functions upon the low plane or the high plane is determined by a fortuitous concatenation of accidents over which he may have no control.

For you the reading of these lines may prove that accident.

If that be so, welcome to super-conscious participation in the comedy and tragedy of man!

PART V
THE PHILOSOPHIC ASPECT

Around the devisers of new values revolveth the world, invisibly it revolveth.

—*Thus Spake Zarathustra*.

CHAPTER XIX
THE CONQUEST OF COMFORT

ALL men crave comfort. But few are capable of experiencing it.

For men are of two kinds: those who can understand, and those who cannot. And only those are capable of experiencing comfort who are capable of understanding it.

What is here said concerning the quest of comfort may mean something to those who can understand. It will mean absolutely nothing to those who cannot.

For

> . . . No secret can be told
> To any who divined it not before;
> None uninitiate by many a presage
> Will comprehend the language of the message
> Although proclaimed aloud for evermore.[47]

•

Life is a sequence: birth, growth, consciousness, joy, pain, reproduction, decay and death.

We have this sequence somehow or other to live. How shall we live it, and what shall we think about it?

There can be no conquest of comfort, even though we surround ourselves with all the comforts which civilization offers us, until we answer this question for ourselves and put into the answer what ever may be needed of the accumulated knowledge of mankind, of personal experience, and of the understanding that makes for wisdom.

Life, it is true, will still remain "a tale told by an idiot; full of sound and fury, signifying nothing," but we will be able at least to console ourselves for enduring it at all.

•

Few indeed are those of us who achieve the privilege of answering this question for ourselves. Most of us never even ask ourselves the question because we accept the answer which society provides for us in conventional custom, conventional law, conventional religion.

For we are born subject to the tyranny of conventions.

We begin to absorb conventions from the moment we take suck at our mothers' breasts. And we continue to absorb them thereafter until we die. We live out our allotted span surrounded, immersed and engulfed by them. It is a miracle if we escape the credulity which makes the masses of mankind believe in them; it is twice a miracle if we develop the scepticism which makes it possible for us to detect the falsehoods in them; it is thrice a miracle if we discover how often they become the barriers to our comfort.

For the society into which we are born is not of any intelligent being's contriving. It is a chaos of irrational, contradictory, cowardly conventions which have acquired validity not because of inherent truth and goodness and beauty but through the inertia of great antiquity and general consent.

If we discover that the conventions which civilization accepts and which civilization generally imposes upon us are merely the compromises of the timid and fearful, stupid and ignorant masses with the ideas launched throughout the ages by exceptional men, we will not hesitate to abandon them and to replace conventions with principles of conduct which represent the deliberate application of wisdom to every phase of life.

•

This is an elemental fact about the good life which our present morality does not recognize. Intelligence is suspected today, on the theological theory, flattering to the inferior masses of mankind, that intelligence is of the devil.

To the herd-minded there is no inconsistency in the belief that men may be intelligent and yet immoral, and good even though they be fools.

Now while intelligent men may live the good life, ignorant and conventional men can never do so. Ignorant men cannot be truly good. They can only be innocent.

To live the good life, we must eat freely of the fruit of the Tree of the Knowledge of Good and Evil.

•

To the herd-minded who accept the conventions because they "know" them to proceed from truth, the universe presents no unsolvable riddle; life no inexplicable miracle; consciousness no impenetrable mystery. For them the riddles of the universe do not exist. Convention fills the infinite spaces of the cosmos for them with a god. It makes life purposeful for them with a promise of paradise. It makes consciousness free for them by endowing human kind with an immortal soul. Why should they therefore spend time struggling to understand life—concerning which they think they already know the truth?

Unfortunately for ourselves and for mankind, even the quality minded are influenced and governed by whole encyclopedias of equally false facts, false hopes and false fears. This is our poignant tragedy: that so many of us potentially capable of understanding, accept these armies of conventional falsehoods because we dare not take the time to question them.

We never get to ask "What is truth?" because we can not spare the time to ask "What is falsehood?"

We have not the time—the time to read, to converse, to work, to play—which is necessary to acquire wisdom.

We cannot—because we are too busy.

We are too busy, in this particular civilization, keeping our factories producing—telephoning, dictating, conferring, producing and marketing, advertising and selling, financing and profiteering—to devote time to the acquisition of wisdom. And so we continue the dupes of the colossal delusion that the conquest of comfort consists of nothing but the accumulation and consumption of the creature comforts that our factories produce.

•

Not every man is capable of understanding. Men are born with different potentialities for acquiring wisdom. The idiot is born with zero potentialities. The perfect man with one hundred percent.

Both throughout their lives react to their environments, but their reactions to them—even when their environments are identical—are different. A piece of quartz may be subjected to all the artistic polishing of the most skillful lapidary; it will never become a diamond. The final result of the polishing—the quartz's reaction to it—is conditioned by the original stuff of which the gem is composed. The moron may be educated to the *n*th degree, he remains a moron even though educated. So it is with *every* man's reaction to environment. Let his environment be what it will, his reaction to it will vary with his potentialities. And since potentialities are unknowable, the ratio of the influence of potentiality upon the reaction to environment is indeterminable.

How much of his potentialities each man realizes is determined by his environment—the effect upon him of his family, school, friends, work—by the totality of all the circumstances and conditions of his life. These determine what sort of man he will finally become, and how much understanding he acquires, much as the diamond polishing determines what sort of diamond will finally emerge from the rough, but potentially beautiful, gem. This environmental polishing process is man's real education. It is real education as contrasted with the academic education to which the term "education" is generally confined.

What each man manages to extract and to incorporate into his personality from exposure to his environment determines the extent to which he realizes his potentialities. More than his potentialities however, nothing that he may do and no educational process—nothing in his environment—will enable him to realize. The *quartz,* no matter how much it be polished, can never be anything more than perfectly polished *quartz.*

•

Reduced to a mathematical equation we may say:

$$R = x{\cdot}P{\cdot}E$$

in which R represents man's reaction to life—the individual's reaction to environment—his real education—expressed in percentages of perfect reaction; P represents man's potentialities—his inherent capacity for acquiring knowledge, intelligence, wisdom—

expressed in percentages of perfect potentiality; *E* represents the individual environment—home, school, church, work; parents, friends, associates; party, religion, nationality—the totality of his circumstances and conditions—expressed in percentages of perfect environment; while *x* represents the ratio of the influence exerted by his potentialities upon his reactions to environment—the effect which his capacity for learning has upon what he learns from his environment.

•

To illustrate: two men begin life with different potentialities: Mr. Potentially Inferior begins with 10 percent of perfect potentiality; Mr. Potentially Superior begins with 100. Environment now determines for them how much of their potentialities they will realize.

Mr. Potentially Inferior, if he encounters an environment only one percent perfect, will be educated to only a portion of his possibilities. But if he experiences an environment of 10 percent, he will fully realize his potentialities and attain to a reaction to life of 10 percent of possible perfection.

If Mr. Potentially Superior passes through life in an environment of only one percent, he may not even develop to the degree that Potentially Inferior does in an environment of 10 percent, in spite of the fact that he has ten times the potentialities of Potentially Inferior. But if Potentially Superior's environment is 10 percent, or the same as Potentially Inferior's, Superior will be many times wiser than Inferior because his enormously greater aptitude for wisdom enables him to extract much more from the same educational opportunities.

If Potentially Superior's experiences are, however, only one percent; if they are such that he passes through life in an environment which fails to develop his possibilities; if he lives in a crude environment without contact with the accumulated wisdom of the ages, in spite of his high potentialities he will probably be an illiterate, untravelled, ignorant man; a mere rough diamond. He will be one of mankind's "mute, inglorious Miltons."

But if Superior's experience were to be just the opposite; if he were to live in an environment which developed his potentialities and if every circumstance of his life combined to develop his capacities; if he found in various individuals, various books and various experiences those burning flashes of insight which make life forever afterward more comprehensible, then he would far surpass Inferior.

For Inferior's reaction to life, no matter what his educational opportunities, can never get beyond 10 percent of possible perfection. Superior, however, can assimilate when Inferior no longer can. He can learn from environments of more than 10 percent—indeed, if he has a potentiality of 100, he will never stop learning and will become wise to a degree that is inconceivable to the man of such limited potentialities as Inferior.

Inferior can never rise above the herd. Inferior's capacity for climbing out from the overwhelming mass of falsehoods with which all men are environed is too small to enable him to really understand.

But Superior can. He has the necessary capacity, if he is given, or gives himself, the chance. He can Begin his warfare upon the all-encircling falsehoods of our civilized conventions with some assurance that he will someday attain wisdom *if he is free to make the necessary effort.*

And he must make that effort.

For Superior is potentially a man of wisdom. He must make himself wise in actuality because every potentially wise man is confronted by the alternatives of suffering frustration, or of securing the freedom to live wisely.

•

In nothing is the difference between the inferior average man and the superior exceptional man more clearly revealed than in the complacence with which the average man accepts the falsehoods of our conventions, and the energy with which the superior man tries to free himself from these conventional falsehoods—these innumerable falsehoods asserted as facts, accepted as facts, generally acted upon as facts but which a little investigation reveals as incompatible with the facts they purpose to describe or explain.

Fortunately these falsehoods, which constitute what may be called the barriers to wisdom, (and therefore to comfort), usually reveal themselves in self-contradictions. The comparison of one group of conventional beliefs with another tends to reveal these contradictions. Through such comparisons conventional false hoods can be made to destroy themselves. The destruction of the more important of these barriers to wisdom is therefore an essential first step towards the attainment of wisdom itself.

•

It is a futile waste of time for us to look to modern "applied" science for wisdom. modern science has been made the hopeless serving-maid of the modern factory. It is concerned with the problem of how the factory can be made to produce and distribute more and more, not the question of how we should live and what we should think about life.

As to "pure" science—well, its so-called laws of nature may tell us how we live but they do not tell us how we *should* live. They may tell us how we think, but they do not tell us what we *should* think.

For science seeks no further than its natural laws. It seeks these laws as if there were such things as natural laws.

Nature, however, knows no laws. Nature is as sublimely indifferent to us and our concerns as is god himself.

What we call natural laws are merely our own interpretations of nature's undesigned and inexorable sequence of changing appearances. The uniformities and the regularities which we think we have found and which we assume to be universal and immutable and which we dignify by the name of natural law—these sequences which we apprehend and measure and record most of all need rationalization.

We have too credulously accepted the idea of inexpugnable natural law.

We have assumed that without it there could be no scientific ordering of knowledge.

Yet a metaphysic which begins with the negation of natural law furnishes us just as sound a basis for an understandable universe as does one which begins with the affirmation of natural law. And such a metaphysic may actually aid us in arriving at a better statement of the question of the absolute itself.

There is no more reason why we should accept the *prevalence* of law and order than there is reason for us to accept the *absence* of law and order. One hypothesis is just as reasonable as the other.

The view of nature as a series of events occurring in an in variable order without the intervention of mutable personal agencies is of very recent origin. Before the age of Newton and Darwin practically all men thought of nature—as the savage still thinks—as mutable, local, irregular and nonsequential. And men begot, lived and died in spite of the fact that they thought of the world as the plaything of propitiable supernatural beings. Now we have universally accepted the idea of law, and are blind to the fact that what we call law, is simply the ideas of a particular set of thinkers at a particular time.

Ultimately we shall discover the natural law itself can only be relative—and law therefore only to us.

•

Assume that the universe is chaos—that there is no ultimate order to it whatsoever. What we apprehend as orderly—the sequence of causes and effects to which we give the name of natural law then becomes sequential only to us. It is orderly only in our *minds.*

The universe is *apparently* orderly, not *necessarily* orderly.

The sequences which we see have order, universality, immutability only relatively to our point of observation—relative to us and our limitations in time and space and understanding. *But, they may have no sequence at all viewed from the standpoint of eternal time or infinite space.*

We are creatures that pick out of all the chaotic facts and incidents which we apprehend certain ones apparently related to each other causally, and upon the basis of these identified relationships we build our magics and religions, our sciences and philosophies. To us they have a well-nigh absolute validity. But no matter how valid to us, they do not preclude the possibility that there may be no design, no order, no uniformity, no law, no inexorability in the totality of all events in all time and all space.

The consequence of this assumption must be considered: why does the attainment of some sort of order have such an importance to us? Why science and philosophy? Why our unending effort at understanding?

The answer is twofold: order, even if it is of our own devising, has for us a survival value, and to the extent of its correspondence with truth it makes real comfort possible to us. The wiser we are, the profounder our knowledge, the deeper our understanding, the greater are the probabilities of our survival and flic greater are the possibilities of our conquest of comfort. If we touch a hot stove with our fingers, we discover a natural law, if we may use the term natural law a little freely: fire invariably burns flesh. It always has burned it; it always will. The comprehension of sequences of this sort contributes manifestly both to survival and comfort even though they leave untouched the ultimate reality of what takes place when flesh is exposed to fire.

It is even possible to argue that every animate creature, and perhaps in some way everything inanimate as well, survives and is comfortable only if it develops for itself apparently inexorable sequences in nature, and adapts itself to them. For the evocation of a relatively orderly scheme in nature according to which it then governs its own existence is not an exclusive prerogative of human beings. Each creature which evokes a routine that enables it to adapt itself to the minor changes in the sequences of nature survives and lives more comfortably than it otherwise could. But the moment some major sequence develops which negates what seemed to it an immutable state of affairs and which is beyond its range of adaptation, discomfort sets in and destruction begins.

The whole universe is filled with things, animate and inanimate, intelligent and unintelligent, and of every gradation between these extremes, which are ceaselessly adapting themselves to their environments—which invent sequences to assist them in the process of adaptation—sequences to some of which mankind gives the august name of natural laws—and yet the existence of all these orders, laws, religions, philosophies, conventions, traditions, customs—the existence of all these patterns of being and action with which life is guided and governed—does not reduce by a particle the probability that the totality of all the events in the universe is chaos.

Mankind's patterns have validity for man only to the extent to which they contribute to his survival and comfort.

•

In far the greatest number of its manifestations human life is governed by what might well be called race-patterns. These patterns become life-routines, life-habits and life-instincts.

In all the lower, the physiological aspects of life, the race-patterns are well-nigh absolute. And we observe them instinctively. But in the higher, the conscious aspects, the race-patterns are subject to change by the individual. Yet even on these higher planes of being and action where wisdom can function for us, most of us tend to accept the conventional patterns, many of which are manifest barriers to the comfortable life. Most of us endure the discomforts which they inflict upon us because we are not sensitive enough to be conscious of them, or because we believe the discomforts inescapable and so deliberately accommodate ourselves to them.

Most of us tend to depart in no way from the patterns which the masses of men have somehow or other accepted and to which they have given a false validity though conventionalization. We travel with the stream of conventions and not against it or even at an angle to it. We hew no new paths—adopt no new ideas and ideals—create no new folkways—devise no superior patterns for our own conduct—make no intelligent effort to attain comfort because we are not free to do so.

Only as we free ourselves from servitude to arbitrary and non-creative routines; from conventions which do not contribute to comfort—only as wc give ourselves the time and leisure necessary to develop wisdom, do we begin consciously to create patterns of our own and so take on one of the attributes which give dignity to the conception of deity.

We may be interested in the qualitative aspects of living, but if we are not free to devote ourselves to their cultivation we can never succeed in the conquest of comfort.

•

Ultimately the ideas of quality-minded men—the ideas of the men who are free to devote themselves to the application of wisdom to every aspect of life—are absorbed into the race and culture patterns of all mankind. Their ideas are imposed through the agency of conventionalizations upon mankind and accepted by all types of men. The pattern which a Havelock Ellis creates for conduct; which a Michelangelo creates for art; which a Charles Darwin creates for philosophy, is first accepted by the alert and intelligent minority; it is then conventionalized, and so ultimately imposed upon all mankind.

Today modern art is sweeping over America like a rash. Quantity-minded men are persuading and making the herd minded accept modern art. The masses are accepting a new style in art, precisely as they accept a new style in dress, because they cannot avoid doing so. And ultimately they acquiesce in the im position, enjoy it, rejoice in it and even defend it. They do not, of course, understand the ideas which intrigue the proponents of modern art any more than they understand Ellis, or Michelangelo, or Darwin, but some trace of the ideas of the quality minded survives in the conduct of the herd, and if the ideas are good, quality-minded men may inwardly rejoice at the grim irony which enables them in this round-about fashion to impose upon all mankind their methods of enduring life.

•

"In the beginning" man lived briefly and flamingly. Instinct reigned undisputed. Man was the creature of his elemental needs, and was whipped and driven by blind biologic and physiologie necessity. Only when the quality-minded began to find themselves sufficiently free for the consideration of how men should live and what they should think, did the conscious patterning of conduct for survival, for comfort, for understanding begin.

These free men—or partly free men—who could give at least some time to the cultivation of wisdom, are the men who formulate what we may call mankind's laws of normality: norms deduced from the study of the necessities of human beings; norms which must be observed if men are to live comfortably; norms the violation of which are followed by premature decay and premature death.

It is just as natural for human beings to be diseased as to be perfectly healthy; to decay as to grow; to die prematurely as to the of old age. But it is not just as *normal.*

To the extent of his ability to formulate these norms and thus to introduce more intelligence into existence on his little speck of the universe, man is god.

He becomes the creator of that which did not exist before.

He imposes an order which he has created upon the universe.

For the norms which he creates tend to affect and modify mankind's subsequent being and action, and thus to introduce a design, a law, an order in the universe when otherwise there would have been only chance and chaos.

Confucius, Socrates, Schopenhauer; Darwin, Newton, Copernicus; Phidias, Michelangelo, Rembrandt; Wagner, Beethoven; Goethe, Voltaire, Shakespeare—men like these are not godlike; they are by the supreme test of creativity the only gods there are.

•

These norms are slowly and with great difficulty being established by men who are free to study man as an animal, as a creature who strives to satisfy his needs and desires and as a self conscious being.

Man is an animal, with animal appetites and animal limitations. By finding out what is essential to the normal functioning of man as an animal, we can determine what we ourselves should eat and drink; what we should do to keep physiologically comfortable.

Man is a necessitous creature. He needs food, clothing and shelter; he needs companionship, marriage, parenthood and he needs knowledge.

By finding out how man functions when he normally satisfies his needs or desires, or how he malfunctions when he fails in doing so, we can determine how we should secure our living; what sort of social life we should lead; how we should educate ourselves.

Man is a self-conscious being. He is forever seeking to justify his existence, his struggles, his pains, his joys; forever striving to explain his being through philosophy.

By finding out what is man's place in nature; how he struggles for survival and what pains and joys are normal to that process, we make understanding possible and so attain the wisdom which alone can dignify existence.

•

Without understanding there can be no wisdom.

Understanding must do for the wise man what tradition, habit, instinct, custom, law and convention do for the average man.

The conduct of the masses of average men, their subjective as well as objective behavior, consists of mere trial-and-error reactions to the universe in which they find themselves. Conventional conduct has for them survival value. It is a race-preservation mechanism.

That which convention dictates furnishes a guide to life even to the least understanding average man. The wise man, if he is to survive, must meet the same pragmatic tests for which the conventions were evolved. His conduct may therefore be objectively quite like that which convention dictates. But that makes him only the more unlike the average man. He is like the average man only to those incapable of distinguishing between *motive* and *action*—between conduct which is in one case conscious and voluntary and the other unconscious and involuntary.

Both the average man and the wise man work. Both are objectively performing similar actions. But subjectively their behavior is different. Their motivation is not the same. One works because he has to work. He accepts his "job" without thinking much about the matter. The other works because he has thought the matter through and has deliberately decided that work—of the right kind—is essential to the superior life.

•

Today mankind lives odiously, gracelessly, vulgarly, because the world belongs to quantity-minded men who cannot distinguish between the enjoyment of the comforts of life and the enjoyment of the comfortable life itself.

Life will remain more ugly than beautiful until the quality minded men who can show all of mankind how to live comfortably, are free to be more and more directly the architects of mankind's conventions and the arbiters of its conduct.

Quality-minded men must therefore free themselves more and more from servility to quantity-minded men and to the institutions dominated by the quantity-minded. First, for their own sakes—that they and their posterity shall be comfortable; and then for mankind's sake—that their pattern of living may the sooner be imitated by the masses of men.

For in the conquest of comfort for themselves, they bring about the conquest of comfort for all mankind. How they live and what they think, in spite of the fools, the prudes and the bigots, and in spite of the exploitation of their ideas by quantity-minded men, is ultimately accepted and imitated by the masses of herd-minded men.

It has always been so.

It will always be so.

For it is thus that the ideas of the quality-minded ultimately impose themselves upon mankind.

•

It is an ugly world, my friends. Perhaps it may be made a beautiful world, my friends.

It is an evil world, my friends. Perhaps it may be made a good world, my friends.

It is a foolish world, my friends. Perhaps it may be made a wise world, my friends.

Free yourselves, my friends, and it becomes yours to make it what you will.

•

For thus spake Zarathustra!

Dead are all the Gods: Now do we desire the Supermen to live.

CHAPTER XX
THE BARRIERS TO COMFORT

The Economic Barrier

FIRST comes the economic barrier.

We must live. We must secure food, clothing, shelter—all the essentials of comfort to which the progress of mankind entitles us. We must adopt methods of procuring the things which we desire as well as the things we need. If we adopt an economic policy which provides us three things: security, satisfying work, independence—we procure not only what we need and desire, we provide the conditions for spiritual comfort as well. Without such a policy we may have all the creature comforts of civilization and still be uncomfortable.

Today it is the convention to solve the problem of living by earning money, and to buy with the money what we need and desire. So overwhelming is the force of this convention that even those who inherit wealth in this country feel compelled to devote their time largely to money-making—while those who do not inherit wealth seem unable to think of any other method than that of earning money with which to buy the means to live according to the standard to which they aspire.

But for those of us who aspire to live the superior life, conformity to the convention that we must devote ourselves to the immediate material conquest of comfort, means an almost certain sacrifice of the ultimate spiritual conquest of comfort. Conformity to this convention of our factory-dominated civilization seems incompatible with the security, the satisfying work, and the independence necessary to real comfort.

For us, mere conformity to a scheme of existence which seems designed by the quantity-minded for the exploitation of the rest of mankind is no solution of the economic problem. Only the herd-minded can dispose of their problems by conformity to convention. Only those who are insensitive to the spiritual outrage of a life of insecurity, of inexpressive work, and of subservience to modern business can be comfortable through conformity to the earn-and-buy economy of today. For us, the alternatives of economic conformity or non-conformity represent a choice between frustration or deliberate adoption of an economic policy which makes it possible to secure both the essentials of comfort and the wisdom necessary to their enjoyment.

•

Such an economic policy has been described in some detail in Part IV of this book. No doubt there are other policies which we might adopt to attain the same ends. But whatever the policy we adopt, it should at least equal the one which I recommend in providing security as to the essentials of existence; in providing opportunities for engaging in satisfying work, and in providing freedom to devote time to work and play which is expressive of our real aspirations. All three of these are essential to any conquest of comfort. The last, we must not forget, is most important to those who would live the superior life.

•

So we come to what seems to me the basic principle upon which we must devise a policy which will surmount the economic barrier to the comfortable life. *Economically we must be dependent upon no one but ourselves and those of our own household.* For to the degree in which we are dependent economically upon others, to that degree do we cease to be free to live as we would like to live.

In the feudal civilization of the past we had to work for the nobility, and had therefore to be servants to the nobles and the kings.

In our present factory-dominated civilization we have to work for the factory in order to procure the essentials of life, and so we are servants to the capitalists who own the factories.

In a socialistic civilization we would have to work for the state, and we would become servants to the men who govern the state.

No matter how radically civilization changes, for us dependence always means submission to the conventions, the disciplines, the censorships, the cultural values of predatory, ruthless, acquisitive, quantity-minded human beings who are more interested in the exploitation of their fellows than in the question of how life should be lived.

•

A very homely story from the Old Testament makes it clear that when one man becomes dependent upon another, he may be forced to sacrifice his birthright of freedom and happiness. The story, somewhat freely quoted, is as follows:

> And Jacob had pottage.
>
> And Esau came from the hunt, and he was faint.
>
> And Esau said to Jacob: "Feed me, I pray thee, with that same pottage, for I am faint."
>
> And Jacob said, "Sell me this day thy birthright."
>
> And Esau said, "Behold, I am at the point to die, and what profit shall this birthright do me?"
>
> And Jacob said, "Swear to me this day."
>
> And Esau swore to him and he sold his birthright unto Jacob.
>
> Then Jacob gave Esau bread and pottage of lentils, and he did eat and drink, and rose up, and went his way.
>
> Thus Esau lost his birthright.

Quantity-minded Jacob; how well he knew how to get what he wanted! And Esau, mighty hunter though he was, was shorn of his birthright simply because he had neglected to provide for his elementary economic needs.

•

The legend of Jacob and Esau is an excellent illustration of the operation of one of the most important of all economic laws: the law that *the terms upon which an exchange is made between two parties are determined by the relative extent to which each is free to refuse to make the exchange.* If both are free to refuse, then the exchange will be made on equitable terms. Had Esau been free to refuse to buy, he would have paid Jacob only the reasonable, the market, the competitive, the just price for the food he wanted. But he was not free. He was unable to refuse to buy while Jacob was able to refuse to sell. The one who was "free" (to refuse to make the exchange), dictated the terms of the sale, and the one who was "not free" to refuse, had to pay whatever price was exacted from him.

So it is today. So it has always been and will probably always be.

Certainly in this factory-dominated civilization, the quantity minded, by concentrating upon the acquisition of wealth, naturally achieve a higher degree of freedom to refuse to make exchanges than do we. For to the degree in which we become interested in the qualitative aspects of life, we tend to neglect the acquisition of this freedom. Thus the quantity-minded, who are nearly always free, determine how and when and where we should work, and what we, who are rarely free, should receive for our work. But let us make ourselves free to withhold our services, and we will determine not only the terms for which we work but also the nature and the quality of the work we do.

•

What is more, just as our services as a whole are essential to the maintenance of civilization, so our services individually are important to the factories to which the quantity-minded today devote themselves. Once we are able to withhold our services, the quantity-minded would have to deal with us upon the basis of dependence upon us instead of upon the basis of our dependence upon them. With the reversal of the present relationships of dependents and independents would come a reversal of the present division of the returns from common effort. For to the degree in which we become free to refuse to contribute our services to the enterprises upon which the quantity-minded are engaged, to that degree we become able to dictate terms and to secure a premium price for what we choose to do or choose to produce.

This is a policy which puts self before society, but only because it is the essence of wisdom to put first things first. Civilization exists for man; not man for civilization. Those who contribute most to civilization take only what is theirs in common justice if they organize their lives so that they are able to work as they think best.

Until we have secured the essentials of comfort; until we are able to devote ourselves to satisfying work; until we are free to refuse to work and to play as those with inferior values and with vulgar aspirations would force us to, a less selfish economic policy is neither good for ourselves nor good for civilization.

Only by the deliberate adoption of a policy which provides those of us who aspire to the superior life with the freedom for the expression of our own aspirations can we make civilization less ugly than it is today.

For if we free ourselves through such an economic policy as has been here outlined, the humiliating process of waiting years, generations, and centuries until the quantity-minded find it to their interest to adopt our ideas would be ended. Newer ideas and higher values would much more directly enter into the conventions of civilization. The great lag in time between the conception of new ideas and their acceptance by mankind would be shortened.

Civilization would become less ugly at the same time that life for us would become more comfortable.

The Physiological Barrier

We come secondly to the consideration of the physiological barrier to comfort.

We are animals with an insistent animal need of nutrition and excretion, exercise and rest.

Today we submit to an incalculable amount of physical discomfort because we conform to the conventions as to how we should live and as to what we should do when we are ill. We are the victims of an enormous body of misinformation concerning our bodily processes. Some of this is merely our traditional heritage of ignorance but much of it is the result of deliberate propaganda by those who profit from the foolish habits of eating, drinking, clothing, sheltering and caring for ourselves in which we unthinkingly acquiesce.

Yet an enormous body of knowledge concerning the physiological processes has already been accumulated. Most of us, however, do not have the time to acquire this knowledge, and many of us, even if we were to acquaint ourselves with it, would lack the courage to use it. For we find it difficult to practice what is preached by the men and women who have accumulated this knowledge—not always recognized scientists—when our lives are organized for us, in utter disregard of our normal physiological needs as animais, by the factory-dominated civilization by which and for which we live.

As long as we devote ourselves whole-heartedly to the occupational specialties for which our factory-directed schools have trained us and fill the rest of our lives with the routines which naturally accompany them, it is difficult to develop a conscious policy as to what we should eat and drink and how we should work and rest.

Yet such a policy is essential to the real enjoyment of life.

For man is as artificial an animal as is the dog, the cow or the chicken. Unlike a wild animal, he cannot rely upon his instincts in physiological matters because his instinctive reactions have atrophied during the long ages throughout which he has been domesticating himself. He must substitute intelligence for instinct, or accept the discomforts of contemporary physiological life.

Certainly few of us use our intelligence with regard to this aspect of our lives. We are not supposed to use our own intelligence. We are supposed to leave it to those who specially devote themselves to such matters. We leave it to advertisers to tell us what we should eat and drink; to offices and factories to tell us how we should work, and to doctors and druggists to tell us how we should care for ourselves when we are ill.

Naturally we accept the mental and physical ailments which accompany such living as among the unavoidable ills of life.

•

Our factory-dominated civilization is making us into an over fed, constipated, nerve-racked, physically inferior race. Hospitals, sanitariums, and asylums multiply endlessly. We seem to be sacrificing the abounding vitality we need if we are to be comfortable, to the exigencies of surviving at all under our factory regime.

Consider, for instance, the matter of food and eating.

We eat, not when we are hungry, but when the clock tells us to do so, and without normal outdoor work and play, we eat too often and too much.

We eat too fast. We breakfast too fast because we have to get to work on time; we lunch too fast in so-called "quick-lunches" much as horses eat in their stalls; we dine too fast so that we may the more quickly go out to amuse ourselves.

We eat foods which the factory produces for us and to an ever increasing extent leave it to bakers, delicatessen and restaurants to cook and serve them to us.

But since so much of what we eat consists of foods first devitalized by the factory, we have to turn more and more to doctors, dentists, osteopaths, chiropractors and physical culturists to repair the damage which our dietetic conventions inflict upon us.

For the devitalizing of our foodstuffs seems to be an inescapable accompaniment of our present system of divorcing production from consumption. Producing food in one place and consuming it in another makes it necessary to transport and store (and therefore embalm) foodstuffs which in their normal state decompose with great rapidity. All the skill of modern science and all the ingenuity of modern business are therefore focused upon the development of processes which make it possible to transport foods thousands of miles and to preserve and store them for months and years. Not palatability but salability is the objective of the processing of wheat, corn, sugar, rice and practically all our staple foodstuffs. Our conventional dietary of lean meat, white bread, cooked starches and plenty of fats and sugars, no matter how abnormal physiologically, seems an inevitable consequence.

Is it any wonder that so many of us really die at forty and then rely upon drugs and doctors to keep us existing during the rest of our lives?

•

But when we turn the solution of any of the problems of living over to those who pretend to be able to do what they manifestly are incapable of doing, we invite quackery. The conventional treatment of the commonest, and therefore the most important of our ailments by our physicians, surgeons and dentists proceeds with a disregard of elementary physiological principles almost as complete as that of shamans, voodoo men and other primitive medicine-men. Modern practitioners of the art of healing find it just as profitable as the quacks whom they have supplanted to be blind to the fact, (to which their victims seem equally oblivious), that the real cure for our ills is not to be found in correct medication but in correct living. Their preoccupation with the pathological is really a subtle form of quackery fully as dangerous to our comfort as are many of the recognized forms of quackery.

One of the great disservices rendered us by this conventional medical emphasis on pathology is preoccupation with the germ theory.

In the pre-scientific past, it was difficult enough to see that disease was really caused by some deviation from normal living. As long as disease was ascribed to the instrumentality of demons and devils, mankind devoted itself to propitiating the supernatural agencies which were believed to cause it. But it is almost as difficult for us today to appreciate the importance of normal living now that all disease is believed to be caused by those minute invisible organisms, (popularly called germs), which mysteriously ignore some of us and equally mysteriously seize upon others for destruction. Now that disease is ascribed to the activities of germs, naturally we devote ourselves to the destruction of these malign creatures instead of learning how to maintain health through normal living.

For the amazing thing about our bodies is the remarkable extent to which they are self-protective and self-regulatory. Let us live a normal life; let our bodies function normally so far as nutrition and excretion are concerned; let us work and rest normally and a normal blood-stream is the inevitable result. With a normal blood-stream we will have normal organs, normal muscles, normal bones and normal skins and membranes and these will make short shrift of germs when they do enter our bodies, as enter they will no matter how many antiseptic precautions we may employ.

•

To live comfortably, we need normal exercise and we need normal rest.

But the work which we do today and the rest which we are able to secure furnish us neither.

We spend most of our time indoors, and we herd in cities in

which great crowds, tall buildings, factory smoke and automobile exhausts vitiate the good fresh air and shut out the health-making sunshine. We either do work which uses practically none of our muscles, as in office work, or perform the same operations over and over again, and so use only a few of the many muscles we ought to use. And the tempo of our work, instead of being set by some such rhythm as that of recurring seasons of the year, is set by clocks and machines. We move at the pace which machines dictate or work with papers at a desk at a tension equally abnormal. Business makes us write or dictate large numbers of letters; call and receive dozens of telephone messages; rush here and there in subways, street cars, taxis, autos, trains, and crowd as many human contacts into each of our days as the necessities of the gigantic mechanism of which we are cogs require.

As for our leisure, that too is keyed to a tempo over which we have relatively little control. We read newspapers daily, not one but several, because newspapers must get out edition after edition. We eat regularly—and rapidly—in restaurants in which we have to vacate our seats before the food served us has hardly been ingested, and when we eat at home, rush through our breakfasts in order to catch trains and too often rush through our dinners in order to go to movies, dance halls or clubs to amuse our tired selves. And after this sort of "play" we rush home to a fitful sleep, from which an alarm-clock wakens us to resume the factory dominated rhythm from which there seems to be no escape.

•

Such a regime literally forces us into a physiological life which inevitably proves a barrier to comfort. And there is no hope of comfort until we discover that conformity to a regime evolved by men "who aren't in business for their health," is a sin against the holy ghost.

There can be no real enjoyment of comfort until we discover that the most important thing for which we ought to be in business is our health.

Certainly those of us who aspire to live a superior life must devote more of our thinking to the problem of how to live and less to the problem of how to earn a living.

The Social Barrier

Third comes the social barrier.

We are inescapably gregarious and to enjoy the society of our fellows are confronted with the demand that we conform to the social conventions amidst which we find ourselves. We are expected to sacrifice individual ideas of social intercourse which seem good to us because society cherishes such absurdities as the belief that *strange ideas are essentially bad while familiar ideas are essentially good,* and the belief that *whatever is new is better than what is old not because it is truer, better, or more beautiful, but just because it is newer.* To accept conventions which proceed from assumptions of this kind, (without regard to whether they increase or decrease our own enjoyment of living), is to surrender our birthright of individuality. An unthinking acceptance of conventions which are considered valid not in proportion to their reasonableness, their kindliness, or their beauty, but merely in proportion to the effectiveness with which they impose the ideals of society as a whole upon each individual, makes any real conquest of comfort impossible.

We cannot, of course, entirely ignore the social conventions; we must provide for meeting our fellow human beings. We must work and transact business with them; we must agree with them about political matters, and what is equally important, learn how to disagree with them; we must play with them; entertain and be entertained and give to our children the opportunity for meeting those of the opposite sex so that they may not only mate but also experiment with life; finally, we must be alternately participants and audiences in the play-aspects of life—artists displaying what we have created for the appreciation of others, and audiences appraising what others have created. If we leave the whole of this vast area of life to conventions evolved by the masses of mankind out of the imperfectly understood ideas of quality minded individuals, social life becomes a perpetual crucifixion of the beautiful life.

•

Social conventions we must therefore have, though not necessarily those which prevail at present. We must have them, solely and simply because of their convenience. They make it unnecessary to provide by a sort of special legislation for each occasion upon which we come in contact with our fellow human beings. They save both time and tempers. They eliminate irritations which are inevitable unless human beings are in some kind of agreement as to how they will behave when they have to meet each other.

Conventions of this kind are really nothing other than forms of etiquette. They have no more justification for their being than that which justifies the manners of any polite society. They should be subject to revision, suspension, and revocation, whenever they no longer serve the purpose for which they were originally devised or whenever special circumstances dictate the wisdom of a change in them. Each individual and each group must determine this for themselves, and the deviation and the deviator from these conventions must be judged solely from the standpoint of the purposes and consequences of his conduct.

The formulation of these conventions—the general mould of social life—must therefore be taken from the churchmen, politicians and captains of industry, from the quantity-minded dominators of mankind and assumed by those to whom living is a test of art and of intelligence and not merely the gratification of undisciplined appetite or unthinking acceptance of whatever is.

•

Unfortunately, few of us are really free to experiment in this sense with conventions. Instead of our social life being a deliberate experiment in creating conventions, it involves a repressive conformity to pre-existing patterns.

We stand in abject terror of what "they" will think about the way we live. The terror may be sub-conscious, and the degree to which social pressure influences our actions may not be recognized. Yet it affects practically every moment of our lives. Our treatment of each other, even in such intimate relations as husband and wife and parent and child, is dictated by the conventions of our class. We dress ourselves, we shelter ourselves, we feed ourselves and we entertain ourselves, not the way beauty and comfort dictate as to dress, as to housing, as to food and drink, as to work and play, but according to the conventions which "the crowd" accepts. And we dare not depart from the conventional social form of life; it would mean, not only ostracism from society, but ostracism from business. For conformity to convention is not merely a price exacted of us for acceptance by society; it is a price which we have to pay today if we are to be permitted to support ourselves at all. Plainly, we can indulge in no individual experimenting in social life until we can afford to ignore the conventions of society; until we are independent enough to dictate the terms upon which we will cooperate with the integrated mechanism of business, and until we have provided against loneliness by placing ourselves within a group such as the family in which our own position is so secure that we can dare to be ourselves.

The Biological Barrier

We come fourth to the barrier formed by our civilized sex conventions.

We are biologically incomplete, male or female halves of personality subject to an imperious mandate that we mate and consummate our beings in the reproduction of our own kind. This effort at consummation constitutes our sex-life.

We cannot, even if we try, evade living a sex-life. For if we try to evade it by refusing to live a normal sex-life, we find ourselves rewarded with a redoubled volume of sex of a perverse type.

St. Anthony immured in his solitary desert cave did not escape living a sex-life. He did not conquer sex by repudiating it. He succeeded only in saturating his life with it.

•

In our factory-dominated civilization, mating has to be postponed long after nature most strongly urges us to mate. Marriage is a luxury in which marriageable youth, if it is at all intelligent, hesitates to indulge.

As industrialization becomes more and more complete, and the integration of production makes more and more vocational specialization necessary, the spread between the time when it is easiest for us to adjust ourselves to a mate and the time when our income permits us to marry grows wider.

The more ambitious we are to wrest creature comforts from our complex civilization, the greater becomes the spread. The higher the place we strive to attain in the hierarchy of modern business, the longer is the apprenticeship we must serve at meagre pay, after spending years at school and college earning nothing at all. By postponing the time when earning can begin so long after adolescence, conventional education tends to pervert our entire life. Education, which ought to be a course of instruction in the essentials of the good life, is thus warped into an actual barrier to it.

•

But while industrialization can press us to postpone marriage, it cannot postpone sex-development. Here the church steps in with conventions which forbid all pre-marital sexual experiences. Marriage, says the church, is the only thing that can sacerdotalize sex-life. Between the church with its categories of sin and the law with its categories of crime, the sex-starved followers of convention are impaled either on the Scylla of frigidity or the Charybdis of prostitution.

True, the revolt of womankind, or rather the economic independence which the factory has conferred upon them has encouraged pre-marital sex-experimentation. But while this experimentation does temper the evil of both frigidity and prostitution, it can contribute little to our happiness until the excessive importance which convention attaches to chastity is ended. Its claim that all sex-life must be suspended until we are ready to marry with benefit of clergy must be ridiculed out of existence.

For the church, with its idiotic cry of "unclean," has made us associate the sex-act with a mystic carnality only to be exorcised through sacraments of which the clergy are the dispensers. So pervasive is the association of ideas with which the church has infected western civilization that even irreligious nonconformists cannot entirely escape from the association of sex and evil. Because of its unearthly and unnatural idea that the sex-act is the original sin, the church strives with threats of hell to confine all sex-life within the marital state. As long as the idea prevails that marriage is a sacred and indissoluble union necessary to sacerdotalize the sex-act and justifying the suppression of all extra-marital experimentation, there is no hope that we shall be able to evolve more beautiful sex-conventions. Hypocrisy, jealousy, frigidity, prostitution, abortion—these fruits of our present sex conventions will remain to plague us. The rigors of the marital tie will not be relaxed. Departures from sexual fidelity will continue to have an undue importance for us. And marriage, instead of being a voluntary experiment in the consummation of being, will remain one of the most disappointing of all our institutions.

•

It is not the least of the discomforts we can attribute to this factory-dominated civilization that it has put a blight upon parenthood.

For there can be no true conquest of comfort without parenthood.

Parenthood is a great adventure. It offers us unlimited opportunities for self-expression, yet it is the greatest of all disciplines. Parenthood, through every stage—conception, pre-natality, infancy, childhood, adolescence, mating, and finally the second cycle of life—is potent with joys that can fully compensate us for the pain and suffering which seem invariable accompaniments of everything worthwhile.

But to make parenthood enjoyable, it must be freed from the black curse under which it struggles and labors today. For children today are economic catastrophes. We marry late and have few or no children, for a decent standard of living can be maintained only on condition that we sacrifice our normal life as mates and parents and, for all practical purposes, sterilize ourselves. So we turn to contraception and even embrace abortion, with its risks, rather than burden ourselves with the economic handicap of children.

Birth should certainly be controlled, and the coming of children spaced so as to minimize the unavoidable physical and mental strains upon the mother, but children should not be prevented from coming altogether. Contraception should be used to regulate child-bearing, not to end it. Unfortunately, in this urbanized and factory-dominated civilization, the invention of means for controlling birth, surely one of the greatest steps yet taken toward the realization of a really beautiful civilization, is being used not to increase true comfort, but merely to make it possible for us to sustain life and to secure the things which our factories belch forth.

•

No really beautiful civilization can be built as long as we merely increase population quantitatively. It is quality, not quantity, that is important. Cultural values can be high only when the proportion of individuals of high sensitivity, who are interested in qualities rather than magnitudes, is also high.

It is ugliness and not beauty that is inevitably coming from the present steady increases in the quantity of herd-minded human beings. This is the type of all types which should be encouraged to exterminate itself. Where this type increases rapidly, mobs, not individuals, are created. Politicians profit from the existence of mobs of herd-minded voters; imperialists, from the existence of mobs of herd-minded "cannon-fodder"; churchmen from the existence of mobs of herd-minded worshippers, and business men from the existence of mobs of herd-minded workers and customers.

A fecund population of this type is necessary to a factory dominated civilization with its constant proliferation of factories, first to consume its constantly increasing production of goods, and secondly to furnish it automatons who will contentedly produce and distribute them.

•

Against the family, that remarkable instrumentality slowly evolved to meet the imperious biological mandate that we reproduce our kind, the factory wages a ruthless war of extermination. For the family is essentially centripetal. As long as it creates and produces it tends to be self-sufficient. It tends to absorb itself in the task of making life endurable for its members. It is a conservator of our independence. Industrialism seeks to root out individual devotion to the family and the homestead and to replace it with loyalty to the factory, just as religion seeks to transfer it to the church, and politics to the state and nation. The factory has pretty well succeeded in dissolving the family into its component parts and in transforming the individuals thus produced into malleable mobs who produce and consume, work and play, live and die, all for its glory.

We may think the economic conventions of the day too strong; we may think the satisfaction of sex apart from parenthood more pleasant; we may think the development of our individual egos most important, and on these grounds seek for some novel instrumentality to take the place of the family. But to the degree in which we aspire to the superior life we must intelligently provide for the functions which the family can perform and which no other institution yet devised seems better fitted to perform.

First, the family can provide for our economic functions. It can furnish us a superior instrumentality for securing most of the essentials and many of the luxuries of life.

Secondly, the family can provide for our biological functions. It can furnish us with desirable conditions under which to mate, reproduce, and rear our children.

Thirdly, the family can provide for our social functions. It can furnish us a really satisfying field in which and through which we can entertain, educate and express ourselves.

Given these four factors: (1) ourselves, with aspirations different from our fellows; (2) the rest of mankind, incapable or unwilling to interest itself in our ideals; (3) the present political status and prevailing money-economy, and (4) the existing machines and methods, labor and resources for procuring the essentials of living, and the family seems to me an institution which can perform these three functions far better than the best combination of factory-hotel-laboratory-club which socialization offers.

•

The family is an institution potent for comfort to those of us who value above all else our individualities. Abandonment of the family and the institutionalization of the economic, biological, and social functions the family can so well perform, seem desirable only to those to whom extreme independence has become abhorrent, perhaps because our factory regimentation of life has habituated them to herd-living and inculcated in them a distaste for individual solutions of the problems of life.

That the average man should seek to solve his problems by turning to something exterior and in his opinion superior to himself, is natural. In the past, his problems were solved for him by the nobility and the church; in the present they are being solved for him by our factory-dominated conventions; in the future why should they not be solved for him by a benign and intelligent state? That the herd-minded individual should look to something exterior to himself is only to be expected. But when we look to something outside of ourselves, we abandon our birthrights; we sacrifice upon the altar of conformity the one quality which lifts us above the herd. We blunt our personal reactions to life in compromising with conventions evolved for the exploitation of mobs of individuals, organized crowds, and the populace of a whole nation.

•

The development of a family on a homestead of its own is not only potent with comfort; it is potent with social progress. For the family on its own homestead is a social microcosm. It furnishes us the opportunity to deal with all the problems with which society as a whole has to cope. What is most important, the problems of private property, land tenure, inheritance, rent, taxation, free trade, tariff, law, education as they develop in the life of the family may be disposed of without sacrificing the unique interests of the individual to the supposed interests of the different masses.

Were we to accept the family and not the factory as the true stage upon which to enact the drama of our lives, not only would we be free from the exactions of our factory-dominated civilization but the less independent rank and file of mankind would be tempted to imitate the sort of life that they would see us live in order to win a similar freedom. By degrees their folkways would absorb our conceptions of how life should be lived. More of the ideas of those of us who are interested in the qualitative aspects of life and fewer of the ideals of those who are interested in its quantitative aspects would be accepted by them. And those of us who believe that life is enriched by the degree in which we individually control our environment would be able to nullify the activities of those who believe that the social environment—the factory, the church, the state—should control all of the important activities of individuals.

•

Fear of the high cost of living, a barbaric desire for sex gratification alone, or an overweening concentration upon our own egotistic ambitions may lead us to reject the whole scheme of life for which the family stands.

We may, it is true, refuse to reproduce our kind. Or we may institutionalize the family, as some idealists believe is desirable, and concentrate the actual procreation and education of our kind upon selected individuals. But if we do, each of us, who individually make the refusal, incur the penalties of self-frustration. If we reject parenthood, on the theory that frustration is the lesser evil, then we not only embrace the discomforts of frustration; we reject a way of living which may be made, if we are wise enough, a positive contribution to the enjoyment of life.

Surely it is the part of wisdom for us to take up the family, which is already ours to develop and which requires no preliminary political reform or social revolution, and with all the intelligence we can command transform its potential contribution to our comfort into a reality.

The Religious Barrier

We come now to the consideration of the religious barrier to comfort.

We are fearful; fear is bred, and perhaps, born into us. It is an emotion which we share in common with all animals. We tend to be fearful for the same reason that all animals tend to be fearful; because it makes us run, or strive to destroy, what is strange and therefore probably dangerous to us. We have scarcely ceased from running from unusual noises like thunder; from unusual sights like lightning; above all from unusual ideas like atheism.

But fear is a protective device for us only as long as it remains a device to insure caution. When we become fearful of non-existent dangers; when we begin to fear ghosts, sex, gods, hell and their like, then we transform the figments of our imagination into actual dangers. We make real dangers out of what actually has no reality at all. And fear, which should be an instrumentality for our protection, becomes an agency for our destruction.

•

Religion* is a solace, a habit and an escape. It is a solace for the fearful; a habit which justifies those who do not think, and an escape for them from the hard facts of life.

Yet it is nearly all snare and delusion. It evades the problems with which it purports to deal. It does not settle them. On the contrary, its evasions create more problems than there are to be disposed of originally.

Why is it not wiser to leave unanswerable questions unanswered, than to accept pseudo-answers to them which rarely have much more than their antiquity to recommend them?

Until we utterly and completely exorcise all religion from our being; until we drop all fears, superstitions, rituals, habits which spring from religion, no true spiritual comfort is possible; we are not properly equipped to extract from every moment of life the uttermost of truth, goodness and beauty.

•

Religion first of all invents a god or gods, or mystic powers over and outside of the tangible powers we know.

But whereas both common-sense and science begin with premises and end with conclusions that are demonstrable and tend therefore to dispose of the questions with which they deal, religion with its resort to god raises more questions than it answers. Nothing is gained by shifting the point of inquiry from nature which can be observed, measured and analyzed, to god who cannot be known and concerning whom the lowest savage and the most highly civilized man can speak with equal authority.

What profit is there in disposing of the question of the nature of nature by substituting the question of the nature of god? Nothing is gained, and something very valuable is lost. What is lost in the process is our acceptance of ignorance as a natural state. The superior man knows that he cannot know very much. The more he knows, the more he discovers what he does not know. For him, education is a voyage of discovery which always reveals new and hitherto unknown areas of ignorance. The superior man goes through

* Throughout this discussion, the term "religion" refers more particularly to the theology of the various churches rather than to the very often beautiful "way of life" which those with a flare for mysticism refer to as religion.

life with a host of questions to which he has only provisional answers. He accepts his ignorance as he accepts any other of the inescapable facts of life.

Only the truly inferior man is unconscious of his ignorance.

The more conventional, the more religious, the more ignorant a man is, the greater is his assurance of knowledge. He knows there is a god. He knows what he must do to get into heaven and to keep out of hell. He is a *vade mecum* of such "facts" and not the slightest doubt concerning their verity ever ventures to obtrude upon his assurance.

As we begin to doubt, we begin to understand. The more we doubt and question, the more conscious we become of our ignorance. To accept god is simply to ignore the fact that we do not know the nature of nature.

The physicist who accepts god may be a good physicist. He may be able to restrict his dogmatism to that carefully circumscribed area of his mind which he calls his religious sense. The fact that he has failed to be provisional in religion may not interfere with his being provisional in physics. But it tends powerfully to warp the application of what he knows to the problem of living. It creates in a thousand different aspects of his thinking the habit of being dogmatic—a habit from which we must protect ourselves, if we are to be comfortable, as we must protect ourselves from dependence and disease.

•

How can we avoid being both agnostic and atheistic? We must be agnostic in that we are willing to admit that we may be mistaken about any position we take. But we must be atheistic in that we must deny the existence of any of the gods which man up to the present time has evoked.

"For I the Lord thy God am a Jealous God," says the Bible. This seems to be true of most gods. Once we begin to believe in a god; once we begin to propitiate him; once we begin to resolve our problems by putting the issue and responsibility on god, we put more and more belief, and worship and responsibility upon him. The Bible merely rationalizes the process when it says that we ought to do this because god jealously requires us to do it. The process itself is an indubitable psychological fact; it is an easy way of dodging the need of thinking about life. Once we discover how apparently easy it is, we are tempted to dodge more and more.

How can any intelligent man believe in the existence of a jealous god? About a jealous Jehovah we must be atheists, just as we must be about a triune god consisting of Father, Son and Holy Ghost; just as we must be about gods like Jove and Juno; just as we must be about gods like Kali and Siva or Isis and Osiris.

While we do not have to deny the existence of what is called the supreme power, we very nearly must deny the existence of a supreme personality, of a supreme intelligence, of a supreme goodness. Personality is the sum total of the flavor of a person—of a being that has brains, eyes, ears, nose, mouth, hands, legs; in short, of a man. Take from man all there things—not just some of them—but all of them—above all take from him the limitations inherent in them, and personality disappears. The personality of a painter is a product not merely of his capacity for seeing but of the limitations of his sight. Let him be all-seeing and he would have no more personality than has a photographic camera. By every definition of personality, no supreme being can possibly be endowed with it.

So it is with intelligence and goodness. By every possible definition of the term intelligence, there is no intelligence in the universe as a whole. Intelligence is man's means for rationalizing his reactions to an apparently irrational environment. It is a survival mechanism. Without what he calls intelligence, he could not build and create and live as he does. Intelligence is a harmonizing, a designing, a rationalizing reaction to life. It is a reaction which is evoked inside each individual man, and never quite alike in any two of them. And no matter how much he exerts himself to impress his intelligence upon nature as a whole, in the end the implacable, impersonal and irrational events that we call nature prevail. The music of the spheres is musical only to those who can hear music; to the untrained ear it is merely noise.

Nor can there be a supreme goodness in the universe, by any definition of goodness which is understandable to man. The good man does not brutally, painfully, slowly, tortuously, remorselessly destroy those whom he loves. And certainly he does not do this with the deliberation which would have to be assumed as a part of the proceedings of an all-wise, all-powerful being. Yet this is precisely what god does, has always done, and will always continue to do, except as men's intelligence lessens momentarily the implacable, inexorable, inexpugnable processes of the world god is supposed to have created.

•

Out of our fear and our egotism, religion has evolved immortality. And immortality, of all the ideas with which religion has cursed us, is one of the greatest barriers to the comfortable life. It makes life seem long, whereas life in reality is short—a brief candle, as the poet put it. Being so short, a moment between two eternities of nothingness, life has a sacredness of which religion, with its immortality, robs it.

The doctrine of immortality is a crime against the sacredness of this life.

By making us think of ourselves as immortal souls, religion makes what we do here and now shrink in importance, as the finite shrinks when compared to the infinite. As long as we accept our common mortality—as long as we live upon the theory that this life ends all; each year, each day, even each hour we live has the importance which comes only from the unique and the irreplaceable.

Into this life, into this adventure, into this moment we must therefore put the very best that is in us, and from it we must, by the same token, extract the very uttermost that we can.

•

But of all the weird, horrible, unimaginative inventions of religion, heaven and hell are the most outrageous.

Religion having invented a soul and then endowed it with immortality, some sort of celestial residence had to be devised for the immortal soul. Heaven and hell are really postulates devised to make tenable the prior postulates of religion.

Religion postulated god, and then found that it had to explain why he created mortal man. It explained man by postulating eternity for his immortal soul. But when it postulated an immortal soul, religion found that it had to explain where that soul was destined to go. And so it explained by postulating heaven and hell. Now there is nothing in life, horrible as it is in many of its aspects, that is as horrible as hell, and there is nothing in life, monotonous as so much of it is, that is quite so inane as an eternity of heaven. Heaven does not attract nor hell terrify individuals of discriminating taste.

The doctrine that we are doomed to either heaven or hell has neither the internal validity which can make intelligent people embrace it nor the external value which would make them recommend it for the rest of mankind. There is little evidence that threats of hell or hopes of paradise have made the masses of mankind better, while there is unlimited evidence as to the untold misery of religions warfare, persecution and bigotry for which the doctrine is responsible.

There is not a single good reason why those of us who would be comfortable should give to ideas of this sort a moment's time beyond that necessary for dismissing them.

•

The dictionary tells us what religion is. It says that religion involves the recognition of god as an object of worship, love and obedience; that it is a system of faith or worship. But unfortunately the dictionary does not tell us what it is not. I say unfortunately because religious apologists always go much farther than the dictionary. Sooner or later they always claim that it is also the basis of morality and good conduct.

But the selfsame theory of revelation upon which the Christians base the validity of their moral law, makes valid the moral laws of all religions. The same sort of prophetic intuitions that make Christian canons the moral law, make Mohammedan canons and Buddhist canons and Aztec canons moral law. If all there codes agreed with each other there would be some plausible argument for assuming that there is such a thing as moral law, and that the codes of each of the religions were merely different statements of the same absolute ethic. They do not, however, agree with each other. Worse, they utterly contradict each other. So that we are driven to conclude that no religion speaks with authority upon morality, and that morality has nothing whatsoever to do with the basic fears with which religion itself deals.

We must get rid of religion, among other reasons, because it is a hindrance to the formulation of a morality intelligent enough to make possible the conquest of comfort.

•

There are certain questions which are of tremendous importance. There are other questions which have a reputation for being important, but which are as a matter of fact of little or no real importance at all.

Take the question of foodstuffs and eating. Now there we have a really important question. In some way or other we must answer it daily—not daily but several times each day. It acquires its importance from this, that we must eat or die.

So it is with all the really important questions in life—nature puts them to us, and nature demands that we answer them in some way or other under penalty of the natural consequences of our failure to do so. It is this way with the food supply and eating; with the water supply and drinking; with the shelter which we must erect against the inclemency of the weather.

But there are many questions of little real importance which convention makes loom large in our eyes. These are questions which seem to be important, which have a reputation of being important, which have been made to have a sort of artificial importance but which, in the fundamental sense outlined above, are of no importance at all. We may attempt to answer them or we may ignore them; we may answer them affirmatively or negatively; we may build our whole lives around them or we may treat them as unimportant incidents in life—and nature will exact no penalty for our attitude toward them as long as we do not let them affect our attitude toward the really important questions in life.

Religious questions are of this sort. They are questions which have acquired a factitious importance. We make much of them, not because nature requires that we pay any attention to them, but because convention tells us that we must concern ourselves about them because of the penalties which god is supposed to inflict upon the irreligious after they are dead, and because sad experience tells us that we had better pretend to do so in order to avoid the more tangible penalties which society inflicts upon the irreligious while still alive.

•

The question of god, for instance, is considered an important question. Most of us are born to believe that there is a god, and never really have occasion to ask ourselves the question because our parents or our churches have answered it for us. All that we have to do is to accept it. Some of us, like Cotton Mather, have wrestled with the question in pain and sorrow and acquired a belief in god, while a few of us after similar considerations of the question have finally come to the conclusion that there is no god. Society has said, believe in god or suffer ostracism. The church has said, believe in god or suffer excommunication. Sometimes the state has said, believe in god or suffer prosecution.

Nature, however, has said nothing. The sun shines and the rain falls precisely the same upon believer and upon unbeliever. The foodstuffs they eat will nourish the two precisely alike; the water refresh them alike; the coal and wood warm them alike.

So that in the truest sense this question is an unimportant question, and would deserve nothing at our hands, but for the importance which the masses of men are made to attach to it. If we are to avoid the discomfort of having to conform to their opinions with respect to religion; of being silent about our beliefs; of perhaps having to render obeisance to the church; and worst of all, of contributing to the support of the church and of the institutions which propagate religions ideas, we will have to be economically independent of those who believe in them and of those who use the belief in them to buttress institutions—such as the state—which they control.

Only then will the religious barrier to our comfort really disappear.

•

If we must have the psychic release of genuine religious experience; if we must aspire to something above our individual selves and worthy of our worship, let us devise a new worship of the lares and penates—of the spirit of the home, the family and the fireside. These at least are worthy of consecration at our hands, because they are capable of responding to the best that we may give to them.

If we must have a religion, let it be this religion which conduces to our comfort rather than erects barriers to it.

The Political Barrier

We come next to the political barrier to the comfortable life.

We are born into a political status.

We have no choice about the matter. We are subject, or citizen, or comrade by virtue of the fact that we are born under the dominion of politicians who have constituted themselves into a monarchy, a republic, or a commune. We can change our political status by emigrating from the subjection under which we are born to some other which we may think more desirable, but we cannot free ourselves from subjection to government altogether. In this respect we have somewhat less freedom today than even with regard to religion. We can avoid tithes, in many states, but none of us can avoid taxes. Public opinion has progressed to the point where it recognizes that abandonment of the church is not in itself an evil however sinful it may be from the standpoint of the clergy. But it has not yet arrived at a point where it recognizes that the abandonment of the state is equally free from evil. In deed, the process of turning one's back upon the government, especially during times of crisis, is stigmatized as treason, and the unpatriotic individual who dares to do so is fortunate if he escapes the jailer's and executioner's attentions for his temerity.

But while we may have to consent to a political status and to contribute to the support of the government, we do not need to over-estimate the extent to which politicians and the political state contribute to our comfort.

For government is, at best, a necessary evil. It does not become less evil because it seems necessary.

•

There are three needs of mankind, and therefore three functions, which seem to justify the existence of governments. The first is the protection of society as a whole, and of the law-abiding members of it, from the illegal, and sometimes anti-social activities of individuals. The performance of this function has brought into existence the police powers of the government: law, law enforcement and the courts of law.

The second function is the protection of the government itself, from the attacks of other governments, and by virtue of what is presumably the corollary of self-defense, the function of attacking other governments which may for some reason—good, bad or indifferent—interfere with the activities of the attacking government. The performance of this function has brought into existence the war powers of the government: armies and navies, international law and diplomacy.

The third function is that of rendering various social and economic services which seem, like our schools, too important to entrust to private initiative, or which seem, like the issue of money, too dangerous to entrust to private monopoly. The performance of these functions has brought into existence the social activities of the government: public schools, postal service, streets and roads, fire protection, water supply and a myriad of similar municipal and national activities.

If we admit, for the moment, that these functions are essential to mankind's well-being, it does not necessarily follow that the only way in which they can be provided is through the agency of political government. History, which is one long record of the imbecilities and the injustices of governments, furnishes us good grounds for seeking some alternative solution for them. And the comfort which we as individuals seek makes it very desirable that the alternative should be controlled as far as possible by us personally and not by the community as a whole.

We develop government because it is an agency which generates social control, when we should develop institutions like the family which are agencies for generating self-control.

•

What we call a government is after all nothing but a group of individuals, who, by a variety of sanctions, have acquired the power to govern their fellows. The sanctions range from the fraud of divine right to that of sheer conquest; from the imbecility of hereditary privilege to the irrationality of counting voters. In most cases the extent to which these sanctions produce capable legislators, judges and administrators, will not bear critical examination

Nominally, government exists and functions for the public. Actually it exists and functions for the benefit of those who have in one of these absurd ways acquired power to govern. It is accepted mainly because of the sheer inertia of great masses of people. Ostensibly, of course, it is accepted because it confers a sufficiency of visible benefits upon society to make the officials who operate it tolerated in spite of the selfish and idiotic exercise of the powers conferred upon them.

Unfortunately for quality-minded individuals above all others, government furnishes for quantity-minded individuals the opportunity to sate to the full their greed for wealth and power. Power, for its own sake, is rarely attractive to the quality-minded individual. It is too ineradicably quantitative. The really superior man, just because he is intelligent enough to know the limitations of his knowledge and the fallibility of his judgments, has no taste for the ruthlessness which is essential to the exercise of power.

For government officials must, first of all, maintain power. Only by maintaining power can they have the opportunity to exercise it. Their preoccupation with the arts which lead to power and which enable them to maintain it after they have secured it is inescapable. The ambitions which should animate them and the purposes for which their power should be used have to be subordinated to "practical politics."

Rarely does the true quality-minded individual attain to power. When he does, he is almost compelled to sacrifice the ideals to which he may originally have been genuinely devoted in order to maintain power. He is almost certain to sacrifice them unless his tenure of power is accompanied by a social convulsion which carries his ideals into force almost in spite of what he himself may do. Ordinarily the task of maintaining himself, and his party, in office is so great that the inclination to make wise use of whatever power he secures rarely survives the ordeal.

Generally, the quality-minded man functions in politics only to the degree that politicians find it necessary to use his abilities, and though he sometimes imposes his ideas upon the politicians the process of emasculation to which they are subjected by legislative, judicial and administrative officials so alters them that they defeat the purposes for which they were originally conceived.

A life-long study of politicians, of all quantity-minded men perhaps the most odious, made Henry Adams use these biting words to describe political office, the struggle to acquire it, maintain it and administer it:

> Office was poison; it killed—body and soul—physically and socially. Office was more poisonous than priestcraft or pedagogy in proportion as it held more power, but the poison he complained of was not ambition; he shared none of Cardinal Wolsey's belated penitence for that healthy stimulant, as he had shared none of the fruits; his poison was that of the will—the distortion of sight—the warping of mind—the degradation of tissue—the coarsening of taste—the narrowing of sympathy to the emotions of a caged rat.[48]

•

Incompetent and imbecile, with a saving trace of grandeur this describes government as it is and not as idealists, aristocratic, democratic or socialistic, would have it.

How are we to permit such an institution, (with which we must come to terms) to function in the directions in which it ministers to our comfort and yet reduce the annoyances it can cause us to the minimum? Short of escape to a desert island, how can we live the good life in spite of it?

Economic independence cannot, unfortunately, completely free us from government. But it can enormously reduce the field of activity for government as a whole.

(1) Dependence upon the public services furnished by the government itself or by quasi-governmental institutions operated upon franchises, can be materially lessened. We can furnish our own water supply; our own sewerage system; our own fire protection; our own schooling. Some of these things for which we now turn to the public services we can do completely for ourselves. Others we can do only in part. To the extent to which we enable ourselves to do them, we avoid the annoyance and escape the incompetence of having them performed by the state.

(2) Support of the government through the taxes we pay we cannot avoid, nor can we entirely escape from such forms of government support as military service and jury duty. But in accordance with the illustrious precedents recorded on every page of the histories of government, judicious flattery and bribery of officials can enable us either to eliminate entirely or in large part reduce taxes and similar demands upon us. Fortunately, we have progressed to such a point that it is possible to yield to these various forms of duress without too great suffering. Perhaps philosophy can reconcile us to paying the taxes imposed upon us, even though we see every day how the taxpayers' money is wasted by those who hold political office.

(3) Voluntary contributions to the work of government, such as voting, party work, office-holding, and agitating, educating and organizing reform movements—these can be reduced to almost nothing. An occasional effort in this direction may be justified, but earnest devotion to these contributions to government is almost certain to disillusion and disappoint us.

•

But if we thus abandon hope of achieving much improvement through the agencies of government, is there any field of effort which we can cultivate in order to impose upon society a superior conception of how life should be lived? For the more sensitive we are to the stupidities, the injustices and the ugliness of civilization, the more important it becomes that we give expression to our feelings in some activity designed to correct them.

Such fields of effort do exist, and unlike the field of government, we are temperamentally fitted to engage in cultivating them. Let us make the arts, the amusements, and the educational institutions of society our own, and we will have: first, a channel into which we can pour our own creative instincts, and secondly, a powerful instrumentality for the improvement of mankind. Let these three fields be kept free from malformation by the greedy, the fanatic and the ignorant, and ideas, now neglected, misinterpreted or falsified for the sake of securing and holding wealth and power, will be developed, dramatized and publicized. Let the fine arts end their present status of sufferance at the hands of dealers in antiquities;

let the stage, the concert hall, and the arena be taken from those who cater to the vulgar; let newspapers and magazines declare their independence of the advertising industry, and schools and universities refuse to continue the manufacture of mere specialists for our factory-dominated civilization—let these become the fields of expression of living artists; of those to whom music, drama and the dance are first of all expressions of the creative spirit; of those to whom journalism, literature, art, science, philosophy are fundamentally means to the good life, and we will find that we can safely surrender politics and government entirely to the politicians because we will be able to impose upon them ideas immeasurably superior to those which they now promote.

But to take possession of these fields of activity, we must make ourselves economically free to boycott the quantity-minded individuals who now control them. Once we make ourselves free to engage in or to refuse to engage in work for which we have prepared ourselves and for which we have developed unusual skills, the artistic, amusement and educational institutions will become ours by sheer force of their dependence upon us. With these in our hands, public opinion could be made a civilizing instead of a vulgarizing influence. And the politicians, with their fear of their constituents, would prove just as responsive to an enlightened public opinion as they now do to a vulgarized public opinion. For politicians live by anticipating the direction in which public opinion turns; they do not actually direct its movement.

With these three instruments we could lessen the veneration which gives to the government its present sacred character in the opinion of mankind; we could persuade the public to deny to politicians their ever-increasing tendency to interfere with the rights of the individual, and we could end by so reducing the need of social control as to gradually reduce government and the politicians who operate it to a state of innocuous desuetude.

•

Having failed throughout all history, over and over again, in competition with the quantity-minded for the control of government, it is the part of wisdom to reconcile ourselves to the fact that government is one of the institutions which we cannot directly use to make civilization more beautiful. Above all, we must guard against over-valuing the cultural potentialities of government and of under-valuing institutions like the press, the stage, and the class-room which are so much more adaptable to intellectual, moral, and artistic idealism. By over-estimating the importance of legislative, judicial, administrative, and military activities, we tend to ignore the evil of the prostitution of what might be called our primary fields of activity to the selfish interests of the quantity minded and forget how many of us are forced to prostitute ourselves to the industrial behemoth which they have brought into being, by designing, writing, acting, and teaching what we do not believe to be good or true or beautiful.

As long as we are content to be chained to behemoth, we shall lack both the freedom and the time to make our ideas dominant in the fields of activity where they would contribute most to the individual improvement of mankind and we shall continue unable to refuse to do work which outrages our highest aspirations. But with freedom from the constraints which behemoth imposes upon us as long as we are dependent upon it, we would be enabled to develop the techniques and the disciplines needed to secure control of the institutions which are the most efficient vehicles for projecting ideas into society.

In a society in which the press, the stage, and the class-room were controlled by the quality-minded, leviathan would be reduced to normal dimensions. Control of the irreducible minimum of government remaining would become of little importance because the ideas of the quality-minded, rather than the interests of the quantity-minded, would become of paramount interest to government officialdom.

•

Government derives its potency mainly from two things: ideas and force.

Ideas tend to impose themselves upon those who actually wield the forces of government. It is the fact that ideas possess this power that makes progress possible at all. Whatever we are able to accomplish toward the making of a more beautiful civilization comes from the innate strength and persuasiveness of the ideas which we launch.

What is for us, therefore, supremely important is that we shall be free to experiment with our ideas—all the ideas which occur to us. We must put ourselves into a position where the ideas which interest us can have real opportunity to function.

In a civilization in which the arts, the amusements, and the educational institutions were the forums of its superior individuals, government would shrink in stature and importance, and beauty would develop in myriads of directions in which it is today cramped, cribbed and confined.

•

To free ourselves so that we can devote ourselves to the work we like, would mean that we would be able to develop, to dramatize and to publicize our ideas.

The facile assumption of sovereign power, so flattering to the herd-minded voter, we would lose through recognition of our impotence in directly wielding the forces of government. But we would be compensated for this loss by the real enjoyment we would secure from conscious devotion to what we like best to do.

And because of the indirect influence we would thus exert upon government we would not only be adding to our own comfort but to that of all mankind.

The Moral Barrier

We come now to the moral barrier.

We are creatures which have to be moral because we cannot live without affecting our fellows.

We act. Our actions affect our fellows. But the judgments of society upon our acts, and our efforts to adjust ourselves to these social judgments, make the conquest of comfort impossible for us as long as we are conventionally dependent upon conventional society.

•

For until we can deliberately discipline ourselves to a self consciousness which enables us to utilize moral values of our own devising, we act as conventional morality would have us act; we think of our own actions as conventional morality would have us think, and we judge the actions of others as conventional morality would have us judge them.

If our own actions and our judgment of the actions of others are in conformity with the conventional codes and creeds of so ciety, we are considered moral and we think of ourselves as good. Moral conduct may not make us comfortable—conventionally good people seldom are—but we can at least console ourselves with the conviction of our innocence.

If, however, our actions and our judgments upon the actions of others are not in conformity with the accepted patterns of conduct; if, on the contrary, they violate the accepted standards, then society adjudges us sinful and criminal, and we tend to think of ourselves as bad. Immorality may not make us comfortable—conventionally immoral people seldom are—but in addition we suffer the discomfort of living under a conviction of guilt.

•

No progress over the moral barrier is possible until we have the time and the freedom for two things: the devising of moral values of our own and the development of a self-consciousness which enables us to utilize our own values. Progress over the barrier can then begin because we are ready to abandon the sacerdotalism upon which conventional morality relies to validate its right to speak with authority.

For morality is not absolute. It is relative. The current morality furnishes us no intrinsic evidence of its validity. Tested by its own canons, it is self-contradictory. And the extrinsic evidence is equally disappointing. The will of nature, so far as morality is concerned, is as inscrutable as the will of god is uncertain. Neither sacred scriptures nor pure sciences furnish any evidence of absolute moral authority.

The sense of sin and the conviction of innocence are therefore mistakes. The voice of conscience furnishes no rational guidance upon moral questions. Because our acts are in themselves neither abstractly good nor abstractly bad, conscience must be replaced by values which we ourselves decide are most conducive to comfort.

Every act of ours is a unique event.

It is the essence of conventional morality to ignore this unique ness; to classify our acts and upon the basis of the classification to reward or punish. Whereas in truth we merely act, and it is the consequences of the act upon all involved which are important. Acts which our conventional code calls immoral often have consequences which are good, and acts which are called strictly moral often have consequences which are bad.

The masses of fools stick to morality when every mandate of wisdom cries out that intelligence should be substituted for it.

•

The ten commandments constitute a code that applies to childhood, youth, maturity and old age; to the married as well as the unmarried; to parents and those not parents; to both men and women; to the strong and the weak; the rich and the poor; the stupid and the intelligent.*

It is a code which assumes not only that we are all alike but that we are alike throughout all our life. Yet the assumption is false in both respects. Just as we are, each of us, not alike but different from each other, so individually we are not one unchanging individual, but a succession of different individuals. If we are to develop intelligent principles of conduct for ourselves we must provide for these differences between ourselves and other persons and for the changes in ourselves at successive ages in our lives.

Only a relative morality meets these requirements.

What may be moral in one person, may not be in another; what may be moral at one age, may not be at another.

•

Today we dispose of the problem of regulating our conduct by conformity to conventional morality. And this morality we are told is validated by the supreme ethical and moral value of duty.

---

* In this respect the ten commandments are inferior to much of the law with its distinctions between minors and adults, masters and servants, competents and incompetents. Unfortunately the onward sweep of democracy is emphasising more and more the assumption of the equality of all persons before the law. That is why in this "democratic" country people like to say that ours is a government of laws, not men.

Duty to god; duty to humanity; duty to the nation; duty to family; duty to self—these are the supreme values of our present moral philosophy. Yet if comfort is the great good to be sought, duty becomes a manifestly inadequate value by which to guide our selves. For duty is not an arbitrable ideal. It plunges us into arbitrary decisions concerning mutually irreconcilable alternatives. It validates all moral conduct on the one ground of duty, yet no statement of our duties but contains mutually inconsistent provisions.

It is our duty to live and to support our families.

Yet in time of war, it is our duty to the nation to die.

With such conflicts of duty we torture ourselves endlessly.

Our moral philosophy ought to deliver us from this kind of conflict. It should furnish us a technique for compromising between immediate desire and ultimate interest; between direct contacts with our fellows and remote contacts with them. It should aim at reasoned compromises between what we decide will yield us the maximum of immediate satisfactions and what we believe will insure the maximum satisfaction in the future. It must produce comfort both in time and in space: in time by providing comfort now and in the future, and in space by providing comfort in our contacts as we meet our fellow humans.

The moral judgment, which precedes action, should follow not upon instinctive but upon conscious decision; not upon deliberate effort to act in conformity with the conventional code but upon deliberate effort to determine the immediate and the remote consequences of the acts which we are contemplating. Our acts may seem inconsistent with each other from time to time and from place to place, yet they may be thoroughly consistent from the standpoint of this principle. And if we proceed intelligently, we shall inflict less discomfort both upon ourselves and others than if we try to act in accordance with the prevailing morality. What is more, we shall avoid not only the folly but the hypocrisy of pretending to be unselfish.

We will discover that *the most intelligently farsighted conduct will make us as considerate of others as it is of universal interest that we should be.*

If we are *intelligently* true to ourselves, we will be as just to all whom our acts affect as we can be.

•

Obviously we can devise no such philosophy of morals as long as we permit our conduct to consist of habitual conventional reactions to the circumstances of life. For such a morality implies intellectual self-approval of ourselves and what we are doing. To attain this self-approval we must condition ourselves, as the behaviorists would say, so that our habitual reactions become intelligent rather than conventional; to temper our actions by "sick lying them o'er with the pale cast of thought."

Such conduct may not invariably, it is true, furnish us full gratification. It is utterly opposed to the idea that happiness is only to be found in self-satisfaction. It involves enlightened choices between conflicting desires—neither a full yielding to instinctive impulses nor yet a stifling of all impulse by too great consideration of remote satisfactions. It merely tempers the desire for immediate satisfaction by consideration for the future. It takes into account the fact that we are not only confronted by the necessity of compromising between the present and the future. We are also confronted by the necessity of choosing among hosts of mutually exclusive immediate desires. No matter how our choices are determined—whether we let conventional morality dictate our choices for us or we substitute a personal morality according to which we make our choices—the actual choices in specific instances can be only one of the many conflicting desires with which we are on each occasion confronted.

But choose we must. And if we substitute intelligence for convention, the choice will mean conduct which consciously relates each of our acts to the sequences of life as a whole. To each moral judgment we apply all our wisdom in an effort to extract the utmost gratification both from the particular event and from the sequences of life in its entirety.

We escape the inhibitions which convention imposes even though we deny ourselves the emotional releases of satisfying unrestrained desire. What we lose, however, in superficial satisfaction because of the restraints we impose upon ourselves, we more than gain by the depth of our understanding of all that we do permit ourselves to experience.

•

Such a morality is manifestly impossible as long as we permit ourselves to be intimidated by what religion, what society, what law prescrites with regard to human conduct. We must feel free to act upon our own judgments. Our conventionally-conditioned consciences must be dismissed as guides to conduct.

The sins, the vices, and the crimes, on one side, and the virtues on the other, which have been evolved because of our conventionalization of our survival habits must be replaced with conscious, voluntary, intelligent compromises designed to make life richer, more beautiful, more satisfying both in the present and the future.

For there are no supreme ends which can justify our inflexible adherence to what convention calls duty. The ends which are supposed to justify this adhesion are never noble enough. Conventional morality is for us under a constant obligation to prove that the ends at which it aims are worth the price which conformity exacts of us. It is the greatest of all crimes to sacrifice what makes us happy immediately merely in order to attain an end which our intelligence tells us does not merit the sacrifice, just as it is the greatest of all virtues joyously to sacrifice an immediate desire when we are convinced that the ultimate end fully justifies it.

•

The full application of such a principle to conduct no doubt has shocking implications to the conventional soul. For it implies that not all lying is bad; not all stealing is bad; not all killing is bad; they become good or bad by virtue of their consequences. Moral conduct ceases to be behavior in accordance with the accepted creeds and codes. It becomes a test of our ability to apply intelligence to action—of understanding the immediate and foreseeing the remote consequences of our behavior.

As long as we are afraid of the law, as long as we are afraid of society, as long as we are afraid of conscience, we cannot substitute moral values devised for our comfort for the morality which the quantity-minded minority finds so well adapted to the exploitation of mankind.

But if we are free enough to disregard the opinions of society, clever enough to elude the clumsy activities of the law, and courageous enough to rid ourselves of all fear of that part of our subconscious memory which we now venerate under the name of conscience, we can make the court of intelligence and not the code of morality the supreme arbiter of our conduct.

The Psychological Barrier

We come now to the psychological barrier to comfort.

We are emotional beings. Unfortunately we are seldom very desirable emotional beings. Our minds, just as our bodies, are so far from any well designed norm that our psychological equipment for life probably constitutes one of the greatest barriers to the conquest of comfort.

For civilization tends to make us into emotional illiterates.

By the time we have arrived at the age of discrimination, most of us are emotional ruins—our minds are habituated to react ruinously in situations where above all others they should help us to act with real wisdom.

•

To become psychologically normal we need from infancy contact at first hand with those aspects of life that most powerfully touch the emotions. This contact with reality is the prime essential for a normal emotional education.

But our factory-dominated civilization seems determined to rob us more and more of such an education.

It deprives us almost entirely of all direct contact with birth and death. These crucial events in life are hidden behind the awesome walls of our modern hospitals. Thus we are deprived of the prophylactic influence of naturally accustoming ourselves to them. Birth and dying are the "business" of a professional caste of physicians and nurses. Neither are a part of the normal lives of ordinary men, women and children.

And while the physicians and nurses are calloused by over exposure to them, we are emotionally atrophied because we never experience normal contact with them at all.

This divorce between real life and what we experience of life makes our emotions, which ought to be cushions which relieve us of the jolts and shocks of life, the very sources of the neuroses by which most of us today are plagued.

We have been made emotionally abnormal by deprivations which have dried up our affections; starved our sympathies; made us indifferent to misfortune, and paralyzed our understanding.

•

What the hospitals and modern medicine do to us with regard to birth and death is typical of what is being done to us in regard to other aspects of living equally important to the development of a normal emotional system.

Take work for instance. Let us be deprived of all useful work, and the result is emotionally disastrous. But it is almost equally harmful to our emotional development if we are deprived of certain kinds of work—if we do no manual work; no creative work; no artistic work; no outdoor work; no so-called unpleasant or dirty work. Without experiencing all these kinds of work, it is almost impossible to understand the work of the world, much less to plan intelligently as to how we should ourselves work.

What is true of work is also true of love and sex; of marriage and parenthood; of singing and music; of acting and dancing, and of every phase of life which we can enjoy only if we have been emotionally prepared for it by first-hand experience with it. Normal psychological development is impossible for us if the contact with reality which doing these things represents is taken from us and from our homes, and transferred to specialists and professionalism and to the institutions in which they devote themselves exclusively to perform them for us.

We cannot equip ourselves psychologically for life if we secure our knowledge of it vicariously from books, plays and pictures. No school, no pedagogic system nor textbook can take the place of seeing, hearing, touching, tasting, smelling and feeling for ourselves. Vicarious experience may illuminate personal experience, but it cannot act as a substitute for it. Only by a sufficient amount of personal experience can we acquire the psychological mastery of ourselves and the emotional training which is essential for the conquest of comfort.

If we run from the crassness and the crudity of real life, or if we are shielded from it by institutions which presumably serve us, we become psychological cripples.

Here self-sufficiency can serve us supremely well. It not only releases us from servitude to the factory-dominated civilization which today aborts our psychological development, but it furnishes us in place of it a whole life of emotional education through contact with reality.

And in thus reducing our emotional maladjustment to life and stimulating our emotional adaptation to it, we tend to overcome the psychological barrier to comfort.

The Educational Barrier

We come now to the educational barrier to comfort.

We think and therefore education becomes important. Our thinking is often of a very low order, and the premises upon which we base it generally abound in error. Yet think we do, and the amazing fact is not that a few reason so well, but the fact that even the lowest and most ignorant of men think at all.

It is the possession of this faculty of thinking with its limitless capacity for enriching life which gives to education its great importance.

•

It is the convention today to consider work the business of adults; education the business of children. Because of this we tend to feel that education should be laid aside with other childish things when we grow up. We think of education as a process of equipping ourselves in childhood for our work as adults.

But since our conception of work in this factory-dominated civilization is confined to activities which enable us to earn money, conventional education warps our entire framework of thought in a most unholy fashion. It implants a set of values in us during childhood in which acquisition is exalted and sensitivity blunted. We emerge from our schooling fully convinced that the problem of how to live and what to think about life is nothing more nor less than the problem of becoming successful—of wresting enough things from nature or our fellow men to gratify our needs and desires.

Our education makes us begin life toughened into a quantity mindedness that is in most cases certain to disappoint us because so few of us have the ruthlessness necessary to attain the levels of acquisition to which convention dictates that we should all aspire.

•

As the factory system grows into every nook and cranny of life, the demand for specialization becomes more and more insistent. Education becomes vocational to an ever-increasing extent. It becomes hardly much more than preparation for a specific kind of employment in a civilization which has use only for specifically trained individuals.

True, education has always been to some degree vocational. It was a preparation for a military, a legal, a clerical or a political career not so long ago. But modern education is dominated as never before by the driving need of equipping us for a career of money-making. The matter of equipping us for living beautifully is relegated to a subordinate place when it is not entirely forgotten by our educational institutions.

As long as we think of education as pre-eminently preparation for money-making, we will never adequately prepare ourselves to live the comfortable life.

Conventional education with its bias toward money-making is, to those of us potentially capable of the good life, a dangerous barrier to the conquest of comfort. For conventional education inoculates us so strongly against non-conformity that nothing which we may subsequently experience can furnish us a better set of values than those which now satisfy the masses of mankind.

Conventional schooling makes education, which should be the principal instrument in our warfare upon ignorance, the principal agency in keeping us ignorant.

Instead of education furnishing us keys with which to unlock the doors to ever higher planes of values, it locks them irrevocably against us.

•

Education ceases to be a barrier to comfort only if we can afford to make the whole of life a two-fold process—a process of acquiring facts about living, and of acquiring understanding of their significance. The two processes must continue unremittingly throughout life.

A lifetime devoted to such education may not, it is true, make us perfectly wise, but it should at least make us wise enough to escape from the false values to which the masses of mankind unthinkingly dedicate their existence.

The Individual Barrier

And thus we come to what seems to me the final barrier to the conquest of comfort.

We are individuals, with needs and desires of our own, the satisfaction of which is opposed to and in conflict with much that is necessary if we are to be successful mates, parents and social beings. And the greater our individual endowment, the greater is this antithesis with which life confronts us. We crave the joy which we can secure from doing creative work; we crave the fame it may bring us, the wealth it may secure us and the immortality it may win for us.

And so we are torn between the desire to sacrifice everything and everybody to express ourselves in our personal activities, and the overwhelming instinct to mate and to live the social life which makes normal reproduction possible.If we are to conquer this final barrier to comfort, we must resolve the conflict between our individual desires and cravings for a personal fulfillment, and the demands and limitations which marriage and home and society place upon us. We must end the antithesis between our own ego and the other egos with which it is necessary for us to come to terms.

•

Here it is that friendship can make its great contribution to comfort. For friendship offers us the only satisfying synthesis between ourselves and our fellow human beings.

Friendship is a mutual feeling. It presupposes a friend—one who feels as friendly to us as we feel to him. To function satisfactorily, it must be reciprocal. When we feel friendship for someone who does not reciprocate it, or for large crowds which cannot reciprocate it, friendship ceases to be a normal expression of being. It becomes pathological. The statesman who thrusts his sentiments upon indifferent multitudes; the philanthropist who thrusts his goodness upon indifferent beneficiaries; the lover who thrusts his love upon an indifferent inamorata, are all made a little absurd because of this lack of reciprocity.

Perhaps with intelligence to assist us in our contact with our fellows, we can confine our friendships to those who can feel friendship to us and so permit friendship to really contribute to the resolution of this final difficulty.

•

To make this contribution to comfort by friendships possible, the family circle, which is a small group, rather than the nation, which is a large group, deserves to become the chief object of our devotion.

Today we are told to devote ourselves to the well-being of humanity—in the name of love.

We are told to devote ourselves to the prosperity of the nation to which we belong—in the name of patriotism.

We are told to devote ourselves to the success of the institution for which we work—in the name of business.

But we are not told to what we should devote ourselves in the name of friendship.

For friendship becomes infinitely diffused when we devote ourselves to the institutions to which we are supposed to consecrate ourselves today. In schools it is diffused among hundreds and thousands of pupils; in stores among great crowds of employees and greater crowds of customers; in factories among armies of workers, armies of officials, and armies of distributors. It is dissipated into nothingness among the hundreds of contacts which working in such institutions crowds into our lives, and the conditions which make us think that we have hundreds of friends, destroy the possibilities of any friendships at all.

Friendship develops out of communion with our fellows; and time, the one thing which we cannot spare from our busy lives for so non-productive an activity as getting acquainted with one another, is necessary to the process. In the hurry and bustle; the restlessness and moving from place to place; the intensity of competition and the overwhelming group consciousness of today, we have time only to cultivate crowds. The more efficiently we complicate our lives, the more certainly do we destroy the conditions under which we can really come to know each other. More and more we live in crowded cities, sleep in crowded apartments and hotels, eat in crowded restaurants, work in crowded factories and offices, play in crowded clubs and theatres. And we overlook the fact that we can be in the midst of these crowds—and still be quite alone—tragically alone. To be alone in this sense is the true misery which life can inflict upon us. For the pains of life—the physical ills, the disappointments, the shattering of illusions, the failures cease to be quite so poignant when we can share them with our friends. Just as the joys of life are doubled and redoubled when we can share them, and live them over and over, with our friends.

For the cultivation of friends we need above all time for conversation and freedom to be ourselves—neither of which this factory-dominated civilization dares to accord us.

And in preventing us from developing these aspects of life it destroys the very grounds upon which we, as individuals, can most surely enter into communion with other human beings.

•

If we devote ourselves exclusively to our careers—if we specialize as civilization is pressing us to specialize today—we will find that achievement alone is not sufficient to avoid the curse of frustration. We shall probably end life with the melancholy discovery that success, fame and achievement are not merely vanity, but that they have gratified nothing much more than vanity. We become conscious of the fact that irreplaceable hours have gone, and that however much we may have achieved we have failed to extract from it that which can only come from the understanding of our friends. This is the great frustration—and consciousness of this failure becomes the final tragedy of the super-conscious individual.

If we, however, sacrifice personal achievement for the sake of family and society, again we find frustration. We end with the equally melancholy discovery that even the happiest of families and the greatest successes in society cannot compensate us for the sacrifice of the dignity of living which follows upon the suppression of the artist within us.

•

Civilization becomes beautiful in the degree to which those who are capable of contributing beauty are free to express themselves. To some degree all have something beautiful to contribute. Even the most ordinary of mortals can create beauty through the home while functioning as providers and parents, if given the opportunity and furnished the proper leadership. But those who have something exceptional to contribute; those whom nature has endowed with greater powers than conferred upon average men and women, must be free to express themselves fully, not only for their own sake, but for the sake of mankind.

It is here that the constraint which this factory-dominated civilization imposes upon the exceptional types of men inflicts the greatest of injuries upon not only the individual of talent but upon civilization itself.

For the individual is made to produce not what he can best produce but that which a factory civilization can best utilize. He is either prevented from expressing himself altogether, or his contribution is perverted so that it neither satisfies himself nor lessens the ugliness of civilization. The teacher is made to teach what he knows is not worth teaching; the scientist to discover what he knows is not worth discovering; the artist to paint what he knows is not beautiful; the sculptor to adorn what he knows is not worth ornamenting; the writer to write what he knows is not worth saying.

Beauty, which should be the natural consequence of efforts to capture the significance of what we see or hear or learn within whatever medium we like to use, is sacrificed to the monetary needs of our factory economy. The artistic shams which we are forced to substitute for it may continue to be called beautiful but they are nonetheless innately ugly for from them has been excluded all expression of our truest selves.

•

In the effort to resolve the conflict between the aspirations of our individual egos and the social needs with which we are confronted, we have our choice of three alternative procedures: (1) we can devote ourselves to the cultivation of self-expression; (2) we can devote ourselves to the cultivation of the needs of social life; or (3) we can devote ourselves to some sort of compromise which provides for both.

We reject the first if we sacrifice the development of our capacity for creating beauty in devoting ourselves wholly to the social activities of civilization.

We reject the second if we sacrifice the responsibilities, the disciplines and the possibilities of friendship in our devotion to a wholly individualized career.

We reject neither entirely if we resolve the antithesis between them by creating conditions under which it is possible to devote ourselves to both alternately. Plainly if such conditions can be created, it is the part of wisdom to devote ourselves to establishing them.

We wish to express ourselves and we wish to live. But to live we must mate, reproduce and rear our kind just as we must eat, sleep and clothe ourselves. Both the personal and the social aspects of life must, if they are to be made endurable, be infused with our genius. Certainly, if we aspire to be superior beings, that superiority should be used to ennoble every task in life and not our special talents only.

But today conditions over which we have little control make it exceedingly difficult to ennoble the ordinary activities of life.

We no longer control our lives sufficiently to enable us to infuse our personalities into every aspect of it. Neither in our factory-dominated work nor in our non-creative modern home making, do we find scope for ennobling life.

The conflict exists today because we permit the quantity-minded wielders of power to impose upon us the conventions of a civilization which sacrifices normal life to the satisfaction of their craving for acquisition.

All our work is therefore turned into channels which yield the business world quantitative returns in terms of money. Activities which should be the expression of our noblest ideals become our means for earning bread-and-butter.

From this, one way of escape is for us to become economically secure as to the essentials of comfort.

Let us attain this security and we will discover that it is possible to do what we like on terms which we set forth; to indulge in the luxury of friendship, and to work and play without sacrificing, real comfort on the altars of the conventions of civilization.

•

Some such survey of what I have called the barriers to comfort and some sort of an outline of policies which might enable us to surmount them, (unsatisfactory as this one no doubt is and dogmatic as it must appear compressed into so brief a compass), is essential to the conquest of material and spiritual comfort. For the family and home life here advocated can contribute to freedom, self-expression and comfort only if we avoid all those conventions which have up to the present prevented the home from becoming the means to the noblest triumph over life which man is permitted to achieve by the essential comedy and tragedy of life itself.

Confucius said: "Only two classes of men never change: the wisest of the wise and the dullest of the dull."

The only convention to which we who aspire to the superior life can freely commit ourselves is the convention of perpetually revaluing all the customs, traditions, and ideas which we adopt.

L'ENVOI

I now go alone, my disciples!
Now go ye also away, and alone!
So will I have it.
Verily, I advise you: depart from me,
and guard yourself against Zarathustra!
And better still:
be ashamed of him!
Perhaps he hath deceived you.

—*Thus Spake Zarathustra.*

CHAPTER XXI
L'ENVOI

THE factory has taken us up on an exceedingly high mountain and shown us all the great cities of the world, and the riches within them.

"All these things are yours," the factory says, "on condition only that you bow down and serve me. Abandon strange and dangerous ideas of your own. Think only of my greater glory. Sink your initiative and your individuality in the conventions that sustain me, and riches beyond the wildest dreams of Crœsus shall be yours and your children's."

Thus has the factory tempted us. And thus has it enlisted most of us in its service.

Mercifully, most of us are unconscious of the fact that we have given up our birthrights for a mess of pottage.

•

This is my story.

Why have I told it? With any hope that the masses of men will try the road to comfort along which I have been travelling? No.

Men may be shown the way to comfort.

But they not only lack the will to achieve comfort; they lack even the desire to attain it.

They are the slaves of habits—habits fastened upon them by the unending repetitions of the work they do; by the universal pressure to conform to what their fellows expect of them; by the concentrated energy they put into living the kind of life to which they are predisposed by a conventional environment.

Conventional educations, conventional occupations, conventional experiences, make it difficult for them to be unconventional in thought and almost impossible for them to be unconventional in action.

They are afraid of the economic, social, mental, physical struggle which the adoption of new values is certain to entail.

Above all, they are afraid of abandoning values which they have come to know, for values for which they yearn, but which they do not know.

•

The quest of comfort and understanding is an adventure. It is a high adventure; a dangerous adventure; an adventure in the transvaluation of values.

It is an adventure for freemen, and not for automatons; for skeptical individuals, and not for credulous souls.

It is an adventure essential to sensitive non-conformists.

Unfortunately, our factory-dominated civilization seems to have made most of us incurably conventional.

Most of us have become anæsthetized against the factory and the ugliness, drabness, sordidness of the civilization in which it has enmeshed us.

Most of us have come to accept the standards this civilization imposes upon us.

Most of us are afraid even to consider changing them.

That any considerable number of those who secure the wherewithal to live by serving the factory and who subsist upon what the factory supplies them, should undertake the conquest of comfort would be a miracle.

Why then have I spent all this time to tell the story of my quest for comfort?

First,

> Because a cold rage seizes one at whiles
>   To show the bitter, old and wrinkled truth
> Stripped naked of all vesture that beguiles,
>   False dreams, false hopes, false masks and modes of youth;
> Because it gives some sense of power and passion
> In helpless impotence to try to fashion
>   Our woe in living words howe'er uncouth.

And secondly, again in the words of the selfsame poet: that

—here and there some weary wanderer
In that same city of tremendous night,
Will understand the speech, and feel a stir
Of fellowship in all-disastrous fight;
"I seer mute and lonely, yet another
Uplifts his voice to let me know a brother
Travels the same wild paths though out of sight." [49]

•

And so good-bye.

You probably will continue as before. And so shall I.

But I, at least, am free to continue the quest of comfort on my own small domain—mine as long as I can scrape together the taxes which the state levies upon it.

I, at least, have the opportunity to work out a manner of living for myself without regard to the life that landlords, tradesmen, and manufacturers would impose upon me.

I, at least, can say to the factory:

"Get thee hence. I want thy riches not, because I need them not."

•

A comfortable home in which to labor and to play, with trees and grass and flowers and skies and stars; a small garden; a few fruit trees; a workshop with its tools, and three big dogs to keep the salesmen out—and I, at least, have time for love, for children, for a few friends, and for the work I like to do.

More the world can give to no man, and more no man can give the world.

THE END

REFERENCES

NOTE: —Folio immediately following date denotes the page in the reference book; folio in parentheses denotes the page in *This Ugly Civilization* on which the reference is made.

1. Glenn Frank, *The Magazine of Business*, September, October, November 1927. (P. 47.)
2. M. K. Gandhi, *The Wheel of Fortune,* Madras, 1922, p. 53. (P. 48.)
3. Ibid., p. 14. (P. 49.)
4. Paul M. Mazur, *American Prosperity*, p. 179. (Pp. 60–61.)
5. Dr. E. Schmalenbach, *New York Times*, June 2, 1928, p. 104. (P. 63.)
6. Frederick W. Taylor, *The Principles of Scientific Management*, pp. 104, 110. (P. 79.)
7. Ibid., p. 140. (P. 80.)
8. *The Nation*, April 11, 1928, p. 403. (P. 82.)
9. Frederick F. Rockwell, *Save It for Winter*, p. 1. (Pp. 130–131.)
10. Hubert M. Greist *Women's Wear Daily*, January 28, 1928. (P. 144.)
11. Henry Ford, *My Life and Work*, p. 201. (P. 148.)
12. *Autobiography of R. D. Owen*, p. 13. (Pp. 155–156.)
13. William L. Chenery, *Industry and Human Welfare*, p. 77. (P. 156.)
14. Tench Cox, *View of the United States*, p. 442. (P. 160.)
15. Ibid., p. 443. (P. 161.)
16. William L. Chenery, *Industry and Human Welfare*, p. 18. (P. 161.)
17. Dexter S. Kimball, *Principles of Industrial Organization*, p. 16. (P. 164.)
18. Ibid., p. 17. (Pp. 164–165.)
19. Ibid., p. 16. (P. 165.)
20. John C. Duncan, *Principles of Industrial Management*, pp. 206, 207. (Pp. 168–169.)
21. Henry Ford, *My Life and Work*, p. 106. (P. 169.)
22. Ibid., p. 108, (P. 170.)
23. Ibid., p. 92, (P. 172.)
24. Marlen E. Pew, *Editor and Publisher*, April 7, 1928. (Pp. 173–174.)
25. Industrial Conference Called by the President, March 6, 1920, pp. 32, 33. (Pp. 174–175.)

26. William L. Chenery, *Industry and Human Welfare*, p. 11. (P. 177.)
27. Lewis Mumford, *The Golden Day*. p. 237. (P. 178.)
28. Kenneth M. Goode and Harford Powel Jr., *What About Advertising*. p. 115. (Pp. 180–181.)
29. Herbert N. Casson, *American Review of Reviews*, 1913. (P. 201.)
30. Frederick W. Taylor, *The Principles of Scientific Management*, pp. 7, 8. (P. 202.)
31. Waldo Frank, *The New Republic*, March 14, 1928. (P. 210.)
32. Dr. George B. Cutten, *New York Times*, September 9, 1928. (Pp. 210–212.)
33. Havelock Ellis, *Little Essays of Love and Virtue*, p. 96. (Pp. 213–214.)
34. Charles Laube, *The New York Telegram*, May 25, 1928. (P. 214)
35. Alfred Henry Lewis, *Cosmopolitan Magazine*, v. 45, p. 619. (P. 243.)
36. Ida M. Tarbell, *The History of the Standard Oil Company*, p. 202. (P. 244.)
37. Henry Adams, *The Education of Henry Adams*, pp. 478, 479. (P. 250.)
38. Lewis Mumford, *The Golden Day*, p. 199. (P. 251.)
39. Charles W. Eliot, *The Nation*, July 18, 1928. (P. 253.)
40. Albert Payson Terhune, *The American Magazine*, August, 1928. (P. 261–262.)
41. Henry Ford, *My Life and Work*, p. 103. (Pp. 268–269.)
42. Confucius, *The Analects*, Book I. (P. 270.)
43. U. S. Bureau of Labor Statistics, 1919, p. 187. (P. 305.)
44. Nathan Straus Jr., *New York Times*, May 16, 1928. (Pp. 324–325.)
45. Confucius, *The Analects*. (P. 333.)
46. Henry Ford, *My Life and Work*, p. 105. (Pp. 345–346.)
47. James Thomson, *The City of Dreadful Night*. (P. 379.)
48. Henry Adams, *The Education of Henry Adams*, p. 365. (P. 421.)
49. James Thomson, *The City of Dreadful Night*. (P. 444–445.)

INDEX

D

E

F

G

L

M

N

O

P

R

S

T

Harry Elmer Barnes

Harry Elmer Barnes (1889–1968) was an American historian who, in his later years, was known for his historical revisionism. Barnes taught history at Columbia University from 1918 to 1929. Afterwards, he worked as a freelance writer and occasional adjunct professor at smaller schools. Through his position at Columbia and his prodigious scholarly output, Barnes was once highly regarded as a historian. However, by the 1950s, his anti-war stance had lost him credibility and he become a "professional pariah". Murray N. Rothbard said of him, "It was Harry's passionate commitment to truth that lost for him the applause of scholars and multitude alike and cast him, for the last two decades of his life, into outer darkness."

Barnes published more than 30 books, 100 essays, and 600 articles and book reviews, many for the Council on Foreign Relations journal Foreign Affairs, where he served as Bibliographical Editor.

Bill Sharp

Mr. Sharp has made a keen study of the life and work of Borsodi and Loomis. He wants to not only understand them as people, but to discover the principles underlying their work. His goal is to make those principles more "first person" and practical, and to update the material to reflect nearly a half-century of development in the sciences and social sciences since Ralph and Mildred were at their prime. He has resolved that the story and legacy of Ralph Borsodi and Mildred Loomis is not over.

The first product of this phase of work is the Cove Institute workbook *Self-Reliance* and related programs started in 2018 (www.transitioncentre.org). The Cove Institute was first formed with a mission very close to what Borsodi had proposed. The legacy he and Mildred Loomis left, is compelling and has a lastnig value Mr. Sharp hopes to convey to yet another generation.

Printed in Great Britain
by Amazon

73726198R00272